How and Why Feelings Change

How and Why Feelings Change

Foundations of Emotion in Cognitive-Behavioral Psychotherapy

IAN M. EVANS

OXFORD
UNIVERSITY PRESS

OXFORD
UNIVERSITY PRESS

Oxford University Press is a department of the University of Oxford. It furthers the University's objective of excellence in research, scholarship, and education by publishing worldwide. Oxford is a registered trade mark of Oxford University Press in the UK and in certain other countries.

Published in the United States of America by Oxford University Press
198 Madison Avenue, New York, NY 10016, United States of America.

Library of Congress Cataloging-in-Publication Data

ISBN 9780197825778

DOI: 10.1093/9780197825808.001.0001

Printed by Marquis Book Printing, Canada

The manufacturer's authorized representative in the EU for product safety is Oxford University Press España S.A. of Parque Empresarial San Fernando de Henares, Avenida de Castilla, 2 – 28830 Madrid (www.oup.es/en or product.safety@oup.com). OUP España S.A. also acts as importer into Spain of products made by the manufacturer.

FSC
www.fsc.org
MIX
Paper | Supporting responsible forestry
FSC® C103567

For

LUANNA H. MEYER, PhD

whose pioneering research on children's friendships promoted feelings of acceptance and kindness as priorities in applied behavior analysis for the inclusive education of students with severe disabilities.

CONTENTS

Introduction

There is a bewildering array of psychological approaches to clinical therapy—Hersen and Sledge's (2002) encyclopedia of psychotherapy methods runs to two volumes. There are distinctive schools of thought, such as behavioral, cognitive, socio-cultural, or psychodynamic. Fourteen distinct systems are covered in Wedding and Corsini's *Current Psychotherapies* (2018). Within each system, there are different foundational principles and theories, and within each theory, there are different techniques. In reality, the techniques that psychotherapists use are not as distinct as they sometimes seem, as treatment packages tend to have a limited number of "common elements" (Chorpita et al., 2007). And what appear to be differences are often in the terms used, the constructs emphasized, and the theoretical rationales offered (Goldfried et al., 2011). This is because techniques for helping clients change are somewhat cultish rather than supported by a universally accepted scientific foundation, even those claiming to be "evidence-based." New therapies often have influential leaders, followers, and advocates—offering workshops and training opportunities—backed by studies specifically designed to demonstrate their efficacy. Their effectiveness is usually less well-documented. Only positive outcomes are typically reported, but there is increasing interest in the possible adverse effects of psychological interventions (Klein et al., 2024).

Studies evaluating new treatment ideas are rarely *process* studies demonstrating that a method worked because of the principles expounded. Confounds with powerful influences such as client expectancies, the social role of being a client, and the emotional relationship with the therapist, are difficult to separate. Outcome studies typically do not show if or by how much a new procedure is better than an old one. The "treatment as usual" received by the control group is not usually a well-validated treatment from the previous decades.

This expansion of therapeutic methods and tactics that have an ostensible basis of research support can be confusing for both consumers and therapists. While stauncher academics have argued that only empirically validated methods should ever be used by practitioners, studies of what clinicians do in practice

How and Why Feelings Change. Ian M. Evans, Oxford University Press. © Ian M. Evans (2026).
DOI: 10.1093/9780197825808.003.0001

have repeatedly confirmed that most are self-described eclectics. "I use different techniques according to the client's needs and problems"; "I often introduce a combination of methods"; "I like down-to-earth behavioral approaches, but I sometimes incorporate ideas from psychoanalysis"; "I'm flexible, so I'm always willing to try out a new method after attending a workshop." I have heard these kinds of statements from many fellow clinicians, former students, and colleagues for decades—and I respectfully understand why. Arnold Lazarus (2001), one of the foremost pioneers of clinical behavior therapy, wrote how his experiences with diverse clients led him to rely on a whole variety of different techniques, a practice he called "multimodal therapy."

There is one different approach to formulating and implementing psychological interventions for helping people cope and thrive and manage their lives. Rather than trying to empirically validate each new technique someone devises, the foundational intervention principles could be drawn from current scientific knowledge and an understanding of the many psychological processes that typically influence people (Evans, 1996). Then, based on those scientific principles, methods could be devised with their effectiveness determined for each individual client through careful monitoring (by both client and therapist) of progress towards previously established goals. Long ago in Britain, Monte Shapiro, the leading clinical psychology educator of his day, advocated the concept of the individual client being in an N-of-1 clinical research study (Shapiro, 1969). This became one of the founding principles of applied behavior therapy. There are a few well-known academic leaders in clinical psychology who have long advocated some version of this "measurement-based care" approach (Castonguay et al., 2021; Goldfried, 2011). The most recent and increasingly sophisticated arguments have been offered by Litz (2023a) and Levinson et al. (2025).

And that, all sounds sensible and doable, except that the basic psychological knowledge itself changes rapidly, is complex, not easily learned, and usually taught during an early part of training—in the typical undergraduate psychology curriculum—rather than later in the more applied part of a trainee's exposure to real-life clients. Furthermore, a huge percentage of the psychological research is of only limited relevance to the clinical task of trying to effect change in a client, which is the purpose of psychotherapy. In two previous works, I attempted to fill that gap by summarizing for present and future practitioners of cognitive-behavioral therapy (CBT) the major fundamental concepts from basic and applied psychology having relevance to the design of treatment for any problem.

The first volume, *How and why people change*, explained how therapy can be focused on how to change behaviors (things like skills, habits, impulses, reactions, and so on—what people do) when those facing a problem are seeking treatment. The second volume, *How and why thoughts change*, is focused on how thoughts (ideas, memories, reasoning, decisions, understanding) change. The focus of this third volume in the series, *How and why feelings change*, is on how feelings (emotions, moods, likes and dislikes, values, motives, attitudes) emerge, evolve, and change. Needless to say, human activity always involves all three: overt behavior, internal cognition, and affect, working together all the time. Actions, thoughts, and feelings are not truly separable parts of the human condition, but they have been studied individually as partly separable categories. The theoretical literature still tends to be influenced strongly by a certain intellectual rivalry—cognitive scientists might argue that emotions depend on appraisal and judgment of a situation, behavior analysts emphasize context and consequences over inner thoughts and reasoning, neuroscientists focus on brain activity (especially neural circuits and hormonal), sociobiologists on evolutionary forces, social learning theorists think of modeling, culture, and shared language, humanistic therapists are immersed in constructivist models of meaning-making, and psychoanalytic scholars see emotional forces engaged in battle with conscious thoughts, self-preservation, and social rules. It's a theoretical jungle out there. For both practitioners and trainees, this third book hopes to provide you with a compass, a machete, and insect repellant to make your way through it.

Why use the word *feelings* rather than *emotion*? For the same reason that the title of the first book used the word people rather than behavior and the second title used thoughts rather than cognitions. When clients talk, they talk about what they are doing, what they are thinking, and what they are feeling. Feeling and emotion will be used somewhat interchangeably, but "feeling" emphasizes how an emotion is *experienced* rather than how it is differentiated. The word also allows us to think of other hedonic experiences, such as likes and dislikes, and states of pleasure and pain (sexual arousal, hunger, repletion, and fatigue, for example). The word allows us to consider the opposite of feeling—uncaring, perhaps, or emotional numbness when the emotion may have been aroused but is not felt. Or cannot be aroused at all. In other words, the relevant psychological research is largely about emotions; for those in psychotherapy, the topic is about feelings. The two terms overlap, but not perfectly. Chapter 1 explores the distinction in detail and shows how feelings include related concepts of central importance to psychotherapy: moods, preferences, and sentiments. The distinction between explaining one's feelings and describing them is made. I illustrate the way people use the word feelings to include emotionally significant thoughts, and that we can have feelings about ourselves, even feelings about feelings.

There is another important reason for using the concept of feelings. Both behavior therapy and cognitive therapy have always been about emotions and emotional disorders but discussed using different terms. There are therapists and researchers, claiming to be cognitive-behavioral therapy-oriented, who propose bringing emotion back into focus—but it has never been out of focus (Samoilov & Goldfried, 2000). Treatment might emphasize skill development or rational thinking or social support, but people don't seek psychotherapy because they want to improve their tennis game, learn philosophy, or find a friend. As Lazarus (1989) wrote:

> *The whole raison d'être for entering psychotherapy is that people, or those close to them, are unhappy. What emotions (affective reactions) are predominant? Are we dealing with anger, anxiety, depression, combinations thereof, and to what extent (e.g., irritation versus rage; sadness versus profound melancholy)? What appears to generate these negative affects, certain cognitions, images, interpersonal conflicts? And how does the person respond (behave) when feeling a certain way? (p.5).*

This book is not like one of the many self-help guides for clients on how to handle their emotions. An emotion cannot be intrinsically undesirable. As an issue for therapy, the question is always degree and appropriateness, not the occurrence of feelings themselves. Lack of feeling is dangerous. Strong feelings (passions) are wonderful and make life worth living, but in extreme form can become destructive. This volume is for practicing psychotherapists and those in training interested in psychological knowledge needed for the design and implementation of change-directed interventions for clients in distress. It is about the clients—all clients, as all have feelings—and not about their specific psychopathologies, stages of development, gender, or culture. By reviewing, integrating, and interpreting contemporary (and in many instances historical) information from the psychology of feelings, it is hoped to fill the inevitable gaps in my previous summaries of the principles of behavioral and cognitive therapy. In Chapter 2, therefore, I start with the basics by providing a historically flavored overview of the psychology of emotions and how biological concepts have shaped the development of important principles of CBT.

Early in your exposure to scientific psychology, particularly within learning theory, you will have encountered principles of reward (reinforcement) and punishment as well as approach and avoidance. These constructs are integral to most models of psychopathology, as is the experiential dimension of pleasure and pain. However, the classic research studies you will have learnt about do not always point to an integration of the push and pull of these forces. Newer findings in neuroscience parallel and inform the old foundations of learning theory. Thus, in Chapter 3, I attempt to explain how a focus on feelings enables such an integration. In Chapter 4, I change gears and go forward to the past. Thoroughly explored and well-understood principles of child development provide a solid psychological understanding of children's feelings—how they emerge, are shaped, and expressed. Obviously, feelings also get labeled and defined in childhood, and so Chapter 5 is all about words. But not just words; we need to consider the full panoply of how feelings are communicated.

A fundamental principle of psychology—one particularly well-developed in S—R behaviorism—is that responses occur in contexts and that the many discernable stimuli that constitute an environmental context are what elicit (evoke, trigger) a response. Feelings are no exception, and they are very far removed from the threats to and needs for survival that dominated much of our early evolution. You might not always recognize what it is that has provoked a strong feeling in yourself but it is sure to be something. Sometimes these stimuli are automatic, reflexive, but mostly they are created and altered through learning experiences. This fundamental topic is explored in Chapter 6. In the process, you will see the important connection between principles of conditioning and many therapeutic practices.

Feelings do not occur in isolation or individually or sequentially. One feeling can counteract or interfere with another and both can alter cognition and everyday activities, both complex and simple. You can readily understand that having conflicting feelings is a common feature of human life, and your clients will have them as well. So, in Chapter 7, these complexities are examined, leading to a reaffirmation that feelings are functional—which means psychotherapy depends on them. That stands in contrast to the conventional abnormal psychology language of emotion disorders. Some argue, as in emotion-focused therapy (Greenberg, 2017), the somewhat circular case that exploring emotions will reveal what is important or necessary in clients' lives. While agreeing, however, that emotions are never intrinsically bad, and feelings are wonderful, we can also accept that there are times when their intensity is not at all functional. So, the topic of managing feelings, or self-regulating feelings, needs to be addressed, and I do so in Chapter 8.

In some situations, and many of life's experiences, the circumstances are so detrimental to human development and general well-being that the intensity of feelings evoked is beyond what humans should ever have to tolerate. Psychological "treatments" (psychotherapy) must, under some circumstances, give way to other professional efforts, such as prevention, radical social change, and policies far beyond the typical provision of mental health services to individual clients. Dealing with the feelings that develop in times of trauma and catastrophe is a specialized topic. You will discover that I was a coward and reluctant to go down that professional pathway. But at the same time, it cannot be ignored—intense feelings, great passions, and major social emotions cannot be ignored. The psychology of feelings has relevance for those who work in this area and thus I do touch upon some of the implications in Chapter 9.

Given this wide coverage of topics—I used a projector, not a microscope—pulling together the essential ideas that are directly relevant to psychotherapy is not easy. But in the last chapter, Chapter 10, I tried my best. I even boldly entitled it *Therapeutic inspirations: What changes feelings*, as though there were going to be definitive answers! What I hope you will find by the time you get to that terminal chapter is that the whole topic of feelings will now be so enthralling that you will have the feeling that important insights have been acquired, even though big questions and many future debates still remain.

Putting all this another way, this book is not about techniques of psychotherapy, although some will be mentioned here and there. Neither is it tied to any particular school of therapy, although my bias towards behavior therapy and social learning principles will become obvious. In that sense, the approach is within the tradition of what has come to be called CBT. I rather like bringing back the word "psychotherapy" because the interventions are going to be implemented by non-medical practitioners directly or indirectly using *psychological* knowledge and principles to effect changes for the betterment of people's lives (Persons, 2008). The goal is to make accessible to those psychologists who work with clients, or are in training to do so, what current and past research is telling us about feelings and how to influence them. What, in modern psychology, are the foundational ideas, concepts, and insights about changing feelings for the better that therapists could reasonably draw upon while working within some iteration of cognitive-behavioral psychotherapy?

On a very personal note, I have had the privilege of being around—practicing, teaching, and researching—behavior therapy since its inception in the 1960s. I was doing my PhD at the Maudsley Hospital, Institute of Psychiatry, when the major pioneers in Britain from both psychology and psychiatry—Eysenck, Rachman, Marks, Feldman, and many others—were there, honing their important contributions. Fellow students like Rosemery Nelson-Gray, John Teasdale, Jarg Bergold, Peter McLean, John Gray, and Terence Wilson (in the US) who themselves became leaders in our field were inspirational influences. Rosemery and I even published the first papers in the UK reporting our behavior modification work with autistic children, and we attended the monthly professional meetings organized by the charming and insightful Vic Meyer at the Middlesex Hospital in London. I inherited Cyril Franks' eyelid conditioning lab at the Maudsley, and had a personal acquaintance with Joe Wolpe and Arnie Lazarus, because they too were ex-South Africans. I got my first academic position at the University of Hawai'i because the paradigmatic work of Arthur Staats had originally inspired me in the sixties to understand that behaviorism's foundation in learning theory must include language, imagery, thought, development, and emotion. My point in this shameless name dropping is to explain that I have seen promising ideas and principles fade away, new ones come, old ones rediscovered. But the importance of recognizing and understanding feelings has remained paramount.

1

Why Feelings?

Feelings versus Emotions

In the sixties, an Australian pop group, The Seekers, produced a haunting song called "The Carnival is Over." Someone is leaving, and the lyrics raise imagery of tears flowing like rain, and the beating of a heart as the sound of a drum. Despite kisses sweeter than wine, the joys of love are never permanent. The moment contains many of the elements of what this book is about. There is an event, a stimulus situation—a departure—and an affective (emotional) context: they are leaving someone they love, someone who has given them the feeling of joy. There are physiological responses (increased cardiac rate, lacrimation), which require connections between the central nervous system and the autonomic nervous system. If you ask them why they are crying, they might say "Because I feel sad," nevertheless there is a nostalgic sweetness pervading the scene. There is a cognitive reappraisal of the basic situation—there is the possibility that they will never meet again—and this too changes the significance of the event despite sweet and joyful memories. Feelings (love, joy, sadness, sweetness), contexts (meeting, parting, and the passage of time), and physiological reactions all go together without jarring or ambiguity, as they always do in life.

But what is additionally remarkable about this illustration is that it's just a song. When you listen to it, you hear only words and music and the powerful voice of Judith Durham. In Australia, it is sometimes played at the close of sporting events, at funerals, when people go overseas, and was played when the band finally broke up. The song itself, not any actual event, regularly brings audiences to tears. That is empathy—sensitivity to the feelings of others. We understand and share the feelings of the singer. We accept the concurrent bitterness and sweetness of the moment without a sense of contradiction, and the sadness we share is ironically a good feeling. That is the remarkable psychological phenomenology of affective experience that cannot be reduced to its elements without total loss of meaning and understanding.

Affect is a term used in psychology to include all aspects of emotion. The meaning of the term *affect* in psychology is "*any experience of feeling or emotion,*

How and Why Feelings Change. Ian M. Evans, Oxford University Press. © Ian M. Evans (2026).
DOI: 10.1093/9780197825808.003.0002

ranging from suffering to elation, from the simplest to the most complex sensations of feeling, and from the most normal to the most pathological emotional reactions. Often described in terms of positive affect or negative affect, both mood and emotion are considered affective states" (American Psychological Association, 2015). The term is relevant to a book about feelings because that definition emphasizes the experiences we call feelings, which is in accord with my terminological emphasis on feelings over emotions in clinical treatment contexts. But the term affect is used by clinical researchers, especially in psychiatric and neuroscience studies, to refer to emotion as an entire system, including the mechanisms of reward and punishment, motivation (desires), and needs (Cacioppo & Bernston, 1999, p 133). I will occasionally slip into using the term affect when reporting certain findings. But in clinical practice, it is not a useful term. I cannot think of any occasion in which I have asked a client "How's your affect this morning?"

So why focus on feelings specifically? Aren't they just the same as emotions? Emotions, so essential for survival, evolved to move us to action. They are materially an indispensable feature of our human functioning. The emotions are contained within physical changes in bodily functions, in specific neural networks in the central nervous system (CNS), the autonomic nervous system (ANS), and the enteric nervous system, as well as in the chemical reactions and messaging agents (such as neurotransmitters and hormones) that regulate and control the workings of our internal organs. Because of this, we also experience them, feel them. "They didn't evolve so we could just feel them" (Westlund, 2024, p. 9), but by feeling good or bad, they influence the direction of the actions to which they move us. These topics will be discussed in the next chapter. But in this one, I will consider feelings (the subjective experience of emotion), moods (general, longer lasting, less intense emotional states), and the emotive (affective) properties of things (our likes and dislikes, what we enjoy and what we don't).

In cognitive-behavioral therapy (CBT), *emotion* gets talked about much more than feelings, unlike the humanistic psychotherapies. This is mostly because from the early days, so much of the behavioral approach was clinically focused on commonly identified psychiatric "mental disorders": the strong, unpleasant emotions that people sought help in dealing with, such as phobias and panic attacks, grief and depression, conflict, and anger. And when the focus was more directly on modifying deviant and unacceptable behaviors, emotion was seen as secondary. Managing challenging and aggressive behavior, controlling addictions, remediating skill deficits in learning tasks including social situations, and personal health maintenance—these were the targets for change. When feelings were considered, it was mostly seen as part of motivation to change, because the overt, excess, inappropriate behaviors don't actually make one feel any better, in the longer term.

One of the most important early physiologists to investigate emotion, James Papez (1937) wrote the words that define the present text: "The term 'emotion' as commonly used implies two conditions: a way of acting and a way of feeling. The former is designated as emotional expression; the latter, as emotional experience or subjective feeling ... Emotional expression and emotional experience may in the human subject be dissociated phenomena" (p. 725). In this century, neurobiologists such as Damasio and Carvalho (2013) distinguished between feelings and emotions on the grounds that changes felt in one's body's internal environment (interoception) are feelings, and emotions are responses to exteroception from the five senses, either directly or by recall. But they point out exceptions, like fear (an emotion) caused by cardiac pain (interoception). In any psychological therapy, however, the things clients talk about, complain about, and want to change, are most often their feelings. Feelings are what they experience. Yet the words clients use to describe their feelings can be ambiguous, figurative, and embrace unique features of their experience. Davitz (1969; 1970) asked a group of students to describe their feelings when they were depressed. Some of the words and phrases were "I feel I want to withdraw; tired and sleepy; empty; insignificant; alone; out of touch; not hungry; unable to smile." He pointed out that these words included physical symptoms, self-attitudes, impulses to action, facial expressions, and physiological changes.

The fact that emotions have a physiological identity, which we know a great deal about, is going to be important for understanding feelings in clinical contexts. All emotions have peripheral physiological elements such as tears, sweating, blushing, muscle tension, trembling, smiling, heart racing, mouth dry, stomach contractions, genital tumescence. These responses of the smooth muscles and glands are regulated by the major components of the ANS: the sympathetic, parasympathetic, and enteric. It has been very useful clinically to think that the responses of the ANS were designed (by evolution, not some higher power) specifically to prepare our bodies for action to deal with environmental threats and opportunities—energizing us to flee, to fight, to explore, to bond with others, or to mate. Without the physiological changes that can feel so bad mobilizing us to evasive action, we would also not have feelings that facilitate approach and give us pleasurable sensations such as joy and happiness.

Most of these physical changes within our bodies—the *milieu intérieur* as Claude Bernard (1865) called it—can be sensed, even hormonal ones. Sensations from proprioceptors are usually conscious but not always attended to, and are most probably interpreted cognitively according to the situation, context, or past circumstances. It is these feelings and how they are judged that is the topic of this book, so yes, it is about emotion, but focused on how emotions feel, and how they make you feel beyond the interoceptive sensations themselves or the physiological arousal that supports all behavioral action, which is what emotions are for.

We need these autonomic reactions to function in society because they also communicate what we are feeling. Along with our words, the overt manifestations of these autonomic and motoric responses reveal our feelings to others. The early adaptations of our facial muscles to react rapidly to external events gave us distinctive facial expressions for many different feelings, like happiness, anger, disgust, doubt (disbelief). And all these underlying physiological and behavioral responses can now be readily measured. As a physiologist, Pavlov was originally interested in studying the mechanisms of digestion, which was why he began measuring the make-up of dogs' saliva. When he realized that salivary secretions in the absence of the food that usually elicited them could be a measure of what the dog was feeling—"psychic reflexes" he called them—he recognized that this window to understand expectations was much more interesting. He didn't, of course, refer to them as feelings because we can't really know what a dog is feeling. But we can infer a feeling of hope or positive expectation when the animal salivates merely to the ticking sound of an inedible metronome—if it has been made a predictable signal for a coming tasty treat (Pavlov used "meat powder," whatever that is). Similarly, we can infer a feeling of happiness when a dog wags its tail. Since feelings are intrinsically subjective in humans as well, we can connect physiological changes directly to feelings but not claim they are the same exact thing.

Because humans can express their feelings in words, we have traditionally studied emotions through self-reports, often to the exclusion of any other source of data. This means that people must produce descriptive verbal labels for communicating them, and in this book, we will spend time thinking about the precise meaning of our feeling words. As a quick example, think for a moment about the difference between feeling helpless and feeling powerless. They are definitely not the same, but how would *you* distinguish them? We also need ways of reporting the subjective intensity or level of a feeling above or below a typical resting point. A typical point could also be at zero, insofar as we may never have had a particular feeling before. Some words that seem to imply intensity are deceptive. *Dread* sounds like it might be a stronger feeling of *anxiety*. But although they both involve apprehensive cognitions, they are not the same feeling to begin with. Anxiety refers to feelings about things that might happen; dread refers to feelings about things whose negativity is more certain. You have anxiety about taking exams, but dread tomorrow's calculus test; you are socially anxious but dread tonight's party. The feeling of *terror* seems like it is a stronger feeling of *fear*, but fear is what you feel when you might be in serious danger and terror is what you feel when you are. Feeling of *ecstasy* would seem to be an extreme form of *happiness*, but the word implies that it is a feeling of happiness which is overwhelming rather than joyful. Furthermore, the term has been co-opted by religious faiths to mean an emotional frenzy, a state of rapture. Religion is often invoked in metaphorical descriptions of feelings. *Bliss was it in that dawn to be alive*, William Wordsworth (*The Prelude*) wrote of his feelings about the French Revolution, *But to be young was very heaven!*

The occurrence of a feeling and its intensity level can also be inferred from the individual's bodily changes in a new situation. Many feeling words rely on their symbolic value to convey a specific aspect of body language. "Chipper" doesn't just mean happy, it means having a cheerful, lively, sprightly manner. Someone who comes to the clinic "floating on air" is not just happy, their demeanor is light and bouncy—none of which are perfect synonyms because it is the word *floating* itself that conveys the metaphorical feel. When a person shows assertive or strong affect, we say they *stand up* for themselves and won't take an insult *lying down*, emphasizing the general body postures for feeling bold or timid. Slightly differently, but the same general body-position idiom, is when we say "I can't *stand* [that person]," we mean we can't bear/abide them, won't tolerate them, and don't want to be around or near them. If you "can't *stomach* them," it implies feelings of disgust over and above disliking. Like Pavlov's dogs, we salivate when a wonderful cooking smell emanates from the kitchen, and we express desire by licking our lips and pursing them together.

Because feelings derive from physical manifestations, physical descriptions are often used. When scared, our throats "tighten"; when very sad, we "choke up." Even if you don't have a chronic psychogenic cough (*tussis nervosa*), anxiety may well partially manifest itself by sensations in your throat and airways that give you an urge to clear your throat with a dry cough. Other physical descriptions are symbolic or metaphorical. Freud's patient, whose pseudonym was Cäcilie M., had such a strong feeling about an insulting remark made to her by her husband, that she described it as "a slap in my face." In true Victorian hysteria fashion, she then developed painful facial neuralgia after this incident, but we won't go there; see Reilly (2023) for further details.

Bodily experiences are often used figuratively to convey a full sense of the feeling. For example, we say someone is "hungry for power." In Shakespeare's play *Julius Caesar*, Caesar says of one of those plotting against him "Yond Cassius has a lean and hungry look," implying that the conspirator is starved for power. And in Matthew 5:6 of the New Testament, we are told we should "hunger and thirst after righteousness," an excellent physical metaphor for a powerful longing to live a moral life.

Expression of Feelings

Most people can readily tell you what they are feeling subjectively. They can *self-report* immediately in their own words (narratives), or later verbally by prompts in checklists, questionnaires, and rating scales. A change in someone's feelings can also be detected by an observer from *psychophysiological responses* such as blushing, enlarged veins, or sweating. As we shall see, these emotional expressions have a highly significant social and communicative function. In formal clinical research, we can monitor these precisely with instruments such as the electrocardiogram (ECG/EKG) for heart rate or measure the electrical resistance of skin from sweat gland activity (the galvanic skin response, GSR). You don't need instruments in the typical clinical context, as you can also judge someone's feelings from their overall deportment ("body language") and their *facial expressions* (Jack et al., 2014). Most obvious of all, you can infer their feelings in real life from their direct actions and particularly their social interactions, all of which can be called *action tendencies*. In the research laboratory, we can measure action tendencies more precisely by what subjects are willing to do in contrived situations, such as walking up to a live snake in a glass case.

These four objectively measurable modes of expression (self-report, facial expression, measured psychophysiological reactions, and overt behavior) do not, however, always correspond, correlate, or covary. I have explained in some detail that this is because there are measurement errors in each different facet of the pattern of any unitary emotional reaction (Evans, 1986). Self-report of physiological sensations is different from awareness of and labelling a feeling, and approach behavior can be induced despite high anxiety. An excellent example of this can be seen when Albert Bandura famously used modeling to reduce snake phobias. A measure of treatment success was that participating clients would approach and pick up a harmless grass snake. Photographs of some "successfully treated" participants did show them holding the snake, but with a look on their faces of repulsion and horror. On the other hand, Peter Lang, a major contributor to emotion research from a clinical psychology and treatment perspective, has argued that divergence of measures is because actions, physiology, and subjective experience represent three different "systems" of emotion (Lang, 1995). Modern neuroscientists would agree: Cushing and others (2024) wrote that "dissociations between objective responses and subjective experiences can occur because of different circuits involved" (p. 432). What is especially intriguing from a practice point of view is that in one experimental study, the participants who showed the closest correspondence between self-reported feelings and their psychophysiological responses (heart rate/inter-beat interval, skin conductance level, and blood pressure among others), showed the highest levels of well-being (life satisfaction and low levels of depression and anxiety) (Brown et al., 2020).

The physiological changes that can be called our emotional responses will not correspond perfectly with our feelings as experienced. This can be confirmed by the influence of the context. On the one hand, context determines how we interpret the obvious physiological changes seen in others. Their crying can be tears of joy or of grief or of pathos or of relief. In younger children, we see tears of rage, and in anyone, we can see tears of physical pain. Only the nature of the events that caused them can tell you what they are feeling, and even then, it can be uncertain. There is also a difference over and above the volume of tears between crying and tearing up. And within crying, there are substantial differences between sobbing (often involving gasping and noisy convulsive breaths) and weeping (where the feelings of sorrow may be comparable but are displayed more modestly and less communicatively).

We often rely on the more fine-grained, miniscule facial musculature changes to tell us what someone else is feeling. As an exercise, the next time someone you know well tells you about an incident that happened to them, don't say anything but put on an expression of doubt or disbelief, to see if they notice. If they do, they will most likely say "What? Don't you believe me?" But the larger, major changes are surprisingly similar for vastly different emotions and can often be ambiguous. Thus, when we look at photographs of facial expressions and don't know the context, identifying the feeling being expressed can be difficult, especially when they are both extreme, like rage and ecstasy (Barrett et al., 2011). Recognition of different emotions from photographs is therefore quite limited as a measure of emotion sensitivity. However, it does take understanding, part of what has been called emotional intelligence, to interpret accurately a facial expression or other physiological reaction without knowing the context (Elfenbein et al., 2002). The same challenge is present in reverse. One should be able to judge what a person is likely to feel, regardless of the look on their face, from knowing their specific circumstances, such as when passed over for a job, when seeing someone else hurt, or being given an award they didn't deserve.

Similarly, our own subjective judgment of what we are feeling is itself influenced by the context. We know this from at least two different sources. One is that each of the major emotions we feel do not in fact seem to be accompanied by a unique pattern of physiological change. This will be raised again later, as the search for precise physiological markers of any specific emotion has been long, complicated, and ultimately unsuccessful. The second source for context-dependency of feelings comes from the ingenious work of Schacter and Singer (1962), now considered a classic. They hypothesized that if a person experiences physiological arousal for which they have no immediate explanation, they will identify this state and report their feelings according to the situation and their cognitions about the context at that point of time.

The key manipulation involved administering epinephrine to participants (or a placebo for the controls). An epinephrine injection (a medical form of the hormone adrenaline) will cause an increase in heart rate and blood pressure, pupil dilation, and more rapid breathing, among other physiological effects. Then the participants interacted with a confederate who acted either angry or euphoric. When unaware of why they were feeling general arousal, their observed affect and their self-reported feelings matched the emotion of the confederate. There are subsequent studies of this misattribution effect that make the picture more confusing. There have been failures to replicate the original findings (e.g., Cotton, 1981; Marshall & Zimbardo, 1979), and there's a problem that *any* unexplained or unexpected physiological arousal might be perceived negatively

(Maslach, 1979). But for now, we can stick with the idea that the physiological expression of different emotions might be somewhat similar (excitement and fear, for example) and the way they are experienced, positive or negative, is influenced by the context. Later, I will complicate the picture by reminding you that we have feelings about our feelings—some people like (enjoy) the arousal experienced in potentially dangerous or thrilling situations (being on a rollercoaster or going rock climbing) and willingly expose themselves to scary experiences, especially when the true level of danger is low (like a "haunted" house during Halloween). And we relish the emotional feelings aroused in a thrilling, scary, or sentimental movie.

A further reason for separating the terms *emotion* and *feeling* will become more apparent as we go on, but as a hint, let us think of an example of what are called *soft feelings*. Feeling old is a commonly reported soft feeling with a hint of a negative *valence*. It can clearly have emotive properties but is hardly a distinct emotion the way we think about a sudden innervating force in psychology like fear or joy. Another that really doesn't have much of an *arousal* element at all might be "I feel blessed by good fortune." It is a nice feeling to have, but it is more a cognitive account of a judgment that the good things in your life are not entirely a result of your own doings. Feeling inner peace is a wonderful positively valenced feeling (Lomas et al., 2024) with strong cultural overtones. Its low level of arousal might make it an interesting outcome measure of certain therapies. Following recent conventions in emotion theory, I will usually be referring to *arousal* or *activation* as a synonym for the strength of a feeling, and to *valence* for positiveness or negativeness of the feeling. These two terms are commonly used in any discussion of emotion.

If the words "I feel" or "I'm feeling" can be easily replaced by "I think" or "I'm thinking," this doesn't negate the presence of an experience with positive valence but suggests that the emotional arousal component is small. "I've been feeling for some time that these sessions aren't doing me any good," says your client (rarely, one hopes). The feeling might be disappointment, even anger, but the emotive element can be dissipated by a feeling statement that reflects a thought rather than an emotion. I am cheating a little here because the word *feeling* actually has more than one meaning and is often used in a variety of ways. For example, "I feel like an ice cream" usually means little more than something has triggered the thought of an ice cream, and you have a concurrent desire for one. (The ambiguity potential of this comment is revealed by what we always replied when in elementary school if someone made such a remark: "Really? You don't look like one!")

In addition, the word feeling is derived from one particular sense, that of touch. You *feel* the wind in your face, the softness of fur, the smoothness of someone's skin. Unpleasant tactile sensations can arise from irritation. The word "irritated" was one originally designed for disturbances to your skin or soft tissue—an itch that has to be scratched, or an inflamed throat that has to be soothed, a tickle in your mucous membrane that results in a sneeze. Thus, when you say you feel *irritated* (usually *by* someone or some social context in which others have a degree of control over you), you are using a word both less strong than *angry*, and slightly different in the type of feeling to be conveyed.

We have, furthermore, come to use the term feeling to describe many different sensations other than tactile ones, for instance I feel sick, I feel tired, I feel thirsty. Each of these feeling statements could be replaced with the word *am*—I am tired, et cetera. And we use it as well to describe the identification (experience of) complex and thus highly clinically relevant emotive states: I feel unloved, I feel humiliated, I feel accepted, I feel responsible. Sudden insight—the Aha! experience—is accompanied by combined feelings of surprise, delight, and confidence (Irvine, 2015). The feeling of surprise usually has a negative valence (uncertainty) until you discover the situation is benign, like a surprise party, when it is replaced by a positive feeling of pleasure which is strengthened by the concurrent feeling of relief. The feeling of confidence is one of certainty that the suddenly discovered solution or understanding is basically correct. But while a useful heuristic, insight can mislead because certainty is influenced by past information (Grimmer et al., 2022).

From a consciousness perspective, Hurlburt and Akhter (2006) have also pointed out how people use the word feelings in three quite distinct ways: "(1) to describe bodily sensory awarenesses (e.g., 'I was feeling a tickle in my throat'); (2) to describe emotional experience (e.g., 'I was feeling anxious'); and (3) to describe an inward impression or state of mind (e.g., 'I was feeling that I should take Elm Street instead of Pine Street because there would be less traffic')" (p. 248). As I have explained, however, all three have the identical function of expressing affect—feeling unwell, feeling nervous, and feeling regret/doubt, respectively.

Feeling Descriptions, Metaphors, and Conditions

In every human language, then, we have unique labels for our feelings, and these help to make the emotion conscious. Common feeling terms rely on their historical use and verbal associations. When someone feels *cheerful*, we know it is not quite the same as happy; in archaic terms, they "are of good cheer." When your team scores a goal, you cheer; when the team wins, you give them three cheers. When you clink glasses of alcoholic drinks, you say "Cheers!" When you feel cheerful, therefore, you are in a disposition that is lighthearted, positive, optimistic, successful. Some feeling words are now so archaic that they only get used on odd occasions, like religious festivals—"merry gentlemen" only turn up at Christmas time. Merry is a feeling and a state closely related to gaiety, dancing, music, and being mildly tipsy. And because of that dubious association with having a good time, British people will wish you a more restrained "Happy Christmas" rather than "Merry Christmas," which all Americans will wish you, unless they are trying to be sensitive of your personal religious beliefs and feelings, in which case they will wish you "Happy Holidays."

There are some feeling words that seem to be more a description of the person's general affect than of what they are consciously feeling. An example that comes to mind is the word morose. We are more likely to say someone is looking or acting morose than for someone to say, "I feel morose." We make the judgment based on their sulky sullen looks, glum and sad demeanor, and their grumpy behavior, for which in the US at least we will call them "Not a happy camper." It might be stronger or more pervasive than sad, but it is definitely different from depression, since there is a strong suggestion that the black cloud hanging over them can be easily lifted. Morose people can be cheered up and cajoled; when they are depressed that's not so easy. On the other hand, moroseness is something of a character style, and people who tend to be pessimistic are called "crêpe hangers" in America. In Britain, people will recognize Eeyore from A. A. Milne's *Winnie the Pooh* as having this style, and thanks to Disney, Americans will as well. I mention some of these iconic symbols because in psychotherapy, depending on your client's background, it is often useful to use well-known personalities and fictional characters to illustrate your point about a feeling that is otherwise hard to depict entirely in words. In therapy one can quietly tease a client and point out an issue without directly criticizing them by referring to well-known icons. "You're being a bit like Oscar the Grouch this morning" will be understood by any American client who has ever watched Sesame Street on television.

Some feeling words capture the action of the person with that feeling more than the feeling itself. Dudgeon is a feeling of indignation but used to reflect an action such as angrily departing from a situation. "He left the meeting in a state of high dudgeon" conveys a *response* of storming out of the room while trying to look dignified. It's an old-fashioned word, and don't worry—no one knows it's origin; we just know that as a feeling, it is always "high." And if he instead "left in a huff," you would know that the feeling of anger was short-lived, and the cause was probably something rather petty. And if something offensive to you was said at the meeting, you wouldn't "storm out" because you would stay in the shadow (Latin: umbra) and "take umbrage" if the remark seemed deliberately offensive to you personally. Some of our feelings can be hurt; in this case, it might have been your pride.

When asked to explain your feelings, you might describe a complex circumstance which made you feel that way. The feeling is simple, but it is based on an essential *logic*. Logic is a technical term for the circumstances which are necessary for a particular feeling (Thomas et al., 2020); I'm not sure it is the ideal term for the defining conditions of a feeling, but I will use it throughout the book. There is a difference in the feeling logic if you say to someone "I feel disappointed" or "I feel let down." If someone promises to take you out to dinner and when you get there, the restaurant is closed, you can say you feel disappointed. You may even be a little sad, but your friend is not to blame, and it wouldn't be fair to say you feel let down. But if you were looking forward to it all week and your friend called and cancelled because they are doing something with someone else, you can certainly say that you feel let down. You can be disappointed also, and sad, but now it is tinged with anger at the betrayal of trust. It was Andrew Ortony who first explored the criteria for a genuine emotion on the basis that one can report both feeling and being something: I *feel* disappointed, and I *am* disappointed, indicates the same emotion (Clore et al., 1987; Ortony et al., 2022). But when we communicate to others, the semantics are different, since the statement of *being* suggests a more discernable focus (such as "I am disappointed" *in you*?), as opposed to one implied ("I feel disappointed" *by what*?).

The notion of a feeling's logic, its necessary contingency rules, will be mentioned a great deal more. For although these logic rules can be described in words, those words are not necessarily experienced or understood by the person with the feeling. They are not the cognitive precursor to the feeling, usually an event is. The nature of the event can be misinterpreted, of course, which is a cognitive process, but it is still the event as perceived that is the trigger for the feeling. It is also important to remember that whether a feeling is below awareness or very strongly felt, it is nevertheless an experience and can be felt quite independently of the words you might have to describe it, or, if you are a child, the words someone else has given you. Feelings are *experiences* and while you may have words to describe them, and poetic metaphors to make them more vivid or precise, the words, the metaphors, the contingency rules (logic) which justify the feeling are not the feeling. The feeling is the experience, and it is not a cognition. Feelings might require a cognitive appraisal of a situation and its meaning, but the appraisal is not the feeling, nor is it the trigger for the feeling.

Identifying and Classifying Emotions

Given that *emotion* is the overarching construct, it is useful to say a few things about current ideas regarding the description, classification, and measurement of emotions. In this section, I establish a few basic ideas about defining and organizing this sprawling topic. How many basic emotions are there and what common dimensions do they have? Is the form of one emotion the opposite of another? Harlow and Stagner (1932) suggested that emotions could best be identified on the basis of a few feeling dimensions. They recognized four differentiable feelings: unpleasantness (in degrees up to pain); the *different* not opposite feeling of pleasure or pleasantness (also a matter of degree); excitement; and depression. They said the tone of emotions was based on these dimensions, which are eerily like the modern dimensions of valence (negative pain and positive pleasure) and arousal (excited and depressed). They further argued that this was why that far it had not been possible to find discrete physiological conditions for specific emotions. Remember, it was Harry Harlow who famously demonstrated that baby rhesus monkeys preferred a cloth-covered surrogate mother to a plain wire one that provided them with food.

From 1932 onward, the apparently simple question of what an emotion is and how many there are has still proved to be quite difficult. Paul Ekman began his illustrious career focusing on facial expressions and bodily gestures, with a special interest in clients who would claim to be feeling a certain way but whose behavior suggested the exact opposite (Ekman, 1964). Soon he became one of the leading psychologists developing a comprehensive descriptive theory of emotions, beyond those of the major "emotional disorders." Based on identifiably different expressions of emotion, he argued that there are seven universal, innate, human emotions (Ekman, 1999). These are anger, disgust, contempt, fear, sadness, surprise, and happiness/enjoyment. He thus simply added *contempt* to the list of six "primary" emotions that Darwin (1872) had already described. Like Darwin, Ekman identified these because, he argued, they are the emotions that have distinct facial expression which are represented similarly across cultures. They are known in emotion theory as basic emotions. We tend to treat the first five of the seven as negative emotions, with even surprise being negative at first for most people. So, are we able to express facially a range of different negative feelings, but have only one or possibly two for pleasurable feelings?

As I will suggest later, "negative" is not in any case a helpful label for *any* emotion, other than conveying a sense that there are times we don't like feeling them. In fact, what makes a feeling positive or negative is related to the object of the feeling. Fear feels negative in relation to things dangerous; amusement feels positive in relation to things funny; surprise is positive when the object turns out to be pleasurable (like a surprise party), and negative when the object is unpleasant (an unexpected letter turns out to be a demand for payment). All feelings are potentially functional, adaptive, and support survival by means of preparation to action.

More recently, Ekman (2003) has suggested that there are varieties of the basic feelings such that there is a family of similar but slightly different members. For positive or enjoyable feelings, this creates some confusion when trying to describe one feeling (e.g., feeling of accomplishment) by means of another (e.g., enjoyment of achieving). Five members of his positive-feeling family are sensory pleasures (e.g., hearing beautiful music, seeing a gorgeous sunset, or feeling your cool satin sheets). The other ones are: interest; excitement (in response to novelty or challenge); relief (to be discussed soon); wonder; bliss; Schadenfreude (German for enjoying the misfortune of one's enemies); elevation (delight in the goodness of others); gratitude; pride in achievement; and pride in the achievement of others. For this last feeling, there is a unique Yiddish word "naches" (נחת) meaning pride and joy, especially the pride parents take in their children.

Another major emotion theorist you are likely to have encountered as an undergraduate in psychology is Robert Plutchik (1962; 1980; 2003). He appears in many introductory textbooks on account of his attempt to organize all the emotions into a wheel—a sort of Periodic Table of the emotions. He is best known for the proposition, like Darwin's, that there are a small number of culturally independent primary emotions. In his system, these are anger, fear, sadness, disgust, surprise, anticipation, trust, and joy. The first four can be considered negative and the last four positive, suggesting that there will always be a distinction between feelings that are positive and those that are negative. But that does not mean that any emotion, even if it feels bad and you'd prefer not to experience it, is actually harmful or undesirable. These emotions are functional: the first four seem to be related to the necessities during our evolution for dealing with an enemy and other dangers, and the last four seem to be related to finding and keeping a mate.

Although the eight primary emotions can be arranged in the wheel, feelings located opposite each other are not all polar opposites. Indeed, this is only true of joy (happy) and sadness. This is probably because the identification of an emotion as primary was based on distinguishable facial expressions. Thus, although we can be surprised, and show it, anticipation is only its antonym in the sense that an event should cause surprise only if you weren't anticipating it. However, the possibility of pairing two emotions (that they can co-occur) allows one to generate a new feeling. Thus, joy and trust combine to feel love; anger and disgust combine to feel contempt, and so on. The suggestion that surprise and fear combine to create the feeling of awe seems to me to confuse surprise with novelty and fear with potential threat. For example, gazing for the first time at the Grand Canyon and witnessing a flight of military aircraft could both give a feeling of awe, one dramatic and the other terrifying depending on where you are. Indeed, the maverick psychiatrist Thomas Szasz (1988) made the cogent argument that surprise cannot be considered an emotion at all, but an arousal reaction to a cognitively unexpected event that enhances and magnifies the primary feeling about the event. An actual danger that takes us by surprise intensifies fear. Thus, generally speaking, predictable and anticipated negative events that are realistic will elicit anxiety but can be more easily managed. Surprising, unanticipated positive events and rewards are experienced more positively. A valued gift given unexpectedly is received with extra pleasure since it creates a previously unrecognized need and satisfies that need at the same time (Szasz, 1988; paraphrased from pages 220–221).

One feature of Plutchik's model is that levels of arousal (feeling intensity) begin to converge with the degree of negativity. For example, the primary emotion of disgust derives from sensations arising from our digestive system: "That turned my stomach," "It left a bitter taste in my mouth," "His behavior was repulsive, made me want to throw up." The extreme version of this emotion of disgust in the wheel is listed as loathing, which means to feel abhorrence, hateful, intense dislike. From the items associated in the wheel, we have the implication that loathing includes utter disgust, detestation, and intolerance.

In modern culture, it is interesting to compare the different list of primary emotions to the seven emotional reaction icons or emojis used for rating postings in Facebook. Liking something is symbolized by a thumbs up image, which has made an originally American GI gesture into a universal sign for approval. Loving something is a beating heart, and caring is depicted by hugging a heart—this emoji being added by Facebook during the COVID-19 pandemic. The other four feelings are depicted as facial expressions: crying face for sadness, laughing (guffawing really) for amused, eyes raised and mouth wide open for amazement ("wow!"—a mildly positive feeling of awe?), and a red, frowning, vigorously shaking face for feeling angry. Needless to say, despite somewhat matching theorists' ideas of universal feelings, seven emojis is hardly nuanced communication and often ambiguous. In Facebook, one can *like* the message because it's clever or true, but be very *angry* about the content of the material being communicated. On the plus side, however, having amusement represented seems an advance on the emotion theorists in psychology, especially as easily recognized facial expressions was one source for considering an emotion primary and universal. Laughter is surely one of the most easily identified expressions of being amused, even though one can laugh sardonically or in a hostile way. And being amused is certainly different from feeling joyful.

Self-conscious and Interpersonal Feelings

There are various other anomalies with Plutchik's wheel of emotions. Shame and guilt, for example, do not appear. Shame and guilt are included, however, in the categories of a third leading emotion theorist, Carroll Izard. He suggested that there are ten primary and discrete emotions: fear, anger, shame, contempt, disgust, guilt, distress, interest, surprise, and joy (Izard, 1977). (If we are going to think of surprise as a positive feeling, perhaps it should be described as amazement, rather than using a word conveying a sense of being startled, which is negative). The definition of *basic emotions* in Izard's system comprises neural, bodily/expressive, and feeling/motivational components, generated rapidly and nonconsciously when a relevant external stimulus is sensed or perceived (Izard, 2007).

By including feelings of shame, guilt, and embarrassment, the list of basic emotions is broadened to include those we label the self-conscious emotions. They arise from the emergence of a sense of self, or more precisely from recognition firstly, that one is different from others (there is me and there is you), and secondly from being observed by others. These feelings in relation to others can be quite complicated. Think, for instance of the feeling of being an imposter. It is commonly expressed—even given the status of a syndrome—when someone senses they are receiving more recognition and acknowledgment than they deserve. It is tied closely to uncertain feelings of self-esteem but always context-related, when one's performance is being scrutinized and positively evaluated.

From an evolutionary perspective, these self-conscious feelings relate to the need to be accepted by others in your group whom you depend upon, and on the conventions and acceptance rules around privacy and decency your group has developed over time. Middle-class British people of the mid-twentieth century often report that when growing up, their parents emphasized the importance of not making a show of themselves, talking too loudly, or dressing flamboyantly: not "making a fuss"—anything that would attract attention from others. Note that self-directed feelings, such as self-loathing or self-admiration, are not just self-*conscious* feelings, but self-*referenced*. To the extent they can be detected by others, these differ in their degree of social acceptance. Various forms of self-deprecation (like self-pity) are disliked socially because they seem manipulative and designed to elicit sympathy from others.

There has, however, been an increased interest in self-deprecating feelings in recent years thanks to the emergence of Compassion Therapy, originally introduced by Paul Gilbert (1989). There are various current iterations of the idea, but the essence of all of them is the importance of treating oneself with "loving kindness," being less judgmental and less critical regarding one's own flaws and inadequacies, as well as seeing the connection between oneself and all humanity. In Neff's (2003) 26-item Self-Compassion Scale, thirteen have the word "feeling" or "feel," thus providing a helpful operational definition of someone's tendency to be too hard on themselves. Obviously self-compassion and self-acceptance must be modulated since extreme self-admiration is damaging. Nobody likes show-offs. Narcissism is a socially distasteful trait and in its overly dominant form can be a personality disorder. Reflection on mistakes and using self-awareness to be a better person is also important. Gilbert's (2005) comprehensive volume on the concept of compassion and its use in psychotherapy is useful reading for all professional psychology trainees and practitioners.

When being the center of attention is enjoyed by an individual for whatever reason, it often results in a positive feeling called pride. One form of feeling proud is often accompanied by particular body postures. "Puffing out your chest" is commonly mentioned and frequently seen in my culture, whereas acting "cocky" captures the posture and strutting of a bantam cock. Pride feelings also elicit excessive behaviors which can be characterized negatively by others as "showing off" and, when verbal, as "boasting." When, for whatever reason, being noticed by others is not enjoyed, we call these shy or bashful feelings, yielding a potential dynamic (emotional cause) for avoidance of social situations which can be problematic (think social anxiety disorder).

If this dislike of social attention (not enjoying being noticed socially) is strong, feelings of embarrassment occur even if the person has not objectively done anything embarrassing. Sometimes social attention can be excessive and perhaps not entirely deserved, which is a classic trigger for mildly pleasurable coyness. But if the person is observed engaging in a behavior usually considered within the culture to be private and inappropriate in public, the immediate feeling is acute embarrassment, often but not always revealed by such distinctive physiological events as blushing. Blushing is a non-voluntary response of the sympathetic branch of the autonomic nervous system, in which increased adrenalin or neurons in the dorsal hypothalamus causes cutaneous vasodilatation of the face, neck, and ears (Drummond, 2013; Mathis & Kenny, 2018). People don't feel embarrassed when alone and in private but recalling an embarrassing situation will feel very much like the feeling of the original event. If the behavior observed by others is not only embarrassing but also proscribed by one's social group as harmful, it is experienced as feeling ashamed. Feelings of shame can persist long after the public attention or even if the action was not discovered by anyone at all. Shame, as Tangney (Tangney & Dearing, 2002) once explained, is accompanied by the cognition "How could *I* have done that!" That cognition is a handy way of separating shame from guilt, where the cognition is closer to "How could I have done *that*!"

Although those explanatory phrases are often repeated in order to capture the difference between the two feelings, it is not a complete picture from the point of view of the necessary conditions or *logic* of these feelings. Both are based on the negative affect derived from the threat of rejection or abandonment by one's social group. In guilt, there is an implicit threat of punishment for an action, suggesting that the sensation of guilt is derived from anxiety conditioned to an offense by previous punishment. Shame involves fear of rejection for actions taken. The body language is that you hang your head, you need to be submissive so you are not abandoned. Children who have been sent to boarding schools by their parents at a young age, before one cannot fully understand why it might be necessary, often report they felt shame for the first few years as they felt abandoned by their parents who for some reason did not want them.

Feelings of Self in Comparison with Others

There is another cluster of powerful feelings not closely tied to a primary emotion but derived from the recognition of self in a social context and the importance of having feelings for and about others. These have been described by Jonathan

Haidt as the *moral* emotions as they are in response to situations that do not directly impact the self (Haidt, 2003). I have had clients who have expressed burdensome, chronic feelings of being responsible for some seriously negative outcome, but without feeling guilt or shame since their action (or more often lack of action) was, at the time, without malice or harmful intent. One example is of a client, Jim (not his real name, of course), who was an academic, teaching engineering at my university. He self-referred, telling me he was feeling chronic guilt. He had a student, Alan, in the ROTC program who had just been offered a commission in the US Army Corps of Engineers and was being assigned to an interesting but potentially dangerous short-term deployment in another country as soon as his BSc was awarded. But in the final exam of the final course needed to graduate, Alan did unexpectedly poorly. Jim told him he would have to repeat the class, which would have prevented him from graduating. Alan pleaded with him to look again at his exam and see if he could not revise the grade upward just enough to pass. Alan emphasized how graduating and getting commissioned was an outstanding opportunity for him. Jim was persuaded, re-marked the exam, and adjusted his grade to a narrow pass. Alan graduated and went off to the military assignment. But two months later, just as his unit's work was completed and they were about to return home to their base in the USA, Alan was killed by enemy sniper fire. Jim knew that he was not the cause of Alan's death, but the therapeutic focus was to move away from guilt to an analysis of his overwhelming feelings of responsibility, having gone against his better judgment regarding academic standards.

There is a very commonly expressed feeling that is not typically identified in lists of self-conscious emotions, but which belongs in that category. This is feeling sorry. Like so many feeling terms, sorry has at least two meanings. One is that one feels sorrow for others' situations. You could, for example, know that someone is grieving because they have lost a friend. You could have some awareness of what that feels like and you could express sympathy for them ("I'm so sorry for your loss"). If you knew the person who has died, you might also share the feeling of sorrow, in which case both of you would feel sad and express that feeling ("Mary's departure makes me very sad too"). If you know someone is suffering and you feel sorry *for* them, it can be tricky to express that feeling, as if it borders on the feeling of pity which is not usually welcomed by the recipient of the feeling. The feeling is resented by others unless it is accompanied by active attempts to help ameliorate the other person's loss—the verbal form "take pity on ..." reveals a lack of redress.

It has become standard practice to define empathy as being able to "put yourself in the other person's shoes." What does that mean? Does it mean you have the ability to recognize how someone might be feeling in a certain situation, or does it mean you are able to make yourself feel the same way even though you have not shared the same experience? The latter is often assumed to happen, but the former is much more common. Therefore, empathy is often not really a feeling at all, but a cognitive understanding, a description of a willingness to consider others. Indeed, saying "I know how you feel" is often an unwelcome comment if the other person has had a dreadful experience, since you cannot possibly share the intensity of the feeling. Where empathy somewhat approaches a feeling state is that if you see people or even animals suffering from hunger, drought, disease, warfare, and other catastrophes, exposure to that knowledge could be a trigger for anger, more likely outrage, and intense feelings of sympathy if the people who are suffering appear to be innocent of any cause. Empathy does seem to be a valuable pro-social cognitive ability for individuals living in interconnected societies to have when judging distant situations and to direct their actions of helping or their policies and their society's actions. It is an important personal ability to understand and then share in another's feelings. The absence of empathic conditions, having a callous disregard for other people's distress, can be related to overpowering feelings of hatred, an issue we will encounter again in Chapter 9. "I don't care" can mean I refuse to think about your distress, or it could mean you are so inconsequential or so disliked that I can even feel some secret pleasure in seeing your suffering. The pleasure is kept secret because it is socially unacceptable; where it is allowed to be accepted, the feeling is often one of gloating, which is taking active pleasure in someone's distress due to prior feelings of hatred or hostility or condescension.

The other meaning of sorry, derived from the first, is when you are apologizing for something. Saying sorry in conflict situations, like a domestic or marital argument, has powerful de-escalating power when words spoken or negative behaviors are regretted. It usually depends on the other person or persons believing you are sincere and that the "sorrow" feeling about your behavior is genuine. Parents often train their children to "Say sorry!" when they have done something wrong, and any negative outcome is the child's fault. Apologizing for things that are not your fault is, in most cultures, seen as a sign of weakness. There is a standing joke among people in Britain, for example, that an English cultural characteristic is to constantly apologize for minor things, like inadvertently bumping into someone. The amusement arises when one apologizes, "I'm so sorry," when it was the other person who bumped into you.

Gratitude and Trust

There are some important feelings related to one's dependence on others and their dependence on you. Feeling grateful requires recognition that something has been done for you requiring generosity or sacrifice on their behalf. Parents quite often explain to children how others have benefited them directly, but there is a risk that excessive gratitude can lead to lower self-confidence. The nature of gratitude is better understood by children when they are encouraged to be generous to others but not to expect anything in return. Feeling generous is often related to feeling confident about one's own resources. In children, this pro-social behavior is studied experimentally by seeing how willing children are to share their winnings in a game with someone else. The range of variables influencing such behavior is considerable.

When attempting to increase a client's access to positive feelings, gratitude, while ostensibly positive in valence, is a tricky feeling in countries or societies that value an individual's sense of independence. New Zealand culture contains a powerful image of the totally self-reliant Kiwi bloke, who is "rugged and practical—fixes anything, strong and tough, keeps his emotions to himself, usually scornful of women" (Phillips, 1987, from the book cover). The United States is particularly imbued with mythology around the self-made man, that hard work is all you need to get ahead. Frank Sinatra sang that he "did it my way." Some politicians are only able to support basic social welfare programs if these are described as "a hand up, not a handout." Much of the animosity towards Black American history by some conservatives in the USA is that people don't want to be reminded that the wealth and lifestyle of their forebears were based on the exploitation of slave labor and resentment of the liberal argument that the "playing field is still not level." When one lives in relative luxury in comparison to other parts of the world, it is difficult to feel grateful for running water, steady electricity supply, and surplus quantities of food. Nevertheless, if used carefully, encouraging clients to recognize their interdependence on others in one's society can promote simple acts of kindness and showing gratitude.

Another feeling not derived from strong emotional responses is the interpersonal feeling of trust, usually directed towards another individual in such a way that permits positive approach behavior, compliance, acceptance, and reduces feelings of suspicion. This is a self-conscious feeling because it is an "I" feeling in juxtaposition with "You." In other words, the person is in a social context in which certain behaviors are (and always were in human history) important for effective group functioning and constructive interpersonal relationships. Trusting others is itself a positive feeling and if it is justified, it leads to further positive affect—as noted above (positive approach, cooperation, reduced hesitancy in acceptance). These consequences of feelings of trust are often exactly what will benefit the therapeutic relationship and interactions, both directly by making the therapy and therapist more positive and indirectly in terms of making compliance with therapeutic suggestions more likely.

While we usually think of the self-conscious emotions as all relating to the primeval importance of being accepted in a social group, there is another cluster of feelings having less socially cohesive overtones. In situations of shortage or resources, survival may depend less on cooperating with others and more on competing with them. Feelings of power and domination and superiority can have the action tendency of bullying and taking advantage of someone else's weakness.

Other Affective Experiences: Moods and Preferences

Mood obviously refers to feelings, but general, ongoing ones. Some feelings are by definition moods. Disgruntled is a good example. It is a state of general negative affect, not directly related to any specific event, and long lasting because its causal elements are chronic experiences of regular irritation and disappointment that things are not going right when they should be. That is why we rarely talk about a mood as anything other than a collective noun for emotions, either negative (disappointed, sulky, peeved, irritable, all at once) or positive (cheerful, contented, satisfied, grateful) that are predominant for an extended time period. The clinically useful Positive and Negative Affect Schedule (PANAS) (Watson, Clark, & Tellegen, 1988) asks people (including children, see Laurent et al., 1999) to estimate how often over a selected period of time they have had any of an extensive list of possible feelings, both positive (e.g., proud, determined, inspired, enthusiastic) and negative (e.g., distressed, upset, afraid, jittery). The important point about the PANAS is it reveals that people can have both positive and negative feelings within the same time frame.

Happiness (subjective well-being) is often studied in psychology as a mood or as a personality trait ("I'm a happy person"). Some cultures, especially Western, educated, well-off societies endorse happiness as a value to be maximized (Krys et al., 2025). However, happiness can also be a discrete, time-limited feeling ("I feel happy at this moment"). In clinical work, the opposite mood, sadness, is most often used for a feeling (I feel sad at this moment"), because if someone is in a sad mood, their affect is more likely to be described as depression. Mood terms are usually broadly evaluative—good or bad—rather than related to a specific feeling. Everybody knows what being in a good mood feels like ('top of the world" and "on cloud nine"), and what a bad mood feels like ("down in the dumps," "in the doldrums," "got up on the wrong side of the bed"). Mood refers to chronic, ongoing, dominant, or hard to interrupt feelings. There may be one contributing event as the trigger, but typically there is an escalation, a cascade, of many similar previous events.

What is so interesting about bad moods is how easily they can alter the affective value of things usually liked and enjoyed. A cartoon in the newspaper comics section called *Family Circus* shows the usually bossy little girl saying to her three younger brothers who are roughhousing: "You boys better be good! Daddy's on a diet again!" (Bil & Jeff Keane, 2025). The beneficial side of this overall influence of moods is that it works in reverse. Things and experiences often disparaged will become more positive and feel more desirable when a strong positive mood can be induced. While feelings typically come and go, low-level feelings can linger, creating mood states making other contrary feelings less likely. How to turn a negative or blah mood into a positive one will be an important source for changing specific feelings in a more positive direction (Evans, Heriot, & Friedman, 2002).

In psychiatry, for a diagnosis of major depressive disorder, the patient needs to have at least one of the two critical symptoms: (1) "depressed mood most of the day ... indicated by ... subjective report (e.g., *feels* sad, empty, hopeless)" (my italics); or (2) "markedly diminished interest or pleasure in all, or almost all, activities most of the day, nearly every day as indicated by ... *subjective* account" (American Psychiatric Association, 2013, p. 160). These two states (depressed mood and anhedonia) seem quite likely to co-exist—although they are different experiences. Feeling sad is not the same as diminished pleasure, a feeling that will be considered in much more detail in Chapter 3, where it will be apparent that it is not the same as diminished interest. All three feelings are different than feeling empty, or hollow inside, as some people describe it. Feeling sad is related to the loss of something valued. Feeling empty seems close to being a client's description of anhedonia, the medical term that has been around since the end of the nineteenth century for loss of interest or pleasure. Feelings tend to be poorly defined in psychiatric terminology. Just to give one example, the widely used Hopkins Symptom Checklist (Derogatis et al., 1974) has twenty-five items, eleven of which start with the word "Feeling." Item # 20, "Feeling trapped or caught" has interesting evolutionary overtones; # 19, "feeling lonely" can be temporary, but the item presumably hopes to capture the negative mood state of loneliness.

Preferences

Preferences—liking and disliking, which is a milder feeling state than loving and hating—are affectively more complicated than they seem. For one thing, when you ask clients what they like and what they don't, there is always the risk of social desirability factors influencing their answer. There are very few things in our experiences that are intrinsically likeable or dislikeable. Some people like oysters, gardening, kickboxing, canaries, spanking, Johnny Cash, pedicures, and ocean cruises. Others dislike those things. If a client tells you she likes pickleball, it probably means she enjoys playing it. If she says she dislikes football, she probably means she doesn't enjoy watching it. Liking something is typically more static, whereas enjoyment is more often a feeling related to an activity—you enjoy a good meal and like asparagus, dislike the flavor of cilantro, like Chablis, enjoy eating out with friends, like the chef. Our personal likes and dislikes are so varied and so idiosyncratic that it is impossible to trace the origins of their emergence, their permanence, and their frequent radical change of valence.

However, there are clues as to the processes involved, and these give insight into ways feeling preferences can change. Factors such as familiarity, the likings of one's family and social group (experiencing shared emotion, as will be discussed later), association with other experiences (a case of bacterial vibriosis will quickly alter your liking of oysters), your core values, the satisfaction experienced or health benefits after an activity, the way an item attracts the positive attention of others—it's a long list and it will become clearer as well as more technical as we proceed.

It seems slightly circular, but why we like things is because they give us positive feelings, and if we have positive feelings, we say we like whatever produces them. The circularity can be reduced by the fact that liking something really means we value and enjoy that thing in a general sense, whereas the feeling might be quite specific. For example, we may really like and value a pair of shoes we have and will wear them as often as we can. But the positive feelings they give might be as varied as physical comfort with no pain when wearing them, or feeling chuffed by the positive comments you get from friends ("Love your shoes, my dear!"), or by making you appear taller, you feel more confident. Liking certain people might be less related to love and attraction and more to feelings of admiration or respect.

In current CBT, there are many therapeutic practices designed to enhance a client's general feeling of well-being by encouraging participation in activities once enjoyed (behavioral activation), and more importantly, engaging again with things liked which give pleasure. Everyday life is full of simple pleasures: a good wine, a brilliant touchdown, beautiful music, a hot shower after a long walk on a chilly day, a cup of strong coffee, a spoonful of creamy peanut butter, a hug from your grandmother. All Eliza Doolittle in *My Fair Lady* wanted was "*a room somewhere, Far away from the cold night air, With one enormous chair, Oh, wouldn't it be loverly*? *Lots of chocolate for me to eat, Lots of coal makin' lots of heat, Warm face, warm hands, warm feet, Oh, wouldn't it be loverly?*" In some ways, her simple pleasures were in contrast to what she had been used to, but any of us might enjoy at least one or two of her listed delights. Novelty is one of our strongest conditions for liking something, and so, unfortunately is familiarity, which has the rather fascinating consequence that tourists' enjoyment of highly varied experiences is far from guaranteed (Volo, 2021).

Liking something is a general term for feelings of attraction that lead to approach (a wonderfully general term and a topic in Chapter 3). But liking entails levels. These levels have names, and in order of intensity, I suggest the list goes something like this: prefer, like, enjoy, attracted to, enchanted by, value, delighted with, entertained by, treasured, captivated by, love, enamored of, fascinated by, want, crave, obsessed with, depend on. Prefer is at the lowest end because it represents a selection from two or more liked things when there is a choice: I like white wine, but I prefer red. When clients go on a diet and give up ice cream, they should select a less preferred but still liked alternative, such as a frozen banana dipped in chocolate. To say you liked a movie or a novel is a bit wishy-washy as a feeling—it is a little stronger to say you enjoyed the movie, or the basketball game, or the ocean cruise, although that is sometimes no more than a summary of pros and cons. You might say you like walking, but you enjoy rock climbing because it gives you a thrill, you were entertained by the play because you got pulled into the emotions portrayed and can experience them yourself vicariously (an extreme form of feelingness when that happens). You are most likely to treasure objects, usually when they have a sentimental value or are a good part of your life story, but you can also treasure your grandfather or your strict piano teacher.

Love, although we can use the term loosely ("I just love my new I-Phone," "Yes, I saw Barbie twice; I love that movie"), is most importantly used for affection towards others. While we recognize that depressed clients might have negative cognitions about themselves ("There is nothing in my future"), not having someone they love who loves them back is surely an equally serious personal circumstance with respect to positive affect. Feelings of love for pets, friends, and family are highly desirable and important for one's happiness. Romantic love, however, offers additional high arousal feelings of excitement and intensity ("falling head over heels" we say) which can be highly positive as hopefully everyone knows or gets to experience (Brogaard, 2015). Romantic love can be a feeling others judge to be irrational, but that is an intrinsic element of the wonder and novelty of the feeling which gives it its power over us (McKeever & Saunders, 2022). The intensity can be problematic if these feelings are not reciprocated. Yet many would agree with Tennyson's words in 1827 that "*I feel it when I sorrow most: 'tis better to have loved and lost than never to have loved at all*," and they serve as a useful cognitive restructuring for a client's feelings of deep disappointment. Feelings of love for your god can be equally intense and are less dependent on reciprocation, which can, frankly, be rather uncertain. However, if expectations of some benefits are not forthcoming, people can experience the same disappointment and feelings of rejection as in other instances of non-reward. Negative feelings like these can lead to loss of faith and challenges to one's beliefs.

Want and *crave* both imply a need which the liked object or experience can satisfy beyond the simple enjoyment value. As we increase the intensity of "liking" anything to feelings of want, need, and crave, you can see my list begins to blend with issues of addictions. In fact, many theorists would argue that liking and wanting are actually two different things, distinct components of the biological affective system (e.g., Robinson & Berridge, 2008). The enjoyment or pleasure comes not simply from sensory pleasure and delight but from the reduction of a strong and unpleasant need and aversive experiences. As you can like cigarettes, drinking cocktails, painkillers, gambling, and many other things that might be considered harmful, it shows that excessive "liking" (i.e., the upper ends of my list of "like" terms) is not always desirable from a clinical point of view. Clients can like things too much. At this end of the spectrum, our clinical task is not to increase liking but to decrease it.

You might have thought in my list of liking-relevant feelings that "value" should not have been there at all. Saying you like something or you value something has different meanings. Value can refer either to an individual's personal principles and standards of behavior, or it can mean the importance, worth, or utility of something. In both cases, it is implicit that we have positive feelings (likings) for what is being valued, but it is the former definition that has become a popular topic within CBT, on account of its emphasis in Positive Psychology as well as in Acceptance and Commitment Therapy (ACT). When thinking of feelings, a client's values can be classified in two ways. One is whether their values are talked about or enacted (whether they "walk the talk")—a critical point of distinction when collaborating with clients in psychotherapy. The other is whether their values are extrinsic (e.g., wealth, personal attractiveness, fame) or intrinsic (community related, self-acceptance, service, loyalty) (Tessier et al., 2021). Differences in expressed values (according to the first definition) is a major feature of cultural differences; things valued (second meaning) represent major individual differences.

Let's quickly look at the opposite dimension of liking, which is disliking. One could make a list of terms for not liking that increase in intensity (arousal) of feeling, but as with my list of liking, there are subtle alterations in the valence of the feeling. They are all negative but carry distinct aspects of unpleasure. Some disliked things, especially ones that are people related, make one feel sad, afraid, or envious. When it comes to objects we dislike, there is often a symbolic connection to disgust. There are probably evolutionary influences for this. I've already mentioned that many positive feelings are symbolically and figuratively connected to the sense of touch. But many feelings of dislike, especially disgust, distasteful, revulsion, are connected to taste sensations (sour, bitter, not sweet), odors (foul, stinking), and consummatory/gustatory and defecation experiences—nausea, vomiting, sick, bloated. For an extended period in human evolution, differentiating edible from nonedible required extensive trial and error experimentation driven by hunger and thirst as powerful sources of motivation. As regional availability and climate conditions vary and change, cultures were able to develop liking for edible things which in other contexts humans could find distasteful. In hot climates, pork and shellfish could make you extremely sick and were therefore discouraged by religion. Improved methods of cooking turned frogs, snakes, and eels into delicacies. When any food began to spoil over time, its unpleasant taste could be disguised with herbs and spices, especially spices like curries and peppers.

Facial expressions are used for communicating dislike (Albohn et al., 2019). Infants do not have an innate feeling of disgust although things too bitter, too sour, or too spicey will be spat out. But it is when a toddler picks up something in the street that a parent will say "No!" and take the object away. They might add "Ooh, yuk, that's disgusting," and make a very distinctive disgust face. It is easy to see the evolutionary significance of this facial expression to communicate to your group that something should not be eaten. Since taste is not the only feature of harmful or poisonous things when ingested, it also may have taken prolonged learning trials when someone got sick and vomited. Through simple classical conditioning, the aftertaste of vomit will be a cue not to eat anything that tastes, smells, or looks like that again. Sometimes what made you sick was too much of something else entirely, like alcohol, but the flavor of that drink or distinctively flavored food eaten at the same time, then becomes highly aversive (Busch & Evans, 1977). You can also change food preferences through verbal and imaginal associations. A newspaper story of salmonella at your local buffet will keep you away from it for a long time; a visit to an abattoir can influence your enjoyment of meat; sweetbreads will taste better than thymus glands and escargot better than snails.

Even within cultures and social groups, a liking for things that initially don't look or taste very good is something acquired over time (Rozin & Schiller, 1980). We often talk of a particular food, work of art, or type of movie as an "acquired taste"—an excellent example of a feeling change, in this case acquiring a new positive one. Often, this is through a process of gradual habituation in which the initial unpleasant experience of the substance is reduced by some form of dilution or modification slowly withdrawn over time. One example is drinking coffee. Everyone I know tells me they like (often say love) a good cup of strong coffee in the morning. Obviously, coffee is an addicting substance, which makes it more pleasant due to its chemical effects, but it does not originally taste good to people, especially children. But it can be watered down, sweetened with lots of sugar, made more palatable by adding cream, so that gradually these modifications are reduced until one gets down to a shot of double espresso, which is relished with delight.

All of these changes provide examples of *how* feelings change. As to the *why*, evolution is no longer a relevant component, but social influence is. Children and young people across different societies start to drink coffee, imbibe beer, chew tobacco, inhale solvents, smoke marijuana, because they see their friends, major role models, and other important social influencers doing the same. Having a bad taste in your mouth or smell in your nose is nothing compared to the feeling of belonging, being accepted, being noticed, feeling tough—competing positive and negative feelings is another *how* of change.

Implications

When first presenting their now well-known concept of *emotional* intelligence, Salovey and Mayer (1990) described the key features in a way that the word feelings could easily replace the word emotion: observing and recognizing your own feelings as they happen; handling your feelings appropriately and realizing what is behind them (understanding their logic); being sensitive to others' feelings, being able to take their perspective and realize that they could be different from your own; and the social relationship skill of helping others manage their feelings. Although the word "feeling" can sometimes be a stand-in for the word "emotion," they are not the same things. It might have occurred to you that love does not appear in any of the lists of primary emotions. But feelings of love are surely among the strongest and most important—and beneficial—of all the feelings that we have. And feelings of hate are the most destructive, whether directed against ourselves or others.

The range of possible feelings is vast. Because they are subjective sensations arising originally from physiological needs and survival demands, we sometime forget they also arise from social or psychological needs characteristic of all humans. Many such needs have been proposed, often related to cultural priorities and spiritual beliefs or organized phylogenetically like Maslow's (1943) hierarchy from physiological to self-actualization. Thinking more from an intrinsic reward perspective has given us insight into three extremely common, maybe universal or innate, psychological needs, identified by Ryan and Deci (2000) as being for competence, autonomy, and relatedness. These elements will crop up throughout the following pages in various guises—feelings of powerfulness, feelings of independence, feelings of love and affection, feelings of belonging. A lot of feelings jostle for being considered primary.

People seek psychotherapy, become clients, and receive diagnoses because unpleasant feelings have come to dominate their lives and are influencing their behavior in undesirable ways. But because these feelings are intense and are themselves uncomfortable (it's an interesting conundrum that you can feel things about your feelings!), clinical research usually refers to *emotions* rather than feelings. Sometimes it is not just one type of emotion, like anxiety, that disrupts behavior, but a general difficulty in managing a range of emotions, such that this type of emotional volatility appears to dominate or disrupt their entire personality functioning. Both the volatility and the effects on normally well-controlled actions are often referred to as dysregulation. The words *feelings* and *emotions* are, therefore, rather easily interchanged, as I will occasionally do. But they mean different things, with emotion being the more general category of the phenomena we're interested in, and feelings being an aspect of emotion, with the foci being on the experience of the emotion, the words we use to describe it, the sensations we are sometimes but not always conscious of, and the evaluative element of emotion.

Feelings and the language of feelings are especially important in therapy. While most of the technical, scientific literature in behavior therapy and cognitive therapy refers only to emotions, the practice of psychotherapy requires referring more often to feelings. That's what clients talk about, what you ask them about, and what they or others complain about. When the focus of therapy is, as it should be, on behavior (what the client does), the implication is that the dynamics (causes and consequences) of the dysfunctional behavior are undesirable feelings (Evans, 1993). However, it is not strictly accurate to say that a feeling caused a behavior, despite feelings usually having closely related action tendencies.

A famous dictum in science is that if something exists, it exists in some quantity and can therefore be measured. I've been throwing around two important measurement-related terms: *arousal*, meaning the strength or intensity of the feeling, and *valence*, meaning whether it is experienced as good (desirable) or bad (undesirable). But arousal has other meanings as well, which we will see in the next chapter, and that challenges its usefulness (K. Smith et al., 2025). And valence sounds subjective rather than a reliable property of a feeling. We need to be cautious about the use of these terms, despite their convenience in referring to two different aspects of a feeling. Most importantly, as I will be explaining throughout the following pages, that the meaning or logic (the conditional requirement) of a feeling results in qualitative differences. As an example, *annoyed*, *angry*, *furious*, and *enraged* are obviously at different levels of arousal of the construct and seem to share the same general valence (they feel bad), but they have very different properties with respect to triggers and likely action tendencies.

Because the topic of feelings emphasizes the valence of our affect and not just the strength, we can include in the analysis of feelings such closely relevant things as moods and preferences—likes and dislikes. This all brings us close to the more fundamental issues of therapeutic intervention which should be thought of as more than symptom reduction. The scientific therapy outcome research quite naturally focuses on symptom reduction as a measure of successful therapy. But clients themselves focus on other things—being happy, feeling fulfilled, experiencing pleasure, enjoying life, being respected and valued by others. Those therapeutic goals are all about feelings.

2

Back to Basics

The Conceptual Nervous System

I do like William James. As a graduate student, I bought both volumes of *The Principles of Psychology* (James, 1890/1950) at a secondhand bookstall on the Portobello Road market in London. Prices were based solely on how wide each book was in inches. The infamous James quote that has been misrepresented to countless students is: "*The bodily changes follow directly the perception of the exciting fact, and that our feeling of the same changes as they occur* IS *the emotion*" (Vol. 2, p. 449). Most psychological textbook discussions of emotion start with a simple interpretation of what has become known as the James-Lange theory because William James and Carl Lange independently proposed it. In its essence, it contends that potentially harmful or beneficial situations (e.g., dangers, desirable objects, required resources, social interactions) elicit an array of appropriate overt actions, notably approach (acquire), flee (escape), fight (resist), or freeze (hide) accompanied by the internal physiological responses necessary for supporting or enabling such survival behaviors. Sensations from these responses (interoception) are felt as the emotion.

There have always been criticisms of this basic idea, even though it shaped the development of that branch of behavior therapy grounded in principles of classical (Pavlovian) conditioning. It has always attracted criticism because the James-Lange theory seemed to imply that whether one feels fear or anger or sexual arousal will depend on unique patterns of physiological changes for each situation. There is plenty of evidence that this is not the case. Furthermore, Walter Cannon and his doctoral student Philip Bard in the 1920s demonstrated that visceral responses (smooth muscles and glands and their hormones) activated by the autonomic nervous system (ANS) were too slow to represent fully the essence of an emotional response. Glands like the adrenal gland secrete hormones such as cortisol and adrenaline which in turn regulate critical changes in blood pressure, increase blood sugar, and a host of other effects—all taking some time. Furthermore, ablation studies showed these endocrine changes were unnecessary for emotions to occur. Following various lines of experimental and

How and Why Feelings Change. Ian M. Evans, Oxford University Press. © Ian M. Evans (2026).
DOI: 10.1093/9780197825808.003.0003

clinical research, Cannon and Bard concluded that impulses from the thalamus represented the central brain activity which elicits an emotion. Since then, much more complex models have emerged.

In this chapter, I will survey some of the physiological constructs and ideas that seem most relevant to psychotherapy. What physiological constructs might be most helpful in that long and tenuous link between neuroscience and clinical practice, if any? After all, plotting the central structures and architecture of the brain doesn't tell you much about past experience. The brain itself doesn't feel things, even though it can absorb and retain vast quantities of information, as Emily Dickinson in her 1896 poem *The Brain* made clear: "*The brain is deeper than the sea, For, hold them, blue to blue, The one the other will absorb, As sponges, buckets do.*" The brain doesn't *have* feelings, despite the dualism that creeps into neuropsychology. Sensations arise from peripheral and internal sensory receptors and proprioceptive feedback from changes in organs. Sweating, heart rate changes, blood pressure rises, rapid breathing (hyperventilation), muscle tension, dry mouth, need to urinate or defecate, loss of appetite, feeling nauseous: these are some of the sensations we feel. If a client says, "I'm always anxious," the reply "Hmm, an over-active amygdala!" is not wildly helpful in psychotherapy.

I don't wish to sound dismissive of scientific discoveries by offering caution regarding reductionism in psychology. In principle, I agree with Arthur Staats about the limitations of attributing causes of behavior to brain, mind, or genes—what he called the Great Scientific Error (Staats, 2012). And I've always enjoyed the comments of Thomas Szasz, whom I heard talk at the University of Hawai'i in the seventies, that those who study brains directly are no more studying feelings and emotions than the engineers who design and build TV sets observe and study the events reported on the screen by newscasters (Szasz, 1975, p. xix). (He also went on to repeat his famous critique of psychiatry, claiming that "consulting a psychiatrist is like calling a TV-repair person because you don't like the program you're watching.") The fact is, however, many new insights have emerged from basic neurophysiology influencing even the most ardent black-box behaviorists throughout the history of clinical behavior therapy. My perspective on these is that certain concepts have become ingrained in our thinking, not because of the details of the research findings but because of a more general picture of the workings of the brain—what Donald Hebb once called so wisely the "C.N.S., the *conceptual* nervous system" (Hebb, 1955).

There are certain concepts from neuropsychology that have had a particularly strong influence on the development of cognitive-behavioral therapy (CBT) as a clinical endeavor. This can be seen via the influence of Hans Eysenck, one of the intellectual progenitors of behavior therapy. Eysenck's (1967) personality theory had a biological basis. I'm going to describe it because it shaped many subsequent developments, even though the details have been corrected and the terminology supplanted. Certain concepts at the time had a profound influence on personality theory and constructs relevant to the emotional disorders as seen and treated in psychotherapy. The ones I think should be recognized historically are as follows: the idea of the triune brain, activation or arousal within the central nervous system, the limbic system as being the neural core of emotional activity, the autonomic nervous system (sympathetic, parasympathetic, enteric) as a source of feelings via interoception, and psychophysiological changes as an indicator of emotion and as objective measures of clinical treatment outcomes. Some modern neuroscientists will gasp in horror at this list, but *conceptual* nervous system models from the Eysenck era are still usefully linked to certain relevant change (therapeutic) principles that need to be mentioned: homeostasis, sensitization, adaptation, habituation, conditionability, and extinction. They are also linked to highly relevant clinical constructs from learning theory like reward and punishment, as well as approach and avoidance, and those topics will be discussed in the following chapter. Additionally, for whatever reason, new developments in "affective neuroscience" have not yet had much direct influence on clinical CBT or psychotherapeutic practice. Looking at the development of new scientific insights in the context of the well-established past might foster the contribution of both to clinical practice.

The "Triune Brain": Arousal and Lability

Aristotle commented long ago that human beings are animals capable of reason. But it took neurophysiologist Paul MacLean to describe the brain as having three structures: the more evolutionarily primitive brain stem, responsible for arousal; the visceral system later called the limbic system deep within the brain (consisting of the hippocampus, amygdala, hypothalamus, and cingulate gyrus, the latter receiving signals from the muscles and viscera) responsible for emotion; and the final overlaying of the neocortex, responsible for higher intellectual functioning (MacLean, 1990). After he studied the brains of alligators, he named the structures in the brain's core and the brain stem as the R-complex. "R" is for reptilian, which captured the public's imagination and made the entire notion of the triune brain common knowledge. It was a happy coincidence that the three parts seemed to parallel Freud's distinction of the id, ego, and superego. In MacLean's model, the three parts interact, but, as in Freud's model, they are often in competition.

It is important to emphasize immediately that modern research and scholarship has discredited most of the specifics of MacLean's "conceptual" nervous system. Although the word "triune" means "three in one," and MacLean never suggested we had three brains, the idea of such distinctive parts is negated by a better understanding of all the interacting structures. Major parts of the brain evolved together, not in hierarchical stages. What parts should actually be included in the "limbic system" is now considered vague, although my good colleague in the '80s at Binghamton University (SUNY), Bob Isaacson, wrote the book on the limbic system and was very clear about its structures, interconnections, and functions (Isaacson, 1982). There is now greater precision how some elements participate in other functions—the hippocampus, for instance, is involved in sensory and episodic memories. There do not appear to be purely emotional circuits in the brain, although the amygdala, with its extensive connections to the cortex, is consistently implicated, especially with respect to fear, the topic of so much of the neuropsychology of emotion (LaBar, 2025; LeDoux, 1996; 2000). Modern critiques (e.g., Steffen et al., 2022) emphasize the brain as having interdependent networks that "integrate interoceptive and exteroceptive information ... while adapting to continually changing internal and external conditions" (p. 9)—not quite so compelling a story as the primitive crocodile in our heads.

Regardless of current research, in his day, Hans Eysenck was greatly fascinated by MacLean's ideas. In the 1960s, as he was developing his magisterial work on the biological basis of personality (Eysenck, 1967), he frequently cited MacLean. (I know because he was my doctoral supervisor during these years.) There had also been a flurry of work on the reticular activating system of the brain stem and more information as to how continuous excitatory input maintains different levels of cortical arousal and that these levels were different in different individuals. He was further struck by the new findings on the importance of the limbic system as the center of emotion in the brain (MacLean, 1955)—and the infamous hypothalamic–pituitary–adrenal (HPA) axis and its relationship to stress (Leistner & Menke, 2020).

Eysenck's biologically based personality theory thus evolved, with two fundamental dimensions of personality: introversion/extraversion and stable/labile emotionally. The arousal system, which refers to neural activity and input to the brain that keeps the brain continually active as an organ (as can be seen from electroencephalogram [EEG] activity and its various rhythms), underlies Extraversion. Extraverted individuals are under-aroused and need to engage in high levels of social and other forms of stimulation to function well. The limbic system underlies emotionality, and people with very active limbic systems will be high on the second dimension which he usually labelled Neuroticism, meaning emotionally labile as opposed to being emotionally stable. Individual differences in basic emotionality are fundamental to understanding any person's psychopathology in his theory, with interactions between arousal and learning experiences being responsible for the different forms of psychopathology. The unique value of personality theory for clinical practitioners is the emphasis on individual differences (the unique person), but along dimensions (types) common to many. Typological theories remind therapists that the stories clients tell about specific causal events in their lives will always have occurred against a background of prior dispositions and vulnerabilities.

One of the most convincing demonstrations of emotionality came from Eysenck's animal psychology laboratory at the Institute of Psychiatry. It involved raising a strain of highly labile (emotionally reactive) rats through selective breeding (Broadhurst, 1975). How this was done is a striking illustration of fundamental research in behavioral psychopathology. How do you decide if a rat is high in "neuroticism" (emotionally labile)? Well, like us humans, when they are in a very threatening situation, they tend to urinate and defecate more frequently. Everyone reading this knows what that's like ("I nearly wet my pants I was so scared"), and you are sure to know that in combat, inexperienced soldiers sometimes have toileting accidents. For a rat, just being in an open and unprotected area is very stressful. Thus, if you place a lab rat in a large circular pen (called an open field in the studies), all you need to do is count the fecal boluses or urine patches seen over a given period. Also, if you are a nervous sort of rat, you won't enter into the center of the open field but will just scurry around the walls of the perimeter. Exploratory behavior requires courage, something again we all know. Observers can track how much the rat moves into the open and use that as another measure of emotionality. Rats with high indices of these two measures can then be selected for breeding, and over time, you end up with a strain of neurotic rats for use in other experiments on anxiety, avoidance, conditionality, and so forth.

Of special interest was what happens when different strains of rat (different personality types) are subjected to conflict situations—a major source of stress for all of us. Hungry rats are taught to press a lever for a food reward (approach activity). Then, the approach to the lever is electrified and made capable of delivering a painful shock to the animal (requiring avoidance or escape). Neurotic rats would stop approaching the lever and starve; others would approach regardless, ignoring the punishment and obtaining the reward, a tendency that reminded Eysenck of people described clinically as psychopaths. Eysenck further suggested that extraverts in typical situations, being under-aroused, would condition poorly, and if they were very low in emotionality (unfearful), punishment would not condition anxiety to the behavior being punished. Feelings of guilt he interpreted as anxiety conditioned to the sensory feedback from punished actions. No such conditioning, no guilt; no guilt, no conscience, therefore psychopathic traits. This is another compelling story for which the evidence is not at all strong but allows for examination of feelings like guilt and conscientiousness and links the origins of such feelings to learning experiences (Evans & Wilson, 2016). The classical conditioning of emotion responses, an easily and convincingly demonstrated phenomenon, had a profound effect on the theoretical underpinnings of early behavior therapy.

Neuroticism as a fundamental personality type also appeared later in the Big Five model of personality. It often describes those low on the dimension as calm, even-tempered, and secure; those high on the dimension are stress-prone, less happy, less satisfied with their lives, anxious, and prone to negative feelings (Lahey, 2009). Scores for Neuroticism on a psychometric measure are considered to be normally distributed; most people fall in the middle of the distribution. Eysenck and his wife Sybil Eysenck (1963) developed a personality questionnaire, a psychometric scale to measure a person's degree of neuroticism (and introversion/extraversion), which went through various versions (see, for example, Furnham et al., 2008). Items in the questionnaires are statements like "My mood frequently goes up and down" and "I often feel nervous." The concept of neuroticism received a major publicity boost when David Barlow (2000) first began to suggest that all the different anxiety disorders had a common underlying structure, namely neuroticism. This was also important for his expansion of treatment protocols in CBT as "transdiagnostic," describing generic approaches to intervention that address underlying vulnerabilities in clients' emotional states. Barlow described neuroticism as "*A dimension of temperament marked by elevated stress reactivity resulting in the frequent experience of negative emotions. This negative affectivity is accompanied by a pervasive perception that the world is a dangerous and threatening place, along with beliefs about one's inability to manage or cope with challenging events*" (Barlow et al., 2014, p. 481).

Neuroticism has therefore emerged as important in the understanding of clinically relevant feelings and their changes in treatment, but the dimension as described by Barlow contains many elements. These are not identical to Eysenck's construct, which was of a personality type with the assumption that it is fixed over time and situation. Scores on neuroticism based on self-ratings do agree strongly with ratings by others. But even then, there is ambiguity in the construct (at least as measured by personality questionnaire). There are two prominent themes in neuroticism questionnaire items: those related to anxiety and tension and those related to worry, fear, and vulnerability (Weiss & Deary, 2020). We will soon encounter hints as to why those two sets of feelings are different.

Further Developments: The BIS, the BAS, and the FFFS

When Eysenck retired, his position as Professor of Psychology at the University of London was filled by his former doctoral student, Jeffrey Gray, who had already made a name for himself by translating into English the work of Russian researcher Teplov on Pavlov's approach to individual differences (Gray, 1964). He followed Eysenck's lead in the development of a biopsychosocial approach to personality, but in light of more information from neuroscience, he elaborated considerably on the nature of fear (avoidance) and reward (approach) (Gray, 1987). Partly from dissatisfaction with the role of conditionability in the origin of anxiety disorders, and partly from newer work on brain connections, Gray originally proposed two systems slightly different from Eysenck's orthogonal dimensions of cortical arousal and emotional instability. Evidence had begun to accrue that there is a central neural activation system of brain components, connections, and pathways. It is activated by positive stimuli and is responsible for reward-seeking. And there is another system that is attuned to threatening situations and prepares the person for inhibition and avoidance of punishment.

In terms of personality characteristics, people whose behavioral activation system (BAS) facilitates approach is dominant are motivated by rewards and are thrill-seeking and adventurous. Gray suggested that if there is a specialized neural system, different people might show different behavior patterns regarding reinforcement, and he called that specific concept *reinforcement sensitivity theory*. People with high levels of impulsivity seek immediate gratification, act hastily, and take risks without thinking about the consequences (Whiteside & Lynam, 2001). Those with a more active behavioral inhibition system (BIS) tend to be anxious and cautious in threatening or unfamiliar situations and are sensitive to punishment. People high in BIS tend to be wary, avoid conflict, and can be easily overwhelmed in stressful situations, but they are also more considerate and empathic. There is a slight degree of connection with the Big Five personality theory in that the BAS seems to blend with both Openness and Extraversion, and the BIS with Conscientiousness, Agreeableness, and Neuroticism. The model was instantly popular, and Carver and White (1994) were responsible for developing the BIS/BAS Scales, a personality questionnaire to measure the two constructs in individuals. As a side note, apart from its value in personality research, I have found this questionnaire useful to administer to those clients who seem personally interested in understanding themselves better. Giving them feedback on their scores helps alert them to their deeper tendencies in reacting to different situations of possible reward or punishment. Many clients, in my experience, enjoy comparing themselves to the normative scores on psychological tests. Eysenck, after all, did very well with his book *Know Your Own Personality* (Eysenck & Wilson, 1976).

Since Gray's early model and widespread interest in the BIS and BAS, there have been at least two new iterations of the basic theory. These modifications have occurred as a result of collaborations among Gray (until his untimely death in 2004) and two other research psychologists, Neil McNaughton in New Zealand and Philip Corr in the UK, as well as advances in understanding of brain mechanisms and the differential influence of anxiolytic drugs on both animals and human behavior. I'm going to summarize the main features of the current theory that seem most relevant to practice. It will not be specifying brain areas or neural systems beyond the basic of the conceptual nervous system. The most recent version of the model proposes there are actually three independent but connected and interacting neural systems in what LeDoux (2012) calls the emotional brain, that have been adapted for survival when faced with threat.

Animal researchers have long been interested in what an organism does if confronted by a threat of serious harm. It can approach and attack the danger (fight), it can run away (flee), or it can stand still or hide (freeze), or if you are a hedgehog or a porcupine, roll up into a defensive ball. Humans can and do all these things when feeling intense fear (think adopting a fetal position), so there is a fear system that controls different patterns of defensive avoidance. We can call this the fight, flight, freeze system (FFFS). Work by my former colleague Robert Blanchard at the University of Hawai'i, which always interested me, showed that what a rat does when facing a threat depends on whether it can identify the source (see a cat), which encourages flight, or cannot identify the exact source (hearing a cat meow), which encourages freezing. Freezing presumably is accompanied by taking stock of the situation, listening, attending, vigilance, checking (think humans with obsessive-compulsive tendencies). Cautious approach to a possible threat is a defensive behavior and it requires stopping and waiting.

Gray and McNaughton (2000) therefore considered that the FFFS could be its own separate system, an escape and avoidance system motivated by fear, not anxiety. The BAS in the newer model continues to be involved in approaching and seeking rewards. But there is always conflict between approach (such as searching for food or mates) and avoidance if the presence of danger (threat) is unknown. The BIS system which can inhibit both unnecessary fleeing and help you stop unrewarding approach is then thought to be more of an anxiety system adapted for cautious approach and capable of resolving an approach/avoidance conflict (McNaughton & Gray, 2024). This position fits with the differential effects of anxiolytic drugs, and the distinctive subjective feeling of anxiety ("angst") (McNaughton & Corr, 2008), supporting the conclusion that fear and anxiety must be two different things, which, of course, every clinician recognizes as correct. However, we do use the two words very casually, even as synonyms. Conscious awareness, in particular, comes later than the reflexive emotional reaction to threat. And, one might add, much later in terms of evolutionary history. Corr (2011) has proposed that anxiety, despite being an unpleasant feeling, is adaptive—keeps us safe. There are both fast defensive responses to danger, and slower, conscious and deliberative processes that allow learning to occur for future functional reactions.

Affective Neuroscience Theory and Polyvagal Theory

The late animal neuroscientist Jaak Panksepp (1992, 1998) coined the term "affective neuroscience" in his pursuit of the specific brain systems involved in discrete emotions and the feelings we've been discussing. He constructed a list of what he considered to be the seven primary emotions (three negative, four positive), which is a little different from the lists of the emotion theorists introduced in Chapter 1. This is partly because his attempt was to cover emotions common to most animals, especially mammals. The ones he hypothesized to be primary are always written in capital letters, as they are the identifying labels for the emotion but *not* supposed to be descriptive of what that emotion is like or for. His list is as follows: FEAR (which includes anxiety, confusingly), PANIC/SADNESS (sad, grieving, insecure, sensitive to rejection), RAGE/ANGER (aggressive, hotheaded); SEEKING (curious, exploring, imaginative), LUST (sexual desire and arousal), CARE (nurturing, warm, sympathetic), PLAY (funny, humorous, jokes around). The descriptive terms and adjectives I've added in parentheses are derived from a personality questionnaire—the Affective Neuroscience Personality Scales (ANPS, Montag et al., 2022).

For some reason, LUST didn't make it into the original development of the ANPS, but it did in a German version (Fuchshuber et al., 2023). Their LUST items are a little quaint but capture perhaps the basic elements of sexual feelings although in a somewhat repetitive way. They are (Google translation):

I find it easy to indulge in erotic experiences.
I have often had negative experiences with my sexuality.
I generally find my sexuality satisfying.
I am not particularly open to sexuality.
I can fully enjoy engaging in sexual activities (intercourse, masturbation, etc.).

I have seen few applications of these phenotypes to psychology-driven principles of personality research, and none cited in the clinical psychology or CBT literature.

Better links may come in time, since if we ignore the precise details of this line of investigation and look at some of the commonalities with other research traditions, especially Eysenck's, there are some interesting overlaps. For one thing, these primary emotions are all supposedly subcortical and their anatomical origins and neuropeptides (neuronal signaling molecules) are surprisingly reminiscent of the triune brain model. For another, all seven emotions are, as has been assumed by all emotion researchers from Darwin onward, evolved from survival needs of any animal living in a group context. I think it is helpful to always think of emotions in terms of their functions: their original value to an organism's survival and especially their well-being has not changed that much. If SEEKING began as the necessity to get about and find food and water and mates, that specific goal-oriented part of it may be less necessary today. Yet, if that emotion is what drives curiosity, creativity, and scientific discovery, then we can all be thankful we have this vestigial element to generate positive feelings to motivate valuable behaviors as well as risk taking activities. Similarly, if CARE began as the need to protect offspring and has evolved into caring for others, nurturing feelings, and sympathy, that is a valuable primary emotion to have. Furthermore, primary emotions should elicit a characteristic emotional-behavioral action pattern, and the emotional networks' connections to secondary and tertiary brain levels should facilitate learning. Thus, cortical control becomes able to regulate emotions (paraphrased from Montag & Davis, 2018, p. 1).

This brings us to consider another link with personality research and clinically relevant individual differences, and that is the neuroscience of Stephen Porges. He has written: "Social connectedness is a core biological imperative for humans, since human survival is dependent on trusted others, is wired into our genetics, and is expressed throughout the lifespan starting from the moment of birth" (Porges, 2022, p. 7). A foundational concept of his work is the "concise and intuitive principle that humans, as social mammals, are on an enduring lifelong quest to *feel* safe" (Porges, 2022, p. 2, my italics). He emphasizes that our bodily expression of feelings is through the autonomic nervous system. He argues that feelings are cortical interpretations of the neural signals carrying information to the brainstem pertaining to the state of our visceral organs. It is a psychophysiological model very much in keeping with much of the material already discussed, namely that intero- and proprioception of physical bodily changes are consonant with our experience of feelings. He coined the term "neuroception" as an ability to detect life-threatening environmental and visceral features, while humans, as with other mammals, are also able to respond instantly to cues of safety as well. This promotes sociability by allowing physical and psychological closeness to others without any anticipation of potential harm. Porges (2022) restated Descartes' dictum "cogito, ergo sum," and expressed his version in French: "je me sens, donc je suis" (if I feel myself, I exist) (p. 5).

A corollary of this perspective is interesting. Throughout this book, I discuss facial expressions, body language, gestures, and other behaviors as being clear indicators of how we are feeling. Of course, we can disguise or inhibit such displays, and not everyone is sensitive to their true meaning. But that aside, the fact we display our feelings is a fundamental reality of everyday life. So ask yourself, how did all those facial and bodily expressions evolve? Darwin saw how they were *derived*: a wolf bares it teeth and we curl our lip. But the origin is different. Before we had words, we could communicate our feelings socially by facial and bodily expression and it was crucial to be able to do so in a group-based society. Correctly understanding expressions was essential for advanced social behavior—for approach when a connection was desired, and even more so to indicate that one's approach was friendly and that the approach of others was safe and unthreatening.

Other bodily reactions and gestures are greatly influenced by modeling—there are numerous articles written about how fist pumping, for example, became a common gesture in competitive tennis matches. It is supposed to communicate a feeling of triumph—excitement at vanquishing a foe and thus an expression of aggression. Such behaviors, as well as leaping, jumping around, and dancing in the end goal area in American football, are all based on ancient needs to communicate size and power. In men, at least, these actions increase testosterone and lower cortisol levels. While they are enjoyed by fans of a particular sportsperson, and thus socially reinforced, the aggressive, manly element of the feeling being expressed is not necessarily appreciated by others.

Ideas such as these place great importance in gaining control of the otherwise bodily defenses demanded from our autonomic nervous system (ANS)—required for flight or fight or mating. Porges proposed that this all-critical regulation could not come top down. An evolutionary survival system must predate voluntary control by the cortex—shades again of the triune brain but even more so of Gray, McNaughton, and Corr. A particular mechanism he proposed is to be found in the vagus nerve, and his theory is called the Polyvagal Theory. I will not go into the origins of his interest in this, which is via the phenomenon of respiratory sinus arrhythmia (which is related to the vagus nerve's connection to the heart). There may also be various details of the polyvagal theory disputed by other neurobiologists (e.g., Grossman, 2023) and to which Porges has replied (Porges, 2023). As with other theories, I will introduce a plausible story from his approach that could be useful to any clinician thinking about clients who have difficulty managing their feelings.

The vagus nerve, the 10th cranial nerve, carries signals between the brain, heart, the digestive system and is part of the parasympathetic branch of the ANS. The ventral path is linked to the nerves controlling the face, as well as the inner ear and larynx. That means it is linked to social engagement, such as listening, vocalizing, and communicating via facial expression. It seems to be able to promote calm behavioral states by reducing activity in the hypothalamic–pituitary–adrenal (HPA) axis and inhibiting sympathetic influence on the heart. In terms of our evolution, it is thought to be the most recently developed system. The second system to have developed is the sympathetic fight or flight system. The first to have developed is the dorsal vagus nerve which is involved in immobilization, which includes all forms of behavioral shutting down: freezing, feigning death, rolling up into a ball if you are a pangolin or a millipede. These three systems offer a different slant to the usual differentiation between only the sympathetic and parasympathetic branches of the ANS, which is in the textbooks but long known to be an oversimplification.

Polyvagal theory asserts that the three systems are hierarchically organized. Also, that the higher neural circuits (most recently evolved) inhibit the lower ones. The lower circuits only become activated when the higher system is inadequate and not able to respond to challenges. When in a safe environment (or one perceived as safe), the ventral vagus nerve system, the newest system to have developed, is able to inhibit fight or flight responses, suppresses the HPA axis, slows heart rate, and allows for eye gaze control, facial expressions, attentive listening, all things necessary for social communication and engagement. The absence of hypervigilance and a feeling of safety are reciprocated between individuals during social interaction. Porges calls this co-regulation. It can be seen occurring between a baby and its mother with touch, melodic vocalization, non-verbal cues, smiling and laughter, all part of feeling safe and happy. Exactly the same co-regulation occurs when children play, unless something occurs to threaten the feeling of safety. "*Feelings of safety reflect a core fundamental process that has enabled humans to survive through the opportunistic features of trusting social engagements that have co-regulatory capacities to mitigate the metabolically costly defense reactions*" (Porges, 2022, p. 13). I would add that psychotherapy also depends on this source of influence.

Autonomic Nervous System

Discussion of the physiological changes we identify as the feelings of fear and anxiety typically focus on the fact that these responses evolved over a long period of time when it was necessary to prepare and energize the body to react defensively when confronting or anticipating mortal danger, or to engage in rigorous positive behaviors to acquire things. All of the changes taking place in our ANS enhance in one way or another the body's ability for intense action, remembering that even freezing for humans is preceded by flight—we run and hide from danger. Fighting to defend yourself from a threatening foe can be in response to feelings of anger or fear, the latter is often used today as an explanation—even justification—for a violent act.

But survival, back in our early evolution, required far more than getting scared and running away or retaliating. We had to obtain and then protect precious recourses such as food and water supplies which sometimes meant competing with others, both human and animal, thus requiring non-anger, positive feelings of success and winning. Conversely, feeling that one has been taken advantage of, feeling that something is ours by right, feeling that something has been taken from us, all generate the physiological changes we call anger, and those prepare us to be aggressive. Anger-motivated fighting is designed to obtain domination over others in order to acquire their possessions or scarce resources that cannot be shared. Thus, we see the physiological pathways around anger, aggression and violence are different from those around protecting ourselves from the aggression or threat of others.

There is a third very obvious survival need, and that is cooperating with others and making friends with those who can assist in protecting you, which requires resisting your own immediate selfish needs and impulses for the good of your group. Our successful evolution also required forming close (i.e., affectionate) personal relationships with those who offer pleasure, including all important procreation requirements: having sexual partners, having children, and protecting them during their more defenseless periods of development. So naturally, we have evolved physiological systems yielding feelings of sexual desire (mating) and feelings of vanity related to being attractive to the opposite sex, as well as love and physical bonding. We also needed to evolve, as did other mammals, feelings of parental protection of one's young (starting with mothering "instincts," but clearly demanding fathers' involvement as well). Since one's young also must be accepted by other adults and older children in one's group, and since the cohesion of one's group is necessary for survival, we have evolved strong feelings of nurturance for others, sympathy for the vulnerable, empathy for those beyond the immediate family, and the importance of sharing. All our feelings described in the psychology literature as being pro-social relate back to the earliest phases of human development in which group solidarity determined population survival.

Language to describe feelings is often connected to our original peripheral, autonomic physiological reactions. Thoughts of something disgusting might "make your skin crawl." You shudder at the thought of something really repulsive and your skin does physically react—a superficial cutaneous reflex. When expressing a feeling about a past event that was unpleasant, it might have "left a bad taste in your mouth." Having an actual bad taste in your mouth is usually the consequence of a past behavior, such as eating something that tasted alright at the time but later left you feeling nauseous—the bad taste is a result of changes in salivary Ph, and the sympathetic division of the ANS makes saliva more viscous, making the mouth drier and less able to help you chew and swallow food. And if one has vomited, an unpleasant experience under any conditions, the foul taste in your mouth lingers on and through simple associative learning becomes a feeling elicited by anything disgusting, not just rotten food.

Interoception and Psychophysiology

Interoceptive and proprioceptive feedback from the ANS reactions is, therefore, one of the crucial control mechanisms we have. Sensations arising from one's bladder or one's rectum tell us that we need to urinate or have a bowel movement. A warm sensation in our face tells us we're blushing; heart beats can be felt, tell us how aroused we are. Hormonal secretions can be readily detected from their effect on other bodily systems. Menopausal decline in estrogen levels interferes with temperature regulation systems, causing very detectible "hot flashes." Adrenaline is released very rapidly with sudden stress, causing muscles to spasm—you may have noticed sudden pain in the small muscles of your back when suddenly scared. And as the adrenal glands sit above your kidneys, the increased blood flow can be detected as deeper discomfort. But the famous "adrenaline rush" can also be experienced as positive excitement. Dunn and others (2010) reported studies that identified "both the generation and perception of bodily responses as pivotal sources of variability in emotional experience" and intuitive decision making (Dunn et al., 2010, p. 1835). We know that the emotions are interconnected in a system that includes central nervous system pathways, hormonal reactions, influences on bodily functions necessary for survival. It is useful to distinguish between the sympathetic and parasympathetic pathways and responses, but they too are interconnected. And physiological processes are subject to processes of habituation and especially inhibition. Together, this provides a picture of the *conceptual* nervous system (CNS), one part of which is the ANS.

Measuring external emotional reactions in clinical research has mostly focused on measuring fear, anxiety, and stress, which can be done with various degrees of directness. Like a rodent in the Open Field, we have all experienced the urge to use a toilet in an emotional situation. A commonly used indirect measure comes from the operant conditioning paradigm and is used to measure the consequences of a prior conditioning experience in which a stimulus like a buzzer is paired with a painful shock. After a few such conditioning trials, thirsty rats lapping at a waterspout will immediately stop doing so when the buzzer is sounded. The phenomenon is called conditioned suppression in the operant behavior literature and as a freezing, checking, sort of response is an excellent measure of the strength of an FFFS response. Salivary pH is a good biomarker for stress, being related to both sympathetic and parasympathetic activity, and saliva cortisol levels reflect things going on in the HPA axis (Ahmed et al., 2023). Physiological changes we can easily sense may be biomarkers to researchers but are feelings to clients.

For a long time in psychological research on emotions, we have relied on direct measurement of detectable changes in the ANS, the classic measures being the same as are used in lie-detection work: HR, heart rate (which can be broken down to the actual form of the atrial and ventral wave form), pulse rate (in beats per minute), breathing rate, blood pressure, and every psychologist's favorite the galvanic skin response (GSR or its shadow, SCL skin conductance level). The GSR reflects changes in the electrical resistance of skin due to sweat gland activity due to stress, anxiety, fear, and even simple orienting towards the source of a stimulus. There are delightful complications with GSR technology and the response as seen on the polygraph record can be measured in all sorts of ways—latency, rise time, height (strength), recovery time, minimum and maximum values. You have to be dedicated to use the measure properly. Computerized analysis of all these response recordings simplifies matters greatly and allows the clinical application of these techniques, especially in feedback studies in which the client is able to see a visual record of what their ANS is doing.

Some new and important measures of emotional responding have also been developed. One of the most important is frontal EEG asymmetry, which is the difference between left and right alpha activity over the frontal regions of the brain during electroencephalographic recording (see E. Smith et al., 2016). Another one used extensively in the past by Peter Lang (1995) is the startle reaction. Any sudden noise or change in stimulus situation will cause a startle reaction. Sometimes, this has been referred to as an orienting reflex because it attracts visual and auditory attention. It is considered a primitive defensive reflex that alerts the organism to possible threats and can also protect some organs, such as a blink protecting the eye. Electrodes placed below the lower eyelid can measure the strength of the response of the orbicularis oculi—the facial muscle around the eye. The speed and size of the twitch to an unexpected stimulus like a sharp noise indicates the level of negative emotional arousal present in the subject. Lang first developed a set of pictorial images that reliably vary on the two dimensions of pleasure and arousal, called the International Affective Picture System (IAPS, Lang et al., 1995). It has over 400 standardized photographs of all sorts of objects that were rated by participants in terms of their pleasantness/unpleasantness and their internal arousal value—the two commonly assumed dimensions of all feelings (valence and activation). The pictures have been further validated against the blink probe, which allows researchers to use ratings of the pictures to investigate subject's feelings for various themes and concepts in the pictures.

The startle reflex has received further attention in the psychophysiological research literature because of a better understanding of the body's reflexes to sudden and intense environmental changes that might represent a threat—the eyeblink, skeletal muscle tension (freezing), and a deep intake of breath. A deep inhalation of a breath then decreases blinking, with the function, presumably, being to improve vision and focus (Leitman, 2016). The sympathetic nervous system releases epinephrine and norepinephrine, which increases breathing, heart rate, blood pressure, and constricting blood vessels in the skin, all helpful for reducing injury and enabling better protective actions. In feelings of disgust, blinking increases. When noxious odors or tastes are experienced, breathing is suppressed, sneezing is possible, rapid eye blinking occurs, and swallowing is suppressed.

One of the most important features of the physiological changes that are (or just accompany?) feelings is that in many social contexts, they are undesirable or unwanted and themselves embarrassing. Crying openly might be judged unacceptably weak in many male cultures; losing control of your sphincter and wetting yourself is obviously awkward in most contexts. Having hands shake noticeably, having a tremor in your voice when giving an important speech, not obtaining an erection because the blood flow is getting oxygen to the muscles are all sometimes unwanted physiological responses, not easily controlled by thoughts. In very scary situations, you may have felt the hair on the back of your neck stand up. It's called piloerection. Goosebumps are caused the same way: contraction of the small muscles at the base of hair follicles. The implications of these reactions being observable in addition to being felt will be raised in more detail in Chapter 7.

Other Nervous System Elements

It is known to all of us that if we hear an unexpected noise, we startle, orient (focus our attention), and then relax if nothing else happens. When the same noise occurs shortly afterward, this pattern is repeated, but after a few times the noise produces no such reactions. We *habituate* to the stimulus. The mechanism that permits this is important, so we are not constantly reacting to random external stimuli of no significance to us. It could be considered a very basic form of learning, in the sense that there is memory involved ("That's the same sound I keep hearing"). We can tell that the phenomenon of not responding to a stimulus is not fatigue or lack of capacity because if another stimulus in a different modality, like a flash of light, occurs to arouse us and then the sound occurs again, we will immediately react to that sound like we did the first time we heard it—some sort of dishabituation has occurred.

Thompson and Spencer (1966) defined habituation as a decrement as a result of repeated stimulation. They noted some other defining characteristics. Rapid frequency of stimulation produces more habituation; weaker stimuli produce greater habituation; and, interestingly, the habituation level may go beyond (lower than) zero or non-occurrence of the response. There are also individual differences in habituation to repetitive stimuli, especially in clients. People diagnosed with panic disorder show a marked lack of inhibition to neutral stimuli (Lader & Matthews, 1968). Individual differences in habituation are important since, as explained in Chapter 6, every feeling has a stimulus that elicits it.

Homeostasis is an essential mechanism whereby the activation of all these internal physiological changes is regulated. However, the usual control mechanisms can be overwhelmed. We can think of control mechanisms as having two forms—the internal regulators of the homeostatic mechanism and the higher level, consciously driven actions learned during development to help regulate intense feelings—to be discussed further in Chapter 8. Both these mechanisms, however, can be overwhelmed by very strong emotional arousal.

In such situations, our overt active regulatory actions are impulsive and extreme because the usual brakes applied by careful decision making and evaluation of circumstances are failing. When we feel a strong need for something, we often call that feeling an urge, a specially strong feeling difficult to resist. Saying

"I have an urge for Scotch" seems to reflect a qualitative difference in intensity than saying "I'd like to have whisky," or "I feel like a whisky." Not surprisingly, therefore, the CBT literature has addressed urges in the context of substance abuse, gambling, and sexual paraphilias.

Within the neuroscience literature, special attention has been paid to what is called "positive and negative urgency." That term is less about the feeling of an urge and more about the prepotent, impulsive responses that are hard to inhibit. For instance, in a positive mood, there is a tendency towards rash actions, engaging in risky (driving too fast) or costly (going on a shopping spree) behaviors. An example of negative urgency would be binge eating when feeling upset. The neuroscience talk is that there is a dysfunction in the neural areas linking cognitive control (orbitofrontal cortex) and emotion regulation (anterior insula). Or maybe, it could be serotonin pathways involved in emotional experience, inhibiting dopamine pathways which leads to deficits in behavioral inhibition. It's a bit of a mystery. The key point is that negative urgency is different from general personality traits such as impulsivity and sensation seeking (Cyders & Smith, 2007) because the specific triggering link is from strong negative affect. As such, it is sometimes suggested that a tendency towards positive and negative urgency could be a feature of some general underlying, trait-like "p factor" of psychopathology (Pearlstein et al, 2024)—if you think there is such a thing.

Emotion Theory Debates

There are two schools of thought in the affective neuroscience world regarding emotions (van Heijst et al., 2023; 2025). One perspective is called basic emotion theory and is revealed in all the approaches to emotion that list sets of distinct emotions. These have been evolutionarily shaped as adaptive, fundamental, universal, and innate emotions. Their identity is based on such criteria as recognizable facial expressions, animal analogs, and the expectation of specific and differentiable physiological patterns in both CNS and ANS for each. The supposedly alternative or contrary perspective is called the constructionist model, proposed by Lisa Feldman Barrett in 2006, and then popularized in a book (Barrett, 2017a) and various podcasts (e.g., Barrett, undated). Broadly, the approach "assumes that emotions are events that are created in the mind of a perceiver to fit a certain situation" (Lindquist, 2013, p. 356). Many aspects of this complex model are controversial—for one excellent critique, see Westlund (2024).

The constructionist model is most likely to talk about *core affect* (Russell & Barrett, 1999) and to assign emotion entities within a framework consisting of only two dimensions, activation (arousal) and valence (positive or negative).

These two dimensions are useful and have been long-standing, and because they are widely recognized, I have already referred to them. But thus far, I have used them only one way, which is as possible properties of *any* feeling. In other words, the same feeling could have different levels of activation (maybe like arousal level, or just the general energizing intensity and magnitude of the feeling) and different degrees to which it is experienced as pleasurable or unpleasurable. I will continue to use the terms that way, with the caveat as we will see later that activation/arousal might not be intrinsic to the intensity of the feeling, and that what may be experienced as pleasurable by some may be a feeling that others call painful. Generally, I would define the positive or negative valence of a feeling by facial expression, verbal report, and approach or avoidance tendencies (pulling towards or pushing away, with certain provisos). The core affect model of the constructionist position, however, uses the concepts of activation and valence somewhat differently. They are defined as coordinates of two poles of the construct (ACTIVATION-DEACTIVATION and PLEASANT-UNPLEASANT) whereby feelings can be placed a priori. The two constructs are represented visually as two orthogonal dimensions (e.g., Russell & Barrett, 1999, p. 808). But these are not dimensions like the orthogonal dimensions Eysenck proposed, which creates meaningful quadrants of four "types" of personality.

It might be interesting to think of all feelings as experiences that can always be rated (measured) on a Semantic Differential. Osgood and colleagues (1957) demonstrated long ago that any construct could be rated on all and every polar opposite descriptive adjectives—beautiful/ugly, hot/cold, rude/polite, and so on. But Osgood argued that all such descriptors fell into one of three overarching dimensions: evaluative (good/bad), potency (strong/weak), and activity (fast/slow). The evaluative dimension looks like valence; the potency dimension looks like the activation/arousal level; and the activity dimension looks a little like the approach/avoidance feature of an emotion, and conceivably the rapidity of the action tendency related to the feeling, which is confounded with emotional activation in the Russell and Barrett (1999) model. In their model, feelings low in activation are things like "bored, relaxed, depressed" and feelings high in activation are "tense, alert, excited, and nervous." A fast/slow interpretation of activity could be thought to refer not only to subsequent behavior but to the feelings themselves that occur suddenly (e.g., feeling disappointed) as opposed to those building over time (e.g., feeling insecure). That interpretation would make the dimension a bit like Kahneman's (2011) famous fast and slow thinking notion. This makes sense, as some feelings are innate and occur rapidly, like feeling afraid, and others build up over time and sequences of experiences, like feeling inconsequential.

My point is that regardless of its content, any feeling can vary on its evaluative, potency, and activity dimensions depending on the circumstances. Thus, guilt feels fairly bad (negative valence), can be strong in people from certain religious backgrounds (high in activation/potency), and is somewhat fast in that it can lead to subsequent action tendencies like confessions and making amends. Feeling angry can sometimes be positive in valence (can solve a problem or diminish a threat), is most functional when not too strong (medium activation/potency), and can lead to action tendencies overcoming a barrier to a goal. The Osgood activity dimension (fast/slow) is more speculative and doesn't fit feelings quite as well as the other two. But having people rate their feeling on a Semantic Differential might have some clinical utility as a measure of change. For now, I will continue to use the terms activation (to mean the overall strength of a feeling) and valence (to mean whether it is a positive feeling or a negative one). And I'll use logic as the term to define the required conditions for the content (theme) of the feeling, and action tendency to refer to the actions usually taken in response to the feeling.

Implications

Assorted aspects of the physiology of emotions have been introduced. Although it is a quite complicated collection, they are all relevant to the origins of CBT and to the kinds of issues that arise when experimental work relevant to clinical treatment is introduced. I fully agree with what Cacioppo (2004) once wrote: "*It is the joint consideration of physiological and psychological perspectives that enriches theory and research on human emotion by reducing errors of operationalization, measurement, and inference*" (p. 241).

But unless one is truly an expert in neuroanatomy and neurophysiology, I tend to think that clinical practitioners and researchers at the more molar level of psychological experiences will gain greater benefit from broad-picture perspectives, much the way that Hebb spoke about the "Conceptual" Nervous System many years ago. Hans Eysenck, who was also no reductionist, relied on the best neuroscience research of his day to conceptualize how hypothetical brain mechanisms could provide a cohesive basis for understanding psychology, i.e., personality differences. Developments in this arena by psychologist researchers such as Gray, McNaughton, and Corr show the advantages of this approach, partially aligning with popular clinical theories such as those of Barlow: that all clients receiving any of the anxiety disorder diagnoses will share the characteristic of being high on an underlying dimension of neuroticism. But the role of the FFFS allows for distinguishing psychoneurotic syndromes as related to anxiety feelings (e.g., social anxiety disorder) or to fear feelings (e.g., panic disorder).

In terms of personality, there is another feature of the BIS, BAS, and FFFS neural systems that is not always explicit. The theory proposes that high BAS is associated with higher positive feelings in response to reward, while high BIS is associated with higher negative feelings in response to punishment. It has become known as *reinforcement sensitivity theory* (Corr, 2004). Given that reward (reinforcement) and punishment plays a major role in all behavioral interventions, it is important to link this concept to the long-recognized differences (especially among children) as to whether reinforcement contingencies are more effective than punishment contingencies. Quay (1988) used Gray's model to suggest that some children, especially those diagnosed with conduct disorder but with low anxiety, would be more motivated (have stronger positive feelings) by reward than punishment (low negative feelings associated with punishment). This concept of reward dominance will appear again in the next chapter.

Another way that physiological models greatly influenced the early development of CBT was the work of clinical psychophysiologists such as Peter Lang and the insights that could be offered by studying the responses of the autonomic nervous system. Because changes in heart rate and sweat gland activity and all the other ANS responses had such noticeable proprioceptive properties, it seemed that psychophysiological measurement would be especially important when translating the work to the clinical context where we deal primarily with subjective feelings.

Thanks largely to new technologies such as imaging, however, affective neuroscience has gone off on its own and sometimes very different directions. Van Heijst and colleagues (2025) have suggested that the two positions are less contradictory than they appear and "that basic emotion theories and the theory of constructed emotion can complement each other because they focus on different features of and questions about affective processes" (p. 1).

After a long history of research and theory on the nature of emotions in psychology, it may come as a surprise that scholars are still in basic disagreement regarding what it is we are talking about. It is my impression from working with trainees that students with little neuroscience background are impressed with the concepts espoused by physiological thinkers like Bessel van der Kolk (2014). Practice-focused students regularly quote his popular position that trauma interferes with brain circuits that involve cognitive flexibility, focusing, and maintaining emotional control. The notion that even in the absence of conscious memories of past trauma, individuals are left with a sense of helplessness and constant feelings of danger. As trauma will not be addressed until Chapter 9, the broader topic of managing clients' everyday feelings will evolve over the next chapters, starting with the fascinating yet still abstract topic of how learning theory links rewards and punishments, pleasure and pain, approach and avoidance.

3

Pleasure and Pain, Rewards and Punishments, Approach and Avoidance

Three Pairs of Opposites

In his book *Pain and pleasure: A study of bodily feelings*, Thomas Szasz concluded in his final paragraph that "*[If] a person is free from pain and anxiety and is not subject to object loss and mourning, he also does not experience pleasure, happiness, enthusiasm, inspiration, and other pleasurable feeling states*" (1988, p. 255). Pain and pleasure are interdependent psychologically. Neurobiologists have identified opioid and dopamine systems that modulate both (Leknes & Tracey, 2008), and more recent evidence revealing that "different classes of neurons control positive and negative motivation, sending opposing signals along a shared motivation-processing brain circuit" (Stephenson-Jones et al., 2020, p. 921). It is from the previous chapter's set of general concepts and insights regarding the functions of the central and autonomic nervous systems that three psychological topics emerge of special relevance to the role of feelings in psychopathology and how to change them therapeutically for the benefit of clients. The three pairs, in the title of this chapter, appear to be polar dimensions and seem closely related conceptually and functionally, but they have very different traditions of theoretical and experimental analysis.

Surely pleasure and rewards go together? Things that are pleasurable are rewarding, and then, logically, we can add approach, since we certainly approach the things that are pleasurable and rewarding. Sometimes the approach behaviors themselves provide pleasure, and when that occurs, we call the activity intrinsically rewarding (Deci & Ryan, 1985). Conversely, punishments are painful, not always in the physical sense but hurtful in the emotional sense. As Panksepp (2015) has written: "We humans have no rewards or punishments that we do not experience affectively" (p. 113). In general, things that hurt us physically and emotionally are things we try to avoid, and one way to achieve that is to cease the behaviors that lead to such discomfort. That, functionally, is what punishment is all about. When an action has painful, unpleasant consequences,

How and Why Feelings Change. Ian M. Evans, Oxford University Press. © Ian M. Evans (2026).
DOI: 10.1093/9780197825808.003.0004

humans and all other animals stop engaging in that behavior. If they do not, it must mean that through some process unknown, things considered painful and unpleasant to the rest of us are not experienced as unpleasant to them. Or it could mean that in addition to the painful consequences, there are others that are highly positive, making the discomfort worthwhile when considered together. Or, now that we have considered inhibitory systems, it could mean that stopping is challenging for some people.

Thus, we have three categories of things that are different facets of the same general phenomenon fundamental to the practice of CBT. We have just seen in the previous chapter, there are areas and connections within the central nervous system which seem to have evolved to "process" rewards and pleasures as well as aversive, potentially punishing, experiences. And these two systems are not the mirror opposite of each other. There are processes dealing with consummatory rewards that are pleasurable because they satisfy physiological needs. There are also processes which respond to potential harm from immediate dangers (fear networks) or imminent harm from potential dangers (anxiety networks). The differences between them might explain why we sometimes approach (to attack) dangerous situations and avoid or flee from others.

Some theorists have taken an information-processing approach: *cognitions* are avoided or disrupted in emotive situations. That is useful to remember in clinical work, since we expect clients who are sometimes in an agitated emotional state in our sessions to pay attention to our wise words and immediately recognize the superior rationality of our pronouncements. When we are exposed to information that is counter to our feelings (i.e., designed to change our preferences), it can be disconcerting. It is even more disconcerting if we are warned that's the goal of the exposure because greater information processing is needed when being exposed to discrepant messages (Cacioppo & Petty, 1981). Cacioppo was known for recognizing that appetitive and aversive inputs are not "processed" reciprocally, so that increasing one is not the same as decreasing the other (Cacioppo & Berntson, 1999). It makes perfect sense, evolutionarily, that positive (safe, appetitive) and negative (threat, pain) affective processing should be segregated and allowed to be activated at the same time. Cacioppo pointed out how this promotes opportunities for the "exploration of novel environments and the pursuit of seemingly hospitable events while fostering vigilance for and rapid retreats from hostile developments" (Cacioppo & Bernston, 1999, p. 133). Clients are typically people who, for whatever reason, have dominant negative affective processing. Decreasing negative feelings and increasing positive ones may, therefore, require two concurrent strategies of change. Well-being and ill-being are not opposing ends of the same continuum.

But we're interested in feelings and how emotions and overt reactions feel. If we are rewarded with something we like and want, we feel pleasure. Sometimes this can be from both the reward and the sense of achievement. Remember that

Henry Murray first suggested that people have a need to achieve; McClelland and colleagues (1953) turned n-Ach (*need achievement*) into a major psychological trait. The need is demonstrated when people take on challenging tasks that are neither too easy nor so difficult they might not succeed, with the reward being achievement for its own sake, affiliation with others, or power. The need to achieve success is related to, but not the inverse of, the need to avoid failure. Fear of failure, a common phenomenon seen in the clinic, is not the opposite side of the coin. Give your child a treat as a reward for accomplishing something and both the treat and experiencing your approval are a source of pleasure. Negative feelings over failing at a given task will be exacerbated if one is sensitive to criticism, or one is overly self-critical. Both feelings may derive originally from parental priorities and harsh reactions to errors (Chong et al., 2020), although whether "error-related negativity" is a fixed characteristic of some individuals seems doubtful.

Things people like and like doing bring them pleasure. That's obvious. To maximize the pleasure, however, one has to attend to these things carefully and one must attend to the pleasurable sensations and concentrate on really feeling them. It doesn't seem that's too hard to do, but people get distracted, have other negative things on their minds, or, what is strangest but clinically not uncommon, it is possible to dislike intrinsically pleasurable experiences and to be fearful of showing one's pleasure. There are religious prohibitions against hedonism, especially concerning sexual pleasure and other appetitive experiences. Lust is one of the seven deadly sins, but then so is gluttony (which includes eating too eagerly, according to Thomas Aquinas), and pride. The related feelings are not discouraged in CBT. Lust might not be specifically encouraged, but savoring the feelings of sensual pleasure (sensate focus, Linschoten et al., 2016) is a major component of Masters and Johnson's (1970) strategies for treating sexual dysfunction.

Pleasure of Rewards and Pain of Punishment

Behavior therapy in the Skinnerian tradition (sometimes called Applied Behavior Analysis, or Behavior Modification) is heavily oriented around the principles of reinforcement. Reinforcement contingencies are powerful methods for influencing behavior, whether you are teaching a pigeon to play ping-pong, as Skinner did, or training a dolphin to jump through a hoop, or ensuring a middle-school student does her homework. Largely because of philosophy of science mandates, behaviorists preferred the term reinforcer to the term reward. And in the process, we lost some emphasis on the reality that for a reward to serve a reinforcing function (i.e., be *effective* in increasing the frequency of the behavior consequated), it has to feel good (have *affective* properties). Behavior analysts do emphasize consequences such as social reinforcement in the form of praise. Early behavior therapists even saw the value of self-reinforcement and pushed for reinforcers to be intrinsic as much as possible (not artificial or material). But rarely was the focus on the fact that these events had to be liked and enjoyed, had to be pleasurable. If a child's undesirable behavior was judged to be "for the attention," it never conceded that it was "for the joy of attention." Thus, the suggested treatment to a parent was to ignore it and to offer attention for alternative more acceptable behavior. We didn't always ask what it was about getting attention from an adult that felt good or why making an adult annoyed might also feel good to some children.

For some individuals, suffering can be rewarding even if not pleasurable in the conventional sense. There are countless risky, life-threatening activities that are enthusiastically engaged in by many. And it is the risk—the possibility of death—that seems to make them exciting. Car racing, for example, has relatively few deaths (an average of about twenty per year in the USA) and safety efforts have brought the number down. But there are still frequent crashes, and it is the excited anticipation of them that may be a factor contributing to its popularity as a spectator sport.

When we bring feelings of pleasure and pain back into the topic of rewards and punishments, we find that reinforcement contingencies represent an interesting matrix. Rewards can follow a behavior. When they do, and when they feel pleasurable, the frequency and probability of the behavior increases (*acquisition* in learning parlance). When rewards no longer follow a behavior, a negative feeling of frustration typically occurs, and the probability of the behavior declines (*extinction*). When a behavior results in a rewarding thing being taken away or removed (response cost), the feeling is painful (might be sadness, might be anger), and the probability of the behavior that led to it decreases. (In therapeutic/clinical contingency management, this might be called *negative punishment*: loss of privileges, removal of points and other tokens earned, and "time out" from pleasurable conditions.) When a behavior results in something aversive, the feeling is negative, discomfort, pain, and the frequency of the behavior decreases (called *punishment*, technically speaking). When the aversive consequence that previously followed a particular behavior is removed, the behavior returns, unless it is replaced by an alternative desirable behavior. When a consistently uncomfortable condition (such as being cold, in pain, or subjected to constant loud noise) is removed, the behavior that led to its removal increases, which is called (confusingly to many students) *negative reinforcement*.

The rewards and punishments used in behavioral research and analysis are not the opposite of each other—the feeling states are very varied. Any food can reward a hungry animal by decreasing feelings of hunger. Only sweet and tasty foods can reward an animal that is not hungry by virtue of the pleasure or incentive value of the food. Giving a child a slap or a spanking might be somewhat painful, but the truly negative feeling come from loss of affection, loss of dignity, feeling of failure, anger—it is actually hard to predict because the liking of whomever is doing the spanking and what the spanking symbolizes for the recipient is rarely known in advance. This is why deliberately painful punishment contingencies, including rewards based on prior deprivation, are unconditionally rejected in modern clinical treatment. Even if they temporarily reduce a socially undesirable behavior, the occurrence of negative feelings is largely unpredictable and never beneficial. Also, the replacement action for a punished behavior—and there has to be one—is unlikely to be something desirable (Berkman & Meyer, 1988).

Why is achievement a great motivator, and why do items like cups, certificates, rosettes, and ugly trophies serve as rewards for hours of practice and hard work? Because the feeling of earned pride is a good feeling. Being appreciated and respected by others whose opinion you value and who are not merely self-serving sycophants is a source of a great deal of pleasure. Psychoanalysts saw the subtle negativity of trophies. The self-satisfied feeling of getting an award was seen as derived from reduced feelings of anxiety and self-doubt. According to Fenichel (1941), a trophy is a symbol of parental authority which the person is now claiming—it's quite a convoluted argument, but one can certainly sense parental pride when displaying their children's cups and trophies on the mantelpiece. Feelings of *triumph* come only from succeeding after a struggle—something (or someone) first has to be defeated. Ancient Rome's famous triumphal marches included captive enemies in chains. Nations often feel collectively triumphant—in London, the Wellington Monument, celebrating victories in the Napoleonic wars, is a huge statue of Achilles. It is made from melted down French cannons, to make the point clear. Toddlers feel triumph when first walking alone without help, older children after their first unassisted bike ride. The logic for feeling triumphant is that an obstacle has been overcome.

Skinner and other applied behavior analysts have always insisted rewards can only be judged by whether they serve the function of increasing the probability of the behavior they follow. The term reinforcement is preferred to the term reward as it has this same degree of neutrality about it—a reinforcement is not something an organism likes or enjoys or wants. It is only that event which increases the probability of the behavior leading to it. That is a totally logical if entirely circular position. But it cuts feelings out of the equation. It is true that not everything reinforcing is pleasurable, and not everything pleasurable is reinforcing. But rewards are felt, or produce feelings, and these feelings can be described in words, expressed facially and physiologically, and thus communicated to others. Furthermore, the most recent physiological models have indicated a clear difference between sensitivity to reinforcers (i.e., rewards) and sensitivity to reinforcement (reward contingencies) (McNaughton, 2024).

There is another loss when thinking of reinforcement in the absence of understanding feelings. When a reinforcement is withdrawn from a previously reinforced behavior, that behavior eventually declines in frequency. Everyone knows that phenomenon (one of the closest things we have to a law of behavior in psychology) is called extinction. But what actually is seen if you observe a trained animal placed on an extinction schedule? If you are lucky enough to have been taught psychology the old-fashioned way by training a rat to press a lever in a Skinner box, you will know that when the pellet of food being used as the reinforcement for the hungry animal fails to drop into the food trough, the animal sniffs all around the food trough looking for it. This is clear evidence of expectation on the part of the rat. After searching for the food, the rat will return to the lever and press it with renewed vigor, sometimes very frequently and sometimes biting it. Humans do exactly the same. When an expected reward fails to materialize, you feel disappointed. When you repeat the behavior that had been rewarded and you still don't get reinforced, you feel frustrated, just like the rat. It is called frustrative non-reward and it is punishing. If a hungry chimpanzee has been working for a sweet cookie as a reward, gets shifted to a lettuce leaf reward, it shows its feeling by refusing to eat it. Disappointment and frustration are both negative feelings. Disappointment melds into sadness and perhaps feelings of self-deprecation—perhaps you didn't deserve a reward. Frustration, a feeling which involves perception that the non-reward occurrence is due to some sort of blocking or barrier rather than a change in the contingency rules, melds into feelings of anger and from there easily into acts of aggression directed at whatever is judged to be the barrier. Or, like the rat biting the lever or the chimp throwing the lettuce out of the cage, the aggression can be directed at nothing in particular—people's feelings of frustration merge into feeling of anger and they just "lash out." Clients sometimes lash out verbally at their therapist or reveal their feelings of anger passively by not showing up for appointments and failing to follow treatment suggestions.

The implication of this in traditional clinical behavior therapy is that clients who are disappointed and frustrated and tend towards aggression will usually be encouraged or taught to overcome the barrier by assertive, not aggressive behaviors (Speed et al., 2018). Or if the non-reward is demonstrably unfair, clients will be taught strategies to help them obtain rewards to which they are entitled. That is one of the reasons why therapy focused on problem-solving skills is so valuable (Nezu & Nezu, 2018). It can often be quite a complex problem-solving process outside the therapist's control, but our task is to encourage an objective and rational pursuit of why the reward did not occur (thinking here of non-reward like not getting a promotion at work because of gender bias, not getting a prize because the rules were changed arbitrarily) and then thinking of possible legal challenges and other credible solutions. Of course, non-reward can be the result of performance that objectively did not reach a certain standard, and then the therapeutic task might be to encourage a second or third attempt (which requires getting past the negative feelings), further practice or greater effort (Dweck, 2006). Just sometimes, feelings of disappointment and failure are simply so strong that it is better to help a client go in totally new directions. This latter strategy often requires working with feelings like loss of pride, shame, and worry about disappointing others, like parents or spouses. It is not easy to give up on past dreams and find rewards in new pursuits. In self-help CBT books and websites, the recommended strategies focus on cognitive restructuring and mindfulness training. It is typically described as allowing you to accept and move on by observing your thoughts and feelings without judgment, thus making it easier to let go of past emotional attachments. One might also consider, by realizing that the actual feelings are informative and motivational, that there are circumstances where feelings of frustration can energize (motivate) seeking new activities with more likely levels of pleasurable rewards.

There is yet another way in which feelings are directly involved in the mechanisms of reward and punishment, and that is when their delivery—rather than their non-occurrence—is unfair. My research group at the University of Waikato in New Zealand became interested in the topic because fairness is a highly valued cultural construct and the phrase "a fair go" is an important value (NZIER, 2024), as it is in Australia. We were interested in children's feelings about unfair reward (being rewarded for something you didn't do, or not being rewarded when promised) and unfair punishment (being punished for something that was not your fault or avoiding punishment by another child getting blamed). Plausible and realistic scenarios of these events happening to a child were designed, and our young participants were asked how the child in the story would feel and how strongly. We could predict it from reinforcement sensitivity theory (Corr, 2004) but from experience predicted that being punished for something you didn't do would be worse than not getting a reward you deserved. However, the reverse was true for boys (showing a reward dominance effect). Girls thought both outcomes would feel equally negative. Some children gave more complex feeling statements based on the understanding of different logics. Not getting a punishment should give a feeling of relief but also guilt that someone else got punished. Not getting a deserved reward could make you feel anger and upset, as well as disappointed and sad. The children all had a sophisticated understanding of what could be done to make the outcome of each scenario fairer (Evans et al., 2001).

As we will see throughout this book, the words clients use to describe or explain their feelings can provide important information about the *logic* of the feeling—the conditions that are necessary for that particular feeling. A particular form of disappointment, one within the general category of non-occurrence of an expected reward, is feeling *let down*. The symbolism is of loss of support and falling or being lowered. Thus, that type of disappointment felt by a client is directed towards someone or some agency or group that failed to provide the expected and deserved support. It can also be self-directed—a common form of apology by a celebrity caught doing something undesirable is "I let myself down and I let my family down." The words themselves have metaphoric implications.

Satisfaction provides another example. A feeling of satisfaction comes from success—a tough job well done. The logic requires prior tension or discomfort. The symbolic association is from a biological satisfaction of a need—a satisfying bowel movement, a satisfying meal after being hungry, or a satisfying orgasm.

Incentives versus Rewards

Incentive is another common term in psychology. The everyday meaning of an incentive is some additionally rewarding consequence of an activity to motivate or encourage us and make us more determined to do something. It usually implies the promise of some extra positive feature of an activity that increases motivation by making the consequences of the activity more desirable. The great learning theorist Clark Hull (1943) realized that some rewards were more effective than others—a sweet tasting food was more reinforcing than an equally hunger-reducing food that didn't taste so good. So, he introduced a hypothetical construct of *incentive*, labelled *K*, which was the overall appeal of the reward (whether it reduced drives or not). An example familiar to all of us is the high calorie, sugary, and salty foods we call "comfort foods." Such foods, sometimes consumed in quantities, reduce hunger feelings rapidly and along with that they compete with the "pit in your stomach" which comes from anxiety and other negative feelings. Incentive is thus an implicit feeling construct—feeling of pleasure—but Hull certainly never called it that. But thinking of its affective role gives greater understanding, such as the pleasurable incentive value of a drug. These feelings can easily be associated with the drug itself, and all cues related to drug use and paraphernalia like hypodermic needles or heating a teaspoon.

Drugs as Rewards

If you are a psychologist, you might predict that drug cues become positive via conditioning of pleasurable feelings. You would then use classical extinction techniques to reduce the positive valence of cues as a component of a drug treatment program (for a review, see Kiyak et al., 2023). If you are a neuropsychologist, you might see the very same process in different words: drug-caused changes to the brain increasing over time as the incentive value of the drug and all things related to it. Robinson and Berridge (1993) called this increase "incentive-sensitization." Incentive sensitization was considered a neural basis for drug craving, and thus, inter alia, addiction. They wrote: "Repeated exposure to potentially addictive drugs can ... persistently change brain cells and circuits that normally regulate the attribution of incentive salience to stimuli" (Robinson & Berridge, 2008, p. 3137). Brain circuits—in this case the mesocorticolimbic dopamine system—become sensitized (hypersensitive), increasing intense wanting for the drugs. Animal research provides support for the model and its ability to explain the transition from liking something to wanting it even if it no longer produces the kind of pleasure that it originally did (Robinson et al., 2022). It is at least noteworthy that the neuropsychology terminology helps focus on the possibility that things can be wanted more, even when they are liked less.

Consider prescription drugs, which are so commonly recommended for the medical treatment of chronic emotion disorders and dysfunctional mood states. Anxiety, depression, and bipolar disorder are mental disorders most frequently treated by drugs, and hundreds of well-controlled trials confirm that they can successfully reduce the symptoms of these disorders, even without the accompaniment of CBT, which is the concurrent psychological intervention most often recommended. Outcome data on the permanence of the medication effects, on the various iatrogenic effects, on patient satisfaction with their medication regime, and benefits for quality of life are less frequently reported. But what is most interesting is the dearth of information on how these medications make people feel. And studies are less informative on how many different medications and dosages are tried before a strong beneficial effect on symptoms is felt, whether research patients can feel the difference between an active drug and a placebo in a trial, as well as what sorts of feelings occur when the medication is no longer being taken.

This stands in stark contrast to illegal or nonprescription recreational drugs such as alcohol, nicotine, marijuana, opioids, heroin, and various psychedelic substances. As these are only rarely prescribed for emotion disorders and are used experientially and as self-medication for their general effect, it is not surprising that their benefits are known largely through the effect they have on general feelings of pleasure, euphoria, and fascinating phenomenological experiences. States of enhanced positive feeling then contribute further to varying degrees of dependency such that they become the only means of achieving any positive feelings. Cravings develop (which can happen for any positive experience as we shall discuss); through mechanisms that are well-known, they become addictive. Stopping using them is accompanied by a raft of different withdrawal "symptoms"—better described as unpleasant feelings.

Satisfied Feelings

The basic behavioral model derived from the major learning theories of the past was that rewards "stamped in" the response that led to them. This could be expressed atheoretically, as Skinner did, as simply increasing the probability of the response in the presence of the context in which it was rewarded. Or it could be expressed theoretically in terms of hypothetical mechanisms for how rewards had their response-strengthening effects. Hull (1943) proposed that learning meant a stronger bond between a stimulus (S) and a response (R), which he called habit strength (sHr), and he initially proposed that habit strength increased due to drive reduction. Rewards work because they reduce drives. In the relevant experimental studies, the drives were typically hunger or thirst. When hunger is reduced, we call it being satisfied. Satisfaction as a feeling is thus possibly the key element of effective reward—we need to feel satisfied. Work is not really very pleasurable and hardly its own reward, but as we all know it can be rewarding, especially when it is satisfying. The feeling of a job well done, seeing the results of your work, fixing something so that a problem is solved, knowing that you are helping others (such as when volunteering to give blood), are all examples of getting satisfaction from activities that are not inherently pleasurable. Feeling satisfied (by analogy to physiological satiation) is closely connected to completion of a task or activity—in the words of the old Lexington cigarette ads, "After action, satisfaction."

Completion of tasks is quite often something clients struggle with, particularly if depressed, or anxious, or perfectionists (people who do not easily feel satisfied with their own performance). Completion of therapy is equally dependent on the client feeling satisfied that they can now move on with their lives. It is thus helpful when assessing a client's therapeutic needs to ask them what things satisfy them: "When do you have feelings of satisfaction? What things do you do or experience that gives you satisfaction?" This makes an interesting alternative to always asking only what they like doing or what gives them pleasure. "I used to enjoy golf," a depressed client might tell you, but what was it that gave them satisfaction: the social camaraderie of their golfing buddies, sinking a long putt, improving their handicap? That would be useful to know.

Knowing what gives your client satisfaction allows a therapist to make a much more nuanced set of suggestions regarding alternative activities that you might be suggesting in a behavioral activation program. Behavioral activation is a helpful component of therapy for depression, but it is not a stand-alone treatment, despite sometimes being described this way in the therapy research literature (e.g., Mazzuchelli et al., 2009). Nursing homes and elder care facilities often look for enjoyable activities that will engage their residents. But they are not always successful in finding age-appropriate leisure pursuits. I carefully observed one elderly couple in a nursing home for whom we were trying to find a new activity both could enjoy. A complex jigsaw puzzle was suggested—large (1000 piece) puzzles are enjoyed by many adults with limited mobility. The husband started out expressing a somewhat derisory attitude—puzzles are just for kids. The wife was pleased to give it a try and had a good strategy for starting out and finding shapes, and she expressed satisfaction (delight) each time a puzzle piece fitted precisely where it should. Thus, long before the puzzle was even close to completion, she was getting the simple reward of satisfaction. The husband also boasted as to how well he was doing when he found a piece to fit, and expressed delight, but that happened only rarely as he was not following any of the matching strategies his wife explained to him. Without the satisfaction of piece-by-piece success, he quickly gave up and said it was no fun. His wife persisted and spent many hours happily completing the puzzle—alone. The therapeutic solution for the next time, to ensure the husband had the satisfying experience of popping a piece into place, was to have the wife complete just enough of the puzzle for finding new correct pieces to be just a little bit easier.

There has long been a controversy in behavior analysis as to whether material rewards (contingency management) given for activities believed to be inherently pleasurable would reinforce the proper behavior wanted. Parents offering material rewards for a child doing their homework each evening might reinforce superficial or hasty work but not the concentrated effort that emerges from genuine interest in the task. Teachers delivering material rewards and token economy programs seemed to encourage compliance more than academic learning (Winett & Winkler, 1972). The controversy becomes more acute around interesting a child in reading. Reading a fun book should be intrinsically enjoyable—an exciting story whose ending the child wants to discover, gaining new information in the case of nonfiction, and encouraging the child's imagination. If parents and teachers offer a financial incentive, such as a money reward for reading five books during the vacation, will that result in reading stopping once the cash reward is no longer promised? How can you arrange contingencies such that money is the incentive to get started, but reading becomes its own pleasure and is accompanied by feelings of satisfaction, enjoyment, and accomplishment?

The designers of video games know the answer. Interesting, easily accessible, highly engaging material devoted to classic themes of adventure (warriors, spies, criminals, raids, superheroes, elite athletes, racecar drivers) or of imagination and love (wizards, princesses, dragons, exotic vacations, treasure, castles, fairies) are constructed in challenging arrangements that ensure immediate short-term success and satisfaction that only get slowly harder over time and thus seldom lead to failure. Add to that mix the fundamental enjoyment of a contest, playing with or against others, keeping a score, getting recognition, and you have a formula that creates, as we know only too well, hours and hours of dedicated but not always productive activity. Such carefully crafted reward schedules lead to behavior with a compulsive quality, not a classic addiction, but one that is hard to stop and thus dominates the person's repertoire and fills time to the exclusion of many other enjoyable pursuits.

Informative work on school children's motivation has been carried out by New Zealand researchers Meyer and McClure. They found that high school students—who were in fact successful and passing courses—tended to have one of two styles of motivation. Some reported that they always tried to do their best, while others reported they only did just enough to get by (Meyer et al., 2009). This meant that there would be serious limitations to a proposed government educational philosophy that had instituted a new system with only pass or fail grades.

This had been proposed as a sort of progressive principle to avoid students being overly focused on competition. There is a culturally derived, liberal attitude that some students shouldn't feel superior to others. But for those students who always wanted to do their best, there was a need for some indication of how well they were doing over and above the bare minimum (doing just enough to pass). Thus, the new grading system could be seen to be discouraging academic excellence, rather than simply increasing educational equity in the classroom. As a result of the research program, the New Zealand Department of Education revised its grading policy without reinstating the old A, B, C, F system by using the following new criteria: Not Achieved (NA), Achieved (A), Merit (M), and Excellence (E). This served the dual purpose of not totally discouraging students who were failing but allowing students with different motivational systems to work harder to achieve feelings of accomplishment and satisfaction (Hodis et al., 2015).

Approach and Avoidance

In the 1940s, an experimental paradigm became popular which has shaped many later developments in behavior therapy research and practice. It started with a device that was called a shuttle box. It consisted of an apparatus for a rat (usually) that had two halves, divided by a barrier that could be raised or lowered. The floor of the two halves consisted of a series of slightly separated metal rods that could be activated by a power source to deliver a painful electric shock to the feet (paws) of the animal subject. The shuttle box had a specific stimulus source, usually a buzzer. The typical procedure was to sound the buzzer for a short period, perhaps a few seconds and then accompany it by the electrification of the bars on the floor. The animal shows signs of severe discomfort, runs around frantically, bites at the bars, and eventually jumps over the barrier to the other side, where there is no shock. At that point, the buzzer is also turned off. After a while, a second trial is conducted. This time, the side the rat has escaped to is electrified, the rat runs around again and once more jumps over the barrier, is now safe and the buzzer turns off. This back-and-forth pattern is why it is called a two-way shuttle box. The same sort of procedure can be done with just one way, or with a lever press terminating the shock and the buzzer. The nature of the escape behavior is probably very important: what is the natural reflexive action of the animal when in foot pain? Probably not to press a level or to jump over a barrier, but probably to run away, which it can't really do in the shuttle box. Furthermore, jumping back to where you once got shocked is unnatural, as opposed to true escape. These features made this device much more complicated than it need be as an experimental procedure.

Furthermore, it permanently confuses the difference between escape and avoidance. Avoidant behaviors are those that occur *before* the painful, aversive experience. It means, ipso facto, there must be a warning signal or recognition that an aversive situation not yet directly encountered is imminent. This must be learned, based on experience, either directly or indirectly. Escape behaviors occur while the aversive conditions exist and by definition are effective in getting away from or ending those conditions. In non-speaking animals, the gold standard indicator they have negative feelings is that they will escape a situation when given the opportunity.

What fairly quickly develops in the two-way shuttle box procedure is that the time intervals between the onset of the buzzer/shock combination and the escape of jumping over the barrier get shorter and shorter. Eventually, the response latency is so short that the rat jumps over the barrier as soon as the buzzer comes on. At that point, the response becomes avoidance, because there is no shock, and the buzzer gets turned off. Eventually, but reluctantly, the rat shuttles back and forth each time the buzzer is sounded and no longer receives any shocks. That can go on for many trials and the question arises is why, when there is no shock, doesn't this behavior extinguish? In the shuttle box, what starts out as an escape response, rewarded by cessation of shock, becomes, if there is a signal, an avoidance response, rewarded by what? Could this be similar to the anxious client that sees something and immediately avoids it by not approaching or actively moving away without coming to any harm? While human avoidance rarely involves jumping over barriers, the shuttle box behavior is described as the neurotic paradox and has been the major construct behind much analysis of behavior therapy and the psychopathology of anxiety.

The original explanation offered as to why the avoidant jumping over the barrier doesn't extinguish is because of two factors (Mowrer, 1947). One is that fear is classically conditioned to the buzzer which makes the buzzer also aversive. Thus, when first jumping over the barrier, there are two sources of reinforcement—reduction of pain (no more shock) and reduction of fear (no more buzzer). Once the behavior is so adaptive that the jumping occurs before the shock, the cessation of the buzzer and the reduction in the unpleasant feeling of conditioned fear are the reinforcement that maintains the avoidance behavior. There are different ways of viewing this whole situation, but the principle which has survived is Neal Miller's (1948): that reduction of a negative feeling, fear, reinforces the behavior that permits it. Thus, if you wanted to extinguish the prolonged jumping behavior, first extinguish the fear of the buzzer. This can be done by preventing the escape/avoidance behavior through raising the barrier so it can't be jumped over and then sounding the buzzer (CS+) *without* any shock (no UCS). Eventually through Pavlovian extinction, the fear elicited by the buzzer will decrease. When it is eliminated completely, the barrier is lowered, and the buzzer sounded, the rat should simply ignore it and not jump over the barrier—if the theory is correct. And that is exactly what happens.

Negatively valenced feelings are usually associated with avoidance and escape; negative valence motivates (moves) us to actions which remove us from the situation that was the source of the feeling. In the passive sense, we are pushed away from the situation; in the active sense, we push unpleasant situations, even thoughts, away from us. Positively valenced feelings are usually associated with approach; positive valence pulls us towards situations and goals that are the source of pleasant feelings. In the passive sense, we are pulled (attracted) towards the sources of pleasure; in the active sense, we pull pleasant situations and objects towards us.

In a rather ingenious way, experimentalists have used this basic formula as a measure of the strength of the positive or negative emotional valence of any concept or thing—objects, pictures of objects, and especially printed words. Anything, in fact, that can be literally moved towards or away from a subject. Using a technique originally developed by Staats (1996), research participants are asked to pull towards them or push away from them the presented item, and the latency (speed) of their responses (like reaction times) can be finely measured. As you would expect, concepts that have a negative valence for the subject are pushed away from them quicker than they are pulled towards them. The reverse of this is true for positive items. This can be used as an objective measure of any experimental attempt to change a person's emotional valence for a given concept (see, for an example, Rinck & Becker, 2007). In principle, it could be used to measure therapeutic change and in research trials it often is. But it would be cumbersome in the clinic, where it is more convenient to rely on a client's willingness to consciously use or ignore a concept within their typical discourse or reported behavior. A client might well say "I still can't watch any movie that I know has a rape scene in it, my feeling is still so negative, even though I know it is just people acting," or might say "I now found it quite easy to invite my ex and her husband to Thanksgiving dinner this year, as the children asked me to; a year ago I'd have felt sick at the thought of it," or might say to you "Please don't ask me today about my son's behavior, I feel so ashamed I'm just not ready to discuss it." Fear obviously motivates escape and avoidance, but not inevitably, since many animals, humans included, freeze in the face of intense threat, as Blanchard and colleagues (1986) showed. Be aware, then, that freezing as a defensive response to intense feelings of fear is a fundamental possible reaction. Rape victims who didn't struggle, soldiers who never fired their weapon in combat, or homeowners who fail to run or flee in the face of an imminent tornado, fire, or tsunami, all provide examples of the paralyzing effect of intense feelings of fear.

Anger and Approach

Anger is usually categorized as a negative feeling, the reduction of which, like the reduction of fear, will reinforce the behaviors that enabled that reduction. But because anger often leads to approach (to attack), not avoidance (to run away), there are some fascinating inconsistencies. Active aggressive behaviors like physical attacks, violence, hurting others, and damaging property have two distinct forms, based on motivation. Proactive aggression (predatory attacks) is motivated by external rewards. At the personal level, this might be seen in crimes of violence, like mugging a stranger; at the level of nations, rewards can be resources, power, dominance, glory, and such things. Reactive aggression is in response to threat and perceived harm—it may be energized by the emotion of anger but is not inevitably evoked by it. If overt aggression is not possible, such as it being prevented by superior force or previous punishment, a feeling of anger persists and is highly aversive. A child might fantasize hurting someone, think of ways of retaliating that might be safer, draw violent pictures, or even feel angry at themselves. Seeing signs of anger turned inwards should signal therapists to explore clients' feelings in considerable depth, making it clear that talking about angry, hateful feelings is acceptable.

Another important feature of angry feelings is righteous anger. If the action tendency for anger is not always negative aggression, it reveals that positive action tendencies are possible. There are many times when the external threat and the agents causing harm are themselves socially undesirable, even evil. Aggression coming from righteous anger and directed against sources of injustice or inhumanity can often be justified. Political protests, acts of sabotage, assassinations could all be considered of social benefit, although the perception of what is evil, unjust, and contrary to human dignity can be highly subjective. There is one other aspect of aggression, both reactive and proactive, in which the aggressive act itself elicits positive pleasurable feelings, even in people who are normally nonviolent. Getting revenge against a bully, someone rejecting, or someone who has betrayed you, is described as "sweet." Even aggression of no moral value, such as bar brawls or rough housing in sporting contests, is described by participants as feeling fun or exciting. Integrating the different forms of this phenomenon, Quansah and Gagnon (2025) have provided a clarifying set of four categories, depending on whether the aggression is reactive or proactive, and interpersonal or intergroup. For instance, the category of interpersonal-reactive seems to fit Chester's (2017) model in which negative affect (anger, maybe shame) occurs first, then the aggressive act, which elicits positive affect. In this way, the aggression serves the personal function of emotion regulation (Chapter 8).

Approach Promotes Good Feelings

There is no simple formula for relating the form of subsequent actions to specific emotions, although the general likelihood that pleasant feelings mean approach or approach intentions and negative feelings mean withdrawal/avoidance is clear and common enough. Valence and arousal continue to be important properties of feelings, but not if context and logic are ignored.

If positive feelings (liking something or someone) typically lead to approach behaviors, and negative feelings (anxiety, irritation, dislike) lead to withdrawal or avoidance, is it possible that encouraging approach to something disliked will change your feelings about that object or situation? We say to people (especially children), in the classic words of the famous Alka-Seltzer advertisement: "Try it, you'll like it." But in the Alka-Seltzer ad, he did try it and even if he liked it, it made him nauseous. Behavioral activation (getting out and doing things) has become a major part of CBT for depression, on the assumption that it will increase opportunity to obtain reinforcement/rewards. But when people are depressed, they resist doing even the things they once enjoyed—claiming they don't experience any pleasure in these activities. But if approach inherently enhances positive feelings, then any strategy that encourages approach activities rather than avoidance can be seen as useful in changing all negative feelings, including those like anger or fear. We encourage children to include others in their social group, and maybe after that they'll end up liking them (feel friendly). Don't wait to like someone first, we advise clients. And on this same dimension, familiarity is most often a circumstance that generates pleasure—yes, boredom is always a risk, but if in doubt recommend to clients that they engage in activities and places they know well. Everyone needs a happy place: make it literally somewhere you go.

The opposite of trying to inhibit reflexive negative feelings in order to reduce their aversiveness is to attend to magnify, and generally focus on the positive sensation arising from pleasurable, rewarding experiences. In everyday language, we allow people to "bask in their glory" as the positive feelings from winning or getting rewarded can be quite short-lived. In contemporary emotion-focused CBT, the idea of savoring positive experiences has become widespread and is a very easy thing to teach clients and encourage them to do—savor the last bite of a great meal, savor the flavor of the ice cream you're eating, savor the beauty of the sunset. Savoring is a form of positive, focused approach—not physical, but sensory. All positive hedonic experiences that elicit positive emotional feelings can be enhanced by focusing one's attention on the experience and not on the surrounding events. Children can be helped to focus on all of the elements of a positive experience in a variety of ways. At the time, be sure to talk about your own pleasure physically ("that left me with a sugary taste feeling," "made my mouth water," "that movie made me feel all warm and fuzzy") and elicit from them sensation words about how an event is making them feel, physically ("that was so exciting, can you feel your heart racing?," "doesn't that music make you want to jump up and dance for joy?" "hmmm, doesn't this ice cream make you want to lick your lips?"

It has been proposed (see, e.g., Higgins, 1997) that individuals have different self-regulatory goals fitting into one of two categories: promotion-focused goals (the strategies just mentioned) and prevention-focused goals. When an individual's self-regulation is promotion-focused, they are concerned with attaining positive outcomes related to good feelings and are thus focused on their ideals, aspirations, and accomplishments. When self-regulation is concentrated on prevention, they are more concerned with avoiding (not experiencing) outcomes eliciting bad feelings. Such individuals are therefore focused on values and standards like responsibility, duties, safety, and protection. While we all want to obtain pleasure and avoid pain, people differ in which of these two goals are more important. Clients seem to fit into the latter category, on the whole. Their activities are motivated by avoiding negative feelings.

We can link these ideas easily and directly to the notion of people, especially children, being *reward dominant*. Reward-dominant children are relatively impervious to punishment and reprimand because adverse feelings are less important than the positive feelings that accompany reward. Risk takers can tolerate the possibility of aversive outcomes because the feelings associated with rewards and success are stronger than those associated with punishment and failure. Thus, we can see there are numerous concepts in personality theory and emotion/motivation constructs which all generally say the same thing—there are individual differences in clients' focus on having positive feelings or avoiding negative ones. The well-known phenomenon of loss aversion is based on people's feelings that losing something, money for instance, will feel worse than the pleasure of winning. Boys with conduct problems tend to be reward-dominant (Wilson & Evans, 2002). The implication is that rewards are rewarding because they bring good feelings, but if avoiding bad feelings is more important to you, it is cautious and avoidant behaviors that will be rewarded, even if they produce less material gain.

Special Salience of Reward Stimuli

One of the things controlling our feelings is that stimuli signaling the coming of reward do acquire for themselves positive affective value. In other easier words, we come to like things that signal or represent other positive things, even if the signal has no other intrinsic value to us and cannot by itself lead to any pleasure or satisfaction. By signaling, we mean reliably associated with, as in pairing a CS and a UCS. Simple association is adequate for a learning effect (Bitterman, 2006), as can be seen in one trial aversive conditioning. More cognitively oriented learning theorists, however, emphasize that the pairing must be done in such a way that the signal *predicts* the reward or pleasure. If the same reward comes frequently when not being signaled, the signal loses its informational value and thus its affective value. Traditionally, we have looked at this effect as simply a nice example of classical conditioning—a previously neutral stimulus (CS) can through associational learning acquire the ability to elicit the same emotional reaction or feeling as the stimulus (UCS) that already has this emotive property, be it food for a hungry animals, an electric shock that produces a pain response, or a deep kiss from a lover. The sorts of things that are reliable UCSs for specific feelings ("eliciting cues," "triggers," various names have been used), and the sort of cues that might most easily be conditioned by pairing with a UCS, will be described in Chapter 6. For now, it is important to introduce a reward-based twist to the story.

In behavior theory, it was Arthur Staats who pointed out that a stimulus which consistently signals the coming of a rewarding reinforcing event will actually acquire more than just turning into a bland CS. In fact, he argued, such stimuli acquire three distinctive properties, First, they acquire, as I've already noted, affective valence—they themselves become liked or feared or whatever. Staats called that an attitudinal function (A), which is what an attitude is, an acquired liking or disliking of something that is not in itself inevitably liked or disliked by most people. Secondly, he pointed out that this previously neutral stimulus is now enjoyed and can now become a conditioned reinforcer (R) or reward in its own right and could be used to shape other completely different behaviors in different contexts. Token reinforcement programs demonstrate the power of this as people will work for the tokens despite them having no intrinsically attractive value. Third, Staats argued that the previously neutral stimulus can acquire the properties of a discriminative (D) stimulus. In behavior theory, a stimulus whose occurrence leads to an approach response is called a discriminative stimulus as it sets the occasion for the reinforced behavior to occur. It's like telling the organism that a reward is available if you respond the right way now. There's no point in expending energy on pressing a lever for food if the next few presses will not be rewarded. To be a truly discriminative stimulus, there have to be learning trials in which only in the presence of this cue will responses be rewarded. That's what allows the animal or the person to discriminate between opportunities to be rewarded and when one's actions will not be rewarded.

As previously explained, neuropsychologists use a different language to describe the same phenomena—always a pity for scientific progress. They say that CSs are "conferred with incentive motivational properties" as they can elicit approach because they become "wanted," "acting as motivational magnets" (that's the A function); they can "act as reinforcers in their own right" (R); and they can "energize actions by eliciting cue-triggered wanting" (D). Phrases quoted come from the excellent summary of the incentive sensitization theory of addiction by Robinson and Berridge (2008, p. 3138).

Implications

The three dimensions discussed are among the most common of the "big" topics in the science of psychology grounded in behavioral and other empirical principles. They are quantifiable elements of the same general topic—we might call it motivation or even emotion. From the many threads of this chapter, with a focus on feelings, we can construct a simple pattern that links pleasure and pain, rewards and punishments, and escape and avoidance into one common matrix.

The attainment or loss of tangible rewards or punishments represents a 2 by 2 matrix which gives rise to a most useful concept about basic feelings. If a reward is signaled as coming, the resulting feeling (expectancy) is hope, the signal itself acquires positive valence through simple associative conditioning, and attainment of the reward results in any additional positive feelings that are relevant, such as being happy, feeling proud, or feeling satisfied. If a signal indicates that a reward is not occurring, or being removed, the feeling is frustration, disappointment, and anger (all negative feelings) and the signal itself acquires negative valence and can elicit negative feelings. If a punishment is signaled as coming, the feeling is fear, and the signal acquires the negative valence of anxiousness. When the punishment comes, the feelings might be pain, hatred, possibly anger—all negative feelings. If a punishment is signaled as not going to occur, or is ending, the feeling is relief, gratitude, thankfulness (all positive) and the signal (sometimes known in therapy as a safety signal) acquires positive valence. Thus, we have two sources of positive feelings, one from gain of good things and the other from the loss of bad things. And we have two sources of negative feelings, one from the gain of bad things and the other from the loss of good things.

It also follows logically that in humans, these same feelings can evoke further actions related to the nature of the reward or punishment. Rewards lead to consummatory behavior and renewed vigor and the response-strengthening effect can be viewed as positive since future similar activities are enabled. Non-reward disappointment leads to response extinction and giving up, passive behavior. With punishment, the negative feeling leads to active aggressive behaviors. Non-punishment relief feelings may be positive, but they do not encourage further action, rather the opposite. We sometimes call these behaviors *defensive* as they are designed in the future to avoid any more punishment. So, from our matrix, not only can we separate all feelings into good or bad, but we can also further separate them into those good feelings which lead to actively desirable behaviors (approach) versus inactive behaviors (passive avoidance), and which negative feelings lead to active undesirable behaviors (aggressive approach) or to "giving up" type behavior (passive aggression). Desirable and undesirable in this context is whatever your social group values.

There is an important caveat to this whole discussion, based on the general principle that the purpose of emotion is to maximize survival by preparing us for actions that are necessary to avoid harm and to approach situations and events that are life-sustaining. As mentioned earlier, evolutionary views always raise the prehistoric threats of wild animals. But other social groups have also been a much greater threat. Those social groups who are dominant and aggressive are able to take advantage and benefit from weaknesses in others. Aggression and violence was rewarded. Anger leading to attacks was never a negative emotion. Feeling displays of loyalty and bravery, honor and pride, and the glory of conquest had action tendencies that were often rewarded much more than kindness. One cannot judge a priori what feelings can be considered pleasurable and which ones can be considered intrinsically negative and to be avoided. Practicing psychologists are typically confronted with negative feelings that the client wishes to change. As we shall see, one way to do so is to counter negative feelings by increasing positive ones. That seems obvious. However, evolutionary and neurological constructs overemphasize the rigid distinction between positive and negative emotions. The valence of a feeling is much more complicated when one considers the social function of emotions and emotional displays. In a major review of the social effects of emotions, van Kleef and Côté (2022, p 647) suggest that there are limits on referring to emotions as positive or negative: "When it comes to categorizing emotions in terms of what they signal socially, the constructs of affiliation, dominance, supplication, and appeasement are preferrable. This is because the implications for others' behavior depends on individual differences and situations" (p. 647). In the next chapters, I elaborate on phenomena relevant to affiliation (infant and child development), dominance (feelings of superiority), supplication (help seeking), and appeasement (regret, shame). When feelings are related more to the welfare and benefit of society or a social group than to yourself, we can think of another category of feelings—moral feelings. Such feelings are very relevant to family life, as will also be considered in the next chapter.

When working with clients, we shy away from the simplistic view that a good life, a happy life, will be one focused on obtaining pleasure and avoiding pain. Many positive feelings have little to do with hedonistic pleasure. We can have feelings of accomplishment that are positive and rewarding, even though the accomplishment might be of little material value. We have comfortable feelings about our identity, whether culture- or gender-related. And in Martin Seligman's (2011) important contribution to what makes living positive, he has drawn attention to the importance of feelings of meaning and purpose in our lives. Such feelings are derived essentially from contributing to something larger than ourselves. In various ways in this book, we will encounter the general benefit for clients of helping them focus on others rather than always on themselves.

4

Development of Children's Feelings

Highlights

In the history of science, Charles Darwin has always been recognized for his outstanding powers of observation as a source of understanding natural phenomena. Both he and his wife Emma kept written notes of their observations of the emergence of feelings in their children. Consider the following charming and insightful passage from Darwin's observations of the development of his son (nicknamed Doddy) from infancy to toddlerhood, published in 1877:

> *A little later (2 years and 7½ months old) I met him coming out of the dining room with his eyes unnaturally bright, and an odd unnatural or affected manner, so that I went into the room to see who was there, and found that he had been taking pounded sugar, which he had been told not to do. As he had never been in any way punished, his odd manner certainly was not due to fear, and I suppose it was pleasurable excitement struggling with conscience.*

Interest in the profound influence of parental feelings on the emotional development of children has been the hallmark of developmental psychology from every school of thought and psychological theory. Early psychoanalysts in particular were fascinated by how children's feelings emerged from intense biological feelings towards parents. But unlike Darwin, there was a fatal tendency to go beyond the observational facts. Social psychologist Roger Brown (1965) included in his textbook a devastating methodological critique of the influences over Freud's analysis of the famous case of Little Hans who had a fear of horses. Freud's information all came from Little Hans' father, who was a student of his and a staunch believer in the validity of the Oedipal complex. The father asked Little Hans many leading questions about "widdlers" and thus introduced his own biases and interpretations. In 1960, Joe Wolpe and Jack Rachman published an article which offered a more plausible alternative explanation to Little Hans' fear being due to castration anxiety. They pointed out that the phobia had started after Little

How and Why Feelings Change. Ian M. Evans, Oxford University Press. © Ian M. Evans (2026).
DOI: 10.1093/9780197825808.003.0005

Hans had been walking with his nanny in the street and witnessed a frightening incident in which a carriage horse bolted and been shot by police right in front of the child. For Wolpe and Rachman (1960), as for me, this was a perfect example of one trial classical (Pavlovian) fear conditioning.

This is not an attempt to resuscitate the old clash between psychoanalysis and behaviorism, although such critiques were influential for behavior therapy's ascendance in psychotherapy. The case is, however, illustrative of the complexities of studying child problems out of the context of family dynamics. A release of documents related to the Little Hans case has revealed all sorts of interesting additional twists and turns in the clinical history (Blum, 2007). Little Hans' father, Max, was a confidant and student of Freud's. What is less well-known is that his mother, Olga, was a patient of Freud's. A talented musician whose career was thwarted, Olga was unhappily married, became depressed after sexual intercourse, and had postpartum depression after the birth of Little Hans' younger sister Hanna. Olga's own father had died when she was an infant, and later in her life, both her brothers committed suicide. There is evidence that she seriously mistreated Hanna, spanking her on her bottom as an infant hard enough to make her scream. Little Hans reported that he liked his sister but also admitted that he wished she were dead and had fantasies of dropping her off the balcony. Olga and Max eventually divorced; Hanna committed suicide. Themes of sibling rivalry, marital conflict, preferential treatment of one child over the other, depressed mother exposing herself to her young son, the role of women in Victorian society are all elements of the damaging emotional dynamics in this family. It allows one to reflect that modern understanding of children's feelings has advanced substantially thanks to scientific developmental psychology.

If this chapter were truly on the psychology of children's emotions, it would be longer than the book itself. My task is to pick from a massive experimental and theoretical literature a few key concepts that help us understand how children's feelings change and why, and to relate these to issues for all of behavioral psychotherapy, not just children. With children as the topic, it gets us away from just worrying about anxiety, fears, and depression, and brings us closer to important *contextual* issues for all clients' feelings, especially the need for positive ones: growth, language development and usage, parenting, families (including their dissolution), and schools. Schools have come into special focus recently thanks to the COVID-19 epidemic that locked out and disrupted schooling all over the world and interfered with social life outside the home—peer friendships, group play, neighborhood interactions. In the USA particularly, but not unknown in other countries (Solly, 2021), mass school shootings raise feelings around safety. And in many parts of the world, even those which are not immediately threatened, young people's awareness of the cataclysmic consequences of climate change have gained new urgency.

Feelings are fleeting. Events that elicit them are unpredictable. Biological differences in emotionality set the boundaries and hundreds of learning opportunities shape the nature and the intensity of the feelings, as do the feelings themselves, which can then determine how the situation and the culture and the ecology provide or fail to provide new opportunities for change. We can think of these influences the way Bronfenbrenner (1979) did: the enveloping ecological folds from micro to macro. But it was always the proximal processes between the developing child and the people in their environment that were critical to his concepts. Or we can think of cumulative and interactional hierarchies of learning experiences, as Staats did (e.g., Staats, 1990). And we should see the two as complementary, not contradictory. None of this is simple, but the broad framework is straightforward.

Developmental processes and the issues for children's feelings might be the name of the chapter, but it is not a separate topic disconnected from the story as a whole. It is not solely relevant to working with child clients; all our clients either are children or were once, and their developmental paths are never irrelevant. Although we still need to understand them better, we do know what experiences are bad for children's emotional development. When the children are young, we can try to mitigate these influences; when they come to us as adults, we can help clients compensate for them. It is inevitable that as children develop, they will be held accountable by their parents for all the things they do that parents dislike. Ensuring that parents understand their role in child development is a first step. A brilliant child psychiatrist who supervised part of my practicum training always asked parents during the first assessment interview whether the child was, quote, "a wanted child," meaning planned. When I asked him if their answer had any influence on his assessment or diagnostic assumptions, he laughed and said, "Not really. Unplanned children will come to be loved just as much. But it makes parents think about their feelings and takes their minds off their child being solely responsible for their own problems."

There are certain areas of influence on children's emotional development that I can highlight. It is not a comprehensive coverage and reflects areas I've had some special interests in. The first is the universal importance of infant temperament, a topic which addresses the fact that at birth (and indeed before), children react emotively to their environment in different ways that can be observed, described, and classified. Second, I will consider the importance of attachment and feelings of security, followed, thirdly, with the influence of parent-training programs and family dynamics. I then touch on the development of prosocial feelings, early peer and sibling relationships, fairness, and the value of play. Fifth, I will describe recent work on how parental language enhances children's emotion competence. Finally, I will explain the role of teachers in kindergarten and elementary (primary) school and the all-important emotional climate of the classroom. I said this chapter should have been a separate book.

Temperament

We don't start at birth with an emotional blank state. Genetics, maternal health and stresses, pre-natal conditions both internal and external (social and cultural) all contribute to individual differences (Padilla et al., 2020). Psychologists are able to select a dimension and within it cluster these differences into meaningful groups. Emotionality is one of the dimensions. We call it *temperament*, and the original grouping that proved useful are the somewhat value laden categories of easy, difficult, and slow-to-warm-up. Buss and Plomin (1984), using wider data sources, proposed that four temperamental types are discernable: (1) infants with a high emotionality, characterized by feelings of fear and frequent mood swings; (2) infants with an active temperament, characterized by high activity and low stability; (3) infants showing a sociability temperament, expressing interest in their surroundings and pleasure from relationships; and (4) infants who are shy, exhibiting tension and withdrawal in social interactions. If you think of infant temperament as personality, you can connect these categories very easily to the revised Gray/McNaughton/Corr ideas. With a little ingenuity, you can even apply these four categories to the dimensions commonly identified in affective neuroscience: (1) and (3) might be the valence dimension, and (2) and (4) the activation dimension, or is that stretching things a bit?

Temperamental differences are broadly about emotional differences, with differences in activity level (motor) and attention thrown into the mix. Descriptions of the babies tend to focus on the negative and include words like frequent crying, being fussy, not easily calmed, reacting badly to new things or new people, and sensitivity to the intensity of stimulus conditions. By the time we get to observe them or hear about them from their parents, all infants have been influenced by the dynamics of their interactions with their caregivers and living environments. And this immediately brings into play the temperaments, if you like, of the adults in the family—think about how different mothers respond to normal difficulties in getting their infants to breastfeed. Parents who rate their children's temperament as "difficult" report more stress and less reflective parenting (Yaakov et al., 2023). As the infant gets a little older, the picture is confused with differences that are more overtly behavioral, such as distractibility and social interactions. Three-year-olds, for instance, can be reliably judged on five temperament dimensions: overcontrolled, inhibited, confident, reserved, and well-adjusted (Caspi & Silva, 1995).

Widely recognized typologies such as this are useful when talking to parents—in fact they emerged from parental impressions. However, there are advantages to thinking less of a category and more of a dimensional approach. If infants and toddlers were assessed on a number of objective emotional dimensions, it would then be possible to look at profiles of traits (like some personality measures, such as the MMPI) which gives a more detailed picture and perhaps identify a few common variants. It also allows one to consider whether extremes of one trait might influence another as well as be more predictive of later emotional issues. Following this research strategy, Planalp and Goldsmith (2020) have reported four key profiles (typical, low negative, withdrawn/inhibited, low reactive) based on six directly observed emotional characteristics: fear, anger, sadness, positive affect, interest, and activity level. The objective measures in this kind of research are interesting. Anger, for example, was assessed when the infant was being restrained in a car seat or their arms were held down by mother when in front of an enticing toy; fear when given scary masks to play with and also when a stranger approaches; and positive affect when mother is playing with a glove puppet with funny voices or a peek-a-boo game from behind a screen.

In addition to motor activity levels, babies' feelings have been measured by coding observations of their reactions to novel stimuli: positive feelings are reflected by smiling and positive vocalizations such as cooing; negative feelings by fussing ("grizzling" in Britain) and crying. But every baby is fussy at times, any baby can be colicky, cry when wet, and all have different sleep patterns. How a parent, usually a mother, responds to these events shapes further reaction patterns. Infant crying—essentially their first means of expressing their true feelings—is distressing to caregivers, and in families with limited resources and harsh living arrangements can be highly aversive (Kiel et al., 2024). Soothing strategies involve some caregiver sensitivity: offering a pacifier if you know the baby is not hungry, carrying, and close skin-to-skin contact are fundamental, gentle rocking and singing lullabies are classics from the old days, tight swaddling is common in many cultures, distraction (mobiles and musical toys), having regular sleep routines, and letting the infant cry until exhausted are all possibilities. The importance of these skills is evident. Persistent crying is a common stimulus for harsh treatment and harmful physical abuse such as shaking. Child abuse can be a tragic example of negative urgency and the action tendencies resulting from parental feelings of rage. But it is equally a consequence of perpetrators not having experiences of holding and caring for their infant, experiences that promote loving feelings. Feelings lead to behaviors, but behaviors lead to feelings as well. Any notion that infant temperament is fixed at birth and stable across time and situation is thoroughly outmoded but remains a meaningful notion for understanding the emergence of more complex feelings (Lengua & Garstein, 2024).

Attachment

If one were to generalize ("transdiagnostically"), our clients, regardless of formal diagnosis or presenting complaints, often have problems with feeling secure, feeling meaningfully attached to others, and feeling hopeful for the future. These are the central feelings across our development, so much so that they could almost represent the unstated universal goals of one's therapy. If these three feelings are strong in your client at the end of therapy—as evidenced by behavior changes—you can quite justly judge the outcome of treatment as favorable.

John Bowlby developed his still influential model of attachment with respect to the mother-child bond as a child psychiatrist working in London at the end of World War II. Separation and loss were dominant experiences and had dreadful consequences for children's development. (It should be said that he always noted he was talking about a mother *figure*, and not only identifying female birth mothers as important.) He collaborated with Mary Ainsworth, who, as a good psychologist, started systematic empirical and observational research. It was she who developed the Standardized Strange Situation Procedure (Ainsworth et al., 1978). Observe the child interacting with their mother, their play, and their exploration. What happens when a mother is with her young child and an unknown person enters the room? What happens when the mother leaves the room? And what happens when she returns? Without going into the details (users of the method need training), secure attachment is recorded when the child interacts with the mother and also plays and explores and relies on the mother as a secure base. Feelings of distress when the mother leaves are easily soothed on the mother's return and play resumes. It's a classic example of emotion and feelings being inferred from emotional expression and also the ability to get on with fun activities—to engage in constructive behavior. If you are securely attached, you feel safe, so you can play and explore and be in a good mood. Children classified as avoidant are preoccupied with the toys in the room, ignore the parent, and don't react emotionally either to the mother leaving or when she returns. Whether such a child feels secure or not, the feeling is not coming from the maternal bond. Other patterns have been described, but from my point of view, the idea that there are clear-cut patterns reflecting distinct types is incorrect: the entire literature on attachment is grounded in a monocultural framework (Keller, 2013).

Even more relevant for thinking about the development of children's feelings was Ainsworth's (1969) focus on maternal sensitivity. Two aspects in particular can be objectively coded: sensitivity to infant feeling signals, and cooperation rather than interference with the infant's ongoing (play) activities. In therapeutic practice, I think simply observing parent and infant or young child interactions in the clinic is most interesting. Watching them interact at home adds even more to one's understanding. I do remember just sitting quietly watching a mother and a three-year old playing together prior to starting a formal assessment (the child's pediatrician had made a referral of suspected autism). At one point shortly after we began, the child sidled up to his mother and in a loud stage whisper, looked over at me and said, "What's he doing here?" I sorely wanted to reply, "Hey, I'm just the Stranger to you!"

The issue for standard attachment research is always the cultural concern (Quinn & Mageo, 2013). Infants around the world are much more likely to receive their nurturing, support, and feelings of security from a wider group of family and community caregivers than in Anglo-European cultures. Once in New Zealand when working with my colleague Averil Herbert, a Māori clinical psychologist, we heard one of the elderly women of her local Māori marae (community compound) explain how Māori baby rearing differed from the White majority: "We're all involved. We pick 'em up." Anyone old enough to remember videos of Princess Diana visiting African communities will know exactly what this means. It is not just adults in the community. Many societies encourage siblings as young as four to serve a caregiving role, which nurtures their feelings as well as developing their skills around caring and responsibility (Weisner & Gallimore, 1977).

The message from attachment research is quite simple. Panksepp's (see Chapter 2) cross-species basic emotions of CARE and PLAY are relevant. It doesn't matter exactly how it is done but when an infant is nurtured in a caring fashion, there are opportunities for learning social skills. Think how quickly babies with responsive mothers learn the emotive reactions (expressions like smiling, cooing, and clinging) that result in reciprocation (smiling, laughing, cuddling, entertaining activities like "This little piggy went to market"). And when babies acquire a feeling of security in a familiar and stable context, this allows more complex activities broadly definable as play: exploring, manipulating, interacting socially first with mothers and other caregivers, playing games like peek-a-boo to make the baby smile and giggle, then play with other children teaching all about others' feelings. And once the attachment to sources of safety is secured, it allows activities roughly definable as SEEKING—exploring and attending to new places, new people, new tastes, and new opportunities, right up to reading, questioning, inventiveness, and, in later life, to scientific research and creative pursuits.

Caregiving (parenting) in this framework doesn't have precise rules (Keller, 2013). Parents need to be responsive to infant needs as expressed by their emotions. A fussy infant is an opportunity to find out why they are not happy, not a stimulus for parental anger, frustration, or dislike (non-acceptance). Being carried and cuddled (and every culture has different ways of doing this) and interacting lovingly contributes to security. We can also recognize that these truisms from research aren't easily implemented by caregivers who are dominated by negative feelings from other sources of stress, poverty, family conflict, lack of support, and nurturing for themselves. This in turn makes it clear that supporting parents at the individual or community level is a major social priority for rearing emotionally competent children.

The larger message from the study of attachment is that feelings of security are of importance to counteract feelings of fear. The helpless human infant is entirely dependent on caregiving by others, a state of affairs that doesn't last forever but continues through life to be important. The emotional systems that neuroscientists have defined and identified don't have content, as content requires hundreds of learning opportunities. But they seem to have evolved to enable humans to look after each other, and to provide the mechanisms for the individual to respond to threats of serious harm. Infants are not born with love of their country or of a particular religion, or a culture, group, or family. Nor are they born with a love of baseball, steak, Renaissance art, or I-phones. But it does seem they are born with the essential survival skills to ensure that someone will look after them. But because it is never guaranteed, the need for security is quickly and easily translated into things becoming important because they provide that feeling of security. The theory of terror management (Solomon et al., 2015) tells us that when people are exposed to thoughts of their own demise, their patriotism is enhanced or triggered, or at least things like national flags and symbols of power to protect you become more positive. Feeling secure is important, both to children and parents. It is not just feeling physically safe that is behind this feeling. The origin is in the survival importance of being socially accepted and thus the fear of being rejected. All our self-conscious feelings derive from threats to being unacceptable and rejected by our designated social group. Teasing and bullying by peers hurts because it places you on the outside. A child doesn't mind gentle teasing by a parent or sibling when feeling secure within the family—it is not a signal of rejection but one of acceptance.

Family Dynamics and Discipline

Insecure parenting is a reminder of an article by Robert Wahler (1980) which was one of the more influential papers written in child behavior modification (therapy) via parent training. Drawing on sound behavioral principles to assist parents manage children's behavior—once they are more independent, from toddlers to teens—has been one of behavior therapy's most important contributions. Principles of positive and consistent contingency management could be summarized by the slogan: "Catch them being good." However, the best therapeutic interventions, teaching workshops, and media programs for parenting skills did not necessarily result in the application and use of these skills. Wahler noted that the failure to maintain the principles was seen most often when working with mothers who were themselves stressed and disadvantaged socially and economically. In particular, many mothers judged to be "at risk" and in need of guidance and support mostly had interactions only with family members and social service case workers who were critical. He called them "insular mothers."

Some of the comments by mothers about their relatives, welfare officers, social workers, and psychologists would be funny if they weren't so sadly revealing:

"She's all the time telling me what to do."

"It's like he thinks he's God Almighty. I don't do nothing right according to him."

"I tell you. She's not only a snoop, she expects me to be perfect."

"I know I'm supposed to do what she says-but she really don't know nothing about kids."

Fortunately, some of these case workers received positive ratings from some mothers:

"I don't know why, but when she comes around, I can just relax."

"You know—we just sit on the porch and talk about nothing."

"You'd be amazed how nice it is to have somebody just listen."

"It's funny. When she comes over, I like to have the house clean—but she's never critical."

These mothers were often describing the same moment-to-moment coercive traps reported by Patterson (Patterson, 1982; Patterson & Reid, 1970). This model describes how if ineffectual responding (e.g., yelling or giving in) to a child's negative behavior (noncompliance or aggression) results in no change or even an escalation, it will eventually produce an aggressive punitive response from the parent, which is reinforced by temporary cessation of the now increased negative behavior. Children use aversive responses to terminate their parents' aversive behaviors. Once we focus more on feelings, however, this much cited standard model can be revised (Moed, 2024). Clearly, if the mother (let's focus on them for this discussion) has strong negative feelings about the child's inappropriate behavior, the more likely she is to want to end it, withdraw, and give in to the child. In addition to the negative reinforcement of escaping the disruptive negative behavior of the child, the mother ends her own unpleasant visceral feelings, which, like for the rat in the shuttle box, reinforces her escape responses (Beauchaine, 2015).

Behavior management programs for children build on the power of reinforcement and token reinforcement and the value of rewarding good behavior, and consequating bad behavior in non-punitive strategies, like time-out or loss of privileges. These general contingency management procedures are highly successful and positive in their approach. But exactly how rewards should be given is not always specified. Erik Erikson (1950) argued that *"Children cannot be fooled by empty praise and condescending encouragement. They may have to accept artificial bolstering of their self-esteem in lieu of something better, but what I call their accruing ego identity gains real strength only from wholehearted and consistent recognition of real accomplishment, that is, achievement that has meaning in their culture"* (p. 145).

There is an interesting dimension of parent-child relationships that seems to relate to feelings in much the same way as moods do (Chapter 1). This is the dimension of warmth vs. hostility, which is a different dimension than the use of positive reinforcement and consistent discipline practices. It is the sort of phenomenon that you feel confident you know it when you see it but is hard to measure objectively and is subject to serious misjudgment across different cultures, contexts, and parenting styles. Past research has suggested that parents rated as warm on self-report questionnaires behaved differently with sons than with daughters when observed in the home. For example, warm mothers' interactions with their sons contained playful joking and expressions of concern, whereas with daughters their interactions were described as less negative but bland (Russell & Russell, 1989). However, contemporary scholarship emphasizes how in many countries major changes in attitudes towards gender equality in families make any generalizations quickly outdated. In an Australian study, mothers who valued gender equality created a positive environment for children by supporting fathers' positive participation in family life (Nunes et al., 2025). Many other studies also recognize that for children with conduct disorders, hostility in parenting can be an effect not a cause. When a child's conduct disorder is accompanied by callous-unemotional traits, all the interactions are even more complicated (Facci et al., 2024).

Parenting programs have become very popular in behavioral psychotherapy, but they are not usually focused on feelings, the importance of warmth and genuineness, or establishing feelings of security through unconditional acceptance. They mostly emphasize contingency management and are focused on negative behaviors such as noncompliance, hyperactivity, rule-breaking, and aggression, what are called conduct disorders. Due to the artificial factor structure of the very widely used Child Behavior Checklist (Achenbach, 1966; Achenbach & Rescorla, 2001), it is now dogma to state that there are two types of childhood problems—internalizing and externalizing. These categories ignore the reality that feelings and their absence underlie overt expressive behaviors that take many different forms. The distinction also ignores the differences in many socially inappropriate behaviors, such as proactive versus reactive aggression (motivated by feelings of fear or anxiety, Dodge, 1991), as well as understanding the "challenging" behaviors of children with physical disabilities and developmental syndromes where failure to learn alternative prosocial conduct characterizes their so-called negative "externalizing" behaviors. Self-injury can arise from lack of communication skills in an unresponsive social environment, and social withdrawal from a lack of social skills in a rejecting social environment.

Missing Elements in Positive Parenting

One of the principle areas where parents' handling of their children's feelings requires sensitivity on their part is how they deal with their child's experiences of success and failure. The research on the foundations of children's motivation to engage in meaningful tasks is rich in understanding of how feedback, whether focused on effort or outcome, makes a substantial difference. Carol Dweck, in particular, made a very important contribution in her work on "mindsets"—people's implicit theories about the nature and origin of ability. Rather than think one has innate and fixed intelligence, she has promoted the importance of children's feelings about their abilities being a function of hard work, good teaching, and persistence. Parents can influence this adaptive mindset (I think of it more as a feeling, or at least an affectively laden attribution) by how they handle their children's feelings following success or failure. From among many, this example is illustrative.

Dweck (2006) describes the story of Elizabeth, a gymnast who does not win during a competition and is "devastated" when she returns home (p. 180–182). This is a strong unpleasant feeling we have all experienced. There are several potential messages her father can give her, according to Dweck's concepts. He could say, "I thought you were the best"; or "You were robbed of a ribbon that was rightfully yours"; or "Gymnastics is not that important"; or "You have the ability and you're sure to win next time"; or "You didn't deserve to win." Dweck contends that this last option is actually the most growth-minded message (although not necessarily put this bluntly). She states that the father actually said to Elizabeth: "I know how you feel. It's so disappointing to have your hopes up and to perform your best but not to win. But you know, you haven't really earned it yet. There were many girls there who've been in gymnastics longer than you and who've worked a lot harder than you. If this is something you really want, then it's something you'll really have to work for." Note that this more growth-minded parental response explicitly acknowledges the feeling of disappointment and normalizes it. The four other possible responses would have discouraged Elizabeth from feeling her feelings.

Disappointment can also be felt by parents, related to their children's achievements. I had a revealing (and learning) experience at a time in my private practice when I was mostly seeing families of children with autism. The Yanagi family (not their real name) was a third-generation Japanese American family living in Honolulu. They had a six-year-old daughter and a three-year-old son, Kenji, recently diagnosed with Autism Spectrum Disorder. He was typical of the classic description of autism that Kanner had made long ago. I was encouraging his parents to engage in a number of fairly standard positive behavior management programs (e.g., Meyer & Evans, 1989; Tellegen & Sanders, 2013) and naturalistic language training (Laski et al., 1988). The whole family came to some of the sessions. Mrs. Yanagi was attentive, took notes, asked questions, and sometimes brought me mangoes from the tree in their yard. Mr. Yanagi was distant, made little eye contact, and never said a word. Recognizing some cultural aspects around gender roles, I decided not to press him and give him time to warm up to me and the clinic setting. But in one session, when I was explaining what I wanted them to do, Mrs. Yanagi burst out saying "There's no point you telling us this Dr.

Evans, my husband won't follow a single recommendation, he just ignores Kenji, leaves everything to me. He hates the boy and blames me for his birth defects." She started to cry. Mr. Yanagi got up, looking very angry, and left the room.

I arranged for an individual session with the father alone. Mr. Yanagi listened quietly when I told him, without criticism, I thought there were complex feelings clouding our sessions. I asked him just to visualize Kenji in his mind as vividly as he could and then tell me what he was feeling. "Sad," he replied. Not being able to judge whether that meant sympathy for Kenji or feeling sorry for himself, without comment I said, "What else?" "Sad," he repeated, "disappointed. Shame." Taking a calculated guess, I replied: "May 5th is coming up. Are you going to fly a koinobori [carp streamer] for Kenji?" His answer: "No. Cannot. He's retarded."

Without giving a blow-by-blow account of that session, careful discussion about feelings revealed the following. He felt because Kenji had a developmental disability, it would be shameful to celebrate the culturally important Boys' Day, and his neighbors would be scornful. He explained that when he learnt they were going to have a son, he started to dream about how he would take him fishing, teaching Kenji how to fish like his father had taught him. He'd even bought some equipment a young boy could use. It was going to be a thrill for him and Kenji to go off fishing in the early morning. He'd built up many positive scenarios in his imagination. Now, he said, "Kenji can't learn anything." At one point, he also admitted that he felt ashamed of his own bitterness, which he tried to justify by deciding his wife must have done something wrong during the pregnancy or had bad family genes she'd never revealed to him. He spontaneously admitted it was small of him to put so much on something "unimportant, like fishing."

The intervention was very simple. "But it *is* important to you, and anyone can understand that. It's your thing," I said, "everyone has expectations for their children." I was quiet for a moment or two and then said: "Do you have to have a high IQ to go fishing? I always assumed all you needed was luck." He bristled and started to remonstrate until he realized I was gently teasing. "Some skills and know-how, needed," he muttered. "OK," I said, "you specify the basic skills—we call it a task analysis—and I'll show you how to teach them to Kenji. There's nothing wrong with your dream. The two of you can go fishing; he will love it if you make it fun, you communicate your own pleasure and enjoyment and show him how proud of him you are. It might need some patience from you, but I thought fishing taught patience!"

The original program I had been devising focused on Kenji's self-help skills, language, and better managing the child's feelings of frustration by understanding the communicative intent of his challenging behavior (Carr & Durand, 1985). But simple yet powerfully deep feelings of disappointment had never been addressed because people aren't supposed to be disappointed that their child has a disability. Family therapy programs, special education principles, and disability advocacy initiatives encourage acceptance and love, but run the risk, if parents don't feel those things at first, of inducing shame. Mr. Yanagi needed his dream to be still possible; to become a reality but with slightly modified elements. Without that, his sadness turned to feelings of blame and anger, and as he withdrew from equitable childcare responsibilities, his wife became understandably more stressed, angry, and critical. Simple unresolved feelings and cultural norms pervaded the family dynamics.

There are many parent-training programs that have been developed recently which have shifted attention from simple (though effective) contingency management to a greater emphasis on parental feelings about their children, parental understanding of children's feelings, and a focus on establishing a more relaxed background mood for the challenge of raising a child. Australian psychologist Matt Sanders, for example, has refined and elaborated his original parenting program (Triple-P: Positive Parenting Program) through systematic evaluative research in different cultural contexts (Sanders et al., 2022). The revised program now includes emphasis on feelings, such as furthering acceptance, tolerance, and compassion towards others, having appropriate expectations, and supporting children's friendships in a safe environment. Another particularly impressive example comes from the work of Wendy Silverman (Silverman et al., 2024) where the standard CBT treatment of anxiety in youth (7- to 16-year olds) was augmented with parental relationship training including greater use of acceptance, more positive reinforcement, and decreased use of psychological control. Her important argument is that if there are positive aspects of effective parenting that are already in place in a family (show appropriate baseline levels), then selectively including such elements in the training package should allow truly effective fine tuning of a treatment in order to achieve better outcomes.

There are unfortunately circumstances in which the simple mutual pleasures of interactions between a young child and parent are disrupted due to a raft of personal and social challenges faced by many who are disadvantaged in today's complex societies. In a cultural context, Herbert's research provided an excellent example of the kinds of support for mothers that might be the essential framework within which to address effective contingency management. Mothers needing parent training are likely to have a slew of negative feelings about the situation and themselves. Some of the young women in Herbert's program had relationship problems with men (the fathers of their children), had already had other children uplifted from their homes by child welfare officers, and were heavy users of self-medication by drugs, marihuana, and alcohol. Their feelings about themselves, as mothers, were ones of deep shame. Their children were challenging, their community critical. How in that context can one best foster feelings of affection for the children, for themselves, and confidence in the value of the programs they were being taught? Parent skill training was introduced as only one day in each week of a long experience on the marae, culturally and spiritually relevant to these women even though their own Māori identities were not well-developed. The other programs were practical: housekeeping, cooking, self-care skills taught by warm but demanding elder women. Parenting skills were barely mentioned. Instead, traditional Māori parenting values were stressed: whakapapa (ancestry), whanaungatanga (family connections and kinship), awhinatanga (guiding and supporting in a safe learning environment), tangihanga (shared grief in mourning), and wairuatanga (spiritual well-being and connection to the world).

This has opened up important lines of applied research in areas of special relevance to clinical work with some of the most challenging caregiving situations there are: foster parenting. Children who need to be placed in foster care have typically gone through some of the most destructive and disruptive experiences for the development of a stable affect system. When parents and families are under stress of violent marital discord, acrimonious separation and divorce, psychiatric disorders including drug problems expanding serious neglect and abuse, the focus of intense emotions is not on the children. In those countries that have the material and political stability to have public and governmental agencies, children in such families are likely to come under the protection of government agencies devoted to childcare and protection. The challenges facing these social welfare agencies are enormous for all sorts of reasons—inadequate staffing, lack of funding, legal entanglements over custody, well-meaning social welfare staff who, like those described by Wahler, are themselves stressed, under-resourced and trained, and unwelcome at times in the deeply personal lives of families in conflict. One major societal strategy for helping children when family care has completely broken down and abuse and neglect are identified is the placement of children with foster families. It is something of society's last resort but has the potential to be positive. Foster parents, however, may have the best intentions but not the training and understanding to provide the best possible childcare in these conditions. As a result, the placements often break down and the child has to be removed to a different family.

For her doctorate, Bernice Gabriel (2017), an experienced clinical child psychologist in my research group, designed and evaluated a training program for foster mothers that focused on their having a better understanding of the foster child's feelings when difficulties in behavior were threatening the placement. She made use of Tarren-Sweeney's (2007) assessment scale, which unlike the standard child behavior checklists addresses such domains as precocious interpersonal behavior, anxious/distrustful behaviors, self-injury, suicidal discourse, and negative self-image. In any family, challenging behavior can be exhibited by any child, but for a foster child who feels emotionally abandoned by parents and has been shunted from placement to placement, only a deep insight into what this means for emotional development will allow foster parents to manage a child's feelings and support positive emotional adjustment. Gabriel described a typical scenario, using the foster mother's words (I've changed some minor details to ensure confidentiality):

> *Sally is a 44-year-old woman who lives with her husband and three children in their late teens. Sally and her husband, Eric, decided to foster a child as they felt that their family had a lot to offer a child in need. The child placed with them is 5-year-old Petra who has no contact with her biological family. She was removed from her parent's care at the age of 3, due to serious abuse and neglect. Petra had a series of failed placements, largely blamed on her challenging behaviors, before going to live with Sally and her family at the age of four and a half. On arrival, Sally described Petra as being 'feral' in her behavior—she ate very quickly, shoveling food into her mouth with her hands. She was not toilet trained and had poor hygiene. Petra was extremely 'non-compliant, very demanding of attention'; Sally described her as 'manipulative'. Petra's tantrums lasted hours and she would become physically aggressive and scream very loudly. While Petra's behaviors had improved a little since being in their care, Sally still felt overwhelmed by her challenging behaviors, and stated that she regularly 'worried we've made a mistake taking her into their care and then I feel guilty for feeling that way'.*

In this scenario, we see the empathic prosocial feelings of wanting and being able to help a child in need. When it proves extremely difficult, Sally faces feelings of failure, regret, and guilt. Rather than discount those feelings, the training program recognized that any well-meaning person would feel the same. The key was to ensure that Sally did not give up, as previous foster parents already had, and that is where the optimistic support of a formal training program comes into play. With disappointment and shattered expectations, Sally was interpreting Petra's behavior in a judgmental way: "demanding attention" which actually reveals an unmet need for acceptance and love, "bad table manners" which reveals a life history of having to fight for your own sustenance, "being manipulative" which really reflects lack of feelings of security from the experience that adults will only treat you with kindness if you are deceptive and pretend to be affectionate. The training program made these simple observations clear to Sally in a non-critical way. Especially important to the placement continuing was for Sally to be made aware of two things: (a) that positive contingency management techniques implemented with patience would quickly improve behavior; and (b) that the destructive effects of abuse, neglect, and the failures and instability of being moved from placement to placement could not be over-emphasized. Success for Sally had to be presented in terms of her resilience and determination to keep trying, not in terms of sudden improvements. With support and insight, Sally was able to see great strides in the establishment of a loving family environment. This is not, as the saying goes, rocket science, but a focus on feelings does shift the design of an intervention towards linking sound behavior management principles with a professional empathy for what clients are going through emotionally.

Woven throughout this book, there is a strong assumption that parenting is a wonderful experience that brings feelings of joy to both the adults and the children. But we know this is not universally true. Parental burnout is composed of four feeling clusters: emotional exhaustion ("I feel completely run down by my role as a parent"); feelings of not being the parent one once was; feeling fed up with one's parental role ("I don't enjoy being with my children"); and emotional distance from one's children ("I'm no longer able to show my children I love them"). The sample items are from a parental burnout assessment questionnaire (Roskam, Brianda, & Mikolajczak, 2018). The feeling phenomenon is different from the feelings that burnout might trigger: regret. The Parental Regret Scale was constructed by the same team of Polish and Belgian psychologists and contains items such as "Having a child (children) was a bad decision," "I feel sad when I think about what kind of life I could have had if I hadn't had a child (children)," and "I feel guilty because I didn't prevent pregnancy" (Piotrowski, Mikolajczak, & Roskam, 2023). Both types of feelings are seldom examined because they seem to violate expected feelings, but even with the most contented parents, such feelings must occur occasionally during stressful times. Interestingly, there is little definitive work on couples who regret *not* having children, although most reports on life satisfaction suggest such regrets are rare or rarely expressed.

Adolescents and Conflicts

The extent to which parents understand and accept their children's feelings seems to make a significant difference to children's emotional development. So, that is undoubtedly a significant way in which feelings change. The developmental stage of the child is important. Adolescence involves many physical changes as well as establishing positive separation from direct parental control. Where conduct problems are beginning to be seen in some teens, they show difficulties in understanding and regulating internal negative feelings or expressing them to parents (Kostiuk & Fouts, 2002). At this age, parents will set limits on adolescents' behaviors at the very time they are evaluating and asserting greater independence. That inevitably raises barriers to their goals and angry feelings as a result. Feelings of anger and contempt are often causes of family conflict (Capaldi et al., 1994). Conflict will inevitably occur in families with teenagers, however in a very creative line of research, Smetana (e.g., 1995) discovered that what parents and teens argued about fell into distinct categories—safety issues, moral issues, family conventions and rules, and personal issues. Teenagers would usually accept a parent's right to impose household rules, require safety, and uphold moral principles, but felt that personal issues like clothes, how to wear one's hair, music listened to, time on cell phones were not decisions parents should control. Thus, the true focus of many arguments was on what domain an issue belonged to—when parents tried to control personal matters, conflict arose. This concept led doctoral candidate Marie Connelly (2001) to conduct an intervention study comparing a problem-solving approach with one that addressed the domain in which the issue fell. Both treatments saw a reduction in conflict, but parents reported a better outcome using the problem-solving approach (which was more likely to involve compromise). The teenagers reported a better outcome using a tactic of establishing which domain the issue was and who had the right to decide (which was more likely to establish their rights).

Prosocial Feelings and Fairness

There is considerable overlap between the issues that arise for parenting skills and the kinds of childhood experiences to enhance the sorts of feelings that promote prosocial behavior as the action tendencies. These behaviors are categories such as helping, cooperating (in both play and learning), taking turns, and following the rules of a game. Feelings that support prosocial skills are caring, feelings of fairness, and self-confidence. It is not obvious to me where these feelings come from in young children. Are they learnt through parental modeling of feelings when someone is hurt, an animal is injured, a pet needs comforting? Are they acquired when children learn that their expressions of affection and caring for a sibling or a parent on request are met with strong approval which is reinforcing? At what point does the much-admired quality of empathy in children mean that seeing your friend in your playgroup being upset makes you upset as well, and should it not mean even more so that you offer support?

A long time ago, Irvin Staub came to the University of Hawaiʻi as a visiting professor and I heard him talk about some research he was doing that fascinated me. He was investigating the conditions under which a child would help another child who seemed to be in distress. The research paradigm was simple. A child is briefly left alone in a room, and sounds are heard of another child crying. Does the child get up, go out, and see if they can help? Many very young children do. But at a certain age, about the time they go to elementary school, they don't. Staub reasoned that this was because they were learning a new social principle—don't interfere with other children, mind you own business. In later years, when they are teenagers, they have learned that that principle has limits, and the over-riding importance of caring for others results in them once again making efforts to help. Positive socialization experiences that directly teach a disposition towards helping behaviors are modified by circumstances. Staub subsequently expanded his studies to explore more widely the origins of harmful as well as altruistic behavior—see, for instance, his major monograph on the topic (Staub, 2003).

Fairness is also a prosocial condition that can be felt. Or maybe, it is unfairness that gets experienced as a negative feeling. Anyone with more than one child in the family will have heard the irate complaint "That's not fair!" Irate is defined in the dictionary as very angry, furious, incensed, but I don't think we typically use it that way. People who are irate are angry about something they perceive as unjust. Maybe the anger can be really strong, but intensity is not the point; irate includes frustration at not being treated properly. And children who are irate about unfairness will turn it into a new feeling when they sulk and flounce and stomp if the injustice is not rectified to their satisfaction.

My research group at Massey University in New Zealand investigated children's perceptions of unfairness as we were interested in the experience of unfairness on family relationships and its importance in positive peer friendships and creating equitable conditions in inclusive classrooms. There are also decades of research on the destructive effects that differential treatment of children within families can have on the less favored siblings (Jensen et al., 2025). Karma Galyer, Kyle Smith, and I looked at four situations which commonly arise in families with respect to reward and punishment contingencies: not getting a promised reward for something good you have done, getting a reward for something you haven't done, getting punished for something you haven't done, and not getting punished for something bad you have done (Evans et al., 2001). Illustrated stories describing incidents such as these were read to elementary aged children who were asked to imagine they were the child in the story: "How would that make you feel, and how strongly would you feel it?" They were also asked how the child benefiting from unfairness would feel (ideally, in *our* moral judgment, they should feel some embarrassment or guilt).

We had assumed, as adults, that getting punished for something one hadn't done would feel worse ("bad," "sad," or "upset" were the words most commonly used) than not getting a reward for something one had done. This was true for girls. Boys, however, thought that missing a reward would feel worse than getting a punishment—shades of reward dominance ideas, or as McNaughton (2024) concluded, *reinforcer* sensitivity. In terms of receiving an undeserved reward, 89% of the children thought the beneficiary would feel happy. But many fewer of these 9- to 11-year-old children thought the child who avoided punishment at another child's expense would actually feel happy about it—in this situation, the positive feeling would be relief, but they weren't quite ready to identify it. At least a third of the children, both boys and girls, felt that a moral sense of an injustice having been done influenced their feelings. A few of the children (kudos to their parents) even stated that the unrewarded act (returning someone's wallet) was the right thing to do and that should be sufficient reward, thus receiving the material reward (or not) was not considered important.

Words and Talk: Children's Emotion Competence

In addition to these indirect sources of influence over children's feelings, there are effective strategies for directly helping children learn about their own feelings and those of others. A fundamental component of children's development is the acquisition of what has become widely referred to as emotion competence. It is usually defined as the ability to recognize and label facial expressions and basic emotions, understand the nature and causes of emotion, learn the skills to effectively regulate emotion, and manage emotional expression in a functional way. An essential building block of emotion competence is that, through the preschool years, children come to understand their own feelings as well as those of others. Understanding one's own feelings is necessary for the larger task of understanding others, since that permits the emergence of empathy—feelings for others' feelings. If we can use words and fantasy to enhance emotion competence, then it becomes a possible therapeutic strategy rather than a deficiency diagnosis which leaves a therapist only longer-term intervention. It also offers opportunity for consultation and shaping of those more potent contexts where such learning occurs—at home with parents and at school with teachers.

Much of the clinically relevant research on children's emotion competence comes from the emotion socialization framework of Nancy Eisenberg (e.g., Eisenberg, 2020). Parents' expression of their own emotions and their reactions to their children's emotions directly influence children's emotional expression and regulation and thus successful adaptation to life. What is particularly important is the way in which parents accept emotions, encourage their expression, and validate the experience of emotion, which means, of course, validating feelings. It was the early work of Paul Harris and Francisco Pons as a joint team from Harvard and Oxford universities that really set the stage for a whole new appreciation of how children's understanding of emotion was determined, not just influenced, by parental attachment, discourse, and communication.

The issue is a bit complicated by the fact that there are nine distinct components to children's understanding of feelings. Pons et al. (2004) developed a way of assessing children's understanding. They used materials developed with more than 100 English-speaking British children between the ages of three and eleven. The components defined are as follows. (1) recognizing and naming basic emotions (happy, sad, afraid, angry); (2) understanding that there are external causes for different feelings; (3) realizing that different people will have different feelings depending on what they desire; (4) a feeling will be based on what an individual believes to be true; (5) understanding that the intensity of a feelings decreases over time and that a current situation can be a reminder and reactivate the original feeling; (6) as children get older, they learn that different strategies can be used to control feelings, first behavioral strategies like covering your eyes, and then using psychological strategies such as distraction and denial; (7) realizing (around the age of five) the way a person is expressing a feeling, or not, might not represent what they are truly feeling and that they might be trying to hide their feelings; (8) at about the age of eight years, children recognize one can have more than one feeling at the same time and even opposite or ambivalent feelings; and (9) at about that same age, children understand that there are negative feelings for engaging in morally undesirable behavior (e.g., lying or cheating) and also that they can have very positive feelings from performing prosocially and morally, including confessing, making a sacrifice, and helping someone.

You can easily see how acquiring such complex emotion comprehension will be related to how others—parents, siblings, friends, and teachers—explain their own feelings. As this is done verbally, it means that parents' use of emotion words in discussions and interactions will be important. (And we should not forget that with less verbal children, such as those with autism, visual materials serve the same purpose—Round et al., 2017.) When interacting with a child, reminiscing about the past, talking about the future, or discussing any current experience involving children's feelings, parents can describe their own feelings, label their children's feelings, and discuss reasons and causes for feelings. As it is very easy to model emotion talk and teach it to parents, this provides a useful supplementary intervention tactic when working with families. New Zealand researcher Karen Salmon has been instrumental in describing and evaluating these tactics. Wareham and Salmon (2006) gave a good example of teaching parents of preschool children how to have conversations that reminisce about past events and how everyone involved felt. In another of her studies, Salmon and her colleagues (2013) showed how coaching preschool children on feeling labels and causes resulted in improvements on knowledge component (1) (recognizing and naming emotions), but not on the others. Developmental level is always a factor in children's emotion comprehension.

The following conversation recorded between a mother and her son was used as an example in the school climate work described in the next section.

MOTHER: *"We're going to the zoo again on Sunday. D'you remember what happened last time?"*

CHILD: *"I was frightened."*

MOTHER: *"Right! You got scared when that lion opened his big mouth and let out a roar. I was scared too. Nearly jumped out of my skin. But then I remembered the strong fence and I knew we were all safe."*

CHILD: *"You said I was brave."*

MOTHER: *"M'hmm. You were. You didn't run. You stayed and watched the zoo keeper give that lion a meal. You got closer to get a good look. That was brave."*

Teachers and Schools: Emotional Climate

During our research project on the emotional climate of school classrooms, I was quietly observing a teacher in a small rural elementary (primary) school in New Zealand. It was the end of the day, and the children were all cheerfully leaving the classroom, somewhat noisily, one by one. Mr. Whetu, the teacher, stood near the door and was calmly saying goodbye to each child. One small, thin boy with a large backpack was leaving. He looked downcast and was talking to no-one. Earlier in the day, we had noticed him being reprimanded for not paying attention or following instructions. As he passed by, Mr. Whetu stopped him. "Tama, I want to talk to you. Come over here out of the way." Tama tensed immediately, looking stricken. But Mr. Whetu crouched down so the two were at eye level and said very quietly, calmly but firmly: "You didn't have a good day today." Tama looked down; he was about to cry. He didn't answer. Mr. Whetu paused, lips pursed, and nodded his head. "Tomorrow will be better. Go home, have a good feed and a good night's sleep. I'm looking forward to seeing you tomorrow. Off you go now," he added, giving Tama a quick fist bump. Tama smiled and trotted out, hitching up his backpack in a confident manner.

It is difficult with words to capture the simplicity and beauty of this interaction, but what we had observed was a dedicated and brilliant teacher who knew exactly how to support a challenging student. He didn't have to ask Tama how he was feeling—his core affect was apparent and the details irrelevant. There was nothing overdone or sugary, nothing patronizing, no remonstrations, criticism, or attribution of blame, just a statement of fact. He showed respect, gave suggestions, and conveyed acceptance. And Tama's feelings changed instantly.

The project that Shane Harvey led in the schools started with another simple incident. A pupil in a different school had been referred to Psychological Services for consistent misbehavior in class. By the time Harvey was able to act on the referral, that school year was over, and the boy had started in the next grade with a new teacher. The new teacher, Miss Y, was surprised: "That boy's not a behavior problem at all. He's fine. He can get excited at times but that's Third Graders for you. Enthusiasm! Good to see!" Harvey interviewed the pupil anyway, asking him frankly why his behavior had changed. His reply initiated our classroom climate project: "I didn't like Mr. X. I didn't care what he thought about me. I really like Miss Y. I want to be good. I want her to like me."

The elaborate program we developed to support teachers to be able to create a positive emotional classroom climate is too detailed to cover here. All the work is described in Evans and Harvey (2012). Most of the material and examples presented in workshops came from spending time in the classrooms of teachers like Mr. Whetu, whom we instantly recognized as being highly skillful in creating a positive emotional climate.

The concept of social-emotional learning programs introduced in a school-wide curriculum to teach about feelings directly has become popular in educational circles. The evidence for their general success is well-documented (Greenberg, 2023). Similarly, there have been school-wide efforts to teach emotional skills. Australia has been progressive in implementing school-wide CBT-oriented programs for the prevention of depression and other mental health concerns. There are, however, as you might expect, too many variables to validate their effectiveness empirically (Gunawardena et al., 2024). There are also many studies over the last twenty years in the USA on teaching mindfulness in schools, especially with adolescents, usually reporting positive results in various aspects of social-emotional behavior. Comprehensive reviews are rather less positive (Nagpal & Radliff, 2024). Some results from a very ambitious British trial of mindfulness-based cognitive therapy showed mixed results with limited success in increasing positive affect (Kuyken et al., 2022).

Focusing on the naturalistic learning opportunities of being in a context that is itself a positive emotional climate appears to me to be a far more useful strategy to allow children's emotion competence to develop. When teachers are charged with implementing a school-based mindfulness program to directly teach emotional skills, the program is highly dependent on their confidence, stress, and their trust in colleagues and school leadership (Braun et al., 2024). While these packaged programs are good to know about for any therapists working with individual child clients who might be experiencing behavioral or emotional problems at school, working with individual teachers will be a more likely intervention prospect. In our research, we regularly found individual teachers who were either already skilled or who responded collaboratively with us as psychologists to design new individual strategies. Gifted teachers understand children's feelings. As one said to us: "*Really listen. Like when you're talking with a kid they actually know that you're talking to them ... and that can be really hard as a teacher because you've got so many noisy distractions. Especially in these critical times when kids are really needy, you know. And feel, feel—just remember that kids aren't ever too big to know that you care ... that is absolutely critical, but it's got to be genuine*" (Evans & Harvey, 2012, pp. 110–111).

In 1988, author Robert Fulghum (1988) wrote the humorous book entitled *All I Really Need to Know I Learned in Kindergarten*. The things he learned are classic: "share everything; play fair; don't hit people; put things back where you found them; say you're sorry when you hurt someone; flush; don't take things that aren't yours." That's not the entire list but it gives you a flavor of an essential psychological truth—the key social and emotional skills are learned early in play groups, preschools, and kindergartens throughout the world. What are typically seen as problems within the preschool child, and later likely to be diagnosed as Oppositional Defiant Disorder (ODD), are the predominance of negative feelings, the tendency to be active and impulsive when feeling positive (known as surgency), and difficulties in deliberately inhibiting action tendencies and emotion expression when feeling cranky (Zastrow et al., 2018). Maria Ulloa demonstrated the benefits of an emotion-focused training program—both for the preschool teachers in the training and the children they were teaching in early childhood programs (Ulloa et al., 2016). The early emotional features of ODD are exactly the affective situations skilled teachers can shape in a positive direction.

Implications

I picked out different aspects of emotion competence at different developmental stages in order to illustrate the critical point: knowing, managing, and expressing feelings require long periods of learning in supportive and caring environments. Cranky, difficult babies don't stay that way; insecurely attached toddlers still grow up to support their friends and play fair. All of the topics discussed have a consistent link. Emotionally competent children who are also curious and kind, and whose feelings are rich and work to their benefit, need security and warmth in their numerous interactions with parents, families, friends, schools, and communities. Children like this will become the parents and caregivers and teachers of the next generation who will behave in the same way.

I have indicated throughout that being able to understand other people's feelings and to know how they will respond to emotionally salient stimuli is an important ability in life, as it is for psychotherapists. From the topics addressed, you can see feelings are always a two-way street: therapist/client, child/parent, teacher/student, individual/friends. Parents' feelings influence their children and vice versa. Rachel Andersen and others (2012) elicited fascinating observations and insights from school children of various ages when they were asked indirectly about how and why their teachers expressed their feelings. One small group of 10-year olds said of their class teacher: "But she still likes all of us." Interviewer asked: "She still likes you even if you are misbehaving?" Students in unison: "Yeah!."

Life isn't always rosy. Understanding the feelings of others also allows one to be interpersonally manipulative. In therapy, we are used to sounding authentic while having an ulterior motive in order to change clients' feelings and behavior in directions we judge professionally to be helpful. And since our motives in doing so are entirely selfless and focused on clients' well-being, we feel little sense of deception when we use our emotional understanding to achieve professional goals. Nevertheless, it can be seen that some people are not as altruistic as most therapists. Any young person is capable of using their emotional intelligence interpersonally in self-serving, Machiavellian, and possibly psychopathic ways (e.g., Bacon & Regan, 2016). The tactics most often employed by individuals scoring high in Machiavellianism tend to be guilt induction, deceit, and ingratiation. They are also likely to exploit friendships and are able to do so because of their ability to stay emotionally detached.

The all-important topic of imaginative play as a key source of affective learning is complicated by the influence of rapid technological change in electronic access to information and social media. While many commentators wring their hands (an expression of anguish more often written about than ever enacted) over children's access to electronic influence, it is difficult to judge what its impact will be. Eighty-five million people are daily active users of the self-styled "ultimate virtual universe" of games and interactive experiences on the platform called Roblox. Forty percent of these users are under the age of thirteen. Compare their experience to my own and even my now adult children's choice of entertainment when alone: being immersed in reading for pleasure. Not struggling with the heavy classics, influential though they too can be, but engaging with imaginative fantasy tales like Lord of the Rings, Harry Potter, The Wind in the Willows, and Watership Down, and reality-focused stories of heroism and adventure like Lassie, The Black Stallion, The Hardy Boys, Nancy Drew, The Famous Five, to randomly name a few. How will the smartphone and iPad generation be different? No one really knows. It's tempting to believe electronic media is harmful. And of course, that judgment is convincing in respect to easy access to explicit pornographic material most of us would feel is extremely inappropriate for anyone, far less pre-adolescents. Ranting about it or demanding greater controls by the huge media companies has no chance of changing the reality of this feature of twenty-first-century society. Its influence, either positive or negative, will never be known, since whatever it is will become the new reality, just like the printing press once created the new reality of easy access to the books just mentioned. The one thing we do know is that if parents abdicate all control of leisure activities, surrender family engagement with the lives of children, and neglect the recognition, understanding, and shaping of children's feelings, the results will not be what parents hope for and value. Whether as therapists we can or even should help families create what *we* consider feelings-healthy environments remains to be seen.

It is encouraging, however, that the children Rachel Andersen interviewed all knew that a teacher could be angry, frustrated, or moody, but that their altruism and love of teaching meant that they could have all these feelings without it ever influencing their liking and acceptance and support for their pupils. When families provide a basic level of care and security, the same ups and downs of parental feelings can occur without long-term harm. This brings us to another important aspect about feelings. How they are expressed can vary greatly—they can be suppressed and masked and exaggerated in order to achieve different effects. We will consider this issue in the next chapter.

5

Words and Deeds

Communicating and Hiding Feelings

Ears Have Walls

I once saw the phrase "Ears have walls" scrawled as graffiti on an exterior college wall in Cambridge, and I decided that Cambridge students must be very thoughtful. When we want to know about feelings, we have to listen to people. And they have to have words. As psychotherapists and practicing psychologists, our clients are mostly individuals, although sometimes families or therapeutic groups. Individual clients spend the large majority of their time within friendship groups and much larger communities, interacting with many people, in the street, in stores, at worksites, places of worship, on vacations, at sporting events, and at community gatherings larger than immediate family. Every interaction involves shared emotions—the expression of feelings and judging, dealing with, and listening to the feelings of all the other people encountered. Recent scholarly interest in "shared emotions" reveals that it is yet another phenomenon that has been described in different ways based on different starting assumptions.

In this chapter, I introduce a variety of topics related to communication and the expression of feelings in social contexts. Social context includes social media. Online activity is especially relevant to the sharing of feelings, communication via emotive language, emotional contagion, and shared emotions—a smorgasbord of topics, indeed, but all directly connected to the one theme of social communication and the varied expression of feelings in order to achieve a given effect. Social media platforms have become a rich source of naturalistic and large-scale data on feelings. When working with any client of any age in almost any cultural setting, it should be kept in mind that they will have an online presence and participation that is highly reactive and affects their feelings in both positive and negative ways.

There are certain experiences relevant here. One is that when people are asked to express an emotion (through facial expressions and other bodily portrayals), they tend to report feeling that same emotion (Coles et al., 2022). Another is

How and Why Feelings Change. Ian M. Evans, Oxford University Press. © Ian M. Evans (2026).
DOI: 10.1093/9780197825808.003.0006

that we have a tendency, one that is automatic and unintentional, to show similar facial, postural, and verbal expressions as others in a socially interacting group. Hatfield and colleagues (1994) called it emotional contagion. Although originally conceptualized as motor mimicry, more recent analyses indicate the phenomenon is a form of social regulation. Contextual information (what is going on or being talked about) is required for mimicry to occur, and it functions to support social bonding and warmth (Hess & Fischer, 2013). This is why emotional contagion occurs less when the extremes of another individual's emotion would overwhelm the observer or the listener. In some contexts, the stimulus situation, such as listening to a bad joke that made the group titter, was not what caused you to smile along with the others, and you may not even feel amused at the time, but you smile anyway in a shared positive valence.

It is also well-established that while facial and other bodily expressions of feelings are typically automatic, people are able to exert considerable control over these expressions and will do so for social and communicative purposes. We can fight back tears, *not* laugh at a tasteless joke, put on a sad face when hearing of someone's illness, pout when you don't get your way, and scrunch up your nose to share your displeasure with others without actually feeling disgust. An interesting aside on emotional contagion is that in FBI (US Federal Bureau of Investigation) training for handling difficult situations, emotional contagion is recognized as a risk, and the advice given includes listening instead of speaking, putting on a calm demeanor, and being aware of the tendency to mimic expressions. This is useful advice for trainee therapists to have had when first encountering angry, agitated, or frightened clients.

The issue of emotional contagion does not really change the link between genuine feelings and the typical expression thereof, but has been argued as a new theory, a "behavioral ecology view" of facial expression by Crivelli and Fridlund (2019). The important principle, it seems to me, is that the expression of feelings, while both automatic (stereotypic) and learned through imitation, has a variety of functions. Most broadly, it has the survival function of preparing the person and others for escape from danger and avoidance of threats, as well as eliciting caring and nurturance from parents and family groups. It also has, therefore, a communicative function that serves others as well as self, and feelings have a social influence function that more directly serves the needs and desires of the individual. None of these purposes of feelings and their expression are incompatible. Problems of a clinical nature arise when they are not serving the intended function: keeping others away rather than attracting affiliation; alienating close relationships when the expression seems deceptive because it doesn't match the emotional circumstances; arousing the body for action when there is no objective danger; producing or failing to produce physiological changes counteractive to achieving a given goal—a circumstances that will be analyzed in much more detail in Chapter 7.

There has been some interest among emotion theorists, especially those with a neuroscience slant, in the well-known fact that people differ in the precision with which they describe their feelings. In simple terms, this can be called lack of emotion differentiation if someone says that they feel bad but can't be more precise as to whether they are sad or angry or disappointed. Kashdan and colleagues (2015) referred to it as an absence of emotion granularity, but there is no specific measure of it, and it is difficult to distinguish emotion differentiation from the well-researched topic of emotion competence. They give the example of someone commenting on their reaction when hearing of the September 11th attack on the World Trade Center towers in New York City: "I felt a bunch of things, anger, confusion, fear. I just felt bad" (p. 10). However, that does not sound to me like a struggle to explain a feeling, but an illustration of the reality that one can feel more than one thing at a time. That seems different from whether a client can make the granular differentiation between a feeling of anxiety and one of trepidation. If you have an extensive vocabulary, you will use trepidation when you have anxiety about a significant action you are about to perform. Nevertheless, Kashdan et al.'s speculation that it would be clinically helpful to encourage greater emotion differentiation in order to transform feelings and thereby reduce psychological problems is certainly in line with one of the key messages of this book about the importance of analyzing feelings.

The Connotative Meaning of Words

Communication of feelings is not just through facial expression, crucial though that is. Words play an equal role, which is why parental emotion talk is so important in early development. Words themselves, however, have affective properties as well as meanings. Arthur Staats (1972; 1990) introduced into behavioral psychotherapy several important insights into the emotional properties of spoken words. Word combinations and their meaning can elicit feelings. That is obvious. But words themselves are emotive separate from their meaning. Words have *connotative* meaning in addition to their denotative meaning. He called this the "attitudinal" property of words. Their positive or negative valence is the most general emotive property. Words like *beauty, love, sharing, organic, low-fat, healthy, kind, success*, and so on all have positive emotive valence. One of Staats' earliest experimental studies, conducted with his wife Carolyn (C. Staats & Staats, 1957), demonstrated in a classical conditioning paradigm that through association with positive words, feelings could be transferred to otherwise more neutral words or objects. Conversely, of course, words like *hate, crime, accident, ugly, starving, parasite, cancer, feces*, all have negative feeling connotations. These simple observations have significance for influencing the feelings of others and for allowing inferences by therapists regarding client feelings not directly expressed. They confirm the importance of therapists being good listeners and paying close attention to the implications of the words and metaphors used by clients to describe their feelings and attitudes. When emotive words are used in conjunction with other concepts and ideas, associative learning is one of the principal ways whereby feelings change (Weiss & Evans, 1978).

Feelings Are Codified by Words, But Felt without Them

There are hundreds of word labels for our many possible feelings. We use these words to communicate our feelings to others. Language also allows us to codify the essential conditions for a feeling to be labelled verbally by a client—the concept of a feeling's logic was introduced in Chapter 1. Language also allows us to define more clearly the nature and origin of the feeling. The example of jealousy's logic I learned from a fascinating talk given by philosopher and social psychologist Rom Harré at Binghamton University (SUNY) where he was an occasional adjunct professor. He explained that the feeling of jealousy (hard to describe but you know it when you feel it) requires that two conditions be met. One is that a person has got or has acquired something that you don't have. And two, you feel that you deserve it equally or more. This describes the essential conditions (logic) for the emotion but that doesn't mean that someone must first say these words or even think them to have the feeling. Young children can certainly feel jealous without having the verbally encoded cognitions described by Harré, but the situation which triggers that feeling *will* meet those criteria.

The logic of envy is slightly different from jealousy—naturally as the two words mean different things and label different feelings. Envy is the feeling only that someone has something that you would like but do not have. Sibling rivalry, not uncommon in families, can arise either from jealousy or envy in the context of competition for special parental attention. These combined feelings occur when one child experiences another child in the family receiving some form of preferential treatment—a trigger that requires the perception (and as they grow older, the label) of unfairness, as described in Chapter 4.

Jealousy as a feeling in romantic relationships has a slightly different logic. It arises from one's caring for a love partner and wanting that to be reciprocated exclusively. If this feeling is too strong, it leads to over-sensitivity to, or misinterpretation of, signs that one's partner is attracted to and becoming emotionally involved with others. It is a good example of a feeling whose "arousal" or activation level (strength of the feeling) can vary from a simple momentary twinge, easily ignored or re-assessed, to a major, pervasive, and expanding feeling whose negativity leads to misjudgment of cues and hypersensitivity to others—essentially a mood with negative urgency. It can be more clinically problematic when, as will be encountered later, one feeling evokes another. The jealous feeling can easily become accompanied by anxiety and anger which can lead to various aversive behaviors. If these behaviors—questioning, doubting, being over-controlling—become excessive, the phenomenon has been called morbid jealousy. Early in his development of Rational Emotive Behavior Therapy, Albert Ellis (1957; 1962) became interested in excessive jealousy, which he rightly described as fatal for good love relationships. He attributed morbid jealousy to concurrent emotions, specifically having strong feelings of personal insecurity such that the person can only feel acceptable when exclusively adored by their partner. As he was also focused on one of his major concepts regarding irrational thinking—that one *must* also feel or not feel a certain way—Ellis observed that morbidly jealous people *had* to feel hostility to any potential rival for their partner and would feel that they *must not* feel frustrated (Ellis, 1996). The angry or anxious component of the feeling comes from a further recognition of the threat of loss, or of being judged less desirable than someone else. Various treatment components were suggested by Ellis. Cognitive interventions included reframing (finding the good sides and not only the bad sides of a partner's friendship with others), disputing irrational beliefs especially the absolutes regarding what *has* to be, and cognitive distractions, such as a focus on pleasurable experiences. Ellis's emotive techniques included emotive imagery (to be considered later), role playing (changing sides so the client acts as therapist as well), humor, and above all unconditional acceptance *by the therapist*. It is interesting, as a historical sidenote, that Ellis was advocating acceptance long before it was picked up and became a thing in later therapies. Ellis also wrote about how he would ask clients *how* they changed their feelings, in order to build-in a commitment to focusing on more rational beliefs. Many of these sorts of techniques, he said, needed to be practiced regularly—a precursor to CBT's emphasis on out-of-office practice as homework assignments (Kazantzis et al., 2010).

There is, however, an issue that should be introduced here. Cognitive neuroscientists often talk about emotions requiring a certain type of thinking or reasoning called *counterfactual reasoning* (e.g., Van Hoek et al., 2015). This is the capacity to move from perceiving one's current environment to one that can be imagined. For example, a feeling of regret requires the ability to infer or imagine how an alternative course of action might have turned out differently than the one taken. Feeling someone or something else is to blame for your own negative circumstance and requires a comparison between two plausible event sequences. Disappointment is a feeling sometimes included in the list of emotions requiring counterfactual reasoning, but I have suggested that it merely requires the expectation of something better, which could simply be a conditioned response based on actual past experiences. I have already argued how the feeling of disappointment requires having prior experiences of success (rewards preceding the no reward condition). In Bandura's terms, there also needs to be a feeling of self-efficacy for the task, which if very high will more likely elicit frustrative aggression when a positive rewarding outcome is not obtained. And if you have ever owned a dog, you know they experience disappointment. Take down the leash from a hook in the mudroom and your dog will perk up, prick up its ears, and wag its tail. Hang it back up again and the dog's ears go down, tail wagging stops, and they slouch back onto their dog bed. Perhaps in addition to positive affect, the leash elicits a sensory image of the coming walk with all its smells. I certainly think so, but that is going to be hard to discover objectively. Maybe dogs have counterfactual reasoning.

Resentment is a feeling that has come into prominence at the population level, where the feeling is suggested as an explanation of voter behavior and populist anger against those perceived as privileged, especially in the United States but in many other countries as well. In Belgium, for example, resentment is predominant in people who are middle-aged, support fringe political parties, and report being excluded from the political system and their values and interests are marginalized (Feitosa et al., 2024). The feeling of resentment is defined as one of bitter indignation at having been wronged or treated unfairly. It is a complex feeling as it contains elements of anger, a perception of injustice based on a feeling of being put down or ignored. It is always targeted: you resent someone or some group or something, but the target can be very broad, like someone might resent principles such as affirmative action, inclusion, civil rights, or "East Coast intellectuals." The feeling does not require the cognitive verbalization of such logics and may be verbalized in less precise ways: "I'm just fed up," or "I'm tired of hearing about ... [slavery, trans people]," or revealed indirectly through the use of emotive-laden (negative connotation) words in discourse, ones like "handout," "welfare," "I worked hard," or "immigrant."

Group Feelings Capture Affective Words

At the population and particularly the racial level, feelings of resentment can relate to historic injustices, systemic discrimination, and group competition. We know that structural inequalities in society lead to feelings of uncertainty, isolation, and alienation (Blustein et al., 2025). Racial resentment has been connected causally to the problem of racial animosity. In the United States, sociologists report that while overt hostility to Black people (endemic during the Jim Crow era) has declined, and prejudicial attitudes are less likely to be expressed directly, racial resentment is a major influence on White attitudes. Often feelings of racial resentment interact with false narratives about unfairness. Simmons and Bobo (2019) write: "Racial resentment is informed by non-racial values about individualism and fairness, hostile racial affect, and beliefs about the continued relevance of race in the US and the sources of racial inequality" (p. 325). These authors conducted a detailed study of the Racial Resentment Scale (Kinder & Sanders,

1996), with the qualitative component revealing themes such as: strong antipathy (negative feeling) towards "special favors"; that minorities should try harder; and a perception of fewer opportunities as a result of affirmative action ("I and other family members have been turned down for jobs and education ... employers have told me they were required to fill their next position with someone of color ..."). (These direct quotes from participants are from pages 349–352.)

It is difficult to know how group-level feelings and attitudes impact clinical work. It is certain to do so at least in contexts where there is a struggle to provide appropriate mental health care to minority groups or groups likely to be marginalized and who are not heavily represented by professionals from the same ethnic and cultural background. Canadian scholars such as Tom Strong have made important contributions to this topic (e.g., Sametband et al., 2024). The challenge is comparable to recognizing feelings of shame that are expressed differently in different cultures, but which can represent a background state of affect that is highly relevant to working with individuals and families given psychiatric diagnoses. In some cultures, feelings of shame contribute to people being unwilling to seek help from a mental health specialist or service.

Verbal encoding of feelings into commonly used words and phrases means that we have the possibility of changing a feeling in someone, not by dismissing it, but by suggesting another way of enciphering it—changing the logic. Societies often express remorse, sometimes formally by apology for wrongdoing, and when people identify closely with the group (nation or culture), individuals may share these feelings. When they do not, they typically have strategies for dismissing past injustices as not relevant to them now, or focusing on mitigating circumstances, such as colonial take-overs benefitting indigenous societies in the long run (de Groot et al., 2021). Personal feelings of remorse for a harmful action are related to but slightly different from a feeling of regret. Remorse, having the connotation of self-reproach, should motivate clients to seek ways of correcting the harm they have done to others. Since that could be seen as therapeutically beneficial, shifting a person's feeling statement from regret to remorse could facilitate remedial actions the person might take to make amends.

Another example of more carefully encoding a feeling can be found in the feeling of nostalgia. The valence of this feeling is slightly ambiguous, another problem with the valence dimension. Is it a positive or a negative feeling? When people feel it, are they saddened, perhaps by the absence of past pleasure? Or can the feeling be positive through one's recall of past pleasures? If the feeling is shared with those who were participants in the original pleasure, it is plainly one of the feelings that van Kleef and Côté (2022) call "affiliation emotions," since they are self-focused but can involve others in recollections of joint positive experiences. Can a therapeutic focus on these past experiences be encouraged as a counteracting influence on feeling lonely or isolated in the present? I think it can. Most cultures have mythical nirvanas which provide a counteracting (see Chapter 7) feeling to sadness, loneliness, and grief. In New Zealand, for example, there was a period in recent history in which most families, even those with limited means, were able to own a second holiday home (called a bach or a crib). Usually very modest, the bach experience was seen as a time of family togetherness, swimming and relaxing, playing board games when the weather was bad. Recalling these halcyon days is commonly adopted by older New Zealand adults as a nostalgic way of recapturing carefree feelings.

If a feeling label has negative denotation similar to other words but a connotation at a different level of emotive intensity, and these levels can be hierarchically arranged, it might create opportunities to dial back the feeling. Let me explain. Where there are different emotion words with very similar meanings, they differ mostly in terms of the intensity of the feeling rather than the precise logic conditions for the feeling. We could, for example, think of gradations of intensity in feeling angry: annoyed, irritated, angered, furious, enraged. Assuming this is the approximate sequence of intensity for people who are prone to anger, it might be helpful to enquire into exactly what irritates or annoys them the least, rather than the most. The aim is to help them realize that an angry outburst, difficult to control, could be forestalled at an earlier stage of just being annoyed. Through insight into what precisely it is that annoys them, they might be able to find ways of removing, reducing, or reinterpreting these conditions. Once serious anger is aroused, rational cognitive thinking or problem solving is much harder to do, so it is much more difficult to analyze the precise conditions that evoked the feelings and thus avoid them in future.

Feelings in Social Contexts

There have been certain interesting new advances in theories of development of children's ability to understand feelings. Using the example provided by Doan et al. (2025), imagine telling a child the following story: "Sally is hungry today. She saw Anne's cookie and stole it. Sally took a big bite," and then asking: "How does Sally feel?" There are a variety of possible answers, and they all depend on the child's cognitive appraisal of others' goals, desires, beliefs, etc. Remember how often I have said that the logic of a feeling (the conditions that determine it) may or may not be understood by others or by the person themselves. I've already pointed out that the logic for the feeling of jealousy includes the person feeling they deserved what they envied in others. But one can feel jealous without forming that cognition. When logic appraisals are made, however, they determine the appreciation of what is possible. Doan et al. (2025) called these "third-person appraisals." If the child answering our question about Sally's feelings knows that cookies taste good and also what "hungry" feels like, they might answer that Sally feels happy. If they appraise that by stealing another child's cookie Sally might get punished, they might answer that Sally feels worried. If they appraise that Sally might know it is morally wrong to steal a cookie, they might answer Sally feels guilty. And finally, if they appraise that Sally's behavior is inconsistent with her own standards, they might answer that she feels ashamed.

As a child's appraisal competencies develop over time, so the sophistication of their answer to the question will develop. As an adult psychotherapist, you would have instantly been able to judge that Sally might feel ashamed. But as we don't know what Sally did actually feel, we also need to recognize that any of the four feelings are possible, as is the possibility that Sally feels all four of them at the same time. If a client describes their own behavior and you ask them how they feel about it, their answer might not be what you expect, but whatever it is, it reveals the client's self-appraisal. If that is inconsistent with your own expectations, you might want to pursue it. When ACT therapists ask a client about their values, it offers more information than just their behavioral goals—it provides insight into why they feel a certain way about an experience or their own behavior: happy or ashamed, or something in-between (worried and guilty). Doan et al. (2025) gave a list of possible appraisal dimensions, which I can summarize as: intrinsic (un)pleasantness; goals and desires; expectancies (novelty, beliefs); agency (responsibility and intentionality); degree of control; morality; social norms; fairness; and consistency with self-image (pp. 133–134).

Precise Definitions

It is important to stress again that a client might not actually be able to articulate the words that define what I have claimed are the necessary conditions of the feeling, especially if the emotive reaction is too generalized. For instance, a client might feel jealousy but expresses it by anger towards their partner. Or they attempt to manage the fear of loss by checking on the partner's behavior or generally objecting to their activities in a controlling manner. As some therapists have noted, if jealousy is fueled by intense need to feel loved, then the emotive cognition is: "I have to be uniquely special to you." If the jealousy is tied to worry about being made a fool of, then the cognition is more like: "I'm afraid of feeling humiliated." (There was a 1957 pop song by the Everly Brothers that had the lines "*I die each time I hear this sound: 'Here he comes, that's Cathy's clown' ...*").

In interpersonal relationships, there is also a strong connection between metaphors we use, words for the feeling, and relevant facial expressions. If the feeling is scorn, it means sneering, looking down your nose at something, and metaphorically looking down on people, including lovers, friends, and family. You look down on people because you feel intrinsically loftier. You feel superior—better than others, higher in ranking. It is a personality trait that influences many attitudes. Measures of this feeling can be quite amusing: subjects are asked to rate themselves on various positive attributes as to how much they have of it compared to the average person. Metaphorically, if you look up to a teacher or older relative, it is because you admire them and feel lower than they are, and casting your eyes upward is a facial expression of adoration, as you will see from any great masterpiece painting of admirers looking at Jesus.

Expressed Emotion

The year I started as a doctoral student at the Maudsley Hospital, Institute of Psychiatry, George Brown, a social psychologist in the Institute's social psychiatry research center, and Michael Rutter (later to become the leading child psychiatrist of his generation) published a fascinating paper (Brown & Rutter, 1966). They reported on interviews with the families of patients in psychiatric treatment, and noted that these family members (spouses, parents, adult children) expressed a variety of feelings towards their ill family members. Sometimes these were strong statements of criticism; sometimes they were subtle comments in which the true feeling had to be inferred from cues such a facial expression and tone of voice. Usually, these were families of patients who had been discharged from hospital care and were now living at home with members of their family. What was especially interesting was those negative feelings, which they called *expressed emotion*, related closely to the likelihood of the patient relapsing—reappearance of symptoms or having to return to hospital.

Since then, there has been a substantial amount of research both on how to define and measure expressed emotion and on why it may have the influence it seems to have. A standard interview protocol was developed and detailed scoring criteria specified, and a training protocol developed in order to obtain reliability in scoring the phenomenon (Leff & Vaughn, 1985). The interview asks a series of questions about the patient, how their difficulties developed, what interactions with them were like, and how everyone in the family was getting along. There is no point asking direct questions about how they feel—social desirability factors are too likely to distort their answers. We now know that family members' feelings cluster into three major groups: critical (e.g., "He just sits around all day and won't help"); hostile, judged from the tone of the comments, which includes rejection (e.g., "She can be annoying. I think she might be happier if they found another placement for her"); and emotional over-involvement, such as exaggerated feelings of concern, or the interviewee getting emotional during the interview (e.g., "I worry about him all the time"). Emotional over-involvement is more often seen in parents than spouses. The extent of these expressed emotions can be scored, and it is criticism that is the most prominent indicator of future relapse.

Jill Hooley, a British psychologist now on the faculty at Harvard University, has been the major force in programmatic research on the phenomenon of expressed emotion. She and others have demonstrated the negative influence of expressed emotion on a wide range of psychological disorders, beyond the original observation with respect to schizophrenia (Hooley, 2007). She has written that "although it [expressed emotion] is measured in an individual, it is thought to reflect disturbances in the organization, emotional climate, and transactional patterns of the entire family system" (p. 331). As such, you can see that this brings the phenomenon into the same realm as so many other causal influences of feelings within social relationships on the well-being of vulnerable people. Rejection and criticism are closely related within emotional climate—it is all connected to the feeling of not being acceptable to others you are close to or depend upon. That is an existential threat. It should be remembered that criticism can be perceived, independent of objective reality, and some people will be more sensitive to it. Given the importance of this feature of family and other social relationships, practitioners who are interested in assessing or measuring family environments have shorter alternatives than the original interview, which requires training. These have been reviewed by Hooley and Parker (2006).

Dominance and Appeasement Emotions

The feeling of disdain has a special role in social interactions. The facial expression is one corner of the mouth raised, without sign of anger or smile, and verbal statements that sound smug and disapproving. The definition of the word usually includes closely related feelings like scorn, feeling removed from, and facial expressions like sneering and rolling the eyes. Together, these represent a certain kind of dislike, which may not be that strong as there are other conflicting reasons for liking someone. Disdain allows one to be dismissive, separating the person expressing it from what is going on around them. Teenagers often show disdain because they don't want to be seen as too young (to participate in childish games) or too old (not to be old-fashioned, or boring). When in couples therapy, facial expressions of disdain like rolling of the eyes, vocalizations we call scoffing, changing gaze to another person like the therapist are partially reflexive and partially designed to communicate. The client's attempt is to bring them into a sort of collusion with the therapist, the implicit message is: "Look what I have to up with! Don't you agree that that is ridiculous? Wouldn't anyone scorn this kind of response from my partner?" Therapists need to keep alert for such expressions of feelings that suggest you are on one side or another. As a male, I typically got "the look" from husbands which seemed to me to be saying: "Look here, Ian, you're also a guy. I'm sure you know what I'm talking about. Isn't this just typical of women?" I imagine that female therapists receive somewhat similar messaging from female clients.

A slightly different, stronger form of disdain is contempt—a primary emotion in most theories (Chapter 1). Contempt for someone who is not personally connected to you requires a cognition (logic) of: "I am better than you and that you are lesser than me." As an attitude to a whole group of people, it does not need a specific trigger, although the most common eliciting feature is someone engaging in behavior that you consider morally wrong. It typically involves a degree of power over the other person and so it seems likely that by feeling contempt for someone more influential or important than you are, you can internally adjust the power balance. Feeling contempt for someone more powerful allows a person to reduce any doubts about their own status. (There will be more to say regarding its significance when we consider John Gottman's work on marital relationships in the next chapter.)

Cultural pressures provide a powerful source of control of feelings. Boys are often expected not to show weakness by crying when hurt or having a sad experience. "Crybaby" is a derogatory label. Some cultures value "the stiff upper lip," meaning not only should you not cry tears, but you should also not reveal the trembling of the upper lip, which Darwin pointed out is what often accompanies sadness and is a precursor to tears.

While crying can elicit derogatory comments, the tears themselves are a potent trigger of feelings for sadness and empathy. Tears often end conflict because the tearful person is showing a level of upset that may make the antagonist decide that the conflict has gone too far. Crying is a psychophysiological reaction that is difficult to control voluntarily, since tears can indicate remorse, mirth, empathy, pain, grief, joy, relief, love, and sympathy. And doubtless other contexts as well, including simply hearing a story, seeing a movie or a play. The tears themselves are more visible indicators of the feeling, and generally, we as observers feel especially upset by someone else's tears, especially children's. Therapists must deal constructively with clients' tears and their apologies for them, as well as their own. Tears can also be viewed as manipulative. There is a common sign in English street markets: "Cry baby, cry; make mummy buy." Think about the difference between a client crying and sobbing. I would suggest that when a client sobs in front of you, their feelings are not just of sadness but contain elements of self-pity and possibly despair. How might such a judgment influence your decisions as to how or whether to comfort them at that moment?

Collective Feelings

Consider shame as a word used in various contexts. We might say of something that shouldn't have happened or didn't happen when it should have: "It's a shame the picnic was ruined by the rain" or "What a shame that I spoiled the soufflе by opening the oven door." It means regrettable; it's a pity; it's unfortunate. We're not actually feeling much regret or pity, but there's a tinge of it, and more importantly no one is to blame—it's just life.

Actual shame—being ashamed—is a very different sort of feeling as discussed in Chapter 1. Its valence is negative, and it is often unrecognized by the person experiencing it. It can form a chronic background, mood-like essence. It is not the same as guilt, but it is close to embarrassment in which as a feeling it further induces a wish to disappear, to hide away, to not show your face: "I wanted the earth to swallow me up" people feeling shame say. As a feeling with strong clinical relevance, it has garnered much scholarly and scientific interest in recent years.

Normally, you are ashamed *of* something (that you have done or said). But shame can also be a mood state, perhaps originating from failing to achieve the high expectations that parents had of you. If what you do is never good enough for a parent to feel proud and to congratulate about, then you feel a failure. This creates an overlap with depression, but it is clearly not the same phenomenon. This makes it difficult to identify through self-report. Shame questionnaires, for example, ask things like "Do you feel worthless?" but those feelings are really from depression. Free floating (mood) shame comes from being criticized no matter what you do, akin to being criticized for who or what you are. This is what happens to members of disadvantaged or colonially dominated peoples—are you really worthwhile? Making people feel ashamed of who they are is the direct cause of the group feelings of cultural shame as reportedly experienced by some colonized peoples in the absence of any immediate wrongdoing. Cultural shame is a term for incipient feelings of awkwardness, low self-worth, or inadequacy experienced by an individual when their culture or cultural identity is devalued.

Anger can also be a group or collective feeling. Obviously one event can anger all members of a large group of people. But groups can also be in an angry mood when they share a series of influential events and physical conditions, like hot weather, or water shortages. It is often very obvious when a whole group is "spoiling for a fight."

Feelings Are Expressed in Images

Most of the discussion has been about feelings construed (the logics) and explained in words, as well as emotion expression through facial and bodily changes and overt behaviors beyond language. A neglected form of expression thus far is non-verbal—it is in visual images from simple drawings to elaborate works of art. Such images are a double-edged sword, since, following from the discussion of cultural shame, negative and stereotyped images of different cultures can elicit strong negative, hurtful feelings in those thus depicted. The other edge of the sword is that, just like a person's facial and verbal expressions of feeling are stimuli eliciting feelings in the observer, so a visual or musical artist's emotive creation will, as it is usually designed to do, elicit strong acceptable feelings in the audience. Picasso's feelings about the horrors of war, oppression, and the suffering of its victims expressed in his 1937 painting *Guernica* are instantly recognized. And it will elicit similar feelings in an observer. Thirdly, the sharp point of the sword comes from the way images can be more evocative than words and are especially useful when a person has limited language ability—such as child clients. Asking children to draw something to *show* their feelings is hardly a popular technique in the CBT assortment of assessment methods and therapies. The problems of over-interpreting are considerable—a child's drawing can be as ambiguous. Nevertheless, there have been many incidents in recent years in the USA in which children have drawn dark images of death and destruction which were not taken as sufficiently important warning signs of later violent behavior. If used cautiously, asking a young client to share their feelings about affectively important topics through art is a possible source of helpful information.

When a client is asked to recall a memory of a negative event that generated an unpleasant feeling, what happens? Is the memory in the form of images including words spoken at the time? Because we ask for a verbal description of the memory, we understand the incident by means of those words, but that does not mean that the memory was encoded in the same words, or even words at all, and there are individual differences in vividness of imagery in autobiographical memory (Yeung et al., 2025). Initially, a client might be unwilling to describe a negative event—they sometimes say "Don't ask me to think about. It was horrible. I'm trying to forget it, I get sad when I think about it, and I get furious. That's all I want to say." These words came from a client who was a nursing student who had been attacked by a patient on the ward during a night shift. She was self-referred to the counseling center because she was thinking of leaving her training program as she was now, in her words, "paranoid" and treating all her patients with suspicion and being anxious about provoking them. Therapist: "Did it make you sad and furious at the time?" Client: "No, of course not. I was terrified. It scared the shit out of me. I've never seen someone so out of control. I thought he was going to kill me." Therapist: "What is it about recalling the details that feels so bad? You're safe here, nothing can happen to you, it's just thinking about it." Client: "It's not the thought. It's like Pavlov's drooling dogs. I picture it, describe it, and the emotion comes flooding back. It's nothing to do with the thought." Therapist: "The feeling is fear?" Client: "Not exactly. It used to be. The same feeling I had at the time. But I hate thinking about it mostly because I get sad and mad." Therapist: "About what?" Client: "Sad because I've lost something. I guess you'd say I've lost my nerve; all patients seem potentially dangerous now, especially when I have to do something that hurts them. And mad because I think my supervisor should have warned me about this patient. Apparently, it's in his record that he has a violent temper. It's silly, I know." Therapist: "OK, that's very helpful. Three important feelings that we need to address. And it's not silly; it's all totally understandable. If you were a little girl and you fell off your bike and I were your father, what would I tell you to do?" Client: "Tell me to get back on it immediately? Extinction! I know what you're trying to say!"

Therapist: "That's the problem of letting nursing students take Psychology 101! But you're not quite right. First, I'd check to see what's hurting, and if you need first aid. Then I'd check the bike to make sure it was safe to ride. Then I'd apologize for not warning you about the curve that was coming. Then I'd tell you that your helmet saved you from getting a bump on the head, but you still have to be careful, and finally I'd ask you to tell me about all the good fun we could have riding again tomorrow. Let's see if we can generalize *those* principles to your serious issue at hand."

Hiding Feelings

Thus far, the discussion of feelings has focused on the *display* of feelings by words or actions or images. Despite the strong emphasis that feelings are subjective experiences, and thus belong uniquely to the feeling individual, the reality is that our feelings are typically enacted in social contexts and typically easily recognized by others. Even though I have identified a certain category of feelings that are best thought of as self-conscious feelings, they are less about the self and more about interactional feelings related to being in the presence of others. Part of the complication of these self-conscious feelings is that people may struggle not to reveal them, which then makes responses like crying or blushing in public yet more aversive—to be discussed further in Chapter 7. Avoidance behavior is also a tell-tale sign. I've had guests praise my cooking, but push the food around on their plate with very little gusto.

So, while I have implied that expressing feelings and recognizing their expression in others are good things, when it comes to social communication and feeling language, there can be major pressure sometimes on keeping feelings private. Deliberately not revealing feelings is something we may want to do. Our efforts may meet with only partial success because how we behave in social contexts is very often strongly influenced by how we are feeling in these contexts.

The topic of our ability to hide feelings links a number of important themes: development of feelings in children, social motivation to mask our feelings (both sensitivity to others and deception for personal gain), and our general ability to exert self-control and control any feeling experience, far less its expression. It is also a lesson in creative research strategies revealing truths about the real world. The story of the relevant studies is this. Imagine you are a child, and your grandparents have just given you a present, beautifully wrapped up for your birthday. You are very excited, and you rip open the paper and find that the gift is just a box of boring old pencils. You have been taught to show appreciation for a gift, but you are very disappointed. Can you hide that disappointment so as not to hurt the feelings of your grandparents? This is the basic procedure that Carolyn Saarni (1984) used in her pioneering studies of children's attempts to hide their expression of feelings. Depending on their age, some children were able to fake their appreciation and say thank you for the gift, with a rather thin smile. Or at least they tried. I know some very polite people who are always gracious regarding a gift, but for whom you can tell instantly don't really like it. Some of the children, however, made no effort to disguise their dislike at getting a few pencils in a tin. These, as you might have guessed, were usually boys. Girls are more likely to be socialized early on to be affiliative and not hurt other people's feelings.

By the time children are six years old, they can understand that someone is covering up their true feelings as well as being able to give reasons why someone might do so, such as not wanting other children to laugh at them. It is possible that this ability comes from being better at reading a variety of facial and bodily cues and detecting when they don't match a given likely feeling context. We often try to smile when in pain, but other actions will reveal our true discomfort. Children also probably realize their own facial expressions and statements of feeling don't always match exactly how they feel—even very young children are known to cry after a minor injury when there is an audience, although they may not be conscious of deliberate deception to elicit sympathy. Harris and Tang (2018) who summarized some of the possibilities also suugested that when parents label children's feelings they may do so inaccurately. If you say to a child "You must be feeling scared" as a part of emotion coaching, but they are not, this further helps to separate the reality of emotions felt from their expression by words or physical appearance. This also raises interesting issues regarding cultural differences. Some cultures avoid open discussion of both mental states and feelings.

Thus, when it comes to masking feelings, there are substantial cultural differences. One interesting example comes from children's expression and regulation of disappointment. Ip and colleagues (2021) compared Chinese, Japanese, and American preschoolers' reactions with the "disappointing gift" paradigm just described. Remember that a complication is the extent to which not offending the gift-giver is considered important by the recipient. When it is, children can give a fake smile (positive expression), as opposed to showing displeasure (negative expression). Children can also express verbal disappointment to a third party. In the study, Chinese and Japanese preschoolers verbally reported more negative feelings than American preschoolers but showed more neutral expressions. Regardless of elements of the task, the Chinese children showed the most neutral expressions (e.g., "poker face"). Culture shapes the expression of feelings but not the nature of the feeling—at least with respect to disappointment.

Enacting Feelings without Them: Caring, For Example

Some actions that we take, often those of social decorum, are habits that may have little affective weight behind them (low affect activation). We do things to make it look like we have a certain feeling, but the level of that feeling is minimal.

In the US, it has become habitual in public discourse to wish someone or some group facing loss and other tragedies our "thoughts and prayers," The now common social expression of concern "You have my thoughts and prayers" which doesn't mention a feeling at all. This comment is trotted out so routinely and unconvincingly that it has become very close to sarcasm. We need to judge a person's level of concern by what they are willing to do in terms of support or assistance. This is not a reflection on anyone's lack of feeling—there are many tragedies and much suffering which is sufficiently remote that we may be troubled by it, but one cannot be anguished about every horror story of human suffering one hears about on the news. What I am suggesting is that both therapists and clients need to be able to distinguish between genuine feelings, lack of feelings, and false expressions of feelings.

In therapy, authenticity of feelings is a complex matter. This is where hiding your feelings and exhibiting false feelings come into play as an issue and a problem. Effective therapists are warm and positive and presumably they are judged by their clients as authentic. But many times, we are not; we are putting on an act in the name of therapeutic influence over the client. We show interest in the ordinary everyday happening of their lives, praise them enthusiastically for minor accomplishments, and, especially in Dialectical Behavior Therapy (DBT) and ACT, communicate high levels of acceptance in order never to hint at rejection, which clients that attract such intervention strategies tend to notice (are vigilant for such signs) and are readily upset when they sense it.

An example of one common feeling can illustrate these arguments further. Caring for or about something is a major feeling. Not caring is judged by others as negative. Children say "I don't care" when the exact opposite is true. There is a Scottish children's rhyme I remember as a child:

Piggy on the railway, picking up stones
Along came an engine and broke piggy's bones
Oh, said Piggy, that's not fair
Oh, said the engine driver, I don't care

Quite apart from the fact that popular children's nursery rhymes are all incredibly dark, the idea that someone doesn't care seems closely related to lack of empathy. When we do care about something, it means we like it in a supportive kind of way: "Take care of the dog, Johnny, he needs a walk," "The house is a mess, and visitors are coming. Don't worry, I'll take care of it." And of course, we have caregivers and care homes, and these are not specifically places of love, but there is acceptance and a sense of responsibility. We should care about the poor and the hungry. So, it is a feeling of responsibility but not necessarily affection, although it can be used that way. And it seems important for people to have things that they care about, as this motivates positive behavior for others, which might be done out of a sense of duty. Your duty is what you should do to justify your existence, it is a type of behavior benefiting a larger group than yourself: your country, your parents, your religion, you have a responsibility in return for something like the care you have received. Do we ever tell clients to do their duty? Probably the exact opposite!

This brings us to a place not often considered in behavioral psychotherapy but very much in the forefront of humanistic schools of thought—the topic of authenticity in both clients and therapists. It is a central topic in existential and Gestalt schools of therapy; it gets short shrift in CBT. It is not even easy to define, unless you are very familiar with Heidegger's work—he argued how much easier it is to conform to the public's societal values than to forge our own trails through life and live according to our own principles and values. Kernis and Goldman (2006) said authenticity is "the unobstructed operation of one's true- or core-self in one's daily enterprise" (p. 294). Burks and Robbins (2012) asked a diverse group of practicing psychotherapists what it meant. One common theme of relevance to this chapter was: *"A matching of one's inner thoughts, beliefs, and feelings with outer presentation and behaviors. In so many words, the participants associated authenticity with honesty, truth, genuineness, realness, and openness"* (p. 85). They then add: *"Contradicting common assumptions, this study's participants believed that authenticity is not necessarily characterized by total openness; instead, it can be opaque or hidden from others. Furthermore, in counseling situations, the overt expression of feelings, thoughts, and honest challenges, which some might think is characteristic of authentic therapy, may not be appropriate with some clients"* (p 101). I have been implicitly agreeing with that latter statement and including parents, teachers, and romantic partners in the general mix.

Shared Emotion

Anyone who has sat face to face with a client and listened to their story will be aware that your own feelings come and go with the client's expressed emotion in the session. You feel for them and their experiences; share in their laughter, commiserate with their losses, feel compassion for their difficulties. At the same time, and in parallel, you have feelings of doubt about the session itself and how you are conducting it. The cognitive expression of such doubts might be self-questioning such as "is it going well; was my last comment necessary; am I losing control of the session by letting him talk so much?" I think it is most likely that you won't actually be saying these phrases to yourself but will be implicitly monitoring your behavior. That self-monitoring can become more self-critical if you are being observed through a one-way mirror by a supervisor or a group of trainees; you may become more aware of your own anxiety or find yourself feeling rushed as you try to get through the treatment plan designed for that session.

If you are a supervisor watching an intern flounder with a difficult client, you share your trainee's discomfort, their anxiety, and their frustration.

Shared emotion as a construct has recently become a thing in psychology, somewhat to the surprise of those of us who still remember the long-standing principles of imitational learning (modeling) and Albert Bandura's (1969; 1971) social learning theory contribution to clinical treatment. Perhaps the discovery of "mirror neurons" has contributed to the general interest. Mirror neurons are those that fire equally when performing an action or watching someone else perform it. There's something similar with affect—it's hard not to smile when someone else does even if you didn't understand the joke. In fact, this is part of what makes shared emotions interesting. In social contexts, you smile when others do, laugh when the crowd is laughing, look sympathetic when someone expresses feelings of pain. These are called reciprocal emotional reactions. This means that often it is other people's feelings that you mirror (share) rather than feeling *about* the thing they have feelings about.

There is also a different situation in which a group of people share emotion (have the same emotional response) to an event because everyone is equally responsive to a common experience—when their favorite team scores a touchdown (a goal, or a try, or a basket), and everyone expresses feelings of delight. This in turn creates a feeling of camaraderie or togetherness as they become aware that they have a common feeling. Salmela and Nagatsu (2017) argue that those types of feeling of shared emotion support individuals' motivation to pursue common actions, to work together in coordination. Michael (2016) proposes a slightly different idea. Observing another's emotional expression (or hearing a verbal report of a feeling) allows the observer to gain information about the other person's feelings and thus how they are evaluating a situation. This improves their common ability to coordinate actions and to cooperate. It is worth reflecting on this when encouraging clients with depression to be more active and to engage in social activities they have been avoiding. The implication is that they should choose activities in which others are likely to display positive feelings. Sporting events are a notable example, because even if your group's team loses, sharing dismay and disappointment with everyone indicates participation and belonging. But other simple situations can have the same function—when watching a comedy show on TV with the whole family, it becomes easier to laugh when everyone else is laughing.

Shared emotions can now be seen as the missing affective link to explain various facets of the therapeutic relationship. Consider motivational interviewing. This was originally described by Bill Miller in 1983 as an extremely valuable tactic to overcome clients' resistance to change or their unwillingness to accept the need to make significant changes in their behavior (Miller & Rollnick, 1991). Expecting someone to change creates a context of feeling criticized which we know encourages resistance. Understanding the client's feelings in an empathic way, and at the same time expressing your confidence in their ability to change, creates the motivational balance that is the essence of motivational interviewing. The dynamics of motivational interviewing have some similarity with the dialectic of the therapeutic relationship in DBT (Linehan, 1993). When working with clients who are hypersensitive to signs of rejection (notably those clients diagnosed with Borderline Personality Disorder), the challenge is to convey unconditional feelings of acceptance at the same time requiring a client to be different—to change and to have different feelings.

In order to navigate our own personal social relationships, it is important to know how other people are feeling. When expressing our own feelings to others, the result will depend on various factors. If we express anger (a dominance feeling), it can motivate cooperation and improved performance if the anger seems appropriate, and we share goals. If our expression of anger is perceived as unwarranted, manipulative, or the desired improved behavior is beyond the observer's ability, it will have the opposite effect. Students have often asked me if it is ever appropriate to express one's inevitable feelings of anger with an uncooperative client. The answer is in the two previous sentences: it depends. Similarly with the expression of positive feelings towards clients and their therapeutic gains. Affiliative feelings of happiness and especially feelings of affection can be misleading. There could be shared emotions, which is not always what you want, particularly if the client interprets their efforts in therapy as trying to please you rather than help themselves. Think about the dangers of children's happiness being a function of pleasing a demanding parent—there is a common source of anxiety, perfectionism, and other issues of over-eagerness to please.

How do children with autism manage to share feelings? It is often reported that they have poor emotion recognition. But the studies of this usually rely on facial recognition (Rump et al., 2009). But recognition from photos has many problems. And in any case, in most social interactions, it is the recognition of feelings that will be more important than recognition of primary emotions. The well-known model of autistic deficits being their lacking a "theory of mind" (Frith & Frith, 2025) (they don't know what others know or are thinking) might benefit from an analysis of people with autism not knowing what others are feeling (Kuusikko et al., 2009). It's difficult to share a feeling if you don't know what it is; something we psychotherapists know only too well.

Implications

The language of feelings is rich in metaphor and sensory symbolism. When someone is being sugary and especially kind and affectionate, we call them sweet, and we give them pet names like "sweetheart," "sugar," and "honeybun." When we say a kind person has "a heart of gold," we are linking two important feeling images—that the heart is the organ of positive feelings like love and that gold is universally valued on account of its sensory properties, its shine, its softness, its weight, its untarnishable permanence. Indeed, gold has been universally valued through the centuries; even in modern science, a "gold standard" anything is one you can trust. An important principle in this chapter, however, is to recognize that while we can describe our feelings in words and also that words define the conditions for a feeling, feelings are not cognitive. They are felt in the absence of any cognitive verbal process like self-talk or self-description. We use words to communicate with others, and we might use the words to explain the feeling to ourselves, but the feeling is raw experience. As such, it may be felt in different ways by different people, which is something we will never know.

The feeling of security is one we considered in the previous chapter as rather important in child development and indeed in later life. But the infant or even the toddler doesn't say to itself "I feel secure"—they reveal it by a calm demeanor, pleasure in contact with a nurturing figure, willingness to take a small risk, and approach an unknown object or person. Thus, the feeling of security might be quite like the feeling of no anxiety or the feeling of satisfaction of hunger while nursing (a feeling that can quickly change when the milk dries up or the baby needs to be burped). The best we can do to understand the child is to focus our attention on what we feel when we say we feel safe or secure—undoubtedly a pleasant feeling, hard to define but one that contributes to relaxation, willingness to say what you think (secure that you won't be rejected by doing or saying something controversial), and showing no need to be over vigilant when outside or overly conscious of possible dangers. When thinking of human evolution before farming even before controlling fire, hunger, and thirst and warmth were constant needs, darkness was always dangerous, and the causes of illness and sudden death were unfathomably scary.

Since feeling secure when very young has such wide implications, we might benefit from practicing trying to notice or produce the same feeling as an adult. You can ask your client "When do you feel secure?" When answered you could suggest "Next time you are in a secure situation try focusing on the feeling. Are you relaxed, feeling safe from harm, able to find enjoyment in simple pleasures?" If the answer is "I never feel secure!" you need to explore what changes need to be made in their day-to-day life strategies that would allow secure feelings to occur. When clients are in objective danger (threatened by a former partner, hold a job that might be eliminated, live in a dangerous neighborhood), it is sometimes possible to help a client work out simple precautions that can be made to increase certainty in their lives and decrease the objective risks of harm, even if you personally would not see the same things as terribly threatening.

Feelings are also expressed in images, such as drawings, something very useful for communicating with younger children and less verbal clients. The importance of this we saw in Chapter 4: when children are able to imagine real things and ones that can exist only in fantasy, they can experience good feelings and regulate the bad. And words, as Staats (1996) described so well, have image properties—their connotative meaning can be in the form of a mental image, which gives poetry and stories their powerful affective properties. Staats also pointed out, long ago, that an object can be identified by the word for it or by a mental image of it, so words and images will have the same function. Mental imagery, being able to imagine something with varying degrees of vividness in the "mind's eye," provides a major source of stimuli for feelings, which we shall encounter in the next chapter. And since some people can recreate reality so well by mental image, the ability to do so provides a major avenue for influencing feelings—changing them in the present time, changing their valence for the future, and putting together new and complex images for novel feelings.

6

Stimuli as Triggers

Automatic and Conditioned

Terminology

What we now call a "Proustian moment" comes from an experience Marcel Proust described in his novel *Remembrance of Things Past*, when the protagonist's dipping a small sponge cake into lime flower tea transported him back to feelings from his past: *"I carried to my lips a spoonful of the tea in which I had let soften a bit of madeleine. But at the very instant when the mouthful of tea mixed with cake crumbs touched my palate, I quivered, attentive to the extraordinary thing that was happening inside me."*

This chapter focuses more closely on the most common events and experiences that reliably produce a strong feeling in people. As this book is about how and why feelings change, we need to better understand triggers (what elicits a feeling or emotion) and where they come from, duration (what causes feelings to persist long after original eliciting event), and susceptibility to unwanted feelings (what individual personality characteristics make one person more likely to react negatively to a situation than another). After all, feelings are not something you plan, as in voluntary activities. They just happen. But they happen for a reason and that reason is almost always a stimulus, whether a thought, or an event, a remark, crumbs in lime flower tea, whatever. And if you don't know why you are feeling a certain way, a little reflection and a dab of feeling intelligence will usually inform you. "Free-floating" anxiety or guilt is certainly a thing that people report, but not because there was no stimulus, only that they couldn't identify one. While it is true that gut and brain inter-communicate neuronally, and the enteric nervous system is a source of many feeling sensations, it is doubtful that this fact supports the popular notion that "having a gut feeling" is somehow informative or valid in decision making (Holzer, 2022). In the previous chapter, the questions were about how feelings are encoded, shared, with or without words, and serve a social function. Now the question is what the feeling is about—of what is it a feeling?

How and Why Feelings Change. Ian M. Evans, Oxford University Press. © Ian M. Evans (2026).
DOI: 10.1093/9780197825808.003.0007

A major consideration before we even start is that feelings themselves can be triggers, so there is great potential for "chain reactions" of feelings causing emotional volatility. CBT treatments for syndromes characterized by emotional instability and inconsistent, ungrounded feelings (such as Borderline Personality Disorder) have opened up new awareness of mixed and confused feelings in clients.

The fact that our feelings are always elicited by stimuli is worth remembering as a foundational concept. The word *elicited* is a semi-technical word in psychology; people don't ordinarily talk that way. You are more likely to say, "You made me angry" than "You elicited my anger." But "made" implies that the other person is the cause of your anger, which is probably not entirely true. "Elicited" (along with psychology-talk synonyms like "evoked," or "precipitated") is preferred because it is not a causal statement or an explanation of why the person feels the way they do.

We are constantly bombarded by external stimuli. From birth, as William James declared, "The baby, assailed by eyes, ears, nose, skin, and entrails at once, feels it all as one great blooming, buzzing confusion." True, but now recognized as superficial. Babies direct their gaze, stare, recognize faces, and discover their toes. Two-month-old infants gaze at people differently than they do at objects and their posture is more relaxed; if a mother is asked to act in an unresponsive manner, three-month-old infants use facial expressions, vocalizations, and body movements to get them to resume their typical responses (Tronick, 1989). It is our adult environments that are particularly rich in visual and auditory stimulation. Loud noises and repetitive softer ones are aversive and increase feelings of tension. Visual arrays from phones and televisions are continuous and enormously varied. People happily walk around in public with earphones or earbuds enabling them to listen to a vast variety of music, podcasts, or telephone conversations. Too much intense stimulation is highly aversive, and people often try to reduce stress by selecting calmer quieter environments like a walk in a forest, sitting in a hot tub, chatting to a friend on a park bench. Monotonous and repetitive stimuli and stimulus arrays can also be aversive, however. Primates, as you might expect, but even lab rats, will work for the reward of just a change in the environment—varying stimuli are reinforcing. As we put together stimuli into perceptions and gestalts, we learn to separate signal from noise, meaning from commotion. We must restrict our attention to some stimuli, otherwise we would simply be overwhelmed. Selective attention and the essential control mechanism of habituation are crucial, but focused attention on things positive sustains positive affect.

To a new discrete stimulus, we will orient reflexively, and our autonomic nervous system reacts. If the stimulus is safe or unworthy of further attention, we will habituate an essential mechanism for functioning. Hang a mobile with specific colors or patterns above a baby's crib. It will elicit a variety of responses indicating feelings of pleasure (increase movement, reaching for the mobile, cooing, smiling). If the increase in activity is detected by a sensor in the crib, and that results in the mobile spinning around a few times, the baby will learn to activate that stimulus change by their movements. But after a while, the game isn't much fun anymore and the baby will not make strong movements. Habituation has occurred. Now you can hang different items on the mobile and the baby's interest is revived, and they once again start making movements directed towards the moving objects. Infant researchers use this simple idea as an experimental tool to learn about what babies can perceive and discriminate. The baby's movement (increased activity) has become an operant response, modifying the environment, and if that is rewarding, the responding will continue. The method also reveals responsiveness and cognitive functions like memory.

Sometimes we have habituated too much or have selected other less pleasurable signals to attend to, which is why it is important to savor our experiences. But if you are reading an important story in the paper, drinking your coffee, and eating a piece of toast and marmalade, all at the same time, which of those elements should you be savoring? Mindfulness trainers want you to be in the moment (to be "fully focused on or mentally involved in what one is doing or experiencing" is the dictionary definition), but which moment?

When we say that feelings are the experience of emotions or emotion-relevant situations, it is important to recognize that people feel these things in different ways. We know how they feel from physical expression and from verbal statements—naming the emotion (feeling rejected) or the cause (you didn't ask me to your party). As some of these feeling statements are going to be sensory—both interoception and proprioception—it seems likely that people will differ in their sensory awareness. Hurlburt and his colleagues (2009) have defined sensory awareness as "the direct focus on some specific sensory aspect of the body or outer or inner environment" and show that moments of sensory awareness happen to everyone even when in the middle of doing something else entirely.

There was a flood of interest in the experience of stimulus deprivation after pilots in highly monotonous conditions and people who were sailing alone around the world started to report anomalous and unpleasant experiences. Some of the research was initiated because of reports of solitary confinement and sensory isolation being used in North Korean prison camps as both punishment and attempts to coerce captives to give up information. At Princeton, Vernon (1965) built sensorily deprived environments in which people could sit in comfortable chairs in the dark in sound-proof rooms. Undergraduates were paid by the hour to spend time this way and volunteers, thinking it would be a very relaxing way to earn a little cash, rushed to sign up as participants. Very few of them lasted more than a couple of hours—they were given a "panic button" to push to be let out and they used it very quickly.

All these phenomena will be familiar to anyone who has an undergraduate degree in psychology. Why it is important to be reminded of these background conditions is that the elaborate contexts of our lives are what we live in, what we respond to, or try to ignore. Modern living environments, especially in cities and suburbs, are complex and demanding but so omnipresent that we sometimes forget, when working with a client, that it may be important to know more about their living conditions. And equally importantly, can they access stimulating environments that are enjoyable in and of themselves and do not require excessive drinking or drug use to have a good time? We need to have pleasure, but we need to find it in pleasing experiences that make us feel good and do little or no harm. It has always fascinated me that in psychotherapy settings, we can sit with a client in our own little controlled environment with comfortable chairs, a potted plant or two, carefully selected pictures on the wall, and listen to a client's story with almost no information about their unique living situations, their work conditions, their hourly experiences of pleasure or pain, unless the client makes a point of identifying these things. And when we have no information, we make assumptions about their lives based on our own experiences and expectations. It's not a fatal limitation of work in an office or clinic setting, but it needs to be attended to if we are going to understand the client's day-to-day drama of feelings, in addition to their activities, which they can usually tell us about quite well, if ever asked.

There Is Always a Stimulus: Internal versus External

There is always a stimulus that elicits our feelings, although it need not be some external physical event. It could be a word or the way you interpreted the word; it could be a thought and the thought that was the stimulus could be something external or even another thought; it could be a vivid visual image either conjured up or recalled, it could be a memory that elicited your feeling, and the memory could have been elicited by a word, an event, or a linked chain of free associations on the analyst's couch.

In Chapter 4, I touched on the role of images, pictures, stories, cartoons, videos, and movies as being a strong source of affective arousal for children, and for adults as well. Good imagination, attention, and suspension of rational understanding about what is possible are all elements that will enhance children's response to stimuli that are external but only symbolic or representational of the real thing. It is even more remarkable to recognize that simply imagining these things can evoke strong feelings. This raises further recognition that we can also imagine what a feeling itself is like. We can increase children's emotion competence (as defined earlier) by asking them to show us what it looks like when someone has a strong feeling like anger or love, and the child correctly acts out facial expression, body language, and relevant emotive words. Can we also enhance feeling comprehension by asking them to explain what a feeling feels like? Ask a child to imagine being happy and ask them what that feels like. In kindergartens and daycare centers across America, you will often hear children being taught the song: *"If you're happy and you know it, clap your hands/give a smile; if you're happy and you know it, you really ought to show it ..."*

Imagination of situations and other people's feelings—really feeling their feeling and not just labeling it—is a foundational process for having empathy for others not in one's own immediate orbit (Loev et al., 2022). When clients explain how they felt after a bad incident or experience, a therapist might reply "I really feel for you." It is a delicate balance of authenticity between expressing the right facial response and words of sympathy and concern (or pleasure, if it was a positive experience) and trying to judge whether the feelings they have just shared are at a level and valence that is appropriate and likely to be helpful in the longer term of coping and managing their lives. We enact feelings and judge theirs at the same time.

This in turn raises some interesting possibilities. Daniel Gilbert and colleagues have introduced the concept of *affective forecasting* (e.g., Wilson & Gilbert, 2005). Essentially, it is predicting how you will feel in the future—important for making life choices and decisions. Others have said that because children and adults can imagine their futures, we are able to engage in a sort of time travel. In my lab, doctoral student Lucia Larroa (2013) conducted an interesting study of teenagers who were asked to develop visual (drawing) and verbal descriptions not of what they imagined their future to be like but what sort of future they considered possible. *Possible selves* is a concept from social psychology in which a person imagining what their future could conceivably be creates a cognitive template, or affective image, against which the value of their current activities and experiences might be judged. Larroa worked with high school students who were disengaged from their schooling, by which it meant they had no enjoyment and felt no pleasure in any formal school activities. This is not depression, simply an absence of positive feelings for the educational experience. In her study, she was able to show that high school students could be helped to imagine a positive possible future, but not, without further assistance, construct the realistic steps that would enable them to achieve it. The exercise allowed pleasurable feelings for a future event to motivate them to engage in less desirable tasks that now felt more positive. It provided a mechanism for transferring positive feelings about what they could imagine becoming onto activities that otherwise appeared irrelevant to their interests. If they thought it was possible that they could have bad experiences in the future, what could they do to make such a picture of themselves less possible?

Affective forecasting is about how someone can imagine feeling about the occurrence of some future event. Incorrect forecasting can have negative consequences. An example Wilson and Gilbert (2005) give is that getting a new puppy might be a lot less attractive and enjoyable than originally imagined by a prospective dog owner. The opposite direction can be seen in clients, who imagine they will feel much worse in any new situation than they are likely to experience. Wilson and Gilbert's research participants overestimated how unhappy they would feel two months after the ending of a romantic relationship. Bias in these feelings forecasts will influence decisions about important actions to take, particularly when clients have limited understanding of why things happen to them. Bias can be in how and for how long a person might feel after an event, as well as a bias these authors call *focalism*, which is the tendency to overestimate how much they will think about an event and to what extent other events will occur to change their situation. Expected pleasures, when experienced, are less pleasurable than when unexpected. Affective forecasting represents another way of thinking about irrational cognitions: it would be constructive to help clients anticipate their future feelings more accurately by explaining the bias, rather than just claiming they will feel better in the future.

Experimental work on emotions has typically relied on specific physical stimuli to elicit an emotion. Unconditioned stimuli in research can be things like specific pictures (those developed and used by Lang), painful stimuli like electric shocks, loud noises like Watson and Rayner's steel bars banged together, and phobic objects like snakes, spiders, and cockroaches. But as has been emphasized—perhaps exhaustingly—feelings in the real world are characterized by the eliciting stimuli being interpreted in a certain way. The many examples I have given of the "logic" of feelings tells us about the conditions for having one feeling over another. If you fail at some task and believe someone else is responsible for your failure, you might feel anger, but if you recognize that it was due to some inadequacy of your own, you might feel shame. The initiating condition was the same in both cases. In clinical work, exploring a client's attributions for a feeling often results in an attempt to have the clients see the situation from a different perspective. A depressed client might express a feeling of failure when encountering a task that has not worked out well, and if they then continue to overgeneralize and say that they are a failure, cognitive therapy proposes that the correctness of the generalization be challenged through rational argument and reasoning. But if the failure of the enterprise can be attributed to something other than the client's sole responsibility, then the feeling of personal failure should be mitigated. The discourse might still be that of cognitive restructuring, but the feeling of failure and perhaps shame or defeated pessimism might be less likely to be the feeling retained, since a more nuanced interpretation of what happened can lead to different, constructive actions in the future. The rational therapeutic response, "Just because you failed at this task doesn't mean you are a failure," is certainly true. But "It doesn't seem likely that the failure was entirely your fault. Can you see other aspects that needed to be present that you had no control over at the time?" might lead to mutual thinking about what could be done in future situations of that kind. Often illogical conclusions and faulty attributions can be challenged at the same time. A third therapeutic response—"Failure is just a feeling. Don't feel bad about it. Accept it and learn from it"—is another strategy in which the negative feelings are not modified by changing the appraisal of the eliciting event but by-passed to weaken their influence on subsequent behaviors. By doing things differently, it is hoped that the negative valence of the negative feeling is weakened and made less influential on your life.

Triggers

Another more modern word for elicit is trigger. In contemporary discourse, feelings are often being triggered. Horror movies and even news reports on TV come with a warning about disturbing images. The realism now possible in films really does create a sense that we already have the science fiction world of feelies as well as movies (Heritage, 2025). Thanks to recent trends especially in American culture, the idea of stimuli "triggering" feelings (inevitably unwanted, unpleasant ones) has become part of the concerns of young people, particularly students. However, the association with some kind of firing mechanism for a gun or a bomb does again place the emphasis on the stimulus being a direct cause of the feeling. It also implies that the feeling reaction is inevitable (once the trigger has been pulled the bullet will follow or the bomb will explode) as well as being intense, explosive, no longer under voluntary control. The idiom of explosion covers the possible reaction of the person, as well as their characteristic traits: people who might be considered over-sensitive to certain stimuli, specially sleights, or challenges, are said to "have a short fuse." Slightly less ordnance related, people can be described as "touchy," as can subjects for discussion, which then call for tact and care. The word itself comes from "tetchy," which means irritable and cranky, but certainly conveys a personal brittleness. And thus, since such affect is always negative, people feel they need to be warned. No one complains that the professor has just triggered a deep understanding of the role of mitochondria in cell development, or a new insightful appreciation of the use of language in *Moby Dick*.

There are other symbolic implications of the word trigger. In firearms, triggers can be too sensitive and be activated by the slightest pressure—so we talk of someone's anger being on a hair-trigger. Firearms sometime discharge even before the hammer is fully cocked, so we talk of people going off half-cocked; someone you're implicitly accusing of exploding uncontrollably in rage you describe as "going ballistic."

In order to protect the dignity and the positive feelings of others, we try to be sensitive to their feelings—even when we don't know them. This is just part of common decency in societal interactions. This kind of sensitivity includes not making prior assumptions about someone based on general characteristics and being aware of the possibility of differences in lifestyle and circumstances. This need became very apparent when we were working with well-meaning teachers who would sometimes talk to their class like everyone had a female mother, a male father, and a house with a white picket fence (Evans & Harvey, 2012). With so many changes in family dynamics and arrangements in modern societies, such assumptions can no longer be made. Somehow the importance of being socially and emotionally sensitive at the group level became known disparagingly as "political correctness" and began to attract a strong negative connotation from people who were unwilling or unable to see the basic value in sensitivity, usually because they disliked the possible differences that were being alluded to. That has become particularly noticeable when the issues are around gender and race.

If there was ever even a mildly pedantic element to some of these sensitivities, people with antagonistic feelings regarding racial or gender equality were quick to pick on some of the more exacting versions. A slow growing tolerance towards people who are transvestites and those who are transgender turned rapidly to hostility in segments of American society, based on social media spreading feelings of resentment when transgender athletes competed in sports (Chan et al., 2024). As mentioned earlier, resentful feelings fuels anger and hostility, even though the situations resented have no direct bearing on the person feeling them.

There are, however, good examples of feeling changes occurring when policies are introduced to ensure general fairness and having teams that embraced and welcomed all team members equally. As an overall conclusion, being part of a like-minded group and sharing activities and interests is extremely valuable for people who experience discrimination, are socially anxious, or have negative feelings about themselves. A qualitative study conducted in Ireland summarized the issue well: "[The findings exemplify] the social and cultural capital embedded within LGBT networks and the contributory role of interest groups, established by, and maintained for, LGBT communities, in enhancing social connectedness" (Ceatha et al., 2019, p. 15).

Resentment over accommodating opportunities for people with disabilities is not unknown. We have already seen how children have strong feelings about what is fair. Salisbury and her colleagues (Salisbury et al., 1997) studied elementary (primary) school children's feelings regarding fairness of different classroom situations involving children with and without disabilities. The children were read illustrated stories of things that commonly happen to children in classrooms and then asked to judge if the situation was fair or unfair and how the character in the story would feel. Later, using the school children's acute sense of fairness, the team taught the children how to develop solutions to problems which could quite naturally occur in inclusive classrooms—solutions that had to be fair to everyone, disabled or not. What was interesting was the enjoyment the students showed when catching a teacher or other adult in the classrooms behaving differentially to the children with disabilities. They became the fairness police and relished the role. Sometimes, the unfair situation was when a teacher showed preferential positive treatment to a disabled peer. By helping teachers recognize this and make changes, the other students reduced their occasional feelings of resentment towards a child with special needs when the latter was being held to a lower standard than they were.

Stimulus Control and Detection

For something to be a stimulus that is sensed, it has to be noticed and attended to. Many are subliminal but can be sensed readily when attention is directed towards them, like the sensation on your bottom when sitting on a chair reading this book—of which you have just this moment become aware. There is a vast literature in experimental psychology on the fascinating phenomenon of signal detection. Faint stimuli, like a blip on a radar screen or a low decibel tone in a hearing test, can be mistakenly detected. One can report having heard something when there was no sound (error of commission) or fail to see a distant approaching missile when there was one (error of omission). There are individual differences in which of those types of errors a person is likely to make. The most interesting feature of this for us clinicians is that after a strongly emotional experience (usually a negative one, but it can be after positive feelings too), people become hypervigilant. They constantly scan their environment for signals of danger and threat. And they are likely to see or hear or feel one when none exists. In experiments, participants are asked to respond as rapidly as possible when they see a fear-eliciting image, like a spider in an array of other neutral images. In many research studies, participants' reaction times to recognizing an image have been used as an implicit measure of a negative feeling. So too with words. In experimental studies of anxiety-induced vigilance and selective attention, speed of recognition of a word is used as the dependent variable. If the letters S_ N_ K_ are presented briefly (tachistoscopically), a phobic subject might read it as SNAKE, and a hungry one as SNACK. A related research strategy is to present an ambiguous word and measure how quickly it is judged: the word BAT means something different to a cricket player versus a person who has fears of the dark, so their speed of deciding whether the stimulus presented is animate or inanimate will differ greatly. This hypervigilance in real life is important to remember when talking to clients about the stimuli that elicit their negative feelings. For example, are socially anxious clients hypervigilant for cues of rejection or dislike?

There are three other fundamental principles regarding the role of stimuli in behavioral psychology that are important for understanding how and why feelings change. One is the concept of stimulus generalization, another the related idea of stimulus control, and third is the fact that discrete isolated stimuli always occur against a background of other more general stimuli, a background that we call the context. Stimulus generalization was first reported in detail by Pavlov. A tone slightly different from the one used as the conditioned stimulus (CS) in the conditioning trials could still evoke a conditioned response (CR), but typically the response was smaller in some way than the original CR. The more different the test stimulus is, the smaller the response is—there is a clear gradient to the point that an only slightly similar stimulus will not evoke the CR at all. Much of our clinical understanding of how feelings are under strong stimulus control comes from conditioning research on generalization.

In human experience, there is always a multitude of possible individual stimuli in any context. It is possible (and indeed essential for survival) to make one feature of the context particularly salient, which is then usually referred to as a discriminative stimulus. Discrimination is kind of the opposite of generalization. Specific discriminative stimuli do not have to be precisely the same, just as long as they are identical on a recognizable dimension. You can teach a rat to respond only to the stimulus of a triangle (something with three corners), regardless of the shape, size, or color of the triangle. Thus, the rat learns the concept of triangularity.

Eliciting stimuli for feelings can be considered innate, reflexive, and essentially unlearned because of their biological ability to be either painful or pleasurable. Fear responses seem to be particularly innate. There are many stories of primates reared in captivity that have never seen a snake reacting fearfully to a toy rubber snake dropped into their cage. And they respond negatively to distortions as well. A toy rubber chimpanzee mask will cause great distress when placed in a chimp's cage. Through modeling, generational transmission of past experiences may be possible. An interesting example of this comes from a recent study of wild animals in a South African game reserve (Zanette et al., 2023). A variety of different sounds were played to animals from hidden loudspeakers in the bush. The animals would be feeding or drinking. A short sharp noise might cause them to stop and look up and orient their ears just for a moment. But when human voices—just ordinary conversational snippets—were played over the speakers, the animals would run off in a mad dash. Voices are a more specific signal, cue, or trigger for danger than almost any other sound, including the growl of a lion. With humans in modern societies, the nature/nurture debate is even more complex. It is much harder to decide if there are any instinctual feelings that are uninfluenced by societal experience. A primary emotion such as love might seem basic, but the stimuli that elicit it are undoubtedly learned. J. B. Watson argued that there were only certain things that would automatically elicit fear or distress in a baby (for instance a loud noise or a sudden loss of bodily support) and that all other things capable of evoking fear acquired that power (control) through learning experiences (Watson & Rayner, 1920). Thanks to social learning theorists such as Bandura (1971) and Staats (Staats & Eifert, 1990), the experiential (learning) component includes both imitational learning and the generalization of verbally encoded rules ("Don't touch that jelly fish on the sand; it will sting you."). Toddlers pick up objects off the ground and sometimes put them in their mouths. Parents and caregivers react with words—"That's disgusting! Spit it out. That was on the ground. Let's go wash your hands. Poopy is dirty." In other words, the experiences of others and of previous generations can, by imitation and similar indirect cultural influences, shape which specific stimuli reflexively elicit which feelings.

While there are many opportunities through learning processes for people to become sensitive to stimuli that are not inherently harmful, it is worth remembering that autonomic nervous system reactions can be considered *unconditioned* responses even if not everyone reacts to them the same way. A good example is when individuals react to the sight of blood with strong feelings of disgust, fear, and autonomic reactions such as fainting. The constellation of feelings when exposed to blood stimuli are not ones easily controlled or willed away. There is a two-phase reaction of initial sympathetic arousal followed by parasympathetic hypotension and bradycardia, resulting in feeling faint or actually fainting (syncope). About 15% of college students are known to have fainting feelings, and about the same number of people volunteering to donate blood. The phenomenon is usually described as a specific phobia. But it is difficult to think of the reaction as the same feeling as a fear. However, as will be discussed, what is certainly possible to fear is that you might faint if exposed to blood-related stimuli. Indeed, people with a fainting history report greater sensitivity to their own physiological arousal (hypervigilance to internal bodily cues). Lumley and Melamed (1992) reported that mildly blood "phobic" volunteers reported feeling faint despite their blood pressure readings showing no significant change with blood exposure. It is a revealing example of social demand characteristics, or perhaps their way of labeling the feelings of general discomfort, disgust, and anxiety. Since the context for seeing blood is often medical (surgery, an accident, or an incident of violence), there is another part of the context which elicits feelings, namely empathy. Blood-sensitive participants in Lumley and Melamed's (1992) study, while not different from controls in general levels of ability to feel for others, showed higher levels of empathic distress for the victims of surgery or accident. This gives insight into how an individual cognitive difference—identification with a victim—might influence a feeling elicited by scenes of bodily harm and mutilation.

The Lessons from Fear Conditioning: Acquisition

In psychotherapy, we have to work with eliciting stimuli whose origins we may never fully know but whose precise nature needs to be discovered and understood. It is largely through the work on phobias by the early behavior therapy researchers that we can confidently talk about the stimuli that reliably elicit feelings and at least one way we know how to modify that relationship. In one of the true classics of psychology, Watson and Rayner (1920) described their demonstration with nine-month-old little Albert B that pairing a loud noise (banging two steel bars together behind his head) after showing him a white rat could induce a distressed, fear-type reaction to the rat that generalized to other white fluffy objects (a fur coat, a Santa Claus mask, a rabbit, etc.). Everyone who has taken a course in psychology knows the study. And you probably know the criticisms, in addition to the problematic ethics (there being no Institutional Review Board approvals in those days). The most relevant of the criticisms is that in one of the very few attempts at replication of the study, it proved difficult to condition a fear reaction to a much more neutral CS—indeed an actually positive and familiar object—that of a child's toy building blocks. That alone has created an interest in whether anything can always be conditioned to anything else. But it cannot be denied that through aversive conditioning trials, one can condition fear to at least some inanimate and objectively non-dangerous stimuli (Field, 2006).

My own personal example of this came after our move to a farm in rural upstate New York near my then university at Binghamton. It was a former dairy farm, and the paddocks were being used by a neighbor to keep a few horses. This meant an electric fence around one of the fields. The neighbor didn't maintain the fence very well and there were frequent shorts when long wet grass touched the wire. Nevertheless, it worked well enough to keep the horses from straying. Our Rhodesian Ridgeback dog, Bogey, however, had lived in the suburbs before we moved in. He loved to run around our 100 acres, but after a few days, the inevitable happened. Sniffing around and exploring as dogs do, his nose touched the fence. His squeals of pain told the story. He was all right, but he never went near a wire fence ever again. One trial learning is a reality. And his fear generalized to anything that looked like fencing wire—even a wire coat hanger inside the house caused an instant avoidance response.

In the laboratory study of fear conditioning with human participants, the "fear" eliciting stimuli (UCS) have typically been a mild but unpleasant electric shock, a loud unpleasant noise, or visually aversive pictorial images. When the UCS is something quite mildly aversive, one does not get a large autonomic UCR, and the dependent variable of the study is often a verbally reported prediction of the probability of the UCS occurring after the CS. The fact that human subjects can state verbally what the contingency is between the CS and the UCS ("I learnt that when the buzzer sounds I will receive the shock") leads cognitive theorists to believe that the appearance of the CR is because they acquire this cognitive rule, or, in other words, they learn not an S-R connection but an S-S connection: buzzer comes before shock. It is true that some participants in such studies can state the rule (verbalize the relationship between buzzer and shock) at about the same time they show a CR (responding to the buzzer with an autonomic response such as heart rate change or galvanic skin response). However, conditioning can also occur without any conscious awareness of the contingency.

As clinicians interested in change, what seems to be of key importance is extinction as a process. Albert B never again was frightened by steel bars banged behind his head and Bogey was never again shocked by an electric fence and certainly not by a wire clothes hanger. So, if conditioned fear was based on a cognitive association between two events, surely a cognitive (verbal) assurance that the two events will no longer be paired would result in immediate cessation of fear? The answer is yes, such reassurance can reduce fears and anxieties. But not always, and it is then that people become clients. This is why a study conducted in Don Levis's lab at Binghamton University is so informative (Unger et al., 2003). The story is essentially this. Volunteers experienced fear conditioning trials in which a tone was paired with an unpleasant shock. After just a few trials, the typical psychophysiological signs of fear appeared whenever the tone sounded. Then, they were told there would be no more shocks, and to make that assurance totally believable, the shock electrodes were removed from their hand. But the next time, the tone alone was presented, the same autonomic fear response occurred. Cognitive awareness that conditions were now safe could not override the S-R association learned during the conditioning trials.

One unreplicated study may not be enough to persuade you. Contingency awareness, threats not yet experienced directly, cognitive expectancies, and people's thoughts and beliefs are undoubtedly important psychological phenomena. But I think findings from the basic fear conditioning paradigm do tell us important things about triggering stimuli. Without going into the details of the studies, the findings especially relevant to clinical work are as follows.

First, if a stimulus used as the CS is not a buzzer or a ticking metronome but a more complex stimulus such as a familiar object, say a hammer, a conditioned "fear" response will be observed to other objects that are tools (a saw, a drill, and so on). Anxiety responses can be conditioned to categories and concepts, which Watson and Rayner demonstrated, except the generalization they reported was on appearance (fluffy white things). With cognitive complexity and verbalizing humans, the generalization in the current example will be to the concept of TOOL. The generalization will be even stronger when in the conditioning trials *different* items that are all tools are used as the CS+. And conditioning to a concept rather than a discrete exemplar will be even stronger when other concepts (say animals) are presented as the unreinforced stimulus (CS-). The proof that fear is conditioned to a construct is that after a number of learning trials, a "fear" response will now occur to a tool never previously presented (e.g., Mitra & Asthana, 2024). Clinically, we can understand this very easily and we also know, in real-life situations, fear will generalize very broadly because of language and human concept formation abilities. A dog-phobic child I encountered had two negative experiences with a large dog, once when he was chased by a friendly sheep dog and once as a toddler when he accidentally opened a door where a harmless family dog had been sleeping but which then jumped up, barking loudly. The child had a strong phobic reaction to all dogs. And since constructs in verbal humans are encoded with words or with rules, he learned the rule that dogs were safer if on leashes being walked in park, but not if they were running around loose. But some people unleash their dog when away from traffic to let them run and play, so he also spent his time on walks with his parents deciding whether a particular dog owner was likely to unleash their pet.

Second, in the lab, one can reduce stimulus generalization across constructs and elaborate ritualistic rules by presenting exemplars that are not followed by a UCS (a CS-). In the example given, we can condition anxiety to a *narrower* construct of SHARP TOOLS by presenting hammers, wrenches, and screwdrivers as the CS-, and knives, saws, and chisels as the CS+. But from this simple example, you can immediately see that human anxieties and phobic responses may be elicited by extremely complicated stimulus displays. One of my adult clients who had severely injured herself after slipping on the wet edge of a swimming pool showed severe anxiety to any puddle of water or wet surface. Finding out through careful assessment exactly what features of any stimulus array evokes a strong negative feeling is important for conceptualizing what it is that is really feared—a caveat we will encounter in several different forms.

Overgeneralization (feeling the same way about a number of different things when only one of them is truly a threat to you) is a major cause of feelings based on prejudice and superstition. As a general rule, overgeneralization can best be counteracted by what is called (oddly enough) discrimination training. This means that while CS+/UCS pairings are presented in conditioning trials, a similar but not identical CS- needs to be presented with no UCS following it. This allows an organism to judge what specifically about the CS+ is signaling threat or danger.

This third important feature of human fear conditioning comes from the systematic work of Peter Lovibond in Australia. Among other investigations, Wong and Lovibond (2018) demonstrated that people with high trait anxiety (labile in Eysenck's terms) showed the same degree of conditioning (both cognitive "expectancies" and GSR responding) to a discrete cue as the CS+. But where they differed from the less anxiety-prone participants was in terms of generalization. When novel test stimuli were presented after conditioning to the CS+, anxious participants overgeneralized. Wong and Lovibond argued that this supported the idea in psychopathology models that overgeneralization is a predispositional factor (a causal factor) for the development of an anxiety disorder. In these sorts of studies, when there is a CS- (not followed by shock), participants try to work out if there is a rule about what type of stimulus is the one that signals a shock coming. When participants in the Wong and Lovibond study did develop a rule, both high anxious and low anxious participants showed little generalization to different test stimuli. "The results are consistent with past findings that have shown increased threat appraisal to ambiguity among highly anxious individuals, and they provide preliminary evidence that over-generalisation of fear in the presence of ambiguity is a vulnerability marker for developing an anxiety disorder" (p. 53).

The Lessons from Fear Conditioning: Extinction

If negative feelings can be acquired through associative learning (conditioning), then it follows that they can also be ... hmm, now comes a critical word: "unlearned?" through extinction. It was Pavlov who was also the first to really show how presentation of the CS without the UCS (a procedure called extinction) will result in a gradual waning of the strength of the response to the CS (the CR) (a behavioral phenomenon called extinction). But whether that phenomenon is *unlearning* or not is tricky. Maybe it is simply that one is learning something different—Pavlov's dog soon learnt the tone-signaled food and so it felt hope and salivated, but now the dog learns that it doesn't signal food any longer and the dog feels disappointment and stops salivating. The tone has become just a neutral sound of no significance. But the tone isn't entirely neutral and what it once promised has not been forgotten. We know this because after a few days since the CR has been fully extinguished, the dog can be returned to the apparatus and the tone sounded again—and low and behold the dog salivates. The CR has returned, although not at its former magnitude. The phenomenon is called spontaneous recovery; Pavlov concluded that the phenomenon of extinction was on account of a buildup of inhibition, which can dissipate. What it tells us clinicians is that even if you have managed to reduce a client's bad feelings in one session, they are more than likely to return.

This is a good moment to say something about one extinction style procedure which we know, beyond any doubt, can be an effective treatment for feelings such as fear (phobias). Psychiatrist Joe Wolpe (1958) developed Systematic Desensitization (SD) on the basis of his learning about the phenomenon of extinction following exposure to a feared stimulus without any horrible consequences actually occurring. But recognize a complexity: fear *is* a very unpleasant feeling. If you expose someone to something they fear, there *is* a horrible consequence: feeling of fear. So, Wolpe proposed that you start the exposure at a level that elicits only mild fear, and then slowly change it. And he thought that one might be able to help keep the fear feeling as low as possible by having the person do something that is calming.

Let me give a simple practical example of this. In Hawai'i, where there are a lot of very large cockroaches, it was easy, back in the 1970s, to find people with cockroach phobias willing to participate in some simple clinical studies by my research group of *in vivo* exposure. You might wonder how fearful they really were. One of our typical participants was unable to enter her house when she came home from work. Every evening, she had to pay the neighbor's ten-year-old to go in first, make sure there were no roaches, and just in case, to spray a can of insect repellant around the kitchen floor. For our treatment trial, we had an enormous cockroach in a glass jam jar with a lid. Low-level exposure involved participants approaching from a distance and stopping when they felt fearful. The exact distance they were willing to approach was a convenient measure of strength of the feeling, as explained in Chapter 3. We also asked participants to rate any feeling of distress on a simple ten-point scale called the Subjective Units of Distress Scale (SUDS), first described by Wolpe (1969). They were also taught to stay calm by taking a big breath and letting it out slowly while saying to themselves "I feel calm and relaxed."

Our whole "treatment" process was exactly analogous to Wolpe's clinical SD procedure. One minor difference was that as a practical matter that most clinical-level phobias are of things and situations not easily put in a jar: heights, germs, deep water, bees, the dark, dogs, flying in planes, giving speeches. But as people can vividly imagine what they fear, they could be exposed to it by vivid mental imagery. Believing that the learning process involved was that of extinction and knowing that Hull (1943) had argued that extinction took place because of a buildup of inhibition, Wolpe wanted some way of fostering the inhibition of fear. Hull theorized that extinction involved reactive inhibition because he was studying overt motor behavior (rats running in a lab alleyway) and thought the inhibition might be a bit like fatigue. The autonomic responses of fear are not easily fatigued, so Wolpe looked around for some other way of inhibiting fear and hit on a deep muscle relaxation technique first described by Jacobson (1938). As he argued, it is difficult to feel relaxed (calm) and fearful (tense) at the same time. Well-practiced deep relaxation and feelings of calmness he argued would then *reciprocally inhibit* the feelings of fear. And so, Wolpe created a hierarchy of stimuli to be imagined, from the least negative (and thus easiest to approach mentally) to the most negative, producing the worst feelings. If the client begins to show distress, the presentation of the stimulus is stopped, relaxation is practiced, and then the stimulus is presented again. Typically, therefore, the client goes through the entire procedure without experiencing intense feelings of fear or anxiety.

The resultant procedure, systematic desensitization, could be precisely described, was easy to do, and could be learned by graduate students in psychology, resulting in an outpouring of research studies and clinical trials that have been reviewed and dissected like no other psychotherapeutic treatment. And the overall results are favorable. SD works. For some people better than others, for some negative feelings better than others, and it doesn't have to be done exactly like Wolpe described. Some clients get *more* anxious when taught to relax or told to close their eyes. Some people don't seem to form vivid mental images very easily or refuse to try because they are so unpleasant from the start. Since there are benefits from variations of the original procedure, the simplest summary is to say that SD might not work through "reciprocal inhibition," but does seems to work through exposure without negative consequences. Is the mechanism or causal process exactly the same as Pavlovian extinction? That is still being debated, often in the same confusing terminology of the distant past (Evans & Wilson, 1968).

One of the most interesting things when doing SD with clients, and the main reason for this lengthy coverage here, is constructing the hierarchy and discovering what clients are actually afraid of and what conditions could already mitigate their negative feelings. Most of our research participants could walk up quite close to the jar with the roach. But if it moved suddenly, a lot of them shrieked, reared backward, and shuddered. Also, after being able to go right up to the jar and pick it up and self-reporting very low levels of fear, we would ask them to unscrew the lid. That they flatly refused. Our volunteer clients weren't afraid of cockroaches. They were afraid of cockroaches running towards them, or over their feet, or, as one volunteer reported, being in the coffee cup she was about to use.

Implosion and Flooding

It is reasonable to claim that Wolpe's technique of systematic desensitization was not only one of the first specific treatment techniques in behavior therapy, but it has also been one of the most successful. Many good studies testify to its effectiveness with adults and children who have reasonably specific fears of circumscribed situations (heights, open spaces, elevators, hospitals), common things (dogs, spiders), and experiences (flying, taking an exam, public speaking). What is also true is that there are numerous good studies which show that doing systematic desensitization in exactly the same way that Wolpe described is unnecessary. Using deep muscle relaxation, presenting the stimuli in real life or in imagination, or going systematically up a hierarchy, does not seem to make much difference to the outcome. And the conclusion that thoughtful clinical scholars like Isaac Marks (1987) came to is because systematic desensitization works by virtue of repeated exposure to the feared stimuli in contexts that do not allow escape or avoidance.

This fits neatly with the observation that in the classic two-way shuttle box experiment, the animal continues to show fear of a buzzer that once signaled shock by its jumping over a barrier into a safe compartment (originally an escape strategy and now one that avoids the shock). The jumping behavior and presumably the fear that motivates it can be reduced quite quickly by preventing the escape (raising the barrier) and continuing to present the buzzer (forced exposure). With specific fears that we might label phobias, the technique of preventing escape but presenting the most feared stimulus (with no actual danger or aversive event accompany it) is called flooding.

In flooding, clients can become extremely upset but are encouraged to continue to face (be exposed to) the terrifying stimuli. The flooding procedure requires some courage on the part of the therapist—I have heard clients beg me not to show any more of "those horrid pictures," "get the cockroach out of here, please," "you've got to let me out of this dark enclosed space," and "I want to go home, now, I hate this busy shopping mall."

If the therapist succumbs to these pleas, the client's strong feelings have led to a positive outcome—they have escaped an unpleasant situation—and thus it would seem, theoretically at least, that their anxiety would be increased as a result, or they would refuse to come back for further sessions. And so it was that most clinicians preferred the slower but less emotion-arousing graduated exposure of the designed hierarchy of stimuli in a safe and calming context.

A specific type of flooding procedure designed to create high levels of negative feelings is called implosion. It was developed by Thomas Stampfl and Don Levis (1967). They introduced the important concept that, for example, when clients experience fear of situations such as heights, they are actually exhibiting fear of being maimed or disfigured by possible injuries. People don't fear swimming in deep water, they fear drowning; they don't fear spiders, they fear being bitten by poisonous ones. This can be extended to feelings of panic when a parent fails to show up on time when, say, collecting a child from school. Here, the context triggers fears of being abandoned. It is likely that social anxiety can be related to fear of rejection by one's own group—you don't have to be a Jungian to see how important for survival that meant to our ancestors throughout extensive periods of human evolution. If being ridiculed or breaking an important social rule evokes threat of rejection by one's immediate family, clan, or tribe, the consequences were severe—and still are. There are many archetypical sources of negative feelings—being lost in the woods, not knowing who or what was lurking in the dark—that occur in fairy stories and fantasy tales across all cultures.

Stampfl and Levis proposed that the desensitization hierarchy would go through successive levels of the situation but be accompanied by images or experiences of increasing harm and catastrophe befalling them. And they further suggested that fears of this kind were rarely based on direct past experience, but on unacknowledged traumatic events, perhaps of abuse. Suppressed fears of harm might include terrors of assault, sexual abuse, being maimed or disfigured, being rejected by loved ones. All of which makes good sense: exam phobia can arise from fear of failure, then fear of being terminated as a student, then fear of not getting a desirable qualification, then fear of being jobless, homeless, and destitute—possible selves. We have lots of good examples in children of imagining outcomes far worse than reality: children who feared injections had ideas that the needle might go right through their arm (McIver, 2011).

Nevertheless, the implosion techniques were controversial. Watching Levis doing the classic implosive method at the Binghamton University (SUNY) training clinic showed just how emotionally upset clients could become. A woman with a bee phobia was presented vivid descriptions at the very top of the hierarchy with being attacked by a large swarm of bees that almost covered her body, got into her hair and her ears and stung her repeatedly. The distressed emotion this elicited seemed to me to be like what earlier therapists had called an abreaction (see Jackson, 1994, for a historical review), with emotional exhaustion at the end.

Levis may not have believed that he was moving the imagery into the realm of unconscious conflict as a psychoanalyst might, but he did make the valid point that what a client might put at the top of the hierarchy was not really what they feared. The woman in the clinic didn't fear a buzzing bee or even getting stung, she feared, according to Levis, being covered in bees (like you sometimes see images of beekeepers with protective gear) and being stung to death. The approach was particularly convincing when working with combat veterans with PTSD. He argued that the stimulus complex of scenes and remembered experiences was *sequential*. One set of remembered cues led to another set, and from there to recall of events and scenes that were not ones that the client might have initially described. This process is not unlike Freud's use of free association as a way of sneaking past ego defenses. But the rationale is very different and the exposure techniques of Levis's revised method was to require recall of all of the sights and sounds and smells of the jungle, words spoken, thoughts elicited at the time, and even memories of the sensations from autonomic reactions and the pain. It is a sort of re-experiencing of the past aversive events when negative feelings were conditioned to very elaborate cue complexes. He argued that self-insight or support from an empathic therapist is insufficient to change negative feelings derived from traumatic experiences such as sexual abuse, harsh punishment, warfare, and natural disasters. "*Rather it is clear clinically that symptom reduction occurs only when the intense affect associated with the controlling memorial cues undergoes extinction via repetition of these cues. That is to say, the laboratory principle of Pavlovian extinction appears to be the corrective therapeutic change agent*" (Levis, 1993, p. 159).

The enormous emotional reaction that can be elicited in clients when implosion and flooding techniques are used can themselves be frightening for psychotherapists used to gentle, humanistic, non-confrontational work. In fact, in my experience, trainee therapists can be quite worried any time clients show strong feelings, especially when angry or "breaking down" in tears. They need to be reminded that displays of strong feelings can not only be cathartic in the short term but also highly indicative of where the client's insecurities and vulnerabilities lie.

Stimulus Control

It is useful to think of minor events that can serve as triggers, because minor events are easier to control or create in therapeutic recommendations. As an example, consider the suggestion to a client who is feeling depressed or in some degree of conflict with a partner that they go out and have a nice dinner somewhere. A lovely meal out with a little wine is a common source of positive feelings in many cultures. But a person in a negative mood can be easily irritated by small innocuous events: the music is too loud, you were kept waiting too long before being seated, your favorite dish is off the menu tonight, the waiter was slow to bring water. In a positive mood, none of these things would be worth getting upset about. So, being prepared for, minimizing, laughing off, or just ignoring any minor negative event could be critical for ensuring that the overall event generates the positive feelings it was designed to do. Feelings are very susceptible to contextual influences.

The phenomenon of habituation can be observed when over time a stimulus that once reliably elicited a response, no longer does so. Measures of the response (its magnitude or its latency) decrease. But it cannot be assumed that the changes are taking place in the emotional output side of the old S-R relationship. It is equally possible that what is being degraded is the potency of the stimulus to produce the response it once did. Instead of the response weakening, it is the stimulus that is weakening. Behavior analysis, and Skinnerian opernt conditioning in general, gave us the extraordinarily useful concept of *stimulus control.* In the conventional classical conditioning paradigm, the responses (especially emotional responses of the autonomic nervous system) were originally reflexes closely tied to the particular stimulus that inevitable elicits it (a puff of air in the eye elicits blinking; a tap on the patellar tendon elicits the leg to jump: a drop of lemon juice in the mouth increases in salivation). After appropriate pairing another, previously neutral, often irrelevant, stimulus will elicit the reflex. This is an unacknowledged fascinating feature of associative learning (classical conditioning).

In the operant paradigm, however, any stimulus that signals the potential occurrence of reward gains what we call stimulus control over lever pressing. Pressing will only occur when the stimulus is presented. It seems that any stimulus can potentially gain control over any behavior. In both cases, we have the fundamental fact that a previously irrelevant or neutral stimulus, not heretofore likely to cause a response, is now able to directly cause a response to occur. It stands to reason that if the clinical need is for the client to no longer react in an undesired way to the occurrence of a stimulus, that one way of achieving this is to degrade the ability of the stimulus to evoke that behavior. Since there is no physiological or inevitable reason why this stimulus elicits a response and since its ability to do so is a result of a learning experience, then we should be able to unlearn it. A large variety of CBT treatments have this intention as their goal: unless you can completely avoid the triggering stimulus in the future, you are going to need to find a way to stop it from triggering a negative feeling.

Clinicians can generalize from these principles. If you want your client to reduce negative feelings by trying new things ("behavioral activation" it's called in CBT), these activities have to be self-selected, safe, intrinsically enjoyable and rewarding, and involving contact with people who will possibly play a meaningful role in the client's life in the future. There is no truly direct "evidence" for this recommendation, but by extrapolation from other situations, it seems reasonable to expect that such conditions have the potential to reduce avoidance, promote contact and thus exposure, and be designed to reduce failure and re-traumatization as much as possible.

Triggers for Hurt and Anger

Thus far in this chapter, the focus has been on triggers for fear and anxiety because so much of early behavior therapy was focused on the direct application of work on fear conditioning. Name calling, teasing about a disability or someone's appearance, subtle (and sometimes not so subtle) racial comments and references to stereotypes are now often described as microaggression (Sue, 2010). They're not always very micro at all. Verbal remarks and snide comments can hurt feelings even if the victim tries to hide it so as not to antagonize the perpetrator further. The old rhyme supposedly designed to build self-assurance ("Sticks and stones can break my bones, but names will never hurt me") is patently false, since it is very easy to hurt someone's feelings by name calling.

Hurt feelings are formally defined as feelings such as shame, loss, and sadness or caused by someone's words or actions that were unfair, rejecting, undervaluing the person, or a betrayal of a trust. Studies show that a wide variety of possible feelings can be triggered by hostile comments disguised as pleasantries and humor. When experiencing such situations, African American college students reported shock, doubt, frustration, anxiety, helplessness, and despair, as well as lower self-esteem and aspirational levels (Harris et al., 2004; Smith et al., 2007). In China, Qi and colleagues (2023) explained how certain cultural attitudes towards children with disabilities led to school children experiencing microassaults (belittling and ignoring) and invalidation through patronizing and overprotection. In New Zealand, our classroom observation studies often revealed hurtful put-downs and stereotypic assumptions in remarks by genuinely well-meaning teachers uninformed of the daily life hardships of low-income and minority group students (Evans & Harvey, 2012).

Anger is another important feeling for which the eliciting stimuli need careful consideration, and anger in turn is linked to the action tendency of aggression. Aggression itself is a powerful trigger for fear in others, and even casual acts of verbal threats and insults play an important role in social interactions. Such behaviors are also commonly observed in families and between marital couples. When working with families, it is always useful to be attuned to teasing remarks and derogatory comments that are clearly hostile, possibly unintentional, but when challenged will be passed off as "I was only joking." I've often heard remarks like: "Jimmy doesn't mind a bit of joshing; he knows I don't mean it, don't you kid?"

In marital (couples) therapy, there has been much lay interest in John Gottman's research which demonstrated that when one partner shows feelings of disdain or contempt towards the other, it is highly predictive of later divorce (Gottman, 1993). This told a catchy story that was easily popularized. However, over a long career of observational research studies of families' and couples' emotional interactions, Gottman has elaborated on the complexities of marital relationships. From these studies, a system of marital therapy has emerged, with books, both scholarly (Gottman, 2023) and popular (Gottman, 1999).

For the more restrained purposes of the present book, there are key feeling-related principles of importance in Gottman's work. Traditional marital therapy focuses on resolving conflict. But as some conflict is inevitable, a preferable strategy could be to reduce the negative affect during conflict. One component of this is to explore the triggers that produced strong negative feelings. Each person will have different triggers (sensitivities) that go back to early experience in childhood. There are, however, discernable categories of triggers, that Gottman has labeled "The Four Horsemen of the Apocalypse." The first is criticism, in which one expresses a concern in the form of a criticism of the other person rather than an explanation of how their behavior made them feel. (The importance of implied or subtle criticism has already been pointed out in the *expressed emotion* literature described in Chapter 5.) The second is defensiveness, which we all know is the urge to protect oneself from feeling hurt or guilt by counter-attacking, dismissing the concern, or minimizing the issue. The third category of trigger is defined as showing contempt (or acting contemptuously) which involves sarcasm, insults (name calling), and any other response derived from a position of superiority feelings, as explained in Chapter 5. These triggers can sometimes appear to be quite innocuous, such as acting more knowledgeable or intelligent. The fourth Gottman calls "stonewalling," defined as emotional disengagement from an interaction. His research has demonstrated that the person who is stonewalling appears detached but is actually showing high rates of physiological arousal, especially heart rates increasing to over 100 BPM.

The therapeutic antidote in this category of response is to teach the self-soothing strategies that have been mentioned frequently already: relaxation, meditation/mindfulness techniques, and possibly encouraging the other partner to distract the "inner dialogue" of the stonewalling partner by asking questions. Gottman has emphasized that in-session therapy, when conflict occurs and negative feelings abound, it is the right time to teach new strategies and skills, rather than the therapist using their influence to reduce or minimize negative feelings.

When we think more broadly about eliciting stimuli for feelings, the triggers for anger are among the most interesting as anger is also a stimulus. Anger evokes and energizes aggressive behavior. Some aggression, even violence, is not reactive in response to anger, but instrumental. Aggressive acts are designed to intimidate, threaten, punish, and control others in order to obtain some benefit (power, money, resources). The aggression that is triggered by anger, at the interpersonal level, starts in childhood as hitting, pushing and shoving, biting, kicking, and pulling hair, and is accompanied by physical reactions of anger—muscle tension, facial expressions, vasodilation, screaming. Subjectively, anger is an unpleasant emotion, and angry feelings can persist long after the event that first elicitied them. And these eliciting events can also be sights of or even verbal reports of harm against others and other misdeeds not directly experienced. You can feel strong anger towards someone you love, and anger elicited indirectly can easily lead to feelings of hate towards those responsible for the reported misdeeds. They are not the same feeling. Anger is always directed towards individuals and what they do (including yourself), whereas hate, being more like an intense dislike, can be directed towards anything, including people. Like fear, they both serve to increase distance between the individual with the feeling and the object of the feeling, but with anger, there is, of course, direct approach as the action tendency even if the act of aggression is use of a firearm. Because of the distancing, there is little chance of having experiences that might lead to the opposite emotions—peacefulness for anger and liking/loving for hate.

Within CBT, working with people who are chronically angry and reactively aggressive has typically been directed towards reducing the strength of the feelings (reducing the arousal) and the self-control of the aggressive action tendency. It is, fundamentally, teaching walking away. Adopting a feelings approach—trying to better understand the trigger—has not been popular for the very good reason that in interpersonal aggression such as domestic abuse, any suggestion that the person who triggered the feeling is somehow to blame is obviously objectionable, even abhorrent. However, trying to understand why the perpetrator of the aggression reacted to a particular stimulus can be explored without in any way communicating that their anger was justified, appropriate, or excusable. Understanding why the person (maybe your client) experienced anger is important. A well-controlled but still angry client who has learned to inhibit aggression is not an entirely satisfactory outcome for psychotherapy.

So, can we make some inferences as to why anyone would become angry? We can go back to one of the oldest ideas around, Dollard and Miller's (1939) frustration-aggression concept, historically mislabeled a hypothesis. That being frustrated (an unpleasant feeling if ever there was one) because one's goal has been blocked is a matter of simple observation. The part that is a hypothesis is that frustration leads to aggression through the elicitation of anger, and that leads to aggression, after which there is a cathartic release of tension.

Aspects of the model that have received the greatest challenges over the years are that expressing anger does not end aggression, and acts of aggression, by being reinforced, are increased over time. Furthermore, feeling frustrated does not necessarily lead to angry affect—quite often individuals will withdraw. Having one's goals repeatedly blocked can lead to giving up and feelings of helplessness and hopelessness. It was Martin Seligman, of Positive Psychology fame, who first made a name for himself by suggesting that the experience of unavoidable shocks in a shuttle box led rats to cease making escape behaviors—learned helplessness he called it—a key paradigm for understanding depression (Seligman & Maier, 1967). While the learned helplessness model has been criticized and reformulated a number of times, and the reformulations criticized as well, the point I think to be important is that much attention was paid to cognitive attributions by humans, and insufficient attention to the raw feelings of helplessness.

Comparison with Soft Feelings

In the first chapter, I suggested that there are feelings which might be called soft in that the experience of them is hard to describe in sensation terms. Cushing and others (2024) have proposed that further understanding of "subjective affective experience" (i.e., feelings!) can be gained by not only having individuals report the strength of their feeling but also their confidence in that report: whether they are actually feeling it or just thinking about it. As feelings are so often reported as verbal thoughts, one can see that the distinction is a difficult one. But soft feelings have triggers too, and if a client can identify them, it allows therapists a chance to influence the valence of the feeling from negative to more positive. There are certain feelings many people report at one time or another that clearly have mildly negative valence for most of us, but if experienced more strongly can have somewhat unfortunate action tendencies. Feeling old is one such soft feeling that can be used as an example.

In one sense, feeling old has a metacognitive element, related to becoming aware suddenly of a discrepancy between self-perception and a corrective experience. The experiential trigger varies with one's age. If you are indeed old, the trigger might be a sensory or physical (e.g., muscular, or balance, and coordination) weakness that interferes, perhaps for the first time, with completion of an ordinary, everyday task, which then alters a self-perception. If you are still only middle-aged, suddenly feeling old can be triggered when a much younger person (students especially!) brings to your attention that you are not up with current trends—your clothes look old-fashioned, your musical taste is from the past before they were even alive, and even if your technical equipment is new, you are not fully aware of its functions. Basically, any sign that you are no longer "with it" will trigger feelings of being old. In both cases, the only negative action tendencies can be characterized as trying too hard: if you then go to extremes to look younger (plastic surgery) or engage in risky pastimes. It is not clear whether feeling old derives from more primal fears of death or simply the loss of a virile self-image. It is more likely that feeling old reflects loss within the three basic psychological needs recognized by Ryan and Deci (2000), as mentioned in Chapter 1—for competence, autonomy, and relatedness. These can be challenged by the natural ageing process unless individuals find new ways to meet the need. While ageism (negative social stereotypes and discrimination) is associated with harmful feelings of lesser well-being (Kang & Kim, 2022), it is clear that there are numerous practical life and health realities associated with old age that have the potential to make a person vulnerable to negative feelings over and above the negative social attitudes prevalent in some societies.

Changing the Stimulus Value of Mental Imagery

Because the early days of behavior therapy relied so much on the stimulus properties of imaginal scenes in systematic desensitization, much was learned about individual differences in ability to obtain vivid images. George Betts had published his Questionnaire upon mental imagery in 1909 (see Evans & Kamemoto, 1973; Sheehan, 1967) emphasizing that mental images could be represented by all the senses: the whistle of a train, the taste of ginger, the touch of sandpaper. The vividness of flashback memories often involve strong smells, sounds, and visual scenes, all eliciting particularly strong feelings, as Don Levis emphasized. To enhance positive feelings, therapy techniques like savoring should encourage clients' attention to be focused on all sensory modalities possibly relevant to the full pleasurable experience of the moment.

As in the Proust story at the beginning of this chapter, literature excels at creating images that drive our feelings and often illustrate that essential link with memory emphasized by the neuroscientists (see, for example, LaBar & Cabeza, 2006). Wordsworth gives us a second excellent example in his poem *Daffodils*, often mocked by literary critics but with elements of great psychological insight. When wandering ("lonely as a cloud"), he tells us he came across a vast display of wild daffodils. These are given powerful images of quantity ("crowd," "host," stretching "in a never ending line") or *potency* in Osgood's terms; *activity* ("fluttering and dancing," "tossing their heads in sprightly dance"); and positively *evaluative* ("out-did the waves in glee," and were so "jocund," the observer could not feel anything but happy and carefree, "gay"). Because of this experience, the vivid images in memory that "flash upon that inward eye" later filled his heart with pleasure. One might say that Wordsworth more than "gazed and gazed"; he savored this experience by attending to the important elements and the accompany feelings, both of which were stored in memory.

So often in the clinic, we are more likely to see the influence of vivid sensory memories on clients' negative feelings simply by encouraging detailed recall (mental image) of an unpleasant past event. I had one client, a fifty-year-old university professor who described to me a recurring image that he couldn't get out of his head. It wasn't his reason for therapy and the topic came up more or less by chance. He had once seen a TV news report from the ten-week 1982 Falklands War fought between the United Kingdon and Argentina. The report included vivid scenes of fighting in a location called Goose Green. One scene showed a wounded British paratrooper being rushed in a stretcher to an emergency field hospital. This is how my client described the image he saw:

> *"The man was on a stretcher, and it was bouncing along as the two stretcher bearers were running fast. The man's foot had been blown off and all his flesh had been stripped off his leg up past his knee. You could see his tibia and fibula bones totally stripped—they looked just like a chicken bone after eating a chicken leg. And because what was left of his leg was elevated, his leg bones were just waving up and down grotesquely while he was being carried. I can see it vividly while I am telling you this—imagine a chicken leg or a turkey leg after dinner just waving around. I've seen people injured, I've seen accident victims a few times, but they are always inert, lying somewhere, not having a stripped limb waving around in the air. It was terribly disturbing to me. And I'm not British, I had no interest in who won the war, and later I heard over 300 Argentinian sailors died when the Brits torpedoed their battleship. But somehow the image of a man who was still alive was seared in my brain. I don't think of it often; it has nothing to do with my depression over Marcia leaving me, but when I do think of it, it can still arouse feelings of horror and disgust."*

It was not the focus of my therapy and I only spent a little time suggesting that without any available facts, he could create his own story: imaging the man had been given morphine, doctors were able to amputate his leg just above the knee and later fit him with a prosthetic leg, and that paratrooper was now living happily in the English Lake District where he enjoys leisurely walks and spends happy hours with his friends in the local pub grumbling about his sacrifice to Margaret Thatcher's Falklands War. My client laughed, said he would try, and never mentioned this experience again. Lang had reported that physiological arousal to mental imagery of aversive scenes would increase if the verbal description to induce the image included statements like "You're breathing hard; your heart's pounding" (Ji et al, 2016). My client's use of words of horror and vivid associations with animal bones would surely have been a factor maintaining his feelings over such a long time period. At about this same time, however, Kavanagh et al. (2001) reported a follow-up of an earlier study, on imagery interference. When participants generated negative autobiographical episodic memory images, and at the same time engaged in finger tapping or lateral eye movements, the vividness of their negative memories was reduced, along with their affective valence. You might immediately see the similarity between this laboratory study and the somewhat controversial CBT technique called Eye Movement Desensitization and Reprocessing (EMDR) therapy. While reviews of this technique (Jeffries & Davis, 2013) have concluded that lateral eye movements are important, current clinical practitioners have assured me confidently that alternating left/right tapping movements are now more often used with similar success (Vogelman-Sine, 2025).

Implications

You may be wondering why I focused so much attention on very old and traditional procedures like SD. One reason is that as this prototypical formal intervention method in behavioral psychotherapy could be easily be learned, was very specific, had a sound theoretical rationale, and solid evidence for its effectiveness. But the aspects of teaching relaxation, developing hierarchies, and using imagined themes as the stimuli for feelings of fear, all had valuable implications for building a growing understanding of important influences. For instance, we learned that the cue complex that elicits certain feelings, good or bad, can be very explicit. Examples include: the sudden movement of a feared insect, high places without guardrails, the slippery taste inside the mouth of some foods, words used during sexual relations, the smell of particular foods after food poisoning experiences. Once a therapist can understand the critical element of triggering stimuli, suggestions for avoiding these stimuli or de-activating them in some way can be offered.

It is the lab studies of conditioning in humans and animals that have given us major insights into the exact nature of the stimuli to which people react. We know how to make discriminative stimuli narrower and more precise, and we know how to make controlling stimuli broad—even highly abstract categories like "triangularity" can serve as a discriminative stimulus and signal for the humble rat. For stimuli to be signals, they must be attended to as well as separated from the "blooming, buzzing, confusion." Lab studies of clients with specific phobias have proved invaluable in identifying the concepts of selective attention and hypervigilance to cues. Ingenious studies revealed how people with anxieties and fears are vigilant in their natural environments for threatening stimuli but also scan for signs of safety features as well. People without such worried feelings do neither of these things. Threat-oriented attentional bias is seen by some as an evolutionary characteristic to increase chances of survival (e.g., Craske et al., 2009; Öhman et al., 2001) and a causal risk factor for clinical anxiety disorder, and more rarely by others as a consequence of anxiety. Note there is a difference between selective attention and hypervigilance.

It is important to recognize that while all feelings have an eliciting stimulus of some kind, the stimulus cannot be oversimplified as the *cause* of the feeling. It is essential to appreciate this when the topic, as of this book, is about how and why feelings change—"change" obviously includes "occur." It is simply too easy to say, "What you said hurt my feelings/made me angry, so you caused my pain/anger." In behaviorism, we like the term "set the occasion for" rather than "caused." The causes of someone's pain or anger or any other feeling are complex, going back in time to learning experiences and other influences which came together in highly complex pathways to allow the person to feel the pain or the anger or whatever when presented with that stimulus. The stimulus did elicit it, but is not the cause.

This is not merely splitting hairs. If you were the person—therapist, romantic partner, parent, or unaware professor—who said the hurtful words, you bear some responsibility for the pain. You needn't have said them, or not in that way. So, if you were not wanting the other person to feel pain, you shouldn't have used those words. You can set the occasion for another feeling entirely and thus have some control over what another person feels, but there are limits. You cannot escape the causal influences of past learning. In Chapter 8, on the regulation of our feelings, the importance of stimulus control will again be emphasized.

The many ramifications of thinking about stimuli eliciting feelings must include the recognition that feelings, even negative feelings like sadness and grief, are not the same as clinical syndromes in which such feelings predominate, like depression. Grief is easily triggered by discrete events, such as loss of a loved one, or a pet, or defeat such as the loss of a job or a reward. But grief and sadness triggered by events does not routinely lead to depression, unless a generalization is made about the world and the future and yourself in it. That was the genius of Beck's analysis of depression—natural feelings of sadness become problematic only when there are cognitions and erroneous inferences making one vulnerable. An insightful clinical study by Fitzgerald of teenagers in New Zealand is informative (Fitzgerald & Richardson, 2002). Young people diagnosed with clinical depression were able to identify specific events that triggered their syndrome, such as a romantic breakup or a failure of an exam. But the effect of these events on their feelings was not just sadness, but a cognitive construal which Fitzgerald summarized as "the loss of a cherished ideal" about who they were as individuals—suggesting their image of themselves as lovable or intelligent or loyal had been challenged. That automatic thought easily generalized to become a core erroneous belief about themselves and thus a negative self-feeling. There is a close analogy with a phenomenon which will be encountered in Chapter 9. Military veterans report that they behaved in ways that also challenged their own deep personal beliefs and values. Called "moral injury," it has become a major insight about feelings for therapists working with PTSD.

We can take this idea further. As people age, they have more and more general health problems, with increasing experiences of discomfort and loss of vigor being inevitable. These losses can trigger clinical depression, for which the elderly are vulnerable—the more morbidity factors they have, the greater the evidence of depression. Health challenges are inevitable, however the relationship with depression is not. As we get older, we are increasingly able to minimize negative feelings by selective attention to positive stimuli and by avoiding potentially negative situations (stimulus settings), as well as managing sad feelings by turning to others (Seidman et al., 2025). In a large Chinese study, various factors were shown to be significant positive moderators of this relationship: having positive intergenerational relationships; engaging in social activities with peers; and making use of phone or computer technology to access online interactive and informational material—chatting, news programs, playing games, and watching videos (Duan et al., 2024). Sad feelings can often be triggered, but there are also triggers for positive feelings which can counteract the consequences for the individual. The next chapter, Chapter 7, explores the implications of competing feelings, and the following one, Chapter 8, further addresses the all important topic of self-regulation of feelings.

7

Interference and Contradictions

The Enigma of Conflicting Feelings

Thus far in this analysis of feelings, there has been an implicit sense that feelings are discrete events which come and go in some sort of orderly fashion. Nothing could be further from the truth. As cultural anthropologist Lisette Josephides (2005) wrote in her essay on resentment:

> *"[Daily emotions] create a maelstrom of human passions, where resentment blows about with complacency, apprehension and fear darken a brighter mood, greed collides with jealousy, scorn circles around frustration, generosity becomes tainted with hubris and runs into suspicion and wariness."* (p. 71)

It is likely that our simplification is imposed on us as therapists because we are often targeting specific, unwanted emotions, like fear, anxiety, or depression, which are strong enough to be causing the secondary distress that brings clients into therapy. Thus, we focus on and treat those narrow feelings, and when we do research, we publish papers according to these same symptoms, one syndrome at a time. The reality of living, however, is we experience a dynamic and reciprocal interaction of emotions and behaviors and changing stimuli and situations throughout each day. As a fascinating example of just this clinical reality, Levinson et al. (2025) presented an idiographic network map of the key features of one client, an eighteen-year-old diagnosed with bulimia nervosa. Ten of the fifteen "symptoms" are feeling-related: fear of rejection, social appearance anxiety, worry, body dissatisfaction, eating anxiety, disgust, interoceptive awareness, hunger anxiety, social interaction anxiety, and feeling fat.

For this chapter, the inquiry will revolve around a set of slightly narrower issues: one feeling influences another; a person can have two or more contradictory feelings at once (or maybe not); some feelings counteract other feelings; some feelings sit in the background as moods; some feelings can be masked; and some feelings have displays as well as action tendencies which are themselves

How and Why Feelings Change. Ian M. Evans, Oxford University Press. © Ian M. Evans (2026).
DOI: 10.1093/9780197825808.003.0008

uncomfortable or directly disruptive to intended actions. Feelings can also be ambivalent, especially regarding valence (liking and preference). Ambivalence is more often an affective element of cognitive choice, logically weighing pros and cons. But once feelings are centrally involved, past learning and past experiences complicate all judgments, such as feeling guilty about liking something morally reprehensible. And it doesn't need to be a moral issue at all—guilty pleasures, a term which advertising companies love, are things like going shopping, eating chocolate, or watching TV instead of getting an important client report written up. When feelings differ strongly in terms of their valence, like love versus hate, can they co-exist or do they alternate, and if so, do we think of them being in a seesaw-like arrangement, one replacing the other back and forth? Add to that situation the reality that we can easily like and dislike and sometimes love and hate different facets of the same thing, even people.

I once encountered a clinical example that I've often thought about. Celia, a married woman with a young son, was seeing me about issues she was having over decisions she had to make about changing careers. During one session, she interrupted what I'd started to ask her about to tell me of an unusual experience she had had that very morning. She had woken up and just glanced over at her husband who was still sleeping in bed next to her. He was lying on his back, and his face was in full profile. Celia stared at him intently. Then, she suddenly had a strong almost overwhelming feeling of hate. "I instantly realized that I could not bear to look at him. I hated looking at his face. It was the first time I'd ever felt this, just total awareness that I hated him. I'd just never really stared at only his face that way before, and not often in fixed profile like this."

I admit I didn't know what to say. I first reconfirmed that he had never been abusive or hurt her physically in any way. I then unconvincingly suggested that seeing someone sleeping is a distortion of one's usual perceptions, more like the image of someone deceased. We don't normally stare at or look so intently at someone with whom we are not interacting. So, I proposed, his facial image was artificially distorted. I was thinking of the panic with which a chimp responds to a rubber chimpanzee mask. Later, I made suggestions that doubts about her husband's construction business activities had been growing (she was very disapproving of their dubious legality), but without conscious negative affect. Was she in denial that her relationship was unhappy and that she wanted out of the marriage? That tied in somewhat with her anxiety regarding starting a new and challenging career. All these elements seemed to me to play a role, thus allowing her to explore her feelings as honestly as possible. It did, I think, help her make life changes that were good for her. I said very little and none of it looked like CBT. I'm not advocating such passive intervention, nor suggesting my analyses were either profound or valid. But it did convince me that conflicting feelings can be complicated things.

I have already touched on the issue of whether all feelings have genuine polar opposites. It is easy in measurement instruments and rating scales to ask for ratings on scales like good—bad, happy-sad, calm-excited. But for most pairs, despite how easy it seems in the Semantic Differential, the closer you get to the midpoint, the less the move to the extreme of the opposite seems true. What sort of feeling is the midpoint of the bipolar scale HAPPY to SAD? Zero feelings of happy, that is when people say, "I'm *not* happy/I feel no happiness," usually means they are *un*happy. So, shouldn't that be the polar opposite, since being unhappy is certainly not a degree of being sad? You can play this game with any pair of constructs, and it demonstrates how the challenge of scaling feelings informs you of the difficulty of finding any pair of feelings that are truly the opposite or conflicting feeling of another one.

When we ask clients to tell us the opposite of a given feeling they might be complaining about, it tells us more about the precise context to which that feeling is being applied. When a client tells you about a feeling they have, it is equally informative to ask them what or how they would feel if they didn't have that feeling. That gives some ideas about what should be approached rather than what should be avoided.

The simultaneous interplay of feelings—a reality we all experience—places another distinction between the territories of emotion research and the psychology of feelings. Some emotion models, as we have seen, assign only two dimensions to an emotion: its intensity (activation or arousal level) and its valence (positive or negative), physiologically regulated by appetitive, approach systems or the aversive, behavioral withdrawal system. But feelings having contradictory approach and withdrawal tendencies can occur in the same time frame.

We know from work on children's understandings about feelings that children under the age of five or six do not recognize that someone can have two feelings at the same time (Saarni & Harris, 1989). A little later, about the age of seven, they agree it is possible to have two feelings at once, but only if they are of the same general valence—like feeling happy and excited at the same time. Around the age of ten, they understand one can have two opposite valanced feelings at the same time, but only when they are directed at different things: you are happy you are going on a trip to see your grandpa, but sad your puppy needs to be kenneled while you are away. Eventually, by the age of eleven or twelve, children recognize that two opposing feelings can be held about the same event: you are happy that your mother baked your favorite cookies but sad that you can't share them with your friend who is away for the weekend.

Another source of conflicting feelings arises from the common situation in which the triggers for different feelings switch back and forth between current conditions, memories of the past, and uncertainties about the future.

To illustrate this, consider a study reported from Belgium about children in foster care (a specially emotive context, see Chapter 4). The authors studied the feelings of adolescents between ages twelve and eighteen in long-term foster families, using semi-structured interviews (Van Holen et al., 2022). Positive feelings were reported based on their current situation—feelings of pride in how they were coping and happiness with their placements. Negative feelings of sadness and anger were expressed over their past challenging relationships with birth parents, as well as ambivalent feelings of disloyalty. And negative feelings of uncertainty were expressed over their futures, being able to stand on their own two feet, the fate of siblings, and whether there would be negative judgments from society. Of related interest are findings that the young people who were coping best with their negative feelings were those who talked about them with friends and other supporting individuals rather than hiding them.

Some authors have been especially focused on the simultaneous existence of feelings of joy and sadness in one individual. The argument is often that they are both fleeting feelings that do not cancel each other out because they can both act as catalysts for personal growth (Abdusattorova, 2024). Joy arises in moments of unexpected delights, new connections, or achievements, to name a few. Lasting memories of that feeling, especially when shared with others, can alter and color the significance and importance of the original event. Ask your client to recall a moment of joy (use that feeling word) in their recent past and ask them to elaborate on events at the time. This does not involve asking for a complex thought or a cognition but for feeling words around the event, whatever it was: the elements that made them smile thinking about it, for example. Then ask them if there is anything about the memory that makes them feel sad. These might be a feeling they will not see a place or experience closeness with someone ever again. Feelings of sadness should evoke self-reflection regarding their own current status, highlight their own vulnerabilities, and thoughts about changes they might make in themselves.

In the psychology of behavior change, one of the most important concepts was by analogy with the notion of an economy. Behaviors—one's total current repertoire—fill time and space (Voeltz & Evans, 1982). If you stop doing one activity, it means you are doing something else. This simple logical reality had a major influence on the design of behavioral intervention programs—to reduce one undesirable behavior you need to increase an incompatible positive behavior having the same function (meets the same needs or achieves the same goals) as the undesirable one. Can this idea be applied to feelings? If you can't be happy and unhappy within the same time frame, happiness feelings should compete with unhappiness. Many think that is sure to work: if someone feels miserable, all you need to do is cheer them up and make them happy! But feelings are fleeting, they come and go, and even when they go, they hang about in the background. In this chapter, we will try to see if a feelings replacement model holds any water.

Positive Feelings as Antidotes to Negative Ones

If one feeling can strongly counteract another, it would seem we have a major source of feelings change at our disposal. Counteracting anxiety has been the influence explored most intensely, thanks really to the "reciprocal" influence of relaxation and calming thoughts during systematic desensitization procedures. Although not specifically part of Wolpe's original procedure, when using systematic desensitization with fearful clients, we always added the suggestion that they think of a "peaceful, pleasant scene," which in Hawai'i often involved lying in a hammock between two coconut palms listening to the sound of the gently breaking waves (Evans, 1974). The use of imaginal imagery was an early part of behavior therapy and has also provided a useful analogue experimental paradigm to study the effects of one feeling on another.

In an interesting study with volunteer undergraduates as participants, Demorest (2020) induced feelings of anxiety by having them recall, re-experience, and write about a significant past experience in which they were anxious. That was followed by a similar task in which the feeling was one of love, happiness, or compassion, depending on the group they were in. Each of these inductions in past research has been shown to reduce prior anxiety, and this was true in Demorest's study as well. However, she found that happiness and love yielded significantly greater reduction than compassion. A similar result was reported when the negative emotion elicited was anger.

The value of somewhat artificial studies such as this is that they offer parametric findings encouraging therapists to use similar induction techniques. In an unpublished study in my lab, we asked undergraduates to recall a time that one or other of their parent's had "hurt their feelings" when they were of elementary school age. A surprising amount of negative affect was elicited. The most common incident reported by these adult students was one where a parent had failed them in some way (forgotten to come to watch them at a soccer game, couldn't make it to the school musical performance in which they were playing an instrument, failed to pick them up from school). The intensity of the grudges they still bore was remarkable, becoming one of our incentives for starting research on children's perceptions of what is fair (see Chapter 4), "unfairness" being mentioned often, along with a mild feeling of betrayal. To ensure that our participants did not leave feeling negative about their parents, they were also asked to describe in vivid detail a time in which they felt positive towards their parents, priming them with suggestions: "Think about something one of your parents has done that makes you feel ... [e.g., immensely grateful]." There were three different primes for a positive feeling: feeling grateful, feeling accepted, or experiencing parental pride. Acceptance was the most effective in increasing positive feelings about parents, but only when the recall was one providing evidence of unconditional love. Interestingly, parents expressing pride in their children elicited positive feelings but not necessarily towards the parent. Parental pride actually seemed to put pressure on these university students—they reported the uncomfortable feeling they had to keep living up to parental expectations.

In the clinic, when clients are particularly focused on negative memories, it is easy to ask them to find positive ones and to make them more salient and emotive by requesting they elaborate in detail on the scene, remember the events, the settings, a humorous incident that occurred. You may remember from cognitive psychology classes the well-established finding of mood congruent memories (Bower, 1981). If your client is in a negative mood, it will be harder for them to recall events that occurred when they were happy. Explain to a depressed client that it is a harmful bias if they say claim cannot remember ever being happy. As mentioned earlier, feelings of nostalgia can be particularly tricky, since although the memory will be of a positive event, there will be an associated feeling of past that is lost, people missed, a time in one's life that cannot be repeated.

A classic example of emotions clashing and thus interfering with each other is the feeling of amusement which results in smiling, guffawing, giggling, and laughter. Parents use this device to distract young children from upset, especially crying (sad feelings and disappointment). Positive feelings are an antidote to negative ones—even though we can have both at the same time. Thus, induction by self or by others of positive feelings represents a likely pathway for regulating negative ones. We will encounter this topic again in Chapter 8 on the regulation of feelings.

Framing and Priming

Before trying to analyze all the complexities of conflicting feelings, it might be helpful to give some examples of how the topic has considerable relevance to the conduct of treatment—doing psychotherapy. I use those words carefully as the two constructs of framing and priming do not represent a formal treatment technique or method. Instead, they offer ideas for interactions with clients that might be useful. If we take the inevitability of conflicting feelings together with the emotive properties of words (their connotative meaning as mentioned in Chapter 5), we can suggest some stylistic properties of therapy interactions that could themselves be therapeutic.

Framing refers confusingly to a number of different things; for an excellent review, see Flusberg et al. (2024). The way we frame our message to others has considerable influence over how the message is received. We are all used to framing in advertising in which words and images are carefully calculated to create positive feelings. A car isn't just a car. It permits a life of carefree leisure, driving on deserted roads in relaxing scenery, to the endless admiration of your friends; or, if you are more influenced by the skills of German engineering, it isn't a car at all—it is an "ultimate driving machine." We also know exactly how political slogans make use of words like "patriot," "murder of the unborn," and "peaceful right to protest" as opposed to "violent insurrection." One item recently popped into my cell phone: "10 signs you have a personality of a lone wolf, not an introvert." The final sign clearly indicates why being a lone wolf was considered superior by the developer of these supposed "signs": "You're not afraid to take the harder road if it means staying true to yourself."

When clients first describe their issues and struggle to explain their feelings, there is usually a high level of specific emotional arousal and that emotional state constrains what else they report, what memories they disclose, and how they listen to and understand what you are saying. Leading questions distort eyewitness memory, as we know so well, and so the way you frame interview questions during assessment will communicate your own feelings to clients. In a random selection of self-therapy manuals, I found feeling phrases like "Breaking free from anxiety!" (implication: anxiety is an external force that has imprisoned you); "A jump-start guide to overcoming low motivation and depression!" (low motivation is just a flat battery); "Choose to live! How to defeat suicide through cognitive therapy" (it's just a choice in a battle); "This cutting-edge psychotherapy ... has been spreading rapidly across the country and the world" (everyone's into this super-sharp method).

I'm not disparaging fellow psychologists' efforts to ensure that their wisdom is fully appreciated (well, maybe a little). We all do use hyperbole, and we all want to frame ourselves and our work and our ideas in such a way as to generate positive expectations, commitment to make the effort to change, and trust in us and our methods without creating dependency. That is essentially what motivational interviewing (Chapter 5) is all about: framing your assessment of the client's needs to them in such a way that they will accept the importance of making big changes as well as reducing their tendency to minimize, deny, and passively resist. As many client's resistance to change is driven by feelings, framing their emotional needs as a process of discovery (SEEKING!) is an important part of psychotherapy symbolism: It will be a journey, you tell them, there will be barriers but hurdles will be overcome or bypassed, and you, the therapist, will be their unflinching guide, using scientifically grounded principles ("proved to work!") to point the way rather than carrying their pack for them, but encouraging them more and more to find other natural supports, so as they approach their goals you will be left behind, waving. I'm sure I've never said it exactly like that to any client, but that is a standard implicit message whereby the whole reason d'etre of CBT is framed.

As mentioned earlier, reframing has long been a therapeutic method, though in cognitive therapy it is usually called cognitive restructuring, and it is thoughts that get reframed. Unlike other authorities, I feel that restructuring is the more useful term for thoughts, and reframing is better used for emotion change attempts. Reframing emotions does not address the correctness or irrationality of a thought but uses emotive language and imagery to alter the affective value (valence) of things, which could be people, or events, or experiences.

Flusberg et al. (2024) in their review of framing mentioned priming as one form. I have been interested in priming ever since conducting a community research project to prevent dropout by elementary-aged school children (Evans et al., 1995). By the time such young students were alienated from school with highly negative feelings, their teachers and their parents had negative opinions of them—and of each other. We were hard-pressed to get acknowledgment of *any* positive characteristics of the students. These teachers' emotional responses towards the most difficult children were characterized by negative labels, readiness to use punitive consequences, and harsh verbal and facial expressions when interacting with them (noticeably different from the way they interacted with other students).

Quite often the expression of their negative feelings was much more subtle—in another context, this would be called expressed emotion (Chapter 5). Simply asking teachers to describe the problem behavior seemed sufficient to further exacerbate their negative trait impressions and overgeneralization of the child's bad qualities. But by always starting each discussion with affective priming—coming up with a positive verbal comment or description (based on a memory, a thought, a vision of a positive future, anything that elicited a positive feeling)—it was possible to focus all participants at a planning meeting on constructive campaigns for change.

Affective priming has been investigated extensively in experimental cognitive and social psychology (Klauer, 1997). The classic emotional priming paradigm was originally described by Murphy and Zajonc (1993), who elicited affective responses by subliminally exposing participants to faces expressing happiness or anger. After this exposure, the participants rated their liking for unfamiliar Chinese characters (the probe stimuli), and these evaluations were influenced by the valence of the primes even though the participants were ostensibly unaware of their nature.

So, here is an established principle from experimental psychology with broad application to the important need to alter the affective value of things in everyday life (Evans, 2010). To take the principle beyond the fleeting effects and artificial conditions of the laboratory into the clinic, I will briefly describe a project conducted in my lab by clinical student Kayla Mackie for her master's and doctoral research (Mackie & Evans, 2013). The context for the study was an effort by the New Zealand government to pass a stricter child abuse law that essentially criminalized physical disciplinary methods such as spanking children by parents. There was an outcry from some segments of the community, particularly from fathers, and we became interested in ways of encouraging fathers to think of more appropriate and constructive consequences for children's misbehavior.

The experiment was to ask the participating fathers to describe how they would discipline their child when given a list of inappropriate behaviors and possible attributions an adult could make to mitigate the seriousness of the behavior—for example: "it was deliberately provocative," "it was an accident," "a child that age wouldn't know any better," and so on. Then on a pretext, they were presented with various types of primes, and then re-tested on how they would respond to a different set of naughty behaviors of their children. The primes were color photographs of fathers interacting positively with their young sons, which our participants were asked to look at and describe. Half of the pictures showed fathers in an explicitly skill-teaching role, and the other half showed fathers protecting their child or rescuing a child from danger.

The evolutionary-relevant pictures of fathers in the role of protectors were not more influential than primes of fathers engaged in play or instructional activities. We had predicted the prime of saving a child in danger would be the most influential because in the public debate, fathers often justified hitting or spanking as necessary to protect children from harm. Positive affective primes were most influential with the few fathers who had more negative attitudes to their children's misbehavior and Mackie speculated that in parent training programs which teach positive discipline strategies, it could be helpful to ensure that parents have positive feelings towards their children, regardless of their problems. By the same token, it would be constructive to spend time talking about their children's strengths before getting into details about their disruptive and difficult behaviors.

It is interesting when doing positive parenting-training programs for children with conduct disorders just how many parents reveal (usually reluctantly) negative feelings towards a difficult child. We're not supposed to dislike our children and such negative feelings, common in marital therapy, are rarely central in work on child rearing practices. As Sandra Azar has long advocated, recognizing, exploring, and modifying parental schemas, especially those dominated by negative feelings, is essential for effective parenting programs regardless of the different theoretical orientations of the therapist (see Azar et al., 2005). This extends the discussion of positive parent training in Chapter 4.

Whenever we work with one person to influence the behavior of another, we starkly encounter these issues of attributions. Attributions are everywhere, but the attributions of parents about their children, teachers about their students, and spouses about their partners jump out at us in psychotherapy as common mediators of conflict. One can have attributions about anything, but the ones I'm referring to are the causal ones: how people explain the causes of someone else's behavior. While attributions are correctly thought of as private cognitive events in psychological theory, they are often expressed overtly in words which then gives rise to, or triggers, a commensurate feeling which changes behavior towards the individual. If you attribute your spouse's irritability to a headache, your feeling should be one of sympathy and caring; if you attribute it to retribution for something you mistakenly did earlier, your feeling might be one of anger. Hooley, whose extensive work on expressed emotion has already been described (Chapter 5), gives the following relevant clinical example:

> *If, for example, an adolescent son or daughter becomes very withdrawn, part of the resulting negative emotion might come from concern about the change. However, some of the negative feelings might also be fuelled by our attributional interpretations. If we believed that the withdrawal was due to deliberate avoidance of us, or as a way of getting out of responsibilities, we might become irritated or annoyed. On the other hand, if the withdrawal was attributed to uncontrollable stress, then we might react with sympathy. Relatedly, if we regarded the withdrawal as being triggered by something we had personally said or done, then we might instead experience feelings of guilt.* (Barrowclough & Hooley, 2003, p. 853)

Thus, attributions can be thought of as self-frames for circumstances and situations that elicit feelings. Changing attributions is therefore one of the ways in which feelings in interpersonal situations can be changed.

Fear of Fear

The physiological, facial, and bodily changes that are emotional signatures (expressions) ensure that feelings are usually public. But their display may have mixed consequences. Sometimes there are social benefits, when displays arouse sympathy, support, caring, and making amends. It is commonly thought of as their chief function—certainly their evolutionary origin. But in some circumstances, the revealing of raw feelings is socially uncomfortable, and the physiological changes interfere strongly with desired or successful performance.

To introduce this topic, let me describe a minor but distressing problem reported by Ella, a client of mine from the very distant past. Only some readers will remember the old days when we usually paid for something by signing a check. And going even further back, there was a time when traveling in a foreign country one had to sign what was called a traveler's check. These all had to be signed when they were issued by a bank, and then later, when cashed, they had to be signed again in front of the merchant, who then compared the two signatures. (Having to sign matching signatures on two different occasions does still take place in some modern contexts—such as voting in the United States, where your signed ballot must match the signature you have on file from your ID.) The demands for this simple task are modest: when you sign the second time, it has to be the same as before. This makes you more conscious of what otherwise is a routine motor act you don't usually think about. If you worry about it, over think it, and get tense from a feeling of anxiety that you might make a mistake, there is a risk you can't sign at all. This is what happened to my client. It ruined one overseas vacation as she was completely unable to countersign her traveler's checks. When Ella returned to the USA, she couldn't sign any check or any other important document unless she was completely alone. It wasn't a major mental health crisis, but it was enough of a need for her to seek help. Attending to well-practiced habits that are usually smooth and reflexive often interferes with them. The issue for Ella was that anticipatory anxiety made her tense, and it was the muscle tension that prevented the smooth act of signing her name. The anxiety was embarrassment—she knew she would fail, she'd look stupid, and people would think poorly of her. There were two therapeutic choices at that point. One would be to teach her to relax despite being anxious, that could be done with standard deep muscle relaxation training. The other would be to use paradoxical intention (Frankl, 1975) to convince her that it didn't matter if her signature was illegible, that lots of people just scribble it down any old way (today, ironically, with one's fingertip on a small screen), and it's just too bad if no one can read it. There are probably a number of other ways of conceptualizing the issues and the treatment, but I chose relaxation training while at the same time convincing her that the exact form of her signature just wasn't that important. It is true within limits for signing most things, but not for everything we do, particularly elite sports where the state of anxiety interferes directly with skilled execution of a complex motor task. (This is especially true when there is a pause or wait period immediately before performing, such as high diving, place kicking in rugby, penalty goal kicking in soccer.)

Ella's anxiety was about the effects of her anxiety. Years ago, Eysenck became interested in this conundrum. He came across and quoted a study reported by a Russian researcher called Napalkov, in which an experimental animal was given one trial of a pairing of a very salient stimulus (CS) paired with a very intense and painful electric shock (UCS). When the CS was presented briefly and alone (no UCS), a little bit later, the dog exhibited a very strong (conditioned) fear response. That was to be expected. But when the CS was again presented alone, one would expect a slight reduction in fear—based on the phenomenon of extinction. But the dog instead showed an even stronger fear response than the previous one, or even the first one. And this escalation continued; no extinction took place. Eysenck (1968) called this the "incubation" of fear. Briefly, his argument was that because the intensive fear response was itself a highly aversive feeling, the conditioned response (CR) itself had now turned into a nocive stimulus (UCS) for fear. Fear evoked fear. An interesting phenomenon and worthy of attention. But when listening to him discuss this, he gave other everyday examples that didn't quite fit the incubation phenomenon. I had worked, quite coincidentally, with one or two clients like Ella who showed a similar fear-of-fear pattern that could be explained more simply by the fact that the negative fear response from the first occasion was socially embarrassing, thus the person felt social anxiety about exhibiting it again. One of my clients was a young man, by chance experiencing indigestion, who had vomited in front of his date when picking her up at her house. While she had been very decent and understanding about the event, the thought of it made him extremely anxious about the next time he was going to see her. Intense anxiety produces nausea, nausea produces vomiting. So, he feared the social consequences of exhibiting fear and because he feared them, he did indeed exhibit them (Evans, 1972).

Stage fright is another good example of dry mouth from performance anxiety causing anxiety for the next time. Anxiety can make it hard to articulate ideas coherently without stuttering and saying too many ums and ers. We call this tongue-tied. Anxiety about talking out results in no talk at all, which adults can make worse with semi-humorous phrases like: "What's the matter? Cat got your tongue?" When working with students at a university counseling center as part of a CBT practicum, we quite often encountered capable students who found it difficult to ask questions in class, or to engage in open discussion sessions. They would construct an interesting question or valuable comment in their mind, but while waiting for a chance to speak, their attention would be focused on how they might come across or whether they'd be able to speak clearly. The standard advice was to focus on their confidence that they had something important to contribute. But the build up of anxiety during the waiting period would often make them feel more and more uncomfortable and these feelings were in exact opposition to being able to think clearly and verbalize their ideas.

Incompatible feelings were part of the original design of systematic desensitization, on the grounds that anxiety and feeling relaxed were incompatible and would thus hasten the extinction of the anxiety. If it is not possible to feel anxious and relaxed at the same time, can progressive muscle relaxation contribute to the extinction effect of repeated imaginal exposure to triggering stimuli? There has long been an assumption one could not be anxious and sexually aroused at the same time, so performance anxiety in males, for example, would mean that while there is emotional arousal, anxiety competes with the physiological requirements of sexual intercourse such as obtaining and maintaining an erection, or of beings so aroused (the sympathetic nervous system) that one experiences "premature" ejaculation. In women, vaginal vasocongestion and vaginal lubrication are controlled by the parasympathetic system as well as being maintained by the neurotransmitter norepinephrine, thus easily disrupted by anxiety. For both men and women, however, as sexual arousal is highly dependent on the presence of appropriate erotic physical stimuli, words, and thoughts, feeling anxious in any way (embarrassment, performance demands) results in that conscious focus of attention now being on the wrong things.

Another good example of the physiological expression of an emotional feeling interfering with automatic reflexive actions is the "shy bladder syndrome." Some men worry when conscious of men waiting behind them for their turn at a urinal. Their anxiety of not being able to urinate readily and quickly causes tension in both the internal and external urethral sphincter, which prevents urinating freely. Difficulty swallowing (pills, or even food) often occurs after one incident of nearly choking and there are hundreds of entries on the internet from adults and parents of children regarding anxiety when swallowing or chewing food. It is sometimes called fear of swallowing, but it is actually a fear of choking, which is a terrifying sensation when something is stuck in the throat and preventing breathing. Anticipatory anxiety about choking directly inhibits normal reflexive swallowing and the fear-of-fear model fits the circumstances very closely (Evans & Pechtel, 2010; Kaplan & Evans, 1978).

Interoceptive (bodily) sensations are part of a feeling state that can be aversive in and of themselves, but it is their expression that can be socially awkward and interfere with performance that is being observed. My model proposed that the critical element of the fear-of-fear phenomenon was when these autonomic responses of anxiety or embarrassment either interfered directly with some usually smooth behavior or would elicit some sort of negative attention in a social context. Van den Hout and colleagues (1987) asked people on a rating scale from zero (no anxiety) to eight (extreme apprehension) of a range of bodily feelings. Such self-reports by patients with anxiety disorders were no different than typical control participants. One exception was shown by those diagnosed with panic disorder. They reported being generally fearful of a raft of bodily sensations, such as palpitations, dizziness, chest pain, trembling, hot flashes, faintness. While many of these autonomic reactions that are part of the expression of fear are intrinsically unpleasant, it is when people have experienced them in public and been embarrassed by them that there is the added anxiety of exhibiting them in the future. People with agoraphobic tendencies engage in many safety-seeking activities, looking for places to escape if need be.

The phenomenon is a consequence of *both* how unpleasant anxiety and fear sensations are and how often they have been experienced in social contexts. We tend to call it fear of fear thanks to the famous comment by Franklin D. Roosevelt's in his inaugural presidential address 1933: "the only thing we have to fear is fear itself." Panic during the great depression had gripped America. But many of the examples I have given are really anxiety about anxiety.

Cognitive Interference

Strong feelings can classically interfere with cognitive tasks as well. One of the best examples is test (exam) anxiety. Fear of failure ironically makes failure more probable. However, there are circumstances in which the opposite is true. Feelings of power, for example, seem to be able to boost a sense of confidence for certain tasks. Feelings of power thus need to derive from the explicit experience of changing something meaningful that appeared not to be under one's control. In people for whom the feeling is limited to certain contexts, such as solving a problem, it is possible to prime a feeling of power simply from words, imposed self-statements, or explicit recall. In one experimental study, a feeling of power was created in two different ways. One prime was asking people to re-arrange jumbled words into a meaningful sentence when the words were power-related, like *control*, or *dominate*. A second induction method was asking participants to write a brief account of a time (incident) they can recall in which they had power over someone else. Generating a feeling of power this way resulted in women participants being less susceptible to stereotype threat-based performance deficits on mathematics tasks (Van Loo & Rydell, 2013).

Some environmental contexts make it difficult to reduce the constant push and pull of stimuli demanding attention. Awareness of this sort of interference can influence the choice of activities one might recommend to a client who is affectively highly aroused. Environmental psychology has offered us clinicians some valuable ideas about what sort of activities clients might select that will have the benefit of being calming and self-soothing. The argument goes (Kaplan, 1995) that some environments necessitate considerable attention to constantly changing conditions—driving, for example, being on your smart phone, and even leisure activities like watching television. They all require wide-band cognitive engagement, and demand direct and effortful attention. Other activities only require attention to "softly fascinating stimuli" and leave room for reflection.

Somewhat predictably, the sorts of activity environmentalists claim will allow time for contemplation, daydreaming, and reflection are things like taking a walk in nature (Basu et al., 2019; Kaplan, 1995). To this, we could probably add activities such as gardening, cooking, and painting, as well as soaking in hot tubs and saunas, running on a treadmill, getting up early to watch a sunrise, or sitting alone and contemplatively in an empty church or temple. It is a useful idea to think of activities that are beneficial to having positive feelings—there's no real rule for every individual, but being able to suggest options with different types of possible benefit seems like a helpful therapeutic tactic.

Incompatible Feelings

Lay people will often talk about love-hate relationships, suggesting that having ambivalent feelings must be quite common. Strong love reactions can turn to strong hate reactions because a failure by a deeply loved person causes more distress than being disappointed by someone whom one barely knows. In military contexts, counteracting feelings are used to manage the inevitable fear of injury or death: everything possible is done to invoke the positive affect feelings of loyalty, patriotism, pride, even the "nobility" of self-sacrifice.

Strong (high arousal, high activation) feelings motivate much behavior, particularly striving to acquire (approach) or lose (avoid) many objects and outcomes. It is equally obvious that strong feelings interfere with the smooth and successful performance of many tasks that are themselves motivated by other strong feelings. To illustrate this conundrum for a therapist, consider one of my clients at a university counseling center some years ago. Kaimanalu, a student in the university's pre-med program, came to the center seeking help with his severe test anxiety. He was being emotionally and financially supported by his family and a local community program. The goal of this community was to increase the number of Native Hawaiian physicians, by identifying bright high school students and offering them support, financial and academic, during their pre-med years. He had just failed a mid-term exam in organic chemistry. Kai reported that his anxiety feelings were so intense that he froze, saying how he just stared at the test pages which seemed meaningless to him. We know that high anxiety in such situations can interfere with crucial cognitive tasks such as attention (especially focus on key relevant elements of the task in front of you) and key problem-solving strategies like self-talk ("What's the problem, what do I have to do here?")

That aspect of his experience was easy for him to describe and easy for me to understand. There were worrying implications for me (therapists worry all the time). He had never failed so badly before; his high-school grades were excellent, which was why he was in the program. So now he was expressing his worry that the same phenomenon would occur the next time. That was a more explicit worry than actually failing this particular course. A make-up test was always possible, and he would even be allowed to retake the course if he failed it outright. But now he wasn't just worried about the test (test anxiety)—he was worried about his test anxiety. A classic fear-of-fear situation. However, I had also asked him, somewhat off handedly, what his hopes for a career as a physician were—what feelings did he have about becoming a doctor, what were his ambitions? The answer was informative. He hadn't ever had feelings like that. He was planning his medical career to please his parents. He wanted them to be proud of him, he feared disappointing them, he felt he had an obligation to follow this path because his community expected it and were helping to finance it. Failure would be a disgrace, quite shameful, but he reassured me that he could tolerate that but couldn't face the disappointment his parents would feel.

This collection of feelings is not conducive to effective study. The goal needs to be more intrinsic, something you want for yourself, something that is interesting to you and that you have passionate feelings for. You study intensely and for long hours because you are absorbed in the material and are exhilarated by the possibilities of this career for helping others. I am just suggesting possible intrinsic motives—there are many feelings that are possible in this situation. But for Kai, the pressure to succeed in something that it turned out he was not fully intrigued by, either for himself or his people, created emotional conflicts that were not conducive to success in passing exams.

How Much Good Feeling Is Too Much?

There are times when the intensity of any feeling, even the best ones, is not beneficial to mental health in the sense of having a good balance of feelings. Intensity, as we will consider in the next chapter, demands the holy grail of *emotion regulation*. As many have suggested, it is the intensity of love and hate as feelings that might contribute to their "shape shifting" ease, one turning into the other in a manner that is surprising at first. Or consider the positive feeling of pride.

Taking pride in one's work, especially when it might seem as a mundane or low-skill activity, is a feeling allowing individuals to set and to strive to achieve personal standards for their work activities independent of external rewards. Self-judging a work output, whatever it may be—graduate paper, cleaning a hotel room, packing boxes for mailing, or pouring concrete foundations for a high-rise—as "good enough" does not produce the feelings of satisfaction most of us enjoy even when doing tasks that we have to do rather than activities we choose for their intrinsic reward value. Pride, which by definition is generated by the feeling person themselves, is a powerful positive feeling for counteracting other negative feelings that might emerge from the difficulty of the task, or highly critical social judgments.

Pride, however, like many of the feelings encountered in this book, is one in which excessive expression is not favored by society. The word hubris is widely used to describe an expression of feeling when it is an extreme or unreasonable degree of pride. When accompanied by arrogant behavior, everyone takes delight in someone's hubris contributing to their decline or upset. And upsets are expected for over-confident people: *pride cometh before a fall* is a handy contraction of the actual biblical phrase from Proverbs, 16:18—"Pride goeth before destruction, and a haughty spirit before a fall." For some reason, gods appear to like people to be humble—humility is valued in most religions. Over and over, we encounter the problem that no feeling is intrinsically bad or good—to serve us well, they must be moderated or modifiable, managed by the person rather than others.

The key to positive pride versus hubris may lie in the extent to which it is not entirely self-focused, such as a person's capacity to feel pride in the achievement of a group. Self-confidence, therefore, can be a provocative feeling. There are lots of times it seems appropriate for clients (like for your own children or graduate students) to have plenty of it. In therapy, I think that the term self-esteem would be considered a more desirable way to label the feeling desired. It is a feeling embedded deep in psychological parlance since we see the harm low self-esteem can have in so many aspects of life, particularly those that society judges as success.

The distinction between feelings for aspects of oneself versus for others is one woven throughout this entire book. Self-esteem is good; selfishness is bad. The difference is the degree to which your feeling disadvantages someone else. Feeling sorry for someone is good (if, as I have argued, it leads to doing constructive actions for that person); feeling sorry for yourself is bad. This seems to be the case even for positive feelings. Empathy is usually considered good, but when empathic feelings are more self-directed, it may be less so. A study relevant to this delicate balance was reported by Jin and colleagues (2025) with a large cohort of preschool teachers in China. They used an adapted version of the Interpersonal Reactivity Index (Davis, 1996), one of the best available self-report measures of empathy. The measure has four sub-scales assessing empathic concern, perspective taking, fantasy (how an imaginal occurrence in a story or novel makes one feel), and personal distress in a harmful situation. In preschool teachers, moderate levels of empathic perspective taking and concern for others allowed teachers to understand and support the feelings of their young pupils. But strong feelings of more self-oriented empathy (fantasy and distress) led to difficulties in boundary setting and emotion regulation as well as emphasizing children's feelings at the expense of emphasizing academic learning. Whether training preschool teachers or clinical psychologists, it might be useful to talk to novices about their feelings for the job, for the client, and for themselves in order for the judgments they make professionally to be balanced between the needed distance and separation from their client's or pupil's concerns and the understanding of their own vulnerabilities and apprehensions.

One Feeling Intensifying Another

The opposite of interference and contradiction is when one feeling serves to exacerbate another. This has already been mentioned implicitly a number of times, especially when thinking about how moods serve to either cloud or intensify feelings of the same general affective valence as the mood. Mood influences memories (in a dark mood, unpleasant incidents from the past are easier to recall) and memories can also be of the feelings, not just the events. There are also chronic feelings, more explicit than moods, that seem to be able to influence the affective value of other feelings. There appear to be different mechanisms for this, so I will first give an example of what I mean and then consider the possibilities.

Let's take the self-conscious feeling that one is being judged. In social situations, one is always subject to probably unconscious evaluations by others in one's company. These affective, attitudinal reactions from one's audience are usually minor and of no importance. But if the audience, through words or nonverbal behavior, gives the impression that one is being judged negatively, it is an unpleasant feeling. But feeling judged when there is no evidence or likelihood of a negative evaluation from the people you are with is an unnecessary and problematic feeling. It is common in people with high general social anxiety—whether a cause or a consequence of their social anxiety is a largely unanswerable question, since the two feelings interact: I feel anxious/I feel judged are two feelings that feed off each other.

That is one way that one feeling intensifies another. But sensitivity to feeling being judged (negatively) can be taken further back to other feelings. Let's start with the context in which one actually is being evaluated. While it can be stressful for all of us knowing we are being evaluated on specific criteria (such as a job interview, or one's creative output being judged, or one's sport performance being timed), the occasion is so common an experience that most people are able to accept this without negative feelings as a standard part of life. When there is doubt about the fairness of the evaluation (biased judges are not uncommon and sources of bias in evaluations are legion), being judged negatively evokes anger. Feelings of being judged and feelings of anger feed off each other.

Feeling judged can generalize beyond the criteria being applied to feeling it is one's personal worth that is being judged, and one's general value is being evaluated. Why does this generalization happen? It appears to be related to strong individual needs to be liked and accepted by others. A need for acceptance and a fear of rejection are two interpretations of the same underlying affect. As mentioned, there is an evolutionary basis for the importance of being accepted in order to have feelings of security. So, there is another circular, catalytic relationship among feelings: feeling insecure—fear of rejection—being judged negatively for who you are—feeling criticized—being hypervigilant for signs of what others think about you—wanting to be liked and accepted—feeling insecure. Clients who have been diagnosed with Borderline Personality Disorder are classically caught up in this web of related feelings. Sensitive therapists, teachers, parents, and romantic partners are all aware that criticism of someone, even if deserved, can signal rejection, which for some children and adults is a painful, threatening experience. Whether patterns of criticism and evaluation early in development contribute to this vulnerability are not known, but it does seem likely that harsh, critical upbringing plays some sort of role in these vulnerable feelings. The nature of the criticism and its deservedness is important, as is children's understanding. For example, children whose emotion competence had developed to the level of understanding that people can have conflicting feeling simultaneously (mixed emotions) were less likely to show resentment of teacher criticism (Cutting & Dunn, 2002). However, children with the highest social/emotional competence levels (better able to take the perspective of others and to identify other's emotions) showed the highest sensitivity to criticism. Cutting and Dunn (2002) are not sure sensitivity to criticism is a bad thing. They ask: "Do children with greater socio-cognitive skills early in life have more fragile self-esteem at a later date, for example? These children may be more sensitive to criticism, but is that damaging, or actually a useful learning experience for an able child?" (p. 857).

A further confusion regarding self-conscious feelings is that one can have feelings about oneself as an individual. Consider self-congratulatory feelings. If focused on a particular *achievement*, such feelings can be considered to be pride. That is an appropriate feeling typically and being positive serves as self-reward. When focused only on the self, we encounter feelings of smugness and inflated self-evaluation. Expression of these feelings to others (even if they have some merit) is not favored in some cultures. In New Zealand, boastful, self-important individuals are labelled "tall poppies," and there is an implicit feeling that they should be quickly cut down to size! Self-criticism is perhaps the opposite and, in some ways, a more damaging feeling, since we know these feelings feature strongly in syndromes like depression. Young women in Spain, who had experienced a background of family insecurity (they reported "Threats of separation, moving to another place, or breaking family ties are part of my childhood memories"), revealed a strong connection between self-criticism and feelings of body dissatisfaction (a subscale of the *Eating Disorders Inventory-2*) (Momeñe et al., 2023). And having feelings of self-compassion appears to be the active ingredient of a mindfulness training exercise. A large-scale study was conducted in Vietnan by Tran and colleagues (Tran et al., 2024) during the COVID-19 pandemic. This was a time of increased anxiety, depression, and stress in university students and the authors showed that reductions in these feelings after a mindfulness training program were mediated by enhanced feelings of self-compassion.

Feelings as Signals

With Chapter 6, it seemed that we have covered all possible aspects of what triggers feelings, and in Chapter 3, we have linked the expression of feelings to specific action tendencies and urges. The essential argument is that these tendencies are directly connected to the feeling and designed to reduce the feeling if negative, and to enhance it if positive. What has not been directly addressed is the role of feeling expressions themselves being a signaling system for subsequent cognitive processes such as choice, decision making, and judgment. CBT has become so entrenched in thinking that cognition causes feelings that we have slightly neglected the obvious: feelings cause cognitions!

In the formal experimental psychology literature, this relationship is known as the *affective signaling hypothesis*. It is mostly studied in the context of cognitive conflict situations. Such conflicts are thought to elicit a generally negative feeling. Its content (logic) is hard to describe, but its effect might be due to both valence (its negativity) and arousal (when it is heightened). Negative affect signals the need for cognitive control. Conventionally, when one is pursuing a goal, the presence of affect is a distraction, and one tries to ignore and control it. The alternative idea states that feelings convey important information about our inner life and thus have a signaling function over many cognitive processes (see Dreisbach & Fischer, 2015). The topic is usually discussed in the context of conflict and error monitoring (Dignath et al., 2020). By this it meant *cognitive* conflict, not the interpersonal ones that are usually of greater interest to clinicians. However, we have various approaches to dealing with interpersonal conflicts and the beginning of negative feelings early in such situations can also serve a signaling function, if attended to. Thus, individuals who are having difficulty managing interpersonal and relationship conflicts could be taught to be more quickly aware of a growing feeling of distress (anger, unfairness, dislike). This can be a signal to change tactics, reduce challenging language, and focus cognitively on what the conflict is actually all about.

Implications

Feelings about feelings might sound like a bit of a head-scratcher. Yet we encounter the phenomenon every day. Some clients find their own expression of pleasure to be uncomfortable, or that a feeling of desire feels unpleasant, because both are judged morally wrong. Some clients feel embarrassed when they feel and express excitement. Some feel enjoyment over a bit of misery. These conflicting or contrary feelings arise from different logics. One feeling is triggered by a certain situation and the presence of this feeling is judged according to another rule or stimulus situation, often social teaching about what displays of feeling are socially appropriate and which are not.

In this chapter, there was particular attention focused on the feeling of fear, as well as the "fear of fear" phenomenon. Its various manifestations offer good examples of the phenomenon of linked feelings because it is always the specific physiological expression of the feeling that is the direct trigger for another feeling. Both the feelings from the autonomic nervous system responses and the disruptive effect of emotional arousal on motor and cognitive performance become aversive. Shaking, blushing, dry mouth, blanking out, sweating, losing an erection, and so on produce interoceptive sensations felt by the individual and easily observable by others.

Eysenck might have argued that probably after one really bad experience, further exposure in perfectly safe situations would not result in extinction of the fear because the conditioned emotional reaction is so unpleasant that they are reconditioned or re-sensitized every time they are again exposed: dogs *should* be feared because every time you see one you feel scared and want to run away; travel by plane is to be dreaded because every time you fly you feel terrified. Fear is incubated by its own aversiveness. I would modify that somewhat by arguing that while fear might feel terribly bad, it is its ability to interfere with socially desirable performance that makes it so aversive, because other fear feelings that are socially acceptable can be enjoyed in other contexts and situations, for example by people who like rollercoasters. Other theorists argue that anxiety results in vigilance for messages of harm (M. Eysenck & Calvo, 1992)—which is also true, but there is also increased searching for situations that feel safe. Steven Hayes (Hayes et al., 1994) might say just feel that unpleasant feeling, don't fight it, don't avoid it.

The literature provides a sort of blend of all these notions: that fearful clients *do* overestimate the link between the stimuli feared and possible aversive consequences of experiencing them ("illusory correlations" we call it), and that biased appraisal *does* come about because the link is expected (a cognition) and the outcome (the fear) *is* itself aversive. I think because you avoid these stimuli as much as possible you don't allow an opportunity to experience safe exposure, and then when you can't avoid it, you find the emotional experience to be highly aversive, not pleasurably exciting.

Cognitive-behavioral psychotherapy for fears, then, has a wide variety of plausible possible tactics. When they're effective, they seem to have these common elements that you can always use: (1) Lower expectations of harm as best you can by telling and persuading the client that their appraisal of the true risk is false, but agree that their fearful feelings about it are real and unpleasant. (2) Explain that if they keep focusing on those feelings, they won't go away. (3) Argue that if they can think differently and thus feel differently about these feelings through various means, even coming to accept them, the feelings won't seem so bad. (4) And so, they should focus on no longer avoiding things they would actually like to do, and exposing themselves as much as possible and as long as the negative feelings are not debilitating. (5) Or, if these things are not that important to them or others, stop trying to engage in them and seek other situations and activities that do give you pleasure and meet your personal goals and ideals about what a good life means. There you have it: therapy for irrational fear in five simple sentences. How you enact them, how you skin the cat, is open, as long as they meet those five conditions. This describes feelings change strategies within the supportive, accepting, and sometimes nurturing environment of individual therapy—it is therapist-directed influence. What can clients do for themselves? We need now to turn to the other side of deliberate change: self-initiated and self-regulatory influences.

8

Self-Regulation of Feelings

Orientation

During World War I, there was a popular British army marching song, with lyrics by George Henry Powell that I heard often growing up because my father, who was born just before that war began, used to sing it around the house when I was a child:

What's the use of worrying
It never was worthwhile,
So, pack up your troubles in your old kit bag
And smile, smile, smile.

It has three lessons for us: worry serves no good function; feelings can be put aside; and one way to do that is to express a contrary feeling. Actually, singing this cheerfully dismissive song helps as well. On social media like Tik-Tok and YouTube, there are literally hundreds of videos of Winnie the Pooh humming and singing songs to build his—and thus his child audience's—self-confidence. In Chapter 4, I argued that a major element of emotion competence as it develops in children is their being able to manage and regulate their feelings themselves to some extent. In Chapter 5, there is a discussion of the pro-social context of feelings with the essential regulatory ability to reveal or hide one's feelings. In Chapter 6, we explored the control of feelings by the stimuli (internal and external) that elicit them, and in Chapter 7, we saw, among other things, how some feelings can have counteractive influences on others, as well as negatively interfere with and constrain constructive and desired behaviors. All of them relate directly to the big question in this chapter of how we can regulate our feelings in a manner that will contribute to desired emotional states and affect-laden valued behaviors. The topic has been brought into even greater focus than before because at least one major direction in CBT, ACT, has as a grounding theoretical principle that it is our struggle to regulate, control, or manage feelings which is the problem, not the solution. However, that cannot apply to one of the major

How and Why Feelings Change. Ian M. Evans, Oxford University Press. © Ian M. Evans (2026).
DOI: 10.1093/9780197825808.003.0009

contexts for emotion regulation—social. When interacting with others, particularly in potential conflict situations, we all need to be continually controlling and regulating our feelings in order to sustain meaningful social relationships, particularly intimate ones.

This chapter would appear to fit in with one of the oldest primary intervention methods in CBT—self-control (Rachlin, 2000). Teaching clients self-management skills is a viable treatment approach for controlling unwelcome and excessive behavior. However, managing feelings is different from the general area of self-control because that topic mostly focuses on managing the behaviors (the action tendencies) resulting from feelings. Supporting environmental, contextual, and lifestyle change is a key feature of all traditional behavioral therapy (Evans, 2005). How to make such changes oneself involves tactics collectively called self-modification (Watson & Tharp, 1977/2007). These wide-ranging techniques include goal-setting, self-observation and recording, self-reward, rehearsing alternative self-talk and cognitions. As children learn motor skills, social behavior, and language, they learn important social abilities such as waiting one's turn, considering the needs of others, good table manners so as not to offend. They learn basic safety rules like looking both ways and not dashing across the road, not touching a stove, and not shooting a toy arrow in the air. All this learning requires complex inhibitory mechanisms as well as learning promotional actions. Play a game like "Simon Says" with four-year-olds and you will quickly see inhibitory mechanisms in action—or not. These inhibitory skills do require feelings regulation, often some modulation of the feeling of excitement: not too high as to be silly, and not so low as to not have any fun.

Self-regulation and control of feelings, therefore, do not include the broad array of behavior management strategies such as learning and applying coping and problem-solving skills. Learning to delay gratification is a popular topic that falls somewhere in between. When Walter Mischel and students (1972) published their findings of the famous marshmallow study of preschool children, it told a great story, often repeated: children differ in their ability to delay gratification. A strategy that assisted them was distraction, such as thinking about fun activities. On the other hand, imagining how good the marshmallow would taste was very unhelpful—savoring is bad in these situations. It was also important to believe the promise of the larger later reward. Thus, there are cognitive expectancy elements in the social paradigm of the marshmallow experiment. The comfortingly optimistic story that the children's ability to delay gratification predicts later feelings of self-worth, coping with stress, and academic success has not withstood critical evaluation.

This chapter must focus more on altering external circumstances, both the immediate antecedents of an undesirable response and the broad environmental changes that are potentially at least within our capabilities. This refers to changing ecologies, situations, and circumstances, including relationships, lifestyles, and one's socio-cultural group, but also to changing more specific behavioral routines and daily habits. However, a thesis of the present book is that feelings are less under our voluntary control than clients and even therapists might hope for. They're very reactive. Some people do cope with many forms of adversity which have the potential to induce severe negative feelings and emotional disorders (considered in the next chapter). And people are more likely to become clients if they lack these types of self-regulatory ability. So, teaching strategies of emotion management is surely a good idea. At the same time, we must take seriously the ACT paradox: sometimes it's struggling to control and minimize negative feelings that sustain the distress.

One of the confusions in the literature, which I am going to try to avoid, is that much of the emotion regulation literature focuses only on voluntary attempts to manage *negative* emotions (Thompson, 1994; Werner & Gross, 2010). It includes methods that seem designed to change the valence of unpleasant feelings along with efforts to limit both emotional arousal and the subsequent action tendencies. But the best definition of emotion regulation includes both negative and positive feelings: "the processes by which individuals influence which emotions they have, when they have them, and how they experience and express these emotions" (Gross, 1998, p. 275). That seems to cover everything. In interpersonal conflict situations, for instance, identified emotion regulation strategies are disengagement (concealment of emotions, being dismissive, and suggesting superficial solutions), aversive cognitive perseveration (ruminating, exaggerated emotional expression, and self-focused thoughts), and adaptive engagement (self-assured expression and acknowledgement of feelings, encouraging discussion and problem-solving focused on positive solutions rather than causes) (Low et al., 2019).

If one looks at "emotion regulation" questionnaires, one gets further insight into what is included in researchers' conceptualization. *The Difficulties in Emotion Regulation Scale* (Gratz & Roemer, 2004), for example, has six factors which doubtless reflect the items selected: (1) non-acceptance of emotional responses (feeling bad about feeling bad); (2) difficulties in engaging in goal-directed behavior ("I can't concentrate on other things when upset"); (3) impulse control difficulties ("I lose control when upset; I experience emotions as overwhelming"); (4) lack of emotional awareness ("I don't pay attention to feelings"); (5) limited access to emotion regulation strategies; and (6) lack of emotional clarity ("I have no idea how I'm feeling." "I have difficulty making sense of feelings"). Like other approaches to emotion regulation, the list contains issues related to (a) what I have been calling emotion competence (understanding your own and others' feelings and being able to regulate feelings by enhancing the good ones and damping down the bad), and (b) the behavioral consequences of having strong feelings—inhibiting desired goal-related actions (approach), facilitating undesired ones (avoidance), or facilitating undesired actions designed to reduce negative affect directly. Sadly, it does not include the all important domain of being able to increase, further enhance, and relish positive feelings.

Back to the Children

It will be clear by now that emotion regulation should not mean suppressing feelings. Thus far, I have been implicitly assuming the functionalist perspective on emotion regulation which gives it the role of maintaining a level of arousal and a balance of valence that is tolerable to the individual and flexible enough to support adaptive behavior (Campos et al., 1989). Karma Galyer and I (Galyer & Evans, 2001) explored this skill in 4–5-year-old preschool children with a pretend play game borrowed from previous research. Active pretend play—just like rough and tumble games previously mentioned—is an ideal context for children to gain mastery of feelings in a safe environment (Bretherton, 1989). Our procedure involved us playing a pretend game using a variety of toys (building blocks, farm animals, toy figures). The game was controlled entirely by the child with occasional prompts. The session was videotaped and later scored objectively. After about ten minutes of play, one of us introduced a crocodile glove puppet, muttering "I'm going to eat everything up" and then grabbing the toys in his mouth. This was much more fun for us than it was for the children, and it certainly activated emotional arousal for nearly all of them. There was high excitement, squealing, and telling the crocodile off. The children's range of responses was fascinating: some were upset and withdrew, some tried to whack the crocodile aggressively, a few ignored it and carried on playing with what toys the crocodile had not managed to grab, some said it wasn't a worry because the crocodile was friendly and just wanted play, some said the crocodile had no teeth. You can immediately see that the best indicator of functional management of feelings was to get excited, imagine the crocodile to be harmless or friendly, and continue to play with the grown-ups by allowing the crocodile into the ongoing pretense. The children who participated in this way were those who had shown good pretend play skills previously and who were reported by their parents to be engaged frequently with their families in make-believe games. Not surprisingly, the quality of pretend play in early childhood also correlates with general social competence (Smits-van der Nat et al., 2024). Studies do not yet determine any causal direction or whether emotion regulation skills mediate the relationship, which is what I would expect.

In a later study, Galyer used an imaginative game to examine how a balance between ignoring a situation and getting over-excited by it was functional by allowing young children to continue playing and interacting socially with an adult (Evans & Galyer, 2009). We were interested in how 4 to 5-year-old kindergarten children managed feelings of uncertainty and the effects of reassuring information. Galyer used an activity that had been described previously by Golomb and

Galasso (1995). The procedure involved playing a game with each child individually. At the beginning of the play session, they were shown an empty box and were reminded it was empty. Then a lid was placed on it, and it was put aside in full sight of the children. Halfway through the play, the adult picked up the box, put it to her ear and said, "Ooh, I can hear something. It sounds like a kitten (or baby dragon). I can hear it purring (or growling)." The children were asked if they would like to listen and some of them did so and continued the pretense by saying they could hear purring or growling. Some of them said confidently it was only a baby dragon, and it couldn't hurt anyone. They were then given a visual, verbal, or no reminder that it was just a pretend game. The box was then put down and the previous play resumed. Some children continued the original game and ignored the mystery box. Some switched to talking about what would happen if the kitten or dragon got out. Some could not contain themselves and lunged for the box, desperately trying to open it. Only the tactic of showing the children that the box was still empty was effective in reducing their feelings of uncertainty and allowed them to continue to play the original game with a friendly adult. Parents often try to give anxious children verbal reassurance about the absence of dangers or bad things happening, but direct experience is potentially much more valuable.

Teaching self-regulation of feelings to children is not a single instructional procedure. It requires repeated learning trials, just like teaching and modeling the basic manners of your culture. Each family, culture, or society has such rules that are specific, even if they have to be repeated over and over again before they become habits. Learning the self-regulation of feelings to meet social expectations, however, requires knowledge of the context, the arousal level that is appropriate, and an understanding of the logic of the feeling. Dressing up, make believe, and fantasy allow for the rehearsal of these competencies in a safe context and offer excellent opportunities for children to understand feelings of others and ways of mastering the negative ones. And to learn new rules from stories. If, for example, you are by yourself and taking a basket of food to your ailing grandmother, you should always be sure to check her teeth and her ears when you arrive and if they don't look quite right, express surprise, and run like hell. Imaginative play requires suspension of physical reality and thus actual harm: a stick becomes a sword, a paper hat a crown, and dolls have names and need medical attention.

In a major summary of his and other's work in emotion theory, and its implications for preventative interventions, Izard (2002) wrote "*Whereas interest engages and sustains the child in exploratory play and gamelike activities, joy provides the reward for the work of play that leads to the achievement of mastery and a variety of skills. Object play has substantial benefits for the development of fine motor and perceptual skills, rough and tumble play for gross motor skills, and pretend play, games with rules and other social play for affective-cognitive skills associated with emotion knowledge and emotion regulation*" (p. 799). Every therapist can offer these words to parents.

Methods and Forms of Control and Regulation

There are four different psychological phenomena that can be identified within the psychology of emotion regulation and (self-)control of feelings.

(1) The first is one mostly explored by neuroscientists. It is about brain mechanisms that might be involved in emotional activation (arousal) when needed, and emotion reduction when not. It is also about what regulates the valence: the replacement of dysfunctional negative affect by positive emotions that increase pleasure by allowing pleasurable activities. Knowing that there are centers and pathways in the brain specialized for dealing with pleasure gives special emphasis to this feeling valence. Does the dampening down of negative emotions require the activation of positive ones, and what inhibitory processes are there to prevent even positive emotions from escalating? (Positive emotions often do escalate, as you know if you have ever been to a birthday party for five-year-olds.) These emotion control questions relate to neural processes and pathways and are not, therefore, subject to conscious experience or control, but the capability of the brain to regulate emotions is thought to be laid down early in development and greatly influenced by the behavioral interactions (bonding) between infants and toddlers and their primary caregivers (Chapter 4). The control is not exactly what psychologists mean by self-control, but more like brain control of itself, incorporating neural processes like homeostasis and habituation, specific inhibitory neurons, and the dampening down of others by neurotransmitter hormones.

(2) The second type of emotion regulation is more clearly *self*-relevant, and it is the deliberate control of contexts, environments, situations, and stimuli that *elicit* emotions. The focus is on the input side of the event and setting up processes like a valve that can turn an emotion on or off for some period of time. It is an on/off valve coming before the tap (faucet). But the control mechanism of the tap also allows one to turn on either hot or cold feelings. If you engage in an activity or even a thought that makes you feel calm and relaxed, you are turning the valve and the tap so the output is a mere warm trickle. Thus, these types of regulatory activities typically favor one feeling gaining ascendance over another through stimulus change (from contexts, thoughts, and memories).

There are, of course, processes of self-soothing an emotional reaction that do not require an explicit strategy or conscious self-control, and these can be seen in infants and toddlers. Babies differ—notoriously, as any parent of more than one child will tell you—in their capacity to self-sooth. Originally, this ability was seen as part of the nine traits specified in the original descriptions of temperament by Thomas and Chess (1977). It contributes to the differences between infants labelled easy as opposed to those described as difficult. As infant temperament came to be seen as an interaction between child characteristics and parental (maternal) responding, it depended on the work of Goldsmith and Campos (1990) to see "temperament as individual differences in tendencies to express the primary emotions" (p. 1945). And temperamental tendencies, far from being present at birth and stable over time, vary across time and situations and, like attachment, are closely related to the responses of the primary caregiver. Nevertheless, there are clear individual differences in infants and toddler's ability to "sooth" themselves, and this in turn influences the responses of the caregivers, who also vary in their skills and strategies for managing babies' affective reactions of distress, tiredness, hunger, boredom, frustration, and so on. In an excellent study, Stern and others (2023) showed that mothers who were capable of recognizing basic positive emotions in their newborn infants (e.g., happiness) showed greater sensitivity in play interactions five months later. Sensitivity was coded using the Ainsworth Sensitivity Scales (see Chapter 4).

(3) The third type of emotion control is the one focused on the *expression* of the emotion as well as the inhibition of expression and actions the emotion usually leads to. It doesn't turn down the feeling—it doesn't affect the pressure controlled by the valve or the warmth controlled by the tap—but it stops the feeling from being displayed and the behavioral consequences of the feeling from being activated. That's a bit like blocking the shower head so nothing comes out even though all the taps are turned on. The urge to actively respond is still there, but the expression and the action tendency are both inhibited. It can also involve the learning of alternative behaviors in response to an unchanged feeling, like feeling angry but changing the action tendency from hitting to assertion. That's like changing the flow from going to the shower head and going to a smaller hand-held shower instead. Teaching pro-social alternatives that have the same function as an undesirable challenging behavior (such as verbally communicating a feeling) is a key component of educative and positive behavior management in children with disabilities (Carr & Durand, 1985). When we talk about self-control in education and behavior therapy, it usually only means controlling or altering the action tendency from the emotion.

(4) The fourth important consideration is personality. We don't want to think only about how an individual manages to control one feeling in one situation. We need to understand the characteristic self-control exercised in all situations. Are some people emotionally more reactive than others? Do they

have less "water pressure" to begin with or valves and taps that are stiff and difficult to turn? I've already explained that all personality theorists would say yes. Ever since Eysenck proposed his theory, we have thought of people all differing on a dimension in which the pressure, the valves, the taps and flow direction are all erratic—unstable, we say.

Thus, with the emotion of anger as an illustration: (1) the neural mechanisms can work to calm it down (this is a non-conscious, involuntary process that is an intrinsic part of brain function); (2) a behavioral mechanism can voluntarily implement things taught by a therapist when feeling anger like calming self-talk, removal from the situation, taking a deep relaxation breath; or (3) the person can exert inhibitory self-control over the expression of anger (the poker-faced, stiff deportment of the soldier being unfairly criticized by the sergeant-major, or the bland in-the-moment non-reaction of the practitioner of mindfulness meditation); (4) the person can take drugs to decrease arousal and enhance inhibition, and learn to avoid high stress situations. Neuropsychologists would probably argue that (4) can be explained by (1) and that you need at least some of the elements of (1) to do either (2) or (3); ACT and DBT would basically favor (3) the uncoupling of emotion and typical action; and traditional BT and CT would emphasize coping strategies and problem-solving strategies to modify the sources of emotion and rehearse alternative actions, as in (2). By now, the reader might agree it doesn't have to be one or the other—that's psychological flexibility on the part of a good therapist! In addition, how does it help a therapist work with an angry teenager still living at home to know that parents' failure to understand and accept adolescent anger not only reduces teens' ability to manage angry feelings but also changes the parents' reactions towards the young person generally? This is the age-old truth of negative bidirectional relationships sustaining family conflict (Otterpohl et al., 2022).

The capacity (physiologically) to be able to modulate both the arousal and the valence dimensions of personal feelings is acquired in early development. By the time any individual, whether a child, a teen, or an adult, becomes a client, the capacity is more like a trait than an isolated skill. And it seems more like a disorder when it would be preferable to have a more even keel than a highly reactive system, to have an emotionally mellow temperament, and to be able to both keep calm in a crisis and also be excited when good things are happening around you. That is what we can call "good" emotional regulation, which always implicitly means by the individuals themselves rather than someone else. Gross and Muñoz (1995) offered a helpful definition of what we're talking about here:

> *The regulation of emotions ... concerns our attempts to influence which emotions we have and how these emotions are expressed. Somewhat more formally, we define the process of emotion regulation as the manipulation in*

> *self or others of either emotion antecedents or one or more of the components of an emotional response—behavioral, subjective, or physiological.* (Gross & Muñoz, 1995, pp. 152–153)

There is one perplexing issue. I've been constantly differentiating—not always consistently—emotions and feelings. So here's the question: is the self-control of feelings different from the self-control of emotions? Let's think of anger because anger *management* is a well-known therapeutic modality. We've already looked at the stimuli that elicit different types and degrees of angry feelings—from being disrespected to having one's goals being thwarted. Imagine a client who admits to being chronically angry at work because he feels his boss is overly critical. One could ask: "How would you feel if *I* criticized you? I've sometimes challenged the things you say and do. How does that make you feel?" You might get the answer "Sometimes it was annoying and made me feel bad, but I know you're on my side and trying to help me, not hurt me. When you called it feedback, it was still hard to take at first, but I realized it was exactly what I needed to make some life changes." From there, you can easily explore whether the client's boss has evil intent, or is trying to be helpful, or is just socially unskilled in giving feedback, and whether the boss has any redeeming features that would compensate for their poor management skills. All that sort of information will guide your suggestions to this client.

What Are We Trying to Regulate?

The standard model when discussing emotion regulation as a psychological construct is to rely on the excellent and authoritative work of James Gross (2015; Gross & Ford, 2024). It is referred to as a process model of emotion regulation as it identifies five strategies that can be introduced at different points in the emotion process. Briefly, the five processes (remembering they are conceptualized as voluntary things a client can actually do) are stimulus selection, situation alteration, attention deployment (focusing or distracting), cognitive change (reinterpreting or altering your thoughts about a situation), and response modulation. The first four of these focus on antecedents, and the last one is focused on the response. That means it's a large category and can mean anything from the physiological responses you feel, to their expression via face, body, vocal tone, to all the responses that occur after the feeling (the action tendencies).

And as we have seen, many of those actions are really designed to alleviate negative feelings. When they do, they are reinforced even if their long-term consequences are negative for the person. These behaviors of "negative urgency" are often the ones that come to clinical attention. From the present perspective on how feelings change, this comprehensive model is over-inclusive, even though it encompasses many valuable intervention techniques and the psycho-education we provide clients about their emotions. It might be helpful to go back to just thinking about the feelings. How do we conceptualize them?

If we were to think of a feeling like any other response, we can imagine it has a latency (how quickly it is elicited), it has a rise time (how long it takes to reach its peak level), it has a magnitude (the height of the response curve compared to the maximum possible), and it has a decay time (how long it takes to decline from its maximum level to its previous resting level). Any one of these parameters can vary and thus the overall strength and duration of a feeling can be judged. But sensitivity might be reflected only by one dimension, say the speed of the response or how long it is before it goes away (equilibrium, the return to resting levels of any physiological change). People who are considered unstable (when we are talking about negative feelings) or sensitive (when we are talking about the moral and self-referenced feelings) might differ from others on any of these dimensions, but we don't really know and most often judge the strength of their feeling from the highly reactive and socially influenced phenomena such as facial expression, words spoken, and actions taken.

Before going further, I need to remind the reader that as we saw in Chapter 1, the word *arousal* has been defined and operationalized in many different ways (K. Smith et al, 2025). It covers related terms like activation, energy, excitement, and ANS levels. I'm using it here in a general sense as a hypothetical construct related to the sense of stirring something up, so that a feeling's quantity or intensity can go from nothing at all to low, to high, to through the roof—a basic scientific scale of quantity!

Processes like self-soothing or telling people to calm down presumably relate to returning to previous levels, which can be low or non-existent. Tactics like avoidance of triggering stimuli relate to the sensitivity to elicitation, getting it going. Stopping a feeling from reaching a peak level of arousal (for negative feelings) or getting one to a peak level (positive feelings) require strategies around focused attention (shifting attention with negative feelings and savoring strategies with positive ones). Sensitivity to the trigger (speed of reaction) can possibly serve as a signal function and assist an individual make a more rapid avoidance or removal of a stimulus before the feeling has a chance to grow. In marital conflict situations, one person might be responsive to early feedback: "I can feel I'm getting angry. That's not necessary. The issue is trivial; I've got to find a way of backing off before I get really mad and say something I regret." But if sensitivity means that a client has hundreds of possible versions of a feeling trigger, then the strategy needs to be discrimination training—learning which versions of the trigger are inconsequential and not worth bothering with. Clients should save their feeling for the major element of the situation, the one that is truly influential. Insults, for example, always vary from the minor, possibly slightly accurate and humorous, to the major, hurtful cutting remarks that threaten your self-concept or insult your family or someone or something else you love. People who are judged to be overly sensitive to criticism react in the same way to all levels of nastiness in the insult. Some people are simply more easily disturbed by criticism of any kind. In intimate relationships, you learn how to give a partner feedback about things that upset you without making the feedback sound like criticism. Parents learn to say: "I'm not saying you are a bad person; I'm saying your behavior was bad." We generally think that that sort of reprimand is more focused and more effective and less likely to harm a child's feelings of self-esteem. All of these matters are widely understood, but by placing them in the context of feelings control, we have a clearer rationale for what we are trying to do in social interactions that involve feelings.

Thinking of the feeling response this way also alerts us to another obvious issue. We are talking about the arousal level of the feeling (its affective strength) regardless of its valence (how good or bad it feels). It is likely that the arousal level of the feeling is influenced by the general arousal level of the individual, either biologically related as Eysenck argued, like a trait, or from current circumstances, like a state, or both. If someone who is already stressed is exposed to a stressful environment, the feeling arousal will be earlier, faster, higher, and longer lasting than if they are not. In conditions like this, one begins to see how certain substances, both medical and recreational, might be called for to lower background affective arousal levels. If you think of the above model of feelings rising and falling, the background, either in terms of chronically stressful conditions or the trait of reactivity essentially refers to the resting level (baseline arousal) before the eliciting stimulus.

Sensitivity Also Refers to Variable Contexts

Just when you thought it might be safe to go back into the water, there is another terminological confusion lurking out in the deep. The research literature on emotion-regulation strategies typically lists a variety of things people do when anxious or depressed, irrespective of whether these "strategies" are helpful or make matters worse. Daniel and colleagues (2025), for example, conducted an ecological-momentary-assessment (EMA) study to investigate whether people with high social anxiety switched from one strategy to another. That is considered to be an undesirable approach to emotion regulation, particularly if people do not give any one strategy enough time for it to be helpful. In their study, they enquired into nineteen "unique" emotion regulation strategies by surveying each participant randomly six times a day to find out what they were doing. The anomaly is that the strategy items included ruminating, planning, thinking differently, drinking, eating, exercising, watching TV, sleeping, getting comfort from others, avoiding people, and so on. These are indeed things people do, but whether they regulate emotion depends on how and when they do them. And from the perspective of this book, most of these strategies have nothing to do with regulating feelings. Some of those strategies I would consider to be efforts to reduce negative feelings that might work short-term but are not permanent changes—like drinking alcohol or eating high calorie snacks. In the current context, these activities are judged as highly negative action tendencies to modify bad feelings. This is not a criticism of the study or its potential value. EMA is a valuable but difficult research methodology, and it is good to see it being used. I'm only pointing out that when our focus is clinical—on why feelings change and how to change them—the "emotion regulation" literature can be far too macro an approach to be of much relevance. If someone has social anxiety, it is probably only when in a discrete and identifiable social situation that their negative feelings are an issue and have to be regulated in order to ensure approach rather than avoidance (if social approach—dating, making friends, joining a group—is the desired goal, which it usually is).

For both self-control and self-regulation, the "self" part refers to some sort of action, including thoughts, that will enable a person to increase or decrease a feeling like one would turn up or down a thermostat or a volume control. There is another rather intriguing element to this. We are all, whether therapist or just some influential person, capable of influencing another person's feelings. On a long-term basis, this is what this book is about. On a temporary shorter-term basis that we hope to become more enduring, however, it is very easy to increase, decrease, or change the valence of someone's feelings. But perhaps not for every person and perhaps not for every situation. And that means there may be individual differences, of huge importance, as to whether a client is susceptible to the efforts of a therapist to regulate their emotion in the short term. It may not be a matter of whether you have the technique, but whether the client is predisposed to change a feeling in response to a therapeutic message or other type of intervention.

As I have argued, the most immediate clinical decision to address is whether we are attempting to actually reduce the negative feeling (the subjective experience and also its autonomic manifestations) or whether we are really trying to teach self-regulation of the potentially harmful overt responses (the action tendencies or behavioral impulses in neuropsychology parlance) that accompany the feeling. Is the goal to manage, reduce, or redirect the avoidance and escape from social and functional life activities in the case of anxiety, the aggression and violent acts in the case of anger, and the withdrawal from pleasurable and needed activities in the case of hopelessness (depression)? The focus is not always clear.

Izard et al. (2008) provided detailed examples of the difference between emotion regulation being a reduction of the feeling and what they call "emotion utilization," using the energy and motivation of the emotion for positive behaviors. Anger arousal can be utilized for positive assertive behavior rather than yelling or hitting. Sadness feelings can be used by teenagers to reach out for support from peers or family members rather than withdrawing from whatever social situation is causing the sad feelings. When we teach a disruptive child to control their anger, we are not directly trying to reduce their experience of anger, nor their blood pressure, muscle tension, or even facial expressions. We are trying to get them to stop hitting or kicking their peers, throwing objects, or shouting profanities at their teachers. "Calm down" as a command to a four-year-old doesn't mean "don't *feel* any anger," it means "stop biting your sister." "Take a deep breath," as a command to exert better control, might be helpful in reducing the autonomic reflexes but it also interrupts any more overt physical reactions.

The idea of emotion utilization provides some nuanced concepts for the design of interventions with young children. An outburst of angry feelings, such as a temper tantrum in a child, does provide a good feeling context for suggesting other positive behavior, including providing an explanation of what they are feeling. One of the most important strategies a parent can use is to encourage the child to verbalize what they are feeling. "Use your words!" is an excellent directive. But if they are overly agitated and reactive, turning down the feeling thermostat could be a useful precursor to using their words. So instructions like "Take a deep breath" or "Hug yourself tight" are effective. I have heard preschool teachers tell children with severe temper outburst to think of themselves like a kettle on a hot stove get hotter and hotter until it burst into steam and the lid flies off ("Keep your lid on" is a common remark in Britain to someone getting angry, usually serving to antagonize them further). Children are then told to take the kettle off the stove or turn down the heat. As Hawai'i is famous for having an active volcano, depiction of fiery eruptions is quite common, so with one child diagnosed with Disruptive Mood Dysregulation Disorder, I compared his outbursts to a volcanic eruption, using the image of bubbling molten lava rising to the surface. "Find a little crack, a little vent, and let the steam escape, and feel that hot lava settle back down inside you." He also drew a picture of a volcano for me and the metaphor became a useful reminder for him to cool down *before* the pressure inside him built up to a point he could no longer control it. I acknowledged that he still had feelings, but they could be regulated. Then he could use his words, and then he could solicit assistance from someone to manage the situation that had provoked the anger in the first place. That later component would be more like a formal problem-solving teaching session.

It is also necessary to bear in mind the principle that angry feelings are not intrinsically undesirable. Appropriate retaliatory or protective actions against someone or something that has harmed a client often needs to be discussed. We teach children appropriate ways to respond to frustration, bullying, and aggression against them, just as we might support and encourage an abused spouse not to simply passively accept domestic violence. "Don't get mad, get even" is occasionally an appropriate goal for a client in therapy.

While this distinction between the feeling state and the overt response to it is important, it is clear that the two are typically so closely linked that it is sometimes not reasonable to try to separate them. Muscle tension and raised blood pressure in rage mean closed fists and striking out responses; sweating palms, fast shallow breathing, and rapid heart rate in anxiety means fleeing; lethargy, fatigue, and tears in hopelessness means passive, inactive submission. Feelings are subjective but their expression and their overt manifestations are objective and generally recognized by others. Verbal statements of one's feelings (but not tone of voice, or shouting) can be inhibited, as can other overt expressions and actions, but the dry mouth, sweating palms, rising nausea, hand tremor, and blushing are reflexive and much more difficult to control voluntarily (i.e., self-regulate).

Stopping feeling worried, therefore, is not quite so easy. But worry, or anticipatory anxiety, as we have seen, does have a preparatory function in certain situations. Physiological arousal when threatened readies you to flee or fight and that purpose has value. Feeling anxious (worried) needs to energize you to take precautions, to prepare for dangers and be ready for threatened events, and then it is certainly useful. Once you have taken precautions, done what you can to mitigate risk of harm, then worry has no function and can be dropped.

That is easy to say, but think how often we do attempt to calm friends, family, children, maybe clients, with "don't worry, everything will be fine," instead of "what exactly are you worried about and what are you doing about it?" which might lead to the suggestions like get a fire extinguisher, change the batteries in your smoke detectors, insist the kids wear their helmets even if they're going for a short bike ride, you can't stop an earthquake but you can have an emergency route planned and emergency supplies on hand. "Someone *might* break into your house, that's true, so why not get one of those household alarms with a camera you can monitor?" Of course there are many degrees of plausibility, but each one has some sort of at least slightly mitigating self-protecting activity. But once these strategies have been exhausted and the situation is totally uncontrollable, then you might as well capitulate and simply "smile, smile, smile."

The Opposite of Struggling for Control: Acceptance

It's an adage as old as the hills that one should change the things we can and accept the things we cannot change. Alcoholics Anonymous added the proviso that we need wisdom to tell the difference between what we can and cannot change. We mean individuals, and there are certainly serious issues like unemployment, poverty, hunger, and climate change that potentially could affect any of us, but which no one person can reasonably expect to alter. Acceptance is a very passive attribute. Should people be encouraged to accept unfair, harmful, unpleasant conditions? Acceptance as an outcome goal in therapy, however, has become very popular as a result of the reasoning in ACT approaches that people should not try to get rid of their unpleasant feelings directly (Baer, 2010). Acceptance is a form of passive self-control; a sort of "grin and bear it" admonition, so that once you give up the struggle to change and do the steps in the therapy, your unpleasant feelings will then decrease. Some people do appear to be very intolerant of experiencing bad feelings and will go to extreme lengths to avoid having them. This is sometimes referred to as experiential avoidance (Hayes-Skelton & Eustis, 2020), but we don't want people to avoid experiences, so it is really no more that differences in one's tolerance of negatively valenced feelings, what used to be called distress tolerance, for which measures have been developed (Simons & Gaher, 2005). The overall goal of ACT is to foster psychological flexibility, and acceptance is one of the six processes that have been introduced in order to achieve this goal. (The other five are defusion, being present, self as context, identifying and clarifying values, and committed action.) Positive feelings like joy and pleasure need to be embraced. Evidence from many sources converges to suggest that a comprehensive goal of all psychotherapy is that people will find and experience pleasure, joy, happiness, and meaning (value?) in many aspects of their lives.

Cheron et al. (2009) developed a paper and pencil questionnaire to measure experiential avoidance in parents (Parental Acceptance and Action Questionnaire, PAAQ). Parents who receive high scores on the construct of experiential avoidance would probably not be high on emotional intelligence and unlikely to enhance their children's emotion competence through the kinds of emotion talk described in Chapter 4. Items such as "It's OK for my child to feel depressed and anxious" (score negative for experiential avoidance) or "If I could magically remove all the painful experiences my child has had in his or her life, I would do so" (score positive for experiential avoidance) are ambiguous, since parents fostering emotion competence are attempting to understand and label their children's feelings and would not wish them to feel pained, depressed, or anxious, but will still recognize that such feelings can be informative, valid, and addressed to reduce their negative impact on behavior. The PAAQ has received positive psychometric evaluation, and it seems to be made up of three factors: flexible parenting, acceptance of their own feelings as parents, and acceptance of their children's internal experiences (Bergman et al., 2024).

While good questionnaires of this type can be very useful, what they often fail to do is clarify the true nature of the construct. The actual parental behavior and feelings that one is trying to understand tell us there are significant differences between experiential avoidance and indifference. Many parents focus constructively on shaping positive, rich, and nuanced feelings in their children. It is hard for me to agree (accept!) that good parents would not *endorse* the (experiential avoidance) item: "I try hard to avoid having my child feel depressed or anxious." There is still much to learn about what are valid, functional, acceptable, and emotionally healthy types and levels of children's feelings during development.

Dissonance and Defense

One of the challenges surrounding the topic of self-regulation and control of feelings is that the emphasis is first on not having a bad feeling, and then having one whose level is tolerable and functional for you (dampening down the feeling or increasing it, whichever is needed to feel good and function appropriately). But clients often report feelings that have occurred and have persisted long after the event that triggered them. There are many important feelings that can continue in a non-constructive way—anger from a distant harm, grief from loss of a loved person, disappointment from an unfulfilled ambition or unrequited love. You cannot eliminate the cause of these feelings, but you try to minimize their negative influence. If ever we needed proof that negative feelings are sufficiently unpleasant that actions which reduce them will be reinforced, then the reality and persistence of defense mechanisms should provide it. The classic psychodynamic strategies are avoidance-based, like denial or projection, or escape-based like reaction formation and rationalization. This changes the discussion from self-control and self-regulation of emotion to a different topic, somewhat more like coping strategies.

Defense mechanisms are generally considered to be psychologically harmful, in that you may superficially feel better, but the cause of your distress has not gone away. Let's consider cognitive dissonance. From Aesop's wonderful fable of the fox and the grapes, children learn the moral that people can often profess disdain for something they actually like, and the implication is usually that they are pretending or deceiving themselves. "Sour grapes" is an accusatory rejoinder that we make when a person expresses dislike for something they can't achieve or obtain. It is clearly a derogatory remark. But thanks to Festinger (1957) and his concept of cognitive dissonance, we can see that the fox could be considered to be using a perfectly legitimate coping strategy when he tells himself (the fox was clearly a male!) that the grapes he couldn't reach must be sour. We have already seen that not being able to get a desired object generates the emotion of frustration. In humans, we might allow that a more common feeling is disappointment. It is a negative feeling. We can reduce the negative feeling by devaluing the thing we can't have. Then you feel better. That seems to me to be a perfectly reasonable "coping" strategy, as long as the cognitive process of devaluing is convincing to oneself. In other words, if you can make a plausible argument to yourself that the object was not worth having, why would you feel disappointed in not getting it?

As parents, not liking to see our children disappointed when they didn't win, or get a prize, or get invited to a birthday party, or didn't like the flavor of a treat they had chosen, we work quite hard to help them make these plausible cognitions, even though we don't find them personally convincing. "Better luck next time. There'll always be a next time;" "You said you didn't like that kid, anyway, why would you want to go to her party?" "If friends treat you like that, they are not true friends and not worth worrying about." "Well, you did your best, and that is the important thing, and we're proud of you." I think I've said all of those things at one time or another—I've even said them to graduate students in a different form: "That's not a highly regarded journal anyway." "There are lots of other graduate schools that offer post-docs." "Don't feel bad about the low return rate, I think your *n* will still be big enough." I was probably no more convinced personally than when I tried to tell my grandchild after her team lost the soccer match: "It doesn't matter whether you win or lose, it's how you played the game!"

Festinger made it clear that the items of information that don't fit together (are dissonant) "may be about behavior, feelings, opinions, things in the environment, and so on. The word 'cognitive' simply emphasizes that the theory deals with relations among items of information" (Festinger, 1962, p. 93). We may need to remember that the recognition that a feeling is dissonant with another feeling, attitude, or value is what generates the new feeling of unease which encourages us to change one of them to reduce the dissonance.

Clients often have quite complex or at least nuanced feelings about themselves that are not always consistent. Thanks to the classic and insightful work of Beck, we recognize that depressed clients typically report feelings of worthlessness and inadequacy. In fact, as cognitive statements, these self-descriptions are synonymous with the core symptomatology of depression. But when you probe for their feelings in a more inquisitive way, it is possible to discover a range of feelings around doubts about themselves—a cluster of feelings often described as self-uncertainty (Hogg et al., 2007). These are feelings of doubt and ambiguity about who they are as a person and about other conflicting feelings and values. They may not describe these feelings in exactly these words. One has to make inferences based on other aspects of their self-report and especially of their social behavior (in direct contact with others). When a person has an adequate level of self-confidence (strong ego, positive self-identity) in the sense of being comfortable with who they are, it is much easier to use a cognitive rationale like the Fox did. The famous American poet and writer Sylvia Plath once remarked "I love my rejection slips. They show me I try." At one level, a negative experience is being muted by an affectively positive value. But by emphasizing how she can turn the probably combined negative feelings of disappointment, frustration, and rejection into "love" adds the level of sarcastic humor that reveals the coping sentiment is valid.

Social psychologists have long been interested in identity uncertainty because, they argue, these feelings lead to seeking close connections with very specific groups of people. Membership in tight-knit groups focused on specific attitudes, values, or world views with ritualistic behavioral rules can reduce feelings of uncertainty due to interdependence among the members and shared identities. The standard Uncertainty-Identity Theory proposes that people join these kinds of groups in order to validate their existing self-concept and to find a social context that is highly predictable and reduces uncertainty. This could be considered as an approach behavior tendency (I like approach/avoidance concepts as you know by now): people join these like-minded groups because the social support and validation of their personal qualities inflates their self-importance and reduces uncertainty (Jost et al., 2007).

An alternative mechanism—or perhaps an additional mechanism—that is an avoidance behavioral tendency, has been proposed by Gao et al. (2024). They suggested that "avoidance-oriented affiliation is a basic safety-seeking behavior driven by a desire to escape self-uncertainty discomforts, such as social isolation and anxiety" (p. 3829). Being socially isolated while feeling uncertainty about where and to what you belong is a highly negative feeling state, perhaps not easily recognized and described as such by a client but clearly a source of general stress and discomfort. Belonging to a group like those described earlier (tight-knit, structured, perhaps led by a charismatic leader or explicit code of conduct) serves as a defensive or coping strategy providing some protection from the threat of isolation and social exclusion, which as we have seen can be considered one of the evolutionarily shaped feelings of threat. In two analogue studies, Gao et al. (2024) confirmed their notion that group affiliation by self-uncertain individuals does not just involve sharing of the group's beliefs, values, and ideas—a somewhat cognitive process—but may also serve the escape function of reducing unpleasant feelings of isolation and uncertainty.

Let me quickly touch on the implications for therapists. One is that feelings of uncertainty about the client's self are worth listening for or probing for. They may be somewhat synonymous with self-reported statements indicating low self-esteem or lack of self-confidence. These are often elicited when changes in behavior patterns, especially social ones, are suggested to clients—a common feature of general behavior therapy. Another implication is that if the client appears to be socially isolated, as so many do, encouraging the joining of an in-person group might be more realistic and effective than encouraging new friends or individual relationships. A third is that groups with the tight structure and priorities discussed here may seem like undesirable cults for vulnerable people to join, or already be participating in. For clients with criminal records, gangs clearly serve the sorts of social functions described. But not all cults have insidious objectives. Many focus on ideas about healthy living and lifestyles, positive religious beliefs, or achieving constructive social objectives through activism.

But some can be risky, especially in the digital age when misinformation can be so readily shared and even be focused on dangerous socio-political objectives.

You need to know if your client is drawn to highly entitative (meaning cohesive, unified entity) groups (Campbell, 1958; Crawford & Salaman, 2012) and actively participates in them. Without judging their appropriateness, try to have a better understanding of how the client's involvement functions to reduce or control their negative feelings about themselves. People with symptoms of depression and anxiety, especially social anxiety, are often encouraged in CBT approaches to socialize more and actively seek out social activities. When you are also focused on their emotional experiences, the precise nature of these social groups and the practices they offer can be more carefully tailored to the presence of negative feelings around self-uncertainty.

Implications

Since it is one way to self-manage behavior and have good self-control, self-regulation of feelings is an important long-standing component of the total collection of self-help and self-modification strategies in CBT (Watkins & Clum, 2008; Watson & Tharp, 1977). In this chapter, the focus was limited to the specific possibilities of regulating and controlling one's feelings. Regulation should be in both directions—reducing unwanted feelings and enhancing pleasant ones. As clinicians, we are accustomed to focusing on reducing the negative feelings of clients. But there is not much benefit in reducing them in the clinic, except as an illustration for clients of what is possible. Our clients might want to feel good at the end of a session, but what they need more is the ability to regulate their feelings in meaningful real-life contexts.

The big issue is to what extent can anyone control their own feelings through efforts of will? If we understand the stimulus situations that elicit a feeling, we can change these by avoiding them or changing some feature that changes their influence. If that stimulus situation is a thought with strong affective properties through the words and their associated meanings, it is usually possible to control our thoughts through distraction or deliberately thinking of something else. These new dominant thoughts and images both remove the negative ones, thus reducing the negative feeling, and increase associated positive ones, thus creating positive feelings.

The direct regulation (inhibition) of the responses of the autonomic nervous system is much harder as they are simply not usually under voluntary control. During the era in which biofeedback became a popular clinical tool, people were able to learn to regulate a number of autonomic responses—slow their heart rate, for example. That required training and practice, but it is not magic, nor is such control unusual. Release of the bladder sphincter was not originally under voluntary control, but through training most children learn to hold their urine even with a full bladder and release it when at a toilet. Increases in breathing rate (the rapid panting of fear, for instance) can be stopped by deliberately focusing on taking deep, slow breaths.

In practice, feeling regulation would also include inhibiting and changing any of one's typical action tendencies or introducing positive new ones (approach rather than avoid, and affective forecasting). The overt action pattern of an intense feeling may be easier to control voluntarily than the feeling itself. Anger management training, as a popular technique for people with violent and aggressive behavior, has its primary focus on control of overt behaviors such as shouting, slamming doors, breaking things, or lunging out. The programs also emphasize stimulus control by means of avoidance—walking away from a provocative situation or avoiding them in the first place. But the increases in blood pressure, flushing of the face, muscle tension, and the reflexive discharge of otherwise inhibited reactions like hitting are much harder to regulate and sometimes impossible to do so. As a skill, self-control of anger feelings requires a range of techniques that include recognition of the need to stop an altercation or other provocative incident before it escalates to a point of no return.

This chapter assumes that feelings themselves can be controlled and managed, but the mechanisms will mostly be through a variety of indirect strategies and not willful inhibition of an automatic physical response. Changing the situation is critical; reducing provocative or feared stimuli through avoidance; using biofeedback techniques to change a feeling response pattern and controlling facial expression may be possible. Practically speaking, then, managing feelings (rather than their consequences, the action tendencies) can be broken down into five basic foci, three of which are stimulus change: selection of stimuli and situations; changing situations (like listening to music); altering the focus of attention. The other two are cognitive reanalysis of what a feeling means and its importance to you, and attempts to reduce the physiological reactions of the feeling state (relaxation, breathing).

The important clinical technique known as relapse prevention, originally developed for problem drinking by Marlatt and Gordon (1985), is partially based on the self-control strategy of avoiding exposure to cues and situations that are highly likely to elicit feelings and urges. Ensuring permanent therapeutic change is difficult and relapses are common (Brandon et al., 2007). The expressed emotion literature (Chapter 5) tells us that harmful negative feelings can be elicited in a variety of situations that are not always under a client's control. But where known stimulus-rich situations can be avoided, avoiding them becomes a major self-protecting habit that many clients need to practice.

Is it possible that people become clients because they have a certain personality profile that makes them vulnerable to poor feeling control as a skill area? Either they are reactive individuals, always reacting intensely with autonomic changes like the neurotic rats in Eysenck's research, or they are overly sensitive to the triggers other people take in their stride. Clients are often seen in clinical contexts when it seems they have some sort of aversion to the sensations of intense feelings; this is beyond fear of fear and something like aversion to affective sensations. ACT theorists and researchers made an important contribution by making experiential avoidance a central feature of many clients' vulnerability. Intolerance of emotional experiences, just like having far too many negative experiences, is an individual difference variable increasing vulnerability to the development of emotional disorders and more resistant to the basic treatment strategies that rely on some element of negative experiences to be tolerated. But is experiential avoidance a general trait of affect activation avoidance, or is it limited to negative valence avoidance? Right now, in my local bookstore, there are eleven recent popular psychology books (written mostly by recognized scholars) on *how to be happy*. Is the focus in CBT, including ACT, largely on how not to be unhappy?

The primary construct variously called emotional stability, emotional flexibility, neuroticism, lability, emotional balance, emotion control and regulation, resilience, and emotion competence as a basic personality trait is central to the core of most of the mental disorders of the DSM-5. It is not necessarily the central *causal* deficit, although in the case of some like certain anxiety disorders, childhood dysregulation, and borderline personality disorder, it might be. A focus on managing one's feelings, the subjective side of emotion, adds a more human dimension to these clinical topics. People who can do so well, in both directions, don't often become clients.

9

The Challenge of Changing Intense Feelings

Orientation

There are two topics that come to the attention of psychotherapists that are so intricately tied to the topic of feelings that they need to be addressed. One is when individuals, often acting alone and not in actual mortal danger, perform lethal acts of violence. The other is when an individual is the victim of violence and prolonged cruelty, is exposed to constant danger and serious threat, or is a participant in dangerous actions such as military combat. The second category is summarized as experiencing trauma, and the varied psychological consequences represent a common pattern: Post-Traumatic Stress Disorder, PTSD. Both topics clearly deserve thoughtful consideration, and, like so many other phenomena discussed thus far, could easily justify book-length scholarship. Indeed, many important books have been written on exactly these areas. For our present purposes, however, with feelings as the subject matter, I will simply raise a few issues that might be relevant to general psychotherapy practice, within our theme of better understanding feelings.

Generalizations can never be made about the clients who fit into either of these two categories. But what they have in common is that they are typically extremely dramatic cases that attract inordinate amounts of public attention. There is deep public interest in why certain individuals behaved the way they did (thinking of my first category), and people are fascinated by the realities of PTSD, a phenomenon that everyone has heard of. This means we all typically have knowledge of situations which is entirely lacking in facts and psychological insights. The public asks good questions, but the comments and replies are often banal: "Her injuries will heal eventually, but her internal scars will remain forever." "Was this a hate crime, terrorism, or mental illness?" "What was his motive? We are awaiting an analysis of what he posted on social media." "Neighbors were shocked that someone who killed so many people could be living right

How and Why Feelings Change. Ian M. Evans, Oxford University Press. © Ian M. Evans (2026).
DOI: 10.1093/9780197825808.003.0010

next door—'he seemed a nice person, was willing to help, but he kept himself to himself, never caused any trouble.'"

Lethal Individuals

There are hazards in professional practice too. We cannot easily determine when we might be presented with a case where there is an enormous risk of the client harming themselves or others. You would think that people who are about to engage in a highly destructive act, to kill someone, or go on a shooting spree would reveal feelings so obvious and blatant that dangerousness can be easily predicted. That is not so. But at the same time, we are faced with an ethical obligation to anticipate, judge, and prevent serious harm to others by our clients.

Everyone involved in clinical practice knows about the Tarasoff case. It is one of the foundational occurrences that influenced professional psychology ethics worldwide: the now accepted imperative of our duty to warn (or better still, a duty to protect). You are sure to have read the succinct words of the California Supreme Court (1974): "The protective privilege ends where the public peril begins." Although there were dissents—one can argue that the prediction of future violence is just too subjective, or the client's right to confidentiality too sacrosanct under any circumstances—the Tarasoff ruling has been enacted into law in many US states and other countries around the world. What is less often discussed in professional circles and ethics classes is precisely what sort of feelings were held by graduate student Prosenjit Poddar that led him to stab and kill Tatiana Tarasoff in 1969. Little is now known about Poddar as his conviction was overturned on a technicality and he was deported back to India, where there is no legal statute or precedent to guide psychology practitioners (Modak et al., 2016). However, we know he had a romantic infatuation with Tatiana, she talked to him but explained she was not interested, he felt rebuffed and began to stalk her, and admitted to his therapist that he had feelings he wanted to kill her. Are inescapable feelings of rejection, not being wanted, feeling despised, or one's talents being unrecognized by those who are inferior, a special collection of dangerous feelings in younger, socially isolated, relatively unsuccessful men?

There are so many cases such as this, it is imperative we better understand why whatever feelings he had led to his overt actions. Feeling rejected; male feelings of possession of women; male feelings of entitlement and anger at being disrespected by women; the thought "if I can't have her, no one else can have her," all come to mind, in an entirely non-professional way, as they can to anyone else reading a newspaper. Is there even any commonality to these acts of violence? In 2001, Los Angeles police officer Geno Colello shot and killed Keith Ewing, who was standing outside watering his lawn. The newspapers called it "jealous rage" because Colello's ex-girlfriend had moved in with Ewing a few weeks earlier.

The case attracted psychologists' attention because Colello's father had contacted his therapist and told him of the threat. His psychologist arranged for hospital admission, but did not warn Ewing, and was sued by Ewing's parents (Edwards, 2006.) In 2006, in New Zealand, University of Otago economics tutor Clayton Weatherston contacted a friend and spent forty-five minutes on the phone grumbling about his ex-girlfriend, Sophie. The friend tried to persuade him to let it go and to get help to stop obsessing about Sophie; Clayton was worried she would say things about him that would mar his reputation and academic standing, and his friend kept telling him this was unlikley. Two days later, however, Weatherston repeatedly stabbed Sophie to death in her bedroom, including mutilating her body, face, and genitals, while her mother was helplessly standing outside the locked bedroom door. The 216 stab wounds were interpreted as a deliberate effort to distort her natural beauty. The first police officer to enter her bedroom stated that Weatherston said "I've killed her" in a "calm, natural tone."

It is the apparent calmness and the "banality of evil" (Arendt, 1951) that can mislead us easily and allow us to misjudge the intensity of a person's level of desperation and disruption of normal feelings. I once experienced an incident that convinced me of errors that are possible in misjudging calm behavior where feeling expressions had been numbed. I was the consultant to a state health department daily kindergarten-like half-day program that admitted hard-to-diagnose children for three months of careful and detailed observation. A pediatrician had asked us to screen for admission to the Center a child with unusual behaviors. The girl, Ara, and her mother Joan attended for the day so we could obtain more details. Joan explained that Ara had been adopted at the age of four from an Asian country. Little was known about her background, but she had habits suggesting she had been abandoned and had spent time living on the streets. Joan carefully and calmly listed a large number of difficult behaviors, night terrors, episodes of violence against Joan's two birth children, and wild tantrums in public places if she didn't get her own way. There was no distinctive pattern and no obvious diagnosis.

At the end of the Center's day, after long interviews and careful observations, I had to inform Joan that unfortunately we weren't able to take in children over the age of five and that we had not previously been aware that Ara was six. I assured Joan I could make a referral to various excellent child psychologists. As they were saying goodbye, I got a strange feeling from Joan's flat but defiant affect that her stoic acceptance of the non-admission was a cover of extreme control. I asked her "What are you going to do now?" meaning the rest of the day. She replied "I'm going to go and buy a gun and I'm going to shoot Ara and then myself. I have to do it to save my husband and my two daughters, whose lives are being destroyed." There was no hint of exaggeration or drama, just a cold, deadpan look. I realized I had completely underestimated the level of stress she was feeling, the uncertainty of lack of diagnostic understanding, and the effects of rejection, since Ara had been terminated from at least three pre-school programs. There was only one of those feelings I could immediately assuage. "I'm going to break the rules. We'd love to have Ara here. We are well staffed with professionals, and we can easily make her feel welcome here. I'll sort it out with the Director. Come back tomorrow. We'd love to have her here; every child here is an enigma, but they are all precious." Joan burst into tears. I added one caveat. "You have made a serious threat that I cannot ethically ignore. When you leave, I'm going to call Child Protective Services and make a report. Nothing will happen unless they doubt my judgment regarding Ara's safety, but they will probably visit you. I want you to pick up Ara right now and hug her, and when you get home, I want you to tell your husband everything that happened today. He or you can call me later today or tonight any time if you feel even slightly out of control." Palermo (2003) has offered important advice to therapists working with extreme family stress: "do not abandon" (p. 53).

The understanding needed to manage situations like this is widely available, but cannot always be accessed by families, and within every community, there will always be various levels of services and opportunities. Even in a country like New Zealand with well-developed and government-funded disability services and expertise, there remain risks when the feelings of desperation of a parent are un-recognized. Casey was a seventeen-year-old with strawberry blonde hair who loved music and dancing. She was also autistic. She painted with pink and gold and heavy black paints and if she couldn't achieve the look she wanted, she would eat her pictures. She had limited language, talked in the third person and only around familiar people. When unable to communicate, she had violent tantrums, biting and kicking and destroying things. Casey "became impossible," stated her mother Janine, who also had two young children aged three and four. "We were just so alone; no one saw her beauty. Casey and I were stuck, we were both exhausted. I begged for help but was told there was no funding. I told them I was afraid I was going to end up killing Casey. It just became impossible, beyond any one human to cope with." Early one Sunday morning, Janine took Casey to a high bridge, hoping she would jump. Casey refused; said she was cold. So, Janine took her down a quiet road, took the cord from her dressing gown, wrapped it around her neck and strangled her.

People who engage in extreme behaviors do not have to be depraved individuals with a history of psychopathy and callous disregard, and they do not have to be enraged and out of control at the moment. Feelings of desperation gave Janine a sense that Casey was so lonely she would be better off dead, although she said later, she knew "it was not acceptable to take a life." Janine was tried for murder, convicted of manslaughter, and sentenced to four years in prison. The New Zealand Court of Appeal reduced the sentence to eighteen months.

Cases that one has not personally dealt with do not constitute scientific and objective evidence. They are illustrative, however, of the difficulty in judging a client's lethality. Filicide, the act of killing one's own child, is a particularly difficult behavior to understand. More than half of them are classified as altruistic—murder committed out of love (Palermo, 2003). Children and adults with disabilities are at elevated risk. The many descriptive terms, labels, and social judgments regarding who is most worthwhile are heavily weighted towards affective properties of dislike, fear, and exclusion. The expressed emotion literature we've considered has mostly been applied to people with serious psychiatric diagnoses but is likely to be evidenced in families with challenging children with developmental disabilities. Efforts to change negative feelings and evaluative statements are surprisingly easy to introduce. The work of Meyer (Meyer et al., 1998) on practical strategies that foster natural friendship between typically developing children and those with disabilities shows levels of acceptance and tolerance quite different from the pessimistic expectations of many adults.

Self-Harm and Suicide

Another practice domain where therapists need to be especially sensitive to certain client feelings is the need to be alert to self-injury and suicide. Much has been written about non-accidental self-injury. It is often argued that when young girls engage in non-accidental self-injury, such as cutting themselves, it is done in order to create a powerful feeling of pain mixed with excitement, in order to alleviate feelings of emotional numbness. This model fits closely with everything in the discussion so far about action tendencies being shaped by whatever overt behaviors will reduce negatively valenced (unpleasant) feelings. In this case, however, one would have to assume that feelings of emotional *numbness* are equally unpleasant. Yet, there is a dialectic here. Activated feelings of negative valence are unpleasant; inactivated feelings of positive valence are unpleasant. But it is a little hard to think that if one's feelings are literally numbed, they can fit that latter state of affairs. Getting a much wider range of a client's feelings, good and bad, situation by situation, is necessary to avoid glib overgeneralizations.

It is necessary to relate this topic to the equally controversial subject of suppression of feelings. Suppression is assumed to occur to the emotion, rather than numbness which is suppression of the feelings (sensations). But this all may be a technicality of whereabout in the emotional arousal loop from threat to overt reaction that interference, blocking, suppression, or numbing can occur. One other way people, especially clients, have learnt to enact this blocking mechanism is by drugs, from alcohol to prescription emotion blockers, to illegal medications for pain. The everyday strategies many people use—e.g., smoking tobacco or marijuana, other drugs, yoga, Pilates—are both positive and negative. Ever since the COVID-19 pandemic, there has been renewed interest within mental health circles in the topic of loneliness, which is both an objective condition (social isolation) and a subjective feeling, not restricted to situations in which other people are not around. It is a feeling of being invisible to all other humans.

Suicidal attempts and ideation are an occupational worry for psychotherapists. Thoughts and possible plans have dominated the implicit professional assessment of risk. Feelings have begun to attract more professional attention. Trimble and Chandran (2021), drawing on data from a large school-based survey by the US Center for Disease Control, found that 36% of high school students reported sad feelings, according to their response to one item: "During the past 12 months, did you ever feel so sad or hopeless almost every day for 2 weeks or more in a row that you stopped doing some usual activities?" Apart from the fact that sadness and hopelessness are two very different feelings, the researchers reported there was an 8–11-fold increased odds of suicide behaviors among both boys and girls who reported sad feelings. A team of researchers in Spain reported a well-controlled study showing that people who had made a recent suicide attempt had high scores on a measure of feelings of emptiness (Pemau, 2024). This is a complex feeling and the measure includes items related to such elements as loss of vital meaning, loneliness, lack of self-direction, and emotional disconnection. Oakey-Frost and colleagues (2022) selected three feeling constructs from previous research and examined their relationship to suicidal ideation and attempts. These were defeat, entrapment, and hopelessness. All three showed independent relationships with suicidal thinking. Feelings of defeat (demoralization) were closely related to entrapment which is a belief construct around motivation to escape internal and external conditions; the hopelessness measure was described from the Beck scale of the same name and is a cognitive measure of expectancies for the future. All the predictive measures used in these studies reflect a general theme that is interesting and provocative, but there is a clear need for greater clarification of the feelings identified to show that there is precision beyond the assumption that what is being assessed is depression.

In Sweden, a study by Högberg and Hällström (2018) is particularly relevant as it was a controlled intervention study of depressed adolescents in a clinical setting. A negative mood and feelings questionnaire and an interview-based suicide rating scale were among the outcome measures. The intervention was called "mood-regulation focused CBT," involving the clients keeping records of emotionally positive memories. Compared to the usual clinic treatment, the therapy reduced depression and suicidal ideation. The elaborate rationale ("counter conditioning with memory reconsolidation") could definitely benefit from a tighter theoretical model and operational definition of constructs, but the general idea fits with one of our themes—that a focus on positive memories is constructive. Recording positive feelings is a good place to start.

Trauma and Feelings

Really terrible things can happen to people. The adjective terrible is derived from the meaning "causing terror." It can be one major event or a series of lesser ones, always being exacerbated by feelings of helplessness and rage, the latter being especially strong when others are harmed. The psychological consequences of natural disasters to which virtually every community on the globe are highly susceptible are well-known (Paton & Johnston, 2017), as are the attitudes and feelings that restrict people's ability to take precautions and adopt preventative strategies (Vinnell et al., 2023). Clinical work with people who have experienced and been harmed by severe physical abuse, sexual violence, combat, displacement as refugees is quite specialized. But it needs at least some conceptual coverage here because feelings are particularly important in traumatic experiences and need to be considered. In this second part of the chapter, I will touch on issues that all represent some systemic feature of emotional experience that dominates and swamps everyday individual and more malleable feelings, especially the ordinary affective reactions to people and places, and experiences of our routine lives.

Child maltreatment has long-lasting, negative effects (e.g., Warmingham et al., 2023). It is quite interesting that recent models conceptualizing the physical and mental health consequences of both acute and historic experiences of trauma identify all of the four resilience factors as feelings states (Marks et al., 2022). They are ones we have encountered already: feelings of trust, safety, autonomy, and trauma awareness, which is van der Kolk's (2014) concept of awareness of sensory-based feelings and the connection between current interoceptive and proprioceptive sensations and past trauma experiences.

In the treatment of PTSD, the approach called Cognitive Processing Therapy (CPT) is considered one of the gold standard treatments, especially for military personnel still in active service (Hass et al., 2025). That is a highly structured living and social environment which interferes with common therapeutic recommendations for activities like meditation or for initiating major life changes. CPT is defined as "helping patients learn how to challenge and modify unhelpful beliefs related to the trauma. In so doing, the patient creates a new understanding and conceptualization of the traumatic event so that it reduces its ongoing negative effects on current life." *Beliefs, understanding, and conceptualizations*! If you have come this far in this book, you might join me in asking, "Hey! What about feelings?" Actually, if you read other accounts and especially clinical case studies, you will see that understanding feelings plays a large role, as does emotional flexibility (feeling about the same thing in different ways). Understanding feelings also means understanding what influences patterns of approach and avoidance, which are what emotions regulate, as we have seen repeatedly in many different theoretical positions.

Moral injury as a component of PTSD is now being more widely recognized and studied (Litz et al., 2009; Litz, 2023b). Conscience—the feelings of discomfort on violating a moral code—might not prevent a person from evil actions, but will, after the fact, have negative emotional repercussions. While important flexible treatment principles have been described and evaluated, the full role of feelings is still to be incorporated. Perpetrating or failing to prevent acts fully discordant with one's strongly held moral beliefs results in feelings of anger, shame, and guilt. These are complex feelings that blend with feelings of alienation, betrayal (by trusted others). Mindfulness and compassion training have been evaluated (Bernstein et al., 2025), but there is clearly room for a fuller examination of the logic of each feeling expressed.

The most common circumstance, of course, is extremely traumatic experiences, such as military combat, physical assault, sexual assault, and any prolonged exposure to stress. The past experiences of every client are relevant and should usually be explored. High stress is often followed by depression, for example. Programmatic research by neuroscientist Pizzagalli (2014), linking basic human and animal research, has demonstrated how both chronic stressors and early childhood adversities, including sexual abuse, appear to increase risk for depression by disruption of the dopaminergic reward pathways touched on in Chapter 2, leading to deficits in reinforcement effects and anhedonia. In psychiatry, the term anhedonia is often used to link three feelings characteristics that have surfaced throughout this book: lack of interest in previously liked activities; experiencing little pleasure in usually stimulating contexts such as socializing, leisure pastimes, and sensory experiences; and a general blunting of such feelings as happy, excited, or enthusiastic.

Bottling and Venting

It is widely acknowledged in our culture that "bottling up" your feelings is less productive than talking about them. Disclosure of your inner feelings is recommended. Talking about feelings, having a good cry with a sympathetic person, and telling your story to a sympathetic listener are all considered therapeutic. And in a general sense, this is exactly what a psychotherapist typically offers. Yet there may be cultural differences in the appropriateness of this personal approach, and individual personality differences in both the acceptability of revealing private feelings, and in the psychological value of doing so.

There appear to be gender differences as well, in that it seems widespread that men are less likely to use distress disclosure as a strategy to feel understood and socially connected. Adherence to traditional masculinity ideology can cause men to conceal from others their psychological distress, possibly believing that disclosing their difficulties would cause others to see them as "weak," or "unmanly."

The limited evidence suggests that when men disclose their distress to others, they feel more understood and less lonely. These are two key feeling states that often make up general psychological well-being. A key reason for this relates to one raised in Chapter 7: specific feelings can cascade into other related feelings. Thus, for instance, feeling understood cascades into feelings of justice (being treated fairly), feeling respected by others, and feeling validated as an individual.

Of relevance to this whole chapter is the type of urgency that is related to maintaining an intense negative feeling through emotive thoughts such as fantasizing. Feelings of intense anger often involve sustained aggressive fantasies. While concepts of catharsis have meant that some therapies encourage such fantasies by victims of mistreatment, there is evidence that such fantasies prolong and indeed amplify aggressive feelings (e.g., Twardawski et al., 2024). This was a stronger effect in those individuals whose anger expression and action tendencies were outward, such as verbal attacks and violent outbursts. However, people prone to anger-in, that is to say holding grudges, suppressing and denying angry feelings, are especially likely to sustain angry feelings with violent fantasies, anonymous posts on social media, and personal writings and drawings. The effects of enacting aggressive displays of anger in therapeutic role playing are more difficult to judge.

Venting as a strategy for emotion regulation—as opposed to regulation skill learning and situational change—has an unusual past in psychotherapy. It is tied to the earliest origins of psychotherapy. Freud's first reported case (it was actually his friend Breuer's case, but they talked together about it) was Anna O. Breuer observed that Anna's complicated symptoms decreased, immediately after sessions in which she talked about past experiences of emotional distress. This is why psychoanalysis was originally called the "talking cure." It was the temporary nature of the effect that convinced Freud that past recall was not tapping into the deeper significance of the memories and past events, which prompted the concept of unconscious feelings and conflicts. But modern psychotherapists also know what surely everyone has experienced at one time or another—that talking to a sympathetic non-judgmental listener about experiences that have upset you provides at least some degree of emotional relief. Everyone who has ever done psychotherapy will know that revelations of thoughts and feelings can induce strong emotions, tears, sobbing, anger, aggressive self-injury. Trainees have to learn how to deal with emotional outbursts in sessions. But only therapists who believe that the greater the emotion, the greater the benefit will actively encourage the most extreme reactions, and do things to clients like holding them, tickling them, or shouting at them, such as Janov's (1970) technique known as the primal scream. Janov became a celebrity, and his book sold a million copies. This has resulted in widespread belief in the general public that this is something typical in psychological therapy. So strong was this impression for a while that it was a regular feature of movies; one of the funniest being in the comedy film *Analyze This*. A therapist, Ben Sobel (played by Billy Crystal), tells mob boss and gangster Paul Vitti (played by Robert De Niro) to "release his anger by hitting a pillow" and so Vitti takes out his gun and shoots a number of rounds into it.

What's Underneath? Explaining Versus Expressing Feelings

Venting of feelings takes us again into the domain of getting at the bottom of things. We have all these words for keeping feelings in: bottling up feelings, masking feelings, suppressing feelings, withholding feelings, denial, swallowing your emotions. What we need are better words for pinpointing those that are the underlying feelings. There is a nice example from one of the many very gifted teachers in our emotional climate of the primary school classroom study (Evans & Harvey, 2012), who told us about something she did in her classroom:

> *We have this thing called 'What's on top?' in my classroom where students sit in a circle and share what's on top. We go around the circle, and everybody has one or two minutes to say whatever they want. It can be anything from 'I went to Pizza Hut last night' to 'It's my birthday in 10 day's time.' ... And sometimes we might even do 'What's underneath?' where if you want to say something that's a little closer to home or something they're not feeling safe about, it's a time where you listen—you're not there to defend yourself, you're not there to give comments, you just listen to what that person has got to say and that is really, really important.* (p. 210)

The discussion thus far has focused on what clients currently have in the way of emotion regulation skills, and how deficiencies in these skills are characteristic of some well-known clinical syndromes. And to the extent we know how individuals can self-regulate, we have various strategies which we can teach to clients as the focus of the therapeutic intervention. There are also some techniques that will regulate emotions in the here and now, and I am thinking of external activities and situations that are commonly used by parents and teachers with children and sometimes by therapists with clients. These strategies are short-term but useful to manage moods and change the feelings atmosphere of a setting. All settings have elements with the potential to foster calm moods and positive feelings, and there are some that also have the potential to foster the exact opposite.

We have already encountered the value of children's art projects in relation to understanding their feelings, but these same kinds of projects have the potential to manage feelings as well. In a neat little study, Drake and Winner (2013) asked one group of children to draw something that expressed their negative feelings at the time (which had been made negative by a mood induction procedure), this was a condition called venting. They asked another group to draw something unrelated to the induced negative feelings (a disappointing event), which was then a distraction group. Mood improved significantly more in the distraction group. In a second study to control for simply drawing something not self-generated, the same procedure was followed, but this time the children were asked to copy another child's drawing. When their pictures were not freely constructed, the mood reduction effect disappeared.

One could argue that induced moods are not powerful feelings for which venting is supposedly useful, but interest is in whether something can work at least temporarily to change feelings. Whether the children learned distraction as a long-term technique from this exercise is not known, but we may assume that such procedures such as distraction could be explained to them as something to do when you are feeling bad. That is a teaching moment I presume many parents and teachers take advantage of (Drake, 2023).

Betrayal and Rejection; Love and Hate

Trust, as I said in Chapter 1, is an essential feeling one must have for others if one's social interactions are ever to be positive. When people have been let down by others, it creates tense mood states of wariness and suspicion. You are put "on guard," you have feelings of mistrust, and you are likely to make cognitive misjudgments and be hypersensitive to other people's harmless mistakes. These feelings can be exacerbated because it feels worse when the trust you once had, a positive feeling of comfort and security, is taken away. This is called betrayal. Feelings of betrayal are intensely negative, beyond the direct harm of the actions. This happens when the indirect harm of the betrayal feeling cancels out the trust feeling, and that is more negative than the betrayal alone. As with all the self-conscious feelings, there can be confusion with the logic (requirements) for the feeling. Since these requirements can be expressed verbally, it is sometimes difficult to know whether the feeling is one of a cognitive recognition or a primary affective experience. It seems to me that it can be both. The person who says to their intimate partner "I feel betrayed" is expressing a feeling, one exacerbated by prior feelings of trust. If, however, they say: "Your seeing X behind my back is a betrayal of my trust in you," they are making a cognitive statement that explains their understanding of a circumstance—a violation of an expected rule of their conduct. If they are upset ("This is devastating. You really hurt my feelings!"), the original cognition is not a cause of the feeling but an accompaniment to it. Their cognitive summary of the situation didn't cause the feeling, their awareness of the action of betrayal did. And since the feeling of being betrayed is extremely negative, it can be an eliciting experience for another feeling.

That might be anger if the person has self-confidence and sad, depressive feelings if the person lacks self-confidence and is prone to feelings of self-blame.

You may have wondered that near the end of a book about feelings, neither love nor hate has had much attention. It is an anomaly of both emotion theory and the application of psychotherapy that these two most fundamental of human feelings get short shrift. Short shrift implies both rapid and unsympathetic dismissal, and that is not fair in this instance. Starting with love, there is a huge psychological literature around love, but the word is not in the index of the DSM-5. Having serious difficulties in forming any close personal relationships (which is not really the same as being able to feel love) is often problematic for people diagnosed with certain personality disorders (Schizoid and Borderline come to mind). Erotomania is a term used for some clients I have encountered with delusional style beliefs that some famous person is or could be deeply in love with them. John Hinckley Jr., who shot at President Ronald Reagan in 1981, had an infatuation with movie star Jodie Foster, writing in one note that he would give up his plan to assassinate the President "if I could only win your heart and live out the rest of my life with you." Again, however, while there is a large volume of material written about this case, the true details of how an individual's mental state became overtaken by one idée fixe are too complex to serve as a meaningful case study.

At the more conventional end of the topic of love, Robert Sternberg, whose triarchic model of practical intelligence might be better known to you, developed a valuable "triangular theory of love" (Sternberg, 1986). He must like models that have three parts. It is a very satisfying model because it is founded on the three easily defined and recognized components of intimacy, passion, and commitment. Intimacy refers to feelings of warmth and closeness, with practical elements of communication and emotional support. Passion, he defined as feelings that one cannot live or even imagine a life without another. It is more emotive. Commitment is perhaps more cognitive as it refers to decisions to stay in a relationship. These three components are the corners of the triangle and thus produce between them romantic love (combined intimacy and passion) and companionate love (combining intimacy and commitment).

It is an excellent descriptive model for most people's experiences of love and its different forms. As long as you don't identify passion only with lust and sexual attraction, it can also be applied to people you don't know, pets, and even inanimate objects. (Sternberg, 2021, has applied it to love for one's musical instrument.) The roots of love as a human emotion are less easily determined. And why it is not considered a basic emotion in emotion theory is perhaps because it is a subjective feeling (being in love, falling in love), has no definable facial or bodily expression, and the possible action tendencies can be infinitely varied. As a feeling, however, it is defined by powerful approach tendencies as can be seen when applying love to a dog's attachment to its owner. And the word is also so widely applied, it is difficult to claim it is one feeling: love of one's country, love of the flag, love of a movie star, love of your cat, love of your trumpet, love of your '68 Oldsmobile Cutlass. In Chapter 1, I stated that liking something was a positive affective feeling that could reflect strong approach and attachment behaviors as well as related feelings of pleasure.

More problematic from a clinical standpoint is the feeling of hate. It is the opposite of love, but like all our supposed polar opposite feelings and positive and negative affect in general, it can co-occur, as mentioned in Chapter 7. The concept of a love-hate relationship is easily recognized. Both love and hate have historic connections to early evolution of humans—for family and friends, love guaranteed acceptance and inclusion, and for enemies who might injure or harm you, hate ensured rejection, dismissal, and destruction. Anger leads to violence too, but only when one's goals are blocked. Hate guaranteed that you were willing to engage in distancing behavior and energized defensive approach and physical attack before an enemy had a chance to do you harm first. This is perhaps the basis for hate as a feeling to be quite difficult to reduce since contact and approach to those hated (which might change the feeling) are quite contrary to the action tendencies of the feeling. The negative urgency of hate is attack, but can lead to impulsive, poorly controlled behaviors that are ineffectual. In the modern world, hate is easily sustained by stories, rumors, harm done to others that one knows of or witnessed, indeed a variety of indirect real and imagined harm and threats.

There is one recent comprehensive and scholarly book on the topic by philosopher Berit Brogaard (2020). She provides numerous examples of unspeakable hate crimes and racial animosity, cruelty, and killings to illustrate her analysis of hate as a non-basic emotion, and I hesitate to even summarize any of her main points. If as a clinician, you encounter clients who are hateful, I assume they are unlikely to be complaining about it. However, it is clearly a feeling that we need to take seriously and to try to understand, especially if one is working with violent offenders (who may in fact not hate anyone) and people who have been brutalized by the experience of warfare, either as perpetrators or victims.

Implications

People often become clients and receive diagnoses because unpleasant feelings have come to dominate their lives and are influencing all of their behavioral activities in undesirable ways. Usually, it is not just one type of emotion, like anxiety, which disrupts behavior, but a general difficulty in managing (controlling, regulating) a range of feelings, such that this type of emotional volatility appears to dominate or disorder their whole personality functioning. And I have been arguing that saying people's lives are dominated by unpleasant feelings neglects a different state: that some people's lives are also dominated by a lack of pleasant feelings. These two states are partially independent—they are not the mirror opposite of each other and one doesn't go up when the other goes down.

There are syndromes involving intense emotions that arise from quite different origins. Cultural backgrounds and group and national experiences provide an emotional context that colors more immediate, subjective experiences. Religious beliefs and values, for example, encompass many aspects of a person's psychological functioning. Devoutly religious people have feelings that are a quantum leap different from those central to the discussion thus far. But they are not usually based on harmful or traumatic experiences, with perhaps the exception of people brought up in cults or in very narrow, controlling family circumstances. And on the other side of the coin, we have people with seriously intense negative emotional existences who have been shaped by personal traumas, such as physical and sexual abuse as children, or having encountered traumatic experiences in dangerous activities such as combat. And there are also the group experiences of warfare with killings, constant bombardment, loss of all sources of security and comfort, and group experiences of natural disasters, drought-related famines, and chronic disruptions from terroristic international disorder and injustice.

Stress, in an odd sort of way, can be seen not as a consequence of emotional feeling, but as a background state that exacerbates them. Stress can be considered to be a general system response to chaos, uncertainty, and resource deprivation, such as food shortages. The stress response is mitigated in such circumstances by social support and having good coping skills not for controlling feelings but for managing stressful circumstances and reducing the chaos and inconsistencies in one's life.

As we are confronted with traumatic incidents in schools and communities, there needs to be some focus on the reality that sitting in schools will be children who have experienced trauma at various levels of severity. All, however, will be characterized by disrupted emotional lives which create a need for care and support that might go further than the ideal emotional climate of a classroom in order to manage feelings. There is not a great deal of formal research on this topic, but the experience of educators is informative as a start. Thus, it is interesting that in her book on trauma in classrooms, Howard (2022) identifies the following topics as priorities: ensuring that learning environments are *perceived* as safe and non-threatening; ensuring friendships and relationships with other pupils as well as adults in schools; and encouraging capacity for emotional self-regulation. These are all priorities that have been advocated throughout this book. The more we can understand the feelings behind inappropriate action tendencies (aggressive and disruptive classroom behavior) and even more importantly, inaction (withdrawal), the better we can design positive classrooms and school-wide climate change.

10

Therapeutic Inspirations

What Changes Feelings?

Trends

Celebrities, especially young ones and musicians, talk about their feelings all the time. *"You can close your eyes to the things you do not want to see, but you cannot close your heart to the things you do not want to feel,"* said movie star Johnny Depp. Singer/songwriter Clairo (Claire Cottrill) took more of an ACT stance when she disclosed in a newspaper interview (Hunt, 2024): *"My femininity, my personality and my interests are all so fluid—sometimes it's hard for me to keep track of all the things I love, and all the things I want to do. I used to struggle with the idea of 'what kind of girl I was', and what kind of parameters I needed to exist within to be accepted. I'm much happier now that I understand that it's never going to be defined."* I am sure the endless barrage of intimate disclosures by the "influencers" on social media contributes to the shaping of people's ideas about feelings and will surely have influenced your clients. The reality is that your clients come to you with a detailed assortment of insights, understandings, and confusions about their feelings. Much of your task as a therapist is to help sort them out—not just to "get in touch" with them but to understand their logic—in a way that allows more adaptive behavior (desirable action tendencies) and a new balance of feelings from the mostly negative to the mostly positive. It's a considerable challenge. Especially so when the previous nine chapters show that our own field of expertise is far from confident about feelings.

For psychologists working within the conventional CBT framework, a new focus on the full emotional experiences of a client does not offer an *alternative* to any of the standard treatment strategies. But it provides a perspective, even an inspiration, by awareness that every client has multiple feelings in their everyday lives, which connect them to you and your feelings in a common humanity. This is in addition to the essential focus on specific concerns and the carefully identified problem areas they are seeking to ameliorate. What I have tried to do is not present any alternative perspectives to the broad range of techniques and

How and Why Feelings Change. Ian M. Evans, Oxford University Press. © Ian M. Evans (2026).
DOI: 10.1093/9780197825808.003.0011

methods of intervention that together can be called cognitive-behavioral therapy. Instead, what I wanted to explore is the potential of embracing, *within* the CBT field, the topic of personal feelings. It is my sense that while these have never been neglected by practicing clinicians, the technical parts of our discipline (the experimental analog studies, laboratory neuroscience, the formal treatment outcome research reports), as well as the core, almost hallowed, principles of applied behavior analysis and cognitive therapy, have not paid enough attention to the vast array of common feelings. Emotions, yes, especially the big four clinical conditions of anxiety, fear, depression (anhedonia), and anger. And we've traditionally identified emotions as the key force causing problems of maladaptive, self-destructive, and challenging overt behaviors which are often the primary targets of treatment. These typical targets should be recognized as positive and negative *urgencies*: the avoidance of places and opportunities, social and interpersonal withdrawal, inaction, excesses of consumption, aggression, and extreme violence. We see that these undesirable behaviors can be a result of the aversiveness of negative, deeply unpleasant feelings, but also the absence of positive, pleasurable feelings that are desirable.

Feelings are shaped and altered by experiences. These experiences can be ongoing or ones from the past. The effects of past experiences are perpetuated by conditioning (learning) and memory. Memories allow for reconstruction of the stimulus properties of the original experience. We can manipulate images (that's why it is called imagination), use the connotative meaning of words, and mentally time travel. We can look back on good times and elicit good feelings. And we can recall bad ones and feel less distress if the stimulus patterns can be altered.

Feelings can and will change. That is a truth that can be advantageous or disadvantageous to all of us and to clients in particular. Therapists know, as some friends and family members do not, that merely telling someone in emotional distress that they will "get over it" is unhelpful. Often it makes matters worse by conveying to the person that they should be feeling something different or could be soon if they really wanted to and are willing to put in the effort. But as we have learned from analyzing all the factors which regulate feelings, the changes that do take place for every feeling are not simply binary. You don't change one feeling by having its presumed opposite. You don't have a feeling one day and not the next. "Getting over it" is a poor metaphor, implying that the feeling will be gone, conquered, pushed down, or left behind. "Learn to live with it" might be better, or "come to terms with it," or for positive feelings, "you'll always be able to feel positive tingles when you think back on these times." I don't want to put words in other therapists' mouths or offer catch phrases that might sound phony to you. How best to offer reassurance that feelings change is really a personal thing. But helping clients to change how they feel is a legitimate goal of behavioral psychotherapy and of this book.

In the early days of behavior therapy, we mostly focused on feelings via the measurement and feedback of autonomic responses (heart rate, GSR, muscle tension, penile tumescence). These are one of the ways by which feelings are sensed, expressed, and revealed. But this focus also seems to have fallen out of favor in CBT. Meditation and spiritual Zen principles are in vogue. Self-compassion and an egocentric mentalism have been elevated. If emotions are preventing us from doing the things we want to do or should do, the rubric goes, then emotions are to be disregarded. But psychotherapists need to be careful not to neglect the good feelings many people treasure but lack—such as security, happiness, joy, love, gratitude, triumph, and a feeling of purpose. Values are important but they are not all equally altruistic. Feeling valuable (of value to others) is important too. Perhaps, as we now consider the rich psychology of feelings alongside the science of behavior and of cognition, greater versatility of intervention strategies can emerge, and a broader definition of socially significant outcomes be used in evaluating their success. Not a set of different or new techniques, but a richer affective context within which they can be practiced.

Theoretical Priorities

If you read the title of this chapter and had a *feeling* of delight that you could skip all the previous stuff and just go straight to what's important to you—novel treatment recommendations—you're in for some *feelings* of disappointment. By now you will know only too well that I'm not in favor of coming up with formulaic techniques or names for therapies. If I suggest to my Australian client that listening to the unique sounds of a didgeridoo might provide a valuable context for managing stressful feelings and enhancing mood (Philips et al., 2019), I am making use of a culturally relevant form of a beloved musical experience that has a long history of influencing people's feelings (Sloboda, 2010). I am not doing Didgeridoo Therapy.

I believe that a clear understanding of the currently recognized principles is what will be most helpful for the design and implementation of your therapeutic strategies. Thinking of therapy as helping people "recover" from mental illness is misleading in so many ways. Outcome research that defines treatment success as being free of X symptoms for Y number of months often misses the point about meaningful change (Meyer & Evans, 1993). It is better to suggest that a key purpose of psychotherapy, especially CBT, is to change clients' feelings to allow them to move forward towards happier (and thus healthier, Steptoe, 2019), more enjoyable, fulfilling, and more engaged lives. Different therapeutic schools depict these treatment goals slightly differently: ACT talks about living the life you value; cognitive therapy's core goal is changing destructive negative thought patterns; the goal of humanistic psychotherapy is to help individuals achieve authenticity and self-actualization; the positive psychology movement prioritizes a life that transcends individual interests. The constructive self-regulation of feelings is lauded in both behavior therapy and psychoanalysis: the influential analyst Otto Fenichel (1941) wrote "*The healthy ego experiences affects, knows them, discharges them and uses them for its own purposes ... he is master of his affects, whereas the weak ego is mastered by his affects*" (p. 59). My hope for psychotherapy is that by focusing more on subjective feelings, there will emerge a balance between the goals of affective, hedonic well-being (pleasure and joy), eudaimonic well-being (a life of purpose and meaning), and evaluative well-being—how your clients feel about their lives in general, separate from the inevitable daily ups and downs of feelings.

This book is about change and therapy as a tool for enabling change. Gross and Muñoz (1995) hit the nail on the head when they pointed out that human emotions are mostly depicted in literature and psychology as powerful and uncontrollable. These two authors argue convincingly that we also have many everyday experiences of being able to change feelings—to calm ourselves down, cheer others up, generate excitement in our children, and take pride in our work. The hitch is that clients are those people whose feelings are typically *less* malleable, less regulated—"psychologically inflexible" if you like. The latter is a key principle in all models of mental health, but one that makes it sound like a permanent imperfection, a trait, rather than the result of situations that trap people in conflicting feelings. People *become* clients because negative, uncomfortable, and distressing feelings dominate their experience of life. Paradoxically, they can even feel bad about their bad feelings. If you want just one general personality characteristic of clients, a version of Eysenck's emotional lability concept is possibly useful: clients have a negatively valenced emotion system which is more readily activated (aroused) than their positive one.

Assuming you would like your therapeutic methods to be, if not formally "evidence based," at least drawn from current psychological science, you might still have been bewildered by the density of all the material available. Research in psychology takes place in silos, as Arthur Staats (1983) spent the last half of his career attempting to correct. Rapidly spread ideas in one area seem to leave other important topics standing in the intellectually unfashionable dust. If you trained in the previous century or are being taught and supervised by someone who was, you will find an interesting if disconcerting phenomenon: there have been huge developments in the past twenty-five years which are very hard to keep up with, while at the same time, many of the new ideas seem remarkably like some of the old ones. New bottling of old wines. But most wines age nicely, and the basic constructs of traditional CBT have stood up well in my opinion.

The striking and important development of an "affective neuroscience" has yet to be successfully integrated with psychological phenomena and remains a separate field of research. Advances have been largely due to the ready accessibility of sophisticated imaging techniques while subjects are engaged in conscious thought and designated mental activities. When I was a student, psychologists interested in the neural basis of behavior had to surgically remove or sever parts of a lab animal's brain (or wait until they saw a patient who had had a discrete injury, like poor Phineas Gage, or a locatable stroke) in order to discover if some cerebral region was important for some psychological function. Imaging changed all that, so radically. It has certain limitations which were clearly articulated by the late John Cacioppo, who actually understood and relished the technology. He wrote:

> *We know already that social cognition, emotion, and behavior involve the brain. The functional localization of component social processes or representations is not a search for "centers." Localized changes in brain activation that differ as a function of a task do not, in themselves, signal a neural substrate. The beauty of a brain image does not speak to the psychological significance of the image.* (Quoted by Vanman et al., 2021, p. 5)

But neuroscience now has many more investigatory techniques than imaging and thus emerges as an exciting promise for our understanding. Popular articles in the media, however, still tend to discuss emotion with reference to raw existence rather than quality of life—quoting the literature on how we are all predisposed to respond in certain ways just to survive (e.g., LeDoux, 2012). Cave dwellers and saber-toothed tigers are inevitably mentioned. In terms of threats, I suspect early humankind were equally worried about the people on the other side of the hill who envied what they had in their cave. And in terms of wellbeing, early humans prospered best when they helped each other, nurtured their infants, warned their children by means of scary stories, and educated each other by sharing useful information. Evolution shaped social affiliation and altruism just as much as aggressive self-interest. It is rare to see any allusion to neurological processes when the topic is positive emotions such as caring, fairness, and joy. There is, however, growing physiological research on the pathways, structures, neurotransmitters, and hormones that relate to happiness or support prosocial behavior and thus, implicitly, prosocial feelings and empathy. There is one substantial review of these neuroscience developments (Alexander et al., 2021) that attempts to link with the psychological literature of positive emotions, but which cites almost none of the scholars represented in this book and neglects the role of experience and learning in "cultivating happiness and wellbeing" (p. 220) as well as cultural differences in the importance of maximizing multiple versions of feelings that constitute happiness (Krys et al., 2025). Further rapprochement could be of considerable benefit to psychotherapy and helping people change. It would advance developments in new pharmacotherapies such as hallucinogens like ketamine, where treatment trials still tend to use symptom checklists as outcomes rather than feeling measures (e.g., Beaglehole, Glue, Neehoff, et al., 2025).

The British neurologist with the eponymous name, W. Russell Brain, once wrote the following words of wisdom.

> *Not only are there twelve thousand million nerve cells out of which patterns can be made, but nervous patters exist in time, like a melody, as well as in space. If you look at a tapestry through a magnifying glass you will see the individual threads but not the pattern; if you stand away from it you will see the pattern but not the threads. My guess is that in the nervous system we are looking at the threads while with the mind we perceive the pattern, and that one day we may discover how the patterns are made out of the threads.* (Brain, 1951, p. 30)

Neuroscience researchers sometimes imply that psychological feelings can be reduced to physiological events without loss of the phenomena of interest. In a major synthesis of his highly influential work, leading affective neuroscientist Richard Davidson (2003) used the word feelings only once, and he put it in quotation marks. He favored the phrase "affective style" to refer to individual differences in emotional valence, reactivity, and regulation (p. 655). Neuroscience terminology for neural events can be misleading. The brain is sometimes depicted as though it were a little person inside our heads that makes decisions and judgments, gives warnings, and sends around messages. Barrett (undated) rightly criticizes phrasing of "an inner beast lurking inside your brain, which is constantly in battle with your more sensible rational self (p.5/11)" but goes on to say, equally metaphorically, "your brain is attempting to make sense of [information] so that it knows what to do next to keep itself alive and well. And it's using past experience to make these guesses." To explain the subjective experience of an emotional state of fear, LeDoux (2000) wrote that when encountering "an affectively charged stimulus, such as a trigger of fear, ... working memory will become *aware* of the fact that the fear system of the brain has been activated" (p. 176, emphasis mine). In describing for the public their creative study of classical conditioning of empathy (Zhang & Hackel, 2025), the second author summarized it as "Just as a dog learns to salivate when a bell signals food, our *brains* may learn to feel good when someone else is happy" (Hackel, 2025, emphasis mine).

In an insightful paper analyzing "how the brain has become an object and target for governing human beings" (p. 3), Rose and Abi-Rached (2014) have argued that neuroscientists and social scientists need to:

> *engage in a ... constructive 'critical friendship' that recognizes the importance of recent advances in neurobiological knowledge, but pays close attention to the justification of the truth claims that are being made .... We must recognize*

> *that neuroscience has not solved the problem of the mind-brain relationship, and that we do not even have the language to begin to translate brain states into mental states*. (p. 18)

As clinicians, we have all encountered clients whose out-of-control reactions do look like there's an inner beast lurking in the brain (Chapter 9). As scientists, we still require subjectivity to understand the phenomenon of feelings: the affective reactions one *experiences*. They are subjective and intrinsically non-rational in that they are not directly controlled by thought, although one might agree with Papez (1937) that "*for subjective emotional experience ... the participation of the cortex is essential*" (p. 726). Emotions are obviously necessary for human functioning and thus ipso facto cannot be good or bad. But they can *feel* bad and are judged undesirable and unpleasant when they occur in such a way and at such intensity that they interfere with personal relationships, the activities you once found rewarding, and the happenings that should be pleasurable. If negative feelings are derived or magnified—as they sometimes are—not from direct experience but from incorrect information about the world, then they can be changed by verbal persuasion, in the form of reasoning, explanation, expositions, education, and rational argument from an influential and trusted source. This is the essence of cognitive therapy (Evans, 2015). If clients, regardless of the negative feelings that push them away from an important activity, can learn to approach and get things done by some form of reward, social or material, then positive changes in their lives occur. This is the essence of behavior therapy (Evans, 2013). Both of these two broad tactics, which when combined we call cognitive-behavior therapy, involve feelings. In cognitive therapy, the key is to alter what we refer to as a feeling's "logic" in order to reduce its valence. In behavior therapy, their activation level is counteracted by the greater power of the pleasure of reward. And thus, it would seem self-evident that a fuller understanding of feelings would enable a CBT therapist (regardless of whether their primary emphasis is on cognitions or behaviors) to be more successful in implementing change. This is the hope (one of the nicest of our feelings!) of this book.

The Importance of Likes and Simple Pleasures

Messages change those feelings that do not have excessively high arousal elements, namely attitudes, likes, and dislikes. Messages can change even when those likes and dislikes are about oneself, which can be the most destructive kinds of feeling when very negative in valence. But for the message to work, the fundamental dynamic and logic of the feeling need to be considered. The role of body dissatisfaction in the development of eating disorders provides a good example. Body dissatisfaction could be changed to positive when some basis can be found for the positive perspective to be genuine or reciprocated socially. Being loved and accepted by others who are important to you would be one source of change; feeling proud about who you are and what you do might be another. If your client has a serious eating disorder, trying to feel positive when one is not can introduce a new set of feelings. Failing to feel what we think we should, or what others expect us to feel, can itself be a feeling that is quite negative (e.g., feelings of guilt, shame, or disappointment). Body neutrality might be a more desirable goal since it means focusing attention and feelings on other aspects of personal satisfaction. Satisfaction follows from achieving worthy goals, which can be defined as those which are of benefit to others, not only ourselves.

Feelings occur before and after all of the activities of life—the daily, ordinary, maybe even trivial ones, as well as the major ones that define one's existence as a person. The feelings that precede an activity serve as drives, incentive motivation, the arousal to act. Feelings therefore serve an important role as primes and as determinants of behavior, especially at choice points. When the choice points are unimportant to living a life—such as should you choose the chicken or the pasta on your next flight—you may feel twinges of regret and make commitments as to how you will behave in the future. But the choices and decisions made in important matters have consequences that will influence your life course: Should you accept the job offer or keep looking for something better? Should you major in computer coding or the classics? Should you file for divorce or keep going to your marriage counselor? When clients are confronted with major choices, CBT approaches are helpful through the mechanism of learning good problem-solving strategies. But the limitations of structured problem solving as a way of resolving external conflict begin to be seen when there are major feeling questions to answer—as there are in the three examples given, and not in the dilemma of the chicken or the pasta. And that is why the valuable and transdiagnostic problem-solving strategies developed by Art and Chris Nezu in CBT have added an emotion focus (Nezu & Nezu, 2019) with strategies "geared to foster adaptive emotional regulation skills" (Nezu, Nezu, & Gerber, 2019, p. 368). The major impetus for this development was the finding that strong negative emotions could simply overwhelm the client's ability to plan and implement a reasoned problem-solving strategy. In addition, however, some strong emotions, such as suicidal despair, *are* the problem (Nezu & Nezu, 2021).

Feelings can be important without strong emotions being involved. As explained, "I feel" can often be substituted by "I am," but also by colloquialisms in which we use words like "I think" or "I want." But that means there is still an affective component in terms of valence, even if there is not much in terms of activation or arousal. After any event or any activity, feelings are the experiential residue that lingers on, allowing us to feel rewarded and permitting the re-evaluation of the desirability of the activity and its consequences. And in addition, of course, feelings accompany any activity while it is occurring, thus serving as internal control mechanisms that prompt continuation of the activity or its termination. Stimuli from a specific context elicit feelings propelling you to action. If the engagement of that action is commensurate with (relevant to) the feeling propellant, then feelings sustain and guide the activity, and if not, then behavior changes to align the goals and the feelings more appropriately. We tend to think that cognitive appraisal of our own performance provides the feedback mechanism for continued activity, but this will only be true if the affective experience is desirable or expected. Cognitivists like to talk about the classic behavioral choice-making situation as WIN-STAY, LOSE-SHIFT. This makes perfect sense except that winning and losing have to be experienced positively or negatively. Wins and losses don't ever matter to an individual unless they are felt (experienced) in certain emotional ways.

This is what makes the idea of reinforcement or reward as an emotional experience so important. We can see this when someone wins something (or is rewarded) and yet it brings no pleasure to them. Will that reward serve as a reinforcement and increase the likelihood of the behavior leading to it being performed again? I think not. But when is a win not pleasurable? Well, it could be that the person perceives they did not truly deserve it, that someone else was primarily responsible for the achievement, or the reward was less than expected (a lettuce leaf instead of a cookie), or the material reward was not accompanied by the social acclaim that was deserved, or by the time the rewards came they were not as valuable to the person as they were once—just one more Oscar to put on the shelf. Feeling blasé can occur when reward schedules are far too rich—something that parents with bored children have perhaps failed to realize.

Some feelings, however, require a specific context to be experienced. Falling in love, for example, a highly pleasurable experience, can only happen if you have actually met someone with whom you have interacted and shared experiences. This would mean that social approach behaviors in potentially friend-making contexts are going to be important for experiencing subsequent feelings of love. Individuals with strong social anxieties need to recognize that their fear of rejection, their dread of being humiliated, their dislike of being judged by others, and all the other feelings that can make up social anxiety disorder are not going to be as aversive over time as being lonely, feeling unloved, or regretful of lost chances for friendship.

In the early days of behavior therapy when the influence of Skinnerian thinking was so strong, syndromes such as depression were judged to be due to low levels of positive reinforcement. The notion did lead directly to the development by Lewinsohn (1974) of the very successful therapeutic principles of behavioral activation. But it wasn't really a causal explanation because it was the depression that rendered potential reinforcements to be unpleasurable and thus unrewarding. If you can increase specific behavioral activities, it is always helpful for clients, but experiencing pleasure seems even more so. We have to get back to helping depressed clients like and enjoy things again.

There is both bottom up (neuroscience) and top down (experiential and phenomenological) scholarly indications that pleasure is an important feeling, not just because it is a "good" feeling but because it is so often a missing element in clients with emotional disorders. They either don't experience much pleasure or the pleasure they do experience is only from activities that are damaging to their overall well-being.

Clients have multiple opportunities to experience pleasure but are distracted. It is worth recommending a calming activity like a walk in the forest that allows for "soft fascination" and contemplation. That is why teaching clients to savor experiences can be so useful. It is a simple strategy, easy to do, and when they remember to do it, results in immediate benefit of positive feelings. We tend to recommend physical sensory experiences to savor: focusing on how food tastes or drinks feel (an ice-cold drink on a hot day) or the satisfaction of a hot shower after a work-out on a treadmill. But even common objects around the house will be things that give pleasure if clients will stop and really engage with them—their favorite picture on the wall bought on that trip to Venice thirty years ago, their coffee mug with elephants on it they got when they took their son to the Bronx Zoo. We have enormous attachments to (liking for) our possessions, however humble they may be, if one is willing to really attend to them. Did you actually look at all the signatures on that presentation baseball in the plastic case that your grandfather gave to you on your thirteenth birthday, which you still have on a shelf somewhere? Surely you have in the back of a drawer the hideous ashtray that was your child's first clay sculpture in kindergarten, carefully wrapped in tissue paper because it is still precious.

We all have favorite things—and there is sure to be more than a few of them! Raindrops on roses, for instance, and whiskers on kittens, or bright copper kettles, and your cozy warm woolen mittens, and if you've ever seen one, maybe you like brown paper packages tied up with strings—a list I have obviously borrowed from *The Sound of Music*. It was William Morris, one of the leaders of the Arts and Crafts movement, who suggested one should only have possessions that you feel to be either beautiful or functional. But having seemingly useless objects around us because of their association with beautiful people and meaningful memories is an important source of delight, and positive feelings that can be shared with loved ones, friends, and family.

What the simple delights that surround a person also provide is another absolutely essential feeling for clients to embrace: a feeling of security, the "comfort of home." ("Oh, Aunt Em, there's no place like home" says Dorothy as she clicks her ruby heels and returns to Kansas!) *Familiarity* is the foundational experience for security, for feeling safe. The unexpectedness of events causes negative feelings. But on the other hand, *seeking* (SEEKING in Panksepp's theory) is one of the most fundamental elements of our evolution and drives positive feelings like curiosity, sexual desire, creativity, and the exciting sense of adventure (Wright & Panksepp, 2012). Savoring requires practice and a focus of attention. It is an essential component of mindfulness training, but many aspects of "mindfulness practice" can be self-absorbing, don't encourage sharing feelings, and may not enhance complex feelings of pleasure. It is high time we gave *feelingness* as much attention as mindfulness.

Social Feelings and Loneliness

It is only a small step from sensory delight and attachment to the objects of one's life to attachment to the people in one's life. How can we enhance the quality of people's emotional ties to significant others and support social connectedness? Loneliness is one of the primary unspoken and undiagnosed symptoms of so many patients who come to therapy via the formal mental health system. It is a feeling that seems to arise from the unmet need to belong. McCleery and Evans (2001) reported a series of single-case outcomes of the then new developments from British psychiatry of using CBT technique to reduce the so-called "positive" symptoms of persons with schizophrenia, such as delusions and hallucinations (Kingdon & Turkington, 1994). We obtained significant reductions in these classic psychiatric symptoms of psychosis. In a more qualitative analysis of how our clients were feeling at termination, however, we found something else. All of them reported that they were still feeling lonely. While Bellack and Hersen (1979) had long ago provided convincing evidence for the value of their focus on social skills for people with serious and persistent mental illness, social skills alone do not guarantee social relationships. Opportunity plus a willingness to connect with others are also needed (Evans & Meyer, 2001), something support staff in sheltered mental health and disability programs have to recognize (Evans & Moltzen, 2000).

There are feelings closely related to liking which have a two-way effect in social contexts. The interaction of environmental influences can be particularly important in enhancing positive feelings. After all, you have to have experienced accomplishments, achievements, and successes to feel positive about ones that enhance your feelings of self-efficacy. Bandura (1977) actually said self-efficacy was a belief, a cognitive event, a thought that "I can do it." It's a good example of the difference between cognitive theorists and behaviorists. I would argue that self-efficacy is more often a feeling—similar to a feeling of competence for a given task. You may *say* you can do a task or are good at it, and you can say it to yourself or others, but to motivate your behavior, you need more than a belief, you need to experience it as a feeling—you can feel efficacious/competent/capable and that's a good feeling to have. Think of the delight a baby shows when it has taken its first independent steps. It is the beginning of a personal feeling of mastery. The delighted praise from a parent is just an extra reward. Difficult or demanding adult activities that require displays of capability are also intrinsically reinforced by feelings of competence, though there's a benefit of further reinforcement when done with friends who will praise you for your accomplishments no matter how small they might appear to others.

Feeling of gratitude is a social feeling with mixed valence. The feeling is not always positive, as gratitude is a feeling that can be used by the powerful to make the less powerful satisfied with what little they have. Making others feel grateful is a manipulative way of ensuring they don't expect or ask for more. Gratitude can therefore lead to passivity and inaction. On the other hand, feeling grateful for what are clearly the privileges and opportunities afforded by the sacrifices and thoughtful consideration of others can ensure a level of appreciation for things you have in life as the result of someone else's hard work and generosity. It is a delicate balance. I would not usually encourage clients to feel gratitude if they are children, but adults might, when savoring, give some thought to the origin of their positive experiences. The key logic of feeling grateful is the nature of the attribution. Making accurate attributions regarding the source of your current status is important for giving appropriate credit and acknowledgment to the work of others, as well as your own contribution. If gratitude leads to greater empathy and appreciation for true causes, it is a socially and personally valuable feeling, but harmful if it does not.

Controlling Feelings by Having Better Ones

Teaching clients how to manage their feelings is a specific form of what we refer to more broadly as coping strategies or emotion regulation. Negative, unpleasant, and persistent feelings that are no longer relevant to the initiating experience do not represent a circumstance that requires coping in the sense of planning behavioral and contextual compensatory change. The feelings may be a consequence of bad circumstances that should have been better coped with, and better coping might have prevented distressing feelings from ever occurring. But once feelings are aroused, different techniques are needed to manage and regulate them. Therapists can teach clients to cope better with circumstances, but it is less easy when the circumstances are internal to themselves, encompassing negative feelings they would rather not have.

I have stressed that feelings are elicited by distinct external events. Many of these are simple external stimuli that our different senses detect. Many feelings are reflexive in quality. The old question as to whether you need to consciously have the feeling of fear before you respond to danger is not a good one. The stimulus is received, and you laugh spontaneously, or cry, or your heart races, your palms sweat. These are reflexive. You don't need to process the nature of the event cognitively or consciously any more than when you see a hazard while driving and you slam on the breaks or swerve without any elaborate judgment of the degree of actual danger. Obviously at some level, the central nervous system is involved but the action is involuntary, not based on a preceding conscious thought or intermediate cognitive processing of which you can be aware. We have fast and slow feelings as well as fast and slow thoughts.

The reflexive nature of those feelings that involve immediate interooception from the physical changes caused by the ANS reacting as it should make them especially hard to self-regulate. And the same seems to be true for the countless soft stimuli that don't cause a psychophysiological response but nevertheless "strike a nerve." Someone's nasty remark in a conversation, a barrier preventing a desired goal response, your ice cream falling to the ground, seeing a person in pain can hurt or arouse feelings that are themselves complex, but their elicitation is simple, immediate, and reflexive in adults just as they are in children. The response to the feeling, shortening it when negative or prolonging it when positive, can be managed easier than the feeling itself, and that is what we learn to do during development—or should do.

Cognitively, interpretations of events determine the precise nature of feelings. If you have the money and the ice cream parlor isn't closed, your dropped treat isn't a tragedy. A colleague's success (promotion, a new grant, a major publication) is a shared experience of pleasure. Or could be experienced as feelings of jealousy and resentment, and if so, we will try to disguise those initial negative feelings when we recognize them as beneath us and unbecoming. In sports, satisfaction can be felt that you played your best even if you came second, or you can feel deep disappointment at what you judge to be a crushing defeat. Does every cloud really have a silver lining? Yes, because every feeling is conditional on circumstances as interpreted by the individual, not necessarily consciously or in words, as I have frequently asserted. In Chapter 1, I asked you to think about the difference between feeling helpless and feeling powerless. The distinction, as you probably worked out, is whether you perceive there is a possible solution to your problem but you don't have it or cannot access it (you are powerless to effect change), or whether you perceive that no possible solutions exist (you are helpless to effect change). In both cases, a client's feeling hinders taking effective action, but their expectations alter the feeling in a subtle way that might be relevant to you as their therapist.

A good example of this processing issue—more serious than the fallen ice cream—comes from a common everyday occurrence of feeling anger while driving. In some situations, other drivers do things that are dangerous or stupid and which interfere with your driving plan (cut you off, stop suddenly, turn without signaling, etc.). An autonomic response occurs rapidly, is felt immediately, and is often followed by an immediate action tendency (negative urgency) such as swearing, shouting, honking one's horn, making rude gestures. The entire pattern is what we call an anger response; when extreme, popular media call it road rage. But the logic of anger requires that the action was a *deliberate* attempt to interfere with you or take advantage of you. If the offending behavior was accidental, anger is not logical and should dissipate rapidly. If the person apologizes, signals they made a mistake, has a learner's sticker, or has an out of state or foreign license plate and you decide they were lost, you will be forgiving rather than angry. That is the cognitive part. Your feeling might change from anger to contempt ("What an idiot!") or to relief ("Thank god I braked in time") or to amusement ("Did you see his look of surprise when he realized he was going the wrong way!"). These cognitive re-appraisals take time, so the anger is still there but the new feelings will build on the arousal from the initial anger, and their negativity will dissipate.

Therapists don't have much control over people's past experiences or their fixed personality characteristics that make them volatile and emotionally reactive. However, there are effective strategies for helping clients manage the level and intensity of their feelings according to some personal principles they may enjoy. And there are examples of how training and skill development reduce negative feelings from uncertain threats and improbable dangers.

Overall, some would argue the general idea should be conveyed to clients that feelings are a good thing to be valued and nurtured and not avoided. Even pain itself, although it is a response that we feel, is a reaction that warns us about physical dangers in the environment, so people unable to feel their pain response are at risk of considerable harm. In the same fashion, disgust and nausea warn us about ingesting or consuming harmful foods a second time. Feelings give richness to our lives and good ones must be treasured. Bad feelings need not always be avoided, as they have the beneficial function of signaling that something is wrong. Bad feelings don't always have to be changed unless they are destructive of good feelings and desired goals.

One feeling often can reduce or enhance another, and so in therapy, feelings about oneself and about one's therapist can be used strategically to encourage the sort of even, balanced, or more passionate feelings that the client desires (trust, affection, liking, for the therapist). Contexts and conditions and past experiences can be redefined logically through reasoning, persuasion, and stories (narratives). These can all be defined as cognitive interventions. But it is the analysis of the logic (the requirement) of a feeling that can sometimes be most easily changed. Because every feeling has a stimulus eliciting it, changing the nature (character) of the stimulus context will change the feeling. If you are alone, it might make you feel lonely if the overall context is lack of available supports. But if you are alone and the context is independence or autonomy (not controlled by, or not responsible for, others), the feeling will be freedom.

In therapy, this re-appraisal is often what we try to suggest. It is not without risks as you are implying your client's feelings are wrong, unnecessary, or inappropriate. They will resist that. Nobody likes their feelings discounted in any situation. Sometime one can express your challenge more reflectively: "Can you think of any other way to explain why X did that/said that to you? What do you think *they* might have been feeling? What might make someone so reactive and sensitive in this situation?" There are ways of introducing alternative logics that don't necessitate a refutation of the client's initial judgment.

Sometimes clients need to be allowed to feel what others feel in a situation, be it elation, triumph, success, satisfaction. Do not let them diminish the value of an accomplishment, however small, and make sure your own praise is genuine and cannot easily be dismissed. By setting and supporting attainable goals, you give the client a chance metaphorically to score a goal, win a cup, receive a prize. This doesn't mean that everyone has to win; the feeling of success will not be very strong, genuine, or deserved unless an element of struggle—something to be overcome—is involved.

We all recognize that our feelings can confuse us. Sometimes they run counter to our values and as a result generate a new feeling of guilt or shame. If our anger leads to thoughts of wishing harm on someone, we can easily feel ashamed that this violates our non-violent, peace-loving, and tolerant values. Sometimes we have uncomfortable feelings and cannot easily identify the source of the feeling so we cannot resolve the origins of distress or conflict—although conflicting feelings are common.

To allow clients to express their feelings, to tell you "what's underneath," is the essence of much of psychotherapy's "nonspecific" effectiveness. A therapist sometimes needs to be judgmental; unconditional positive regard permits honest feedback. But encouraging openness allows the clients to express feelings without monitoring or self-deception. For that, they must be assured of safety from being judged harshly or criticized, laughed at, or despised as would possibly happen in any other social setting. Many social contexts don't encourage expression of feelings—it can be uncomfortable. And feelings that reflect an attitude that might be offensive or threatening to others will give rise to hurt or angry feelings in one's audience. Free speech about one's feelings often comes at a social cost. As a client in therapy, however, you can say what you like, and you can report your feelings. As feelings can be difficult to describe, especially when they are in conflict with each other, it takes time to help a client express what they really feel, especially if they are socially proscribed feelings that the client has spent a lifetime learning not to report. This was one reason that Freud developed the strategy (now largely lost to modern science-based psychotherapy) of having the client lie on the couch with the therapist seated behind, so that the stream of consciousness from the client was more like someone talking to themselves. Even slight body reactions, changes in facial expression can be readily picked up by clients during conventional face-to-face office interactions. If these are detected as signs of disapproval, you lose the chance to hear uncensored feelings described and worked through.

"And when that happened (or when you reacted that way, etc.), how did it make you feel?" is one of the most common questions in all psychotherapy. But whether you listen to and understand the answer, or even get an honest one, is much less certain. Adjectives that describe feelings are complex, as we've seen throughout this book. Feelings are hard to describe. Clients do not always have the vocabulary. Assuming that one of the goals of psychotherapy is to allow clients to clarify their feelings, accept them, resolve conflicting feelings, and to have more of the feelings that help them experience life's rewards, I have to conclude that labelling, defining, and generally clarifying feelings is as good for clients as it is for children. If parents can help children understand a feeling and being able to do so is part of emotion competence, then surely the same notion applies to therapy?

I have proposed that one can also foster conflict between feelings in order to reduce the one that is more negative or not working for the client. But opposite feelings are also tricky. Is the opposite of fear the feeling of bravery? Is confidence the opposite of anxiety, as certainty is the opposite of doubt? If someone feels pride, I have suggested it should be for performance that is worthy of acclaim and respect. If it is, there is surely no harm in a little pride, but if it comes with a feeling of superiority, it leads to arrogance in style and deed, and if it comes with feeling overconfident, hubris often leads to a downfall, or so we hope. But the opposite of pride is humility. Feeling humble allows you to recognize that someone else's accomplishments can outshine your own. Having only one or other of these feelings creates an imbalance so your feeling is out of proportion to the context—being excessively proud or excessively humble is not appealing to others. And feelings like pride tend to translate to overt behaviors towards others that they can recognize—everyone knows the face of feeling smug. Someone who is feeling too pleased with themselves will have a condescending little smile (there's even a smug face emoji for it) and make self-righteous remarks. Smug is the opposite of modest and unsure. And while humility is seen as a virtue, particularly in religious contexts, being excessively humble when one has even some degree of worth as a person will seem to others as disingenuous. Both feelings of pride and feelings of humility require accurate appraisal of oneself and others in terms of accomplishments. A therapist can often help identify accomplishments the client doesn't recognize (like being a good parent) and enable promotion of self-compassion. And this in turn allows clients to feel self-satisfaction. Simple techniques in behavior therapy like encouraging the client to use self-reinforcement help promote the selection of a standard for an accomplishment that is realistic and worthwhile. Young children know that.

There is another part of standard psychotherapeutic fare. Over and over in this book, we have encountered the more dynamic concepts around feelings that are *not* expressed. Not feeling a feeling or talking about it to others doesn't mean the feeling is not somewhere inside us. Freud (1901/2021) proposed that "unresolved" feelings continued to wreak havoc on our psyches. And at some level, we all know that is true. We talk of people "bottling up" their feelings and we don't think it is a good thing because eventually there will be one eliciting stimulus too many, one little back-breaking straw that evokes a flood of difficult to control feelings. Descriptively, it is clear that this is a common phenomenon—the release of pent-up feelings that are then less able to work successfully to guide our actions, motivate us, reward us, bring us joy and happiness. It is a weak excuse, but many a criminal defendant tries to justify some heinous behavior with the claim "I just snapped!"

Everyone in my generation knows of ordinary men and woman, husbands and wives, fathers and uncles drafted into the military to serve their country, coming back from war, and rarely talking about their experiences. Of course, they didn't want to talk and to describe events and conjure up vivid memories because it would inevitably re-kindle (note the use of fire, spark, type imagery in common usage) the most unpleasant feelings imaginable. Old comrades meeting up and telling each other the stories they all already knew was always a safer option because everyone in the audience already knew the feelings that accompanied the action of the stories. Painful feelings do not have to be openly expressed when with others who have had the same experiences.

But in therapy, as in intimate relationships, honest communication of feelings is important. One might need to be a little cautious in expressing hidden feelings to a partner, but one should not have to be guarded when talking to one's therapist. Therapy is a transactional relationship quite different from a romantic relationship or even a friendship. The client has no responsibility of any kind not to shock you, not to hurt *your* feelings, or influence your moral judgment of them as an individual. You may experience all of those things, but they are irrelevant to the relationship because the relationship is always about the client and not your feelings.

Clients mostly like their feelings to be authenticated. Being told that one shouldn't feel a certain way or that a feeling is unjustified is aversive to most people. What upsets one person's feelings may not bother another, so arguing that your client is over-emotional, or too sensitive, or not looking at things the "right" or "rational" way does nothing to effect change. In fact, it mostly adds another source of irritation. Therapists do not have to affirm a client's feelings, nor do we have to validate them. We do have to listen to them, understand them, accept them, and decide whether the client is asking for help in changing their feelings. Once again, we return to the parental role of accepting and labeling feelings to allow the individual to know themselves better. But many clients prefer less analytic, more directive approaches.

Giving and Receiving Pleasure

Neuroscientists remind us we have pleasure "circuits" in the brain. Every human being can do things that generate feelings of pleasure. Why don't we spend all our waking time doing so? Obviously, there are often diminished practical opportunities for obtaining or doing things that give pleasure. We have learnt from early babyhood that many of the things that can produce instant feelings of pleasure are not acceptable to others, and later we learn that they are also harmful for our general health and well-being. We have also discovered that some feelings of pleasure arise from actions that harm other people and empathic concerns about that harm would interfere with feeling pleasure. And we have also learned that by delaying immediate pleasures (gratification), we can ensure greater or more prolonged pleasure later. I don't really need to spell out the general point: while everyone seeks pleasure and tries to have pleasant feelings, we do not do so all the time. For clients in psychotherapy, however, it is often the case that they have very few feelings of pleasure. And for some people, loss of reward feels more negative than gain of one feels positive, as I discussed in Chapter 3 and again with respect to reward dominance in children in Chapter 4. If you want to think as a neuroscientist, clients' defensive and avoidance neural system is more active than their pleasure centers. "Reward positivity" is the name given to greater neural reactivity (measured by EEG) to an outcome of gain (reward) than an outcome of loss (of reward) (Proudfit, 2015).

Increasing pleasure feelings is only rarely listed as one of the goals of individual therapy. Would it not be valuable to think of new or alternative sources of pleasant feelings for every client? Don't we need to activate those pleasure networks in the brain? In behavior therapy, we might interpret this suggestion as increasing a client's schedules of reinforcement, a fundamental component of all behavioral intervention plans. But by emphasizing *feelings* of pleasure, we can enhance the experiences of planned activities. You might give a client a reinforcement survey (Cautela & Kastenbaum, 1967) and use this to make suggestions regarding new activities. These might be enjoyed to some extent, but by encouraging a direct and attentive focus on the parts of that activity that are most likely to be pleasurable, you can make sure that the emotional value of the reinforcer is increased. Too often, I have heard depressed clients report to me "Yes, I tried doing what you suggested and went out for a good dinner with a friend, but I didn't enjoy it much. It just didn't make me feel good." Regrettably, there was no planned focus (on my part) on the elements of the experience that would have produced feelings of pleasure—a great tasting entrée, good conversation, or finding the cocktails were half price during happy hour. (Now you know the things that give me pleasure.)

I have tried to explain throughout that while feelings are the experience of emotion, this does not make them mystical. They are real, whether the emotions being experienced are distinctive and distinguishable primary ones or a generalized reaction that gets interpreted or "constructed" differentially (Barrett, 2006; 2017b). Feelings are very physical, some more so than others: sadness that makes you weep, guilt that makes you gulp, rejection that makes you want to retaliate, jealousy really can feel like a little green worm! We can track areas of the brain that are active when feelings are felt, but not yet track the unique neurochemical and hormonal changes that underly the reactions of the autonomic nervous system. Perhaps we will one day, but we will still need the phenomenology of it all to make any sense of what an experience means to the individual—to gaze at the painting, not analyze its structure.

The Tangled Professional Strands of Feelings Research

You have gamely struggled through the tangle of research traditions, old concepts with new names, different names for the same basic thing, fundamental research studies so obscure that their relevance to clinical practice is opaque, and my own selection of topics influenced by past research interests and unique clinical experiences. Is there any hope of now weaving a meaningful tapestry from these many threads? We have become used, nowadays, to standards in research studies which demand things like replication, raw data available for perusal by others, and announcing your intentions in advance so failures don't just disappear but can become part of the negative evidence for an idea. Maybe, when the studies relate specifically to clinical phenomena and their treatment, practitioners should request another standard. Specification of exactly what domain of practice and clinical realities to which they think their scientific findings will be relevant. Putting it another way, we should be asking questions like "Would the findings of your research contribute to an explicit change in the way we might approach treatment for a client?" Does the research suggest an improvement in past practices that were once hailed as valuable? Are you recommending an adjustment to an old method, or does the evidence support abandoning the old method in favor of a novel approach? Is it the same old wine in new bottles, and if so, what was wrong with the old ones?

The assumption of this book, along with my previous two, is that insightful ideas rather than specific research findings are most likely to influence practicing psychotherapists, even those most committed to evidence-informed practice. I'm hoping that what emerges for you from this collection of topics and principles and research studies boils down to four things: (a) a greater appreciation of the importance of considering feelings in "evidence-based" cognitive-behavioral therapy; (b) greater understanding of where feelings come from; (c) greater respect for the importance and universality of human feelings across all manner of people and cultures; and from these three, (d) enhanced understanding of your own feelings and the role they play in your recognition of others' and your designs for how they might be changed.

For this to happen, the threads must produce a meaningful tapestry, not just be a jumble of constructs. The tapestry, like the great medieval tapestries of old, has to tell a story about human nature that is real, strongly influenced by culture, yet not unique to any one culture. The story should show you what you can do in therapy to lift the life of your client so they can make their own story. What is the framework for this tapestry? It should be that feelings are good and essential. All cultures believe that pursuing happiness and other good feelings is an individual's right as a human, but not at the expense of other people's happiness and well-being. All cultures recognize that there are significant differences among people as to what will make them happy, and all cultures believe happiness cannot be experienced without some unhappy feelings, so they too will need to be experienced in a meaningful life.

One part of the story is that feelings have names and definitions that can be verbalized. I feel secure, which means that I am aware that the people and things that support my existence are reasonably permanent and immutable. I feel rejected which means I see I'm being avoided, and I feel insulted when I perceive criticism as ill-intentioned, and both make me feel sad or angry, sometimes together. I feel fear, which means that I have detected the active presence of dangers that threaten me and other things dear to me. I feel jealous, which means you have something I want and I deserve, maybe even more than you do. I feel anxiety, which means that I am aware of avoidable negative events that have a high probability of doing me harm. I feel joy, which means that the good things I experience make me happy, and I feel gratitude when I recognize that others were responsible for those good things. I feel rage, which means that the anger I feel when goals are thwarted is also felt to be uncontrollable. I feel nostalgic, which means that things from my past, whether people, or photographs, or conversations, or memories, evoke a mixture of great fondness and of sadness that they will not occur again.

Some feelings are strongly influenced by time frames—when the experience occurred and whether it can be repeated. This, as already indicated, is true for nostalgia. It is also true for the feeling of regret, as mentioned in Chapter 5. One can feel regretful about a number of things, which complicates analysis of this as a feeling state. When one regrets an action (or an inaction), it leads quite quickly to regret as a negative feeling. But one can also regret an experience such as missing out, that is less immediately and less directly linkable to one's own behavior. Missing out can be current and is linked to loneliness and immediate disappointment. It can also be a retrospective feeling of having missed out on past events, and research by Hayran and Gürhan-Canli (2022) has indicated that the former is experienced as more negative and with a greater degree of arousal. These same authors proposed that when attempting to deal with distant feelings of missing out, people are more likely to rely on emotion-focused coping. When having current feelings of missing out, however, people will be more likely to use problem-focused coping strategies to redress the situation.

However, and this is critical, the verbalized definitions of the conditions eliciting my feeling (the conscious realization of the feelings) need not occur first for the feeling to be elicited. Our feelings can occur without a conscious prior analysis and justification. It suggests that if a client can verbalize the conditions, such as explaining them to you as the therapist, they then have an opportunity to assess whether the feeling is justified by reality or is more of a shadow of past feelings that were justified at the time. And if they are not justified, there will be a need not to correct the feeling but to alter the reality of their experience—for example, lower anxiety by approaching the things clients think might do them harm and see if they are real, or, for jealousy, focus on the positive things or experiences you have, and make a realistic appraisal as to whether the person you are jealous of is truly less deserving than you, or if feeling shame, don't hide, brazenly display your strengths.

Talk therapy, in which a client acknowledges their feelings to a therapist, or social exchange in which you explain your feelings to a friend, both work (makes one feel better after disclosure) by clarifying the thoughts and actions needing to be changed. Short-term benefits often accrue simply because you let your feelings out, got things off your chest—the psychoanalysts were the first to understand that bottling up feelings, not explaining them or professing them publicly, wasn't good for you. That's why we call that mode of therapy "psychodynamic" because if you block the release of pressure, then things blow (tops, lids, gaskets). But it was Freud who observed with one of his earliest cases (actually his friend Breuer's, who told him all about it) when Anna O. poured out her feelings, the relief she felt was only temporary. Behaviorists think that cathartic relief when negative feelings are expressed, while definitely a thing, can only have longer-term benefits if the circumstances causing the feelings are changed by engaging in new behaviors. It is the essence of the feeling (its definition, its logic) that points to what precisely needs to be changed.

How and Why?

Putting all the bits and pieces of feelings research and theory together to form a meaningful whole is a challenging task. But a few general principles do arise from the multitude of varied material that has been considered thus far. I'll identify the ones I think are key, beginning with the fundamental recognition that feelings are learned: they are acquired and shaped by experience.

Many of the behavior patterns that come to clinical attention and which our clients and usually their immediate society and broader culture consider undesirable are a direct consequence of specific feelings. The outward behavioral *enactment* of an inner emotional feeling, both inappropriate approach and attraction (e.g., sexual paraphilias, addictions, violence) or unnecessary avoidance (e.g., depression, school refusal, distancing yourself from crowds or friendships, non-participation in activities), is typically what treatments are focused on—the targeted behavior to be changed. However you like to conceptualize mental health problems—behaviorally, cognitively, neurologically, humanistically—feelings are going to be crucial and cannot be ignored.

Some problems are not the innate, automatic, or inevitable manifestation of the feeling but have evolved as ways of dealing with unpleasant affect. The treatment focus in such dynamics would best be directed towards more acceptable and less harmful ways of managing negative affect. One way of doing this might be to explain to clients that the way they are interpreting their world is wrong (irrational) and by misconstruing situations their feelings are wrong. Another broad tactic might be convincing clients that having negative feelings shouldn't matter and by struggling with them, they are making things worse. What really matters is that the feelings are making you do things you don't like or stopping you from doing things you do like. Another general approach relies on helping a client focus on the positive things in life, being more attentive to good experiences, being more reflective. Learning new skills also represents a general therapeutic model: learning ways of better regulating feelings, better ways of coping with adversity and stress, and changing environment so that old habits are not evoked in new settings. I imagine you too can express your own general therapeutic tactics in one sentence. But since the ones I've suggested, probably yours as well, are not incompatible, we have to conclude that there is no one global summary possible.

Much fascinating research is devoted to the emotional architecture of the brain. Thinking of the emergence of complex feelings in children, however, and the importance of having emotion competence for becoming adults, seems to me to require placing equal emphasis on learning experiences. We see displays of feelings in others close to us and we try as children to understand them. We learn what our friends like and dislike, and we learn that they probably won't like exactly the same things we do, which then means learning about fairness, cooperation, acceptance, empathy, as well as what might and what won't hurt the feelings of those we spend time with. Think of the importance of these experiences within families, and schools, and teams and other groups for supporting emotion regulation and feeling competence. And then think of children growing up with certain feelings who then become parents and now in turn shape the feelings of their children. Then think of the "traditional" family structures, parental roles, and family values, and see how entirely irrelevant they are to ensuring the depth of experience, background security, and learning opportunities that support positive feelings, empathy, curiosity, tolerance, and understanding of one's own and others' feelings.

A constellation of specific negative feelings and dysfunctional behaviors attracts our attention because it is what the client is complaining about and will fit predetermined categories—the syndromes identified as "mental disorders." However, we need to recognize that a client's everyday experiences and their feelings are much more complicated and richer than the specific occasions on which their pathology emerges. This truism has been illuminated by research paradigms that focus on what the client's life is like, either in general terms or from moment-to-moment sampling. As clients talk about their diagnosable "constellation" (syndrome) and tell you all about what it was like at different times since the previous therapeutic visit (on-going symptoms), your sample of their feelings is quite limited. You will not really know how often they laughed during the week, how many simple joys and pleasures were experienced each day, what potentially hurtful (to their feelings) events they reacted to and coped with or generally managed. It would be helpful to find these things out. Positive psychology approaches encourage a balanced focus of the good as well as the bad parts of life.

This fact in turn supports what any social psychologist will tell you. One's immediate personal relationships and friendships, as well as the emotional climate of the settings at work and at play, will be filled with opportunities for feelings to be elicited, good ones to be relished, and bad ones dealt with. Sometimes climates as broad as political and governmental actions will influence mood states which then make the multitude of potential triggers either more salient (noticeable, observable) or more influential. It is just like physical climates such as a long dark winter, or oppressive humidity and heat, creating a background of discomfort that escalates the negativity of otherwise possibly minor experiences of personal susceptibility.

It is reasonable to think everyone's life is susceptible to current social and physical influences *because* we, like other species, have evolved defensive means of managing threats of harm by active escape, passive avoidance, or cautious approach. And we have prospered by forming effective social groups and needing to respond with joy and love and affection and care in order to be able to rely on others for succor, safety, and procreation. We prosper when individuals share their skills and their ingenuity, and when their creativity can entertain us. And as resources were not infinite, there were times we needed to protect ours by aggression, most effectively when angry feelings are disciplined. While we have discernible biological tendencies along these dimensions, they need to be managed for the benefit of the group. This means we need environments in which we learn to use feelings for our personal benefit and the benefit of others. We all need opportunities to experience and manage feelings in play settings that are not intrinsically harmful but allow for hundreds of learning trials about our own feelings and about other's feelings. Thus, clinical work with parents and families that focuses on positive environments, family activities, outside friendships, and imaginative play, represents one of the most important prevention strategies known. Similarly, with formal teaching (including stories and fables, things read, and things seen on electronic media), there is an essential need for adults and friends who can model different emotional reactions and help everyone understand their feelings better.

When these environments break down (harsh parenting, unresponsive teachers, and social calamities like loss of the security of housing and homes, warfare displacement, and chronic diseases), the effect on feelings and their development can be catastrophic. We have formal methods of intervening with the victims of trauma and traumatic circumstances, but it would be better to avoid those circumstances altogether. It is absurd to think we can help produce coping and positive feelings in societal circumstances that are destructive to all the things we know are needed for positive feelings of fulfillment: security, predictability, novelty, opportunity to feel worthwhile, freedom from want and disease, opportunity to have the same lives of material comfort that modern societies have now permitted for the majority of the humans on this planet.

Feelings have a special place in caregiving contexts, including psychotherapy. We could make an enormous contribution to a society imbued with positive feelings or even negative ones used for socially beneficial purposes simply by ensuring that families function well and understand the importance of feelings. Urie Bronfenbrenner once said "We now know what it takes to enable families to work the magic that only they can perform. The question is, are we willing to make the sacrifices and the investment necessary to enable them to do it?" (quoted by Ceci, 2006, p 174). Families often face considerable economic and social pressures. Parents experience burnout. Every child needs to feel wanted; parental feelings of regret have unknown consequences.

Having said that, the language of feelings rather than emotions allows us to have an extraordinary range of affective experiences, both physical (highly varied foods that taste really delicious) and social/psychological (the warmth and security of a friendship, the intimacy of romantic relationships). We could almost represent the act of doing psychotherapy as a focused opportunity to enrich a client's life of positive feelings and thereby enhance the positive feelings of the others with whom your client interacts. The "social contagion" of feelings is what psychotherapy allows. Even if the "intervention" is a rather mechanical one, like systematic desensitization or rational restructuring, you are affording the client a meta-emotional experience, showing them that feelings can change, that they have agency over their feelings, they are not compelled to feel a certain way or not feel another. This is because you are, through the relationship, your words, and your formal techniques, demonstrating that it is possible. Thus, all our long-standing debates about the nonspecifics in psychotherapy and the role of the relationship and the importance of the therapeutic alliance are quite irrelevant within the reality of emotional contagion and the sharing of feelings. This is not a denigration of all the excellent methods and measures and definitions, classification, and diagnoses of clients' problems, but simply a statement that focusing more on feelings will result in additional benefits. Obviously, there are ineffectual therapies and ineffectual therapists, but there aren't any experiences of psychotherapy that don't produce and change feelings, even if they are not the ones hoped for by either the client or the therapist. It has long been recognized that psychotherapy can make people feel worse.

Does an effective therapist have to understand their own feelings and make proper judgments of the feelings of others? That's one of the oldest questions around. The answer is clear as mud: maybe and sometimes. We've all seen trainees who seem totally clueless socially and emotionally manage to help clients. We don't know yet just how emotionally intelligent one needs to be. But it does seem that the literature on feelings is now more than rich enough for those of you who train the next generation of therapists to attend to whatever part of the curriculum (and practica and supervision) is needed to allow students to feel good about who they are. We want them to feel good about what they can do, and how they can communicate their psychological understanding and insights to the enormous variety of clients whom they might encounter professionally. Training programs have emotional climates just like kindergartens and third grade classrooms and high schools and mental hospitals do. Supervising a trainee therapist requires careful sensitivity to the feelings of the trainee. One's responsibility to the public (future clients, at any rate) demands that we sometimes have to hurt a student's feelings, curb their enthusiasm, analyze their motivation to succeed, assess their emotion competence, and expose them to emotional experiences that are as diverse as those of their future clients. We all have sensitivities, weaknesses, hypocrisies, and hubris. We all can be ashamed or embarrassed, defensive and jealous and feel regret and disappointment, and joy, and gratitude. However good you are, you can never fully know what another person is feeling. Let's be thankful that is true.

What some call "impulsive responses" to positive and negative feelings, others call coping behavior or part of emotion regulation. The same actions in response to strong feelings are also called positive and negative urgency. I have been using the term action tendencies. Actions which reduce negative feelings (escape or avoidance) or enhance and elaborate positive ones (approach) can indeed be described as dysfunctional or maladaptive if they carry their own consequences. If your client binge eats or goes on lavish shopping sprees in response to feelings of distress and rejection, the temporary relief from negative feelings is soon replaced by a second set of new feelings such as guilt, remorse, and self-hatred.

But our understanding of these dynamic processes and the value of having coping skills that reduce negative feelings and enhance positive ones suggests some nuanced tactics that can be recommended. For one thing, if the activation of the pleasure centers, pathways, and circuits in the brain can compete with the defensive (fear and anxiety) circuits, this suggests that whatever activity is recommended in response to negative feelings needs to focus on the element of pleasure. Behavioral activation (encouraging depressed clients to engage in more activities) has well-established benefits. We usually ask the client what things they enjoy doing or used to enjoy doing because we expect these will then be rewarding. But what we should focus on is things that bring pleasure directly. Doing something you generally enjoy does not mean that you will focus on and savor pleasurable experiences. Indeed, if the selected activity for a behavior activation strategy has even the slightest inconvenience, requires the slightest effort, and has occasional barriers, these are the features depressed clients focus on and report back to you the next week: "Yes, I took a walk in the evening like you suggested because I used to love walking, but I got a painful blister in my right foot." "Did you at least enjoy the scenery and admire the sunset?" "It was much too cloudy, and it rained a little." "Did the fresh cool air and rain on your face feel good?" "No, I was worried that my new watch would get wet."

I've had conversations like this with many past clients. Now I think the literature indicates that the activity is *only* of value if it can be experienced with pleasure. Thus, it must be chosen with a major emphasis on what can be positively savored or can be performed at a level which can only be evaluated as an accomplishment. And that requires it to be judged favorably (intrinsic reinforcement) by the individual or externally reinforced by praise from someone valued.

Why *do* feelings change? It's not that complicated. They change when circumstances most influential to the individual change. These changed circumstances need not be direct, and often they are not, because future affect-relevant situations and conditions can be imagined and past ones remembered. Feelings time travel!

The *function* of feelings (why we have them in the first place) is to ensure our survival and to improve our well-being and that of our offspring and of the community on which we depend, by communicating our experiences to others. Well-being—having the things that are comfortable and pleasurable—makes us feel happy, and when we are happy and feel good, we behave well to ourselves and others. We are good in that we try to give pleasure to others. When we are disadvantaged in some way, cannot obtain life's necessities, and face physical hazards and threats to our well-being and our survival, we have feelings that help us either approach and remove the threat, or if we can, avoid it and not encounter it. We also have evolved feelings that support activities whereby we can reduce our own deprivation by taking resources from others. These feelings provide the energy (the emotion) to engage in the necessary solutions, either approach or avoid—remembering that cognitively re-evaluating (changing something's meaning) is a constructive form of positive avoidance. However, by their signaling of adverse conditions, some of these same feelings have a strong negative valence—not only is the object of the feeling unpleasant, but the feeling is as well. The converse is true—having security, friendships, and all our physical needs met are not only things wanted, but the feelings themselves towards these things also have a positive valence—they feel good.

It is through learning and conditioning experiences that both positive and negative feelings come to be elicited by stimuli (conditions and circumstances) that are not the object of the feeling but signals for it. That means we are constantly subjected to the initiating circumstances for feelings, which is fine when they are mostly positive, but not so good when they are mostly negative. And because these stimuli can be symbols (sounds, words spoken and written, pictures, both still and moving, and imagined mental images), all of these aspects of our immediate environment have different degrees of affective value—different degrees to which they evoke feelings of any kind.

Feelings occur as a result of experience. If you are rejected, you will feel rejection. What you do with that feeling depends on past learning. So, feelings change with experiences and what you do with them depends on what was learned in past experiences. Why feelings change is because the importance, significance, or relevance of the stimulus triggers change. These change through a variety of processes. Maturity, growing up, and getting older alter the affective value of everything as our needs become more and more our own responsibility. Social and community changes that are inevitable over time reduce the prevalence of previous, affective-laden stimuli and introduce new ones. Sometimes these processes are deliberate: we have dissatisfaction with our current experiences and the feelings they generate, and we make focused efforts to change them. If we are not familiar with the how and why of our feelings, these efforts are not always successful and indeed often make us feel worse. When that happens, we seek other possible solutions, which can vary all the way from radical change of relationships, to changing communities and jobs, trying substances that alter experience (including medicines), and if possible, seeking the help of someone with better ideas, such as a religious figure or, best of all, a psychotherapist.

Feelings, being subjective experiences, must be inferred or judged in others (both our own personal social connections and our clients) from what they say and do. In both social and clinical contexts, adults and children may have reason to mask or disguise their true feelings. We all do this, and we understand it when others do too. In therapy, it means we must be alert to this, looking for inconsistencies in talk and behavior and facial expression, and judging the likelihood of a feeling or lack thereof from the context being discussed. Therapeutic skill demands some level of feeling intelligence. It is sensitivity to the feelings of others that seems so essential for therapeutic communication. While a range of facial expressions are similar across cultures, there can still be subtleties and ambiguities. Even distinctive signs like crying can vary greatly in meaning—what feeling they are actually expressing.

The experience of psychotherapy changes feelings—not always successfully but successfully enough to make it a viable method of change when well-intentioned, and—heresy warning!—often regardless of how it is done. But positive results are not guaranteed because no psychotherapist knows enough and because not enough is known. So, we keep looking for better therapists and therapists keep looking for better therapies and better stories for explaining them and justifying them. This book is one such story.

Postscript

Throughout this book, I have attempted to focus only on the needs of individuals who are the clients of clinical psychologists and other mental health specialists. Sometimes I have also considered the feelings of you, the reader, whether experienced in psychological interventions or still in training. What I have struggled to avoid is launching into the complexities and challenges of what are described as cultural feelings or national feelings, the mood of any country faced with the great upheavals of political, social, and economic change. And there continue to be at the present time truly terrible world-wide events of brutal wars damaging entire population centers, dictatorial oppression, famine, disease, all clearly preventable. During much of this book's writing period, the United States of America was experiencing the outcome and longer-term consequences of a dramatic election period, one described by every TV pundit as "the most consequential in any of our lifetime." By the time of the 2024 presidential election in the USA, America was a deeply divided country and is now even more so.

Any social statistic one chooses (longevity, child survival, access to leisure, social equality, standard of living, scientific progress, easily available technical conveniences) indicates that it would be better to have been born in this century or the last third of the previous one than any other time in history. Despite this, there was endless talk about "grievances" even though the USA and many other countries had largely recovered, in terms of objective economic indices, from the serious health, social, and financial crisis of the most recent world-wide pandemic, COVID-19. The results of the previous presidential election (November 2016) in which Donald J. Trump was first elected had come with great surprise on both sides, and a profound realization of two different nations. As one commentator mused: "Who knew that so many millions of White [American] men felt so emasculated by women and challenged by minorities? Who knew that after years of seeming progress on race and gender, tens of millions of

White Americans lived in seething resentment, waiting for a demagogue to arrive who would legitimize their worst selves and channel them into political power" (quoted by Solomon, 2020, pp. 65–66).

Paul Krugman, winner of the Nobel Memorial Prize in Economic Sciences, wrote in his final opinion column for the New York Times: "What strikes me, looking back [25 years ago], is how optimistic many people felt, both here [in the USA] and in much of the Western world ... and the extent to which that optimism has been replaced by anger and resentment" (Krugman, 2024). In my professional past, there was rarely a need to consider political issues in the course of providing psychological services to clients; the ethics of these services were always towards humanity, compassion, and acceptance. The current political circumstances in the USA threaten those values as core principles of diversity, equity, and inclusion are reviled. We know that social inequality contributes to population feelings of alienation and uncertainty.

As the feelings climates of entire nations turn sour and hostile, it is heartening to reflect on the words from 1944 of American singer and political activist Woody Guthrie:

> *I hate a song that makes you think you are not any good. I hate a song that makes you think that you are just born to lose. Bound to lose. No good to nobody. No good for nothing. Because you are too old or too young or too fat or too slim. Too ugly or too this or too that. Songs that run you down or poke fun at you....I'm out to fight those songs to my very last breath of air and my last drop of blood... I am out to sing the songs that make you take pride in yourself and in your work.* (Cray, 2006)

Throughout this book, I have tried to preserve some degree of scientific detachment from these issues at hand. Research in feelings is so broad and covers so many topics relevant to psychotherapy that it is difficult to extract some of the simpler truths. You don't need to be a therapist or psychologist to understand and recognize that feelings are very much on central stage in the human play. And they are not that complicated. Most people emerge from the universal experiences of birth, being parented, making friends, developing a personal system of likes and dislikes without interfering too much in those of others. We know how to hurt people emotionally and we know how to make them happy. We know what social and political policies are good for offering everyone the best possible chance of making their lives something meaningful, lasting, and personally satisfying. We know that personal satisfaction should not come at the expense of the opportunities of others to have the same kinds of emotional experiences. We know much about what is good for babies, good for justice, good for the planet, good for survival. Thanks to the psychology of feelings, we even know something about why we don't always practice those things.

REFERENCES

Abdusattorova, B. (2024). The interaction of feelings: Delving into the depths of happiness and sorrow. *Open Academia: Journal of Scholarly Research, 2*, 44–47.

Achenbach, T. M. (1966). The classification of children's psychiatric symptoms: A factor-analytic study. *Psychological Monographs, 80*, 1–37.

Achenbach, T. M., & Rescorla, L. A. (2001). *Manual for ASEBA school age forms & profiles*. University of Vermont Research Center for Children, Youth & Families.

Ahmed, T., Qassem, M., & Kyriacou, P. A. (2023). Measuring stress: A review of the current cortisol and dehydroepiandrosterone (DHEA) measurement techniques and considerations for the future of mental health monitoring. *Stress, 26*, 29–42.

Ainsworth, M. D. S. (1969). *Maternal sensitivity scales*. Johns Hopkins University.

Ainsworth, M. D. S., Blehar, M. C., Waters, E., & Wall, S. (1978). *Patterns of attachment: A psychological study of the strange situation*. Lawrence Erlbaum Associates.

Albohn, D. N., Brandenburg, J. C., & Adams, R. B. Jr. (2019). Perceiving emotion in the "neutral" face: A powerful mechanism of person perception. In U. Hess & S. Hareli (Eds.), *The social nature of emotion expression: What emotions can tell us about the world* (pp. 25–48). Springer Nature.

Alexander, R., Aragón, O. R., Bookwala, J., Cherbuin, N., Gatt, J. M., Kahrilis, I. J., Kästner, Lawrence, A., Lowe, L., Morrison, R. G., Mueller, S. C., Nusslock, R., Papadelis, C., Polnaszek, K. L., Richter, S. H., Silton, R., & Styliadis, C. (2021). The neuroscience of positive emotions and affect: Implications for cultivating happiness and wellbeing. *Neuroscience and Biobehavioral Reviews, 121*, 220–249.

American Psychiatric Association. (2013). *Diagnostic and statistical manual of mental disorders: DSM-5*. American Psychiatric Association.

American Psychological Association. (2015). *American Psychological Association dictionary of psychology*. American Psychological Association.

Andersen, R. J., Evans, I. M., & Harvey, S. T. (2012). Insider views of the emotional climate of the classroom: What New Zealand children tell us about their teachers' feelings. *Journal of Research in Childhood Education, 26*, 199–220.

Arendt, H. (1951). *The origins of totalitarianism*. Harcourt, Brace.

Azar, S. T., Nix, R. L., & Makin-Byrd, K. N. (2005). Parenting schemas and the process of change. *Journal of Marital and Family Therapy, 31*, 45–58.

Bacon, A. L., & Regan, L. (2016). Manipulative relational behaviour and delinquency: Sex differences and links with emotional intelligence. *The Journal of Forensic Psychiatry & Psychology, 27*, 331–348.

Baer, R. A. (Ed.). (2010). *Assessing mindfulness & acceptance processes in clients: Illuminating the theory & practice of change*. New Harbinger Publications.

Bandura, A. (1969). *Principles of behavior modification*. Holt, Rinehart and Winston.

Bandura, A. (1971). *Psychological modeling*. Aldine-Atherton.

Bandura, A. (1977). Self-efficacy: Toward a unifying theory of behavioral change. *Psychological Review, 84*, 191–215.

Barlow, D. H. (2000). Unraveling the mysteries of anxiety and its disorders from the perspective of emotion theory. *American Psychologist, 55*, 1247–1263.

Barlow, D. H., Ellard, K. K., Sauer-Zavala, S., Bullis, J. R., & Carl, J. R. (2014). The origins of neuroticism. *Perspectives in Psychological Science, 9*, 481–496.

Barrett, L. F. (2006). Are emotions natural kinds? *Perspectives on Psychological Science, 1*, 28–58.

Barrett, L. F. (2017a). *How emotions are made: The secret life of the brain*. Houghton Mifflin Harcourt.

Barrett, L. F. (2017b). The theory of constructed emotion: An active inference account of interoception and categorization. *Social Cognitive and Affective Neuroscience, 12*, 20–46.

Barrett, L. F. (undated). Your brain is not what you think it is. https://www.apa.org/news/podcasts/speaking-of-psychology/brain-myths

Barrett, L. F., Mesquita, B., & Gendron, M. (2011). Context in emotion perception. *Current Directions in Psychological Science, 20*, 286–290.

Barrowclough, C., & Hooley, J. M. (2003). Attributions and expressed emotion: A review. *Clinical Psychology Review, 23*, 849–880.

Basu, A., Duvall, J., & Kaplan, R. (2019). Attention Restoration Theory: Exploring the role of soft fascination and mental bandwidth. *Environment and Behavior, 51*, 1055–1081.

Beaglehole, B., Glue, P., Neehoff, S., Shadli, S., McNaughton, N., Kimber, B., Muirhead, C., de Bie, A., Day-Brown, R., & Hughes-Medlicott, N. J. (2025). Six weeks open-label oral ketamine for patients with treatment-resistant depression, post-traumatic stress disorder, or obsessive-compulsive disorder. *Journal of Psychopharmacology, 39*, 571–576.

Beauchaine, T. P. (2015). Future directions in emotion dysregulation and youth psychopathology. *Journal of Clinical Child & Adolescent Psychology, 44*, 875–896.

Bellack, A. S., & Hersen, M. (Eds.). (1979). *Research and practice in social skills training*. Plenum Press.

Bergman, T. H., Sandred, A., Lindström, T., Lappalainen, A., Ghaderi, A., & Hirvikoski, T. (2024). A psychometric evaluation of the parental acceptance and action questionnaire (PAAQ) in parents of children with and without disabilities. *Journal of Contextual Behavioral Science, 32*, 100757.

Berkman, K. A., & Meyer, L. H. (1988). Alternative strategies and multiple outcomes in the remediation of severe self-injury: Going "All Out" nonaversively. *Journal of the Association for Persons with Severe Handicaps, 13*, 76–86.

Bernard, C. (1865/1949). *An introduction to the study of experimental medicine* (H. C. Greene, Trans.; 1949). Henry Schuman.

Bernstein, A., Aizik-Reebs, A., Phung, Y., Yuval, K., Gebremariam, S. G., & Vujanovic, A. A. (2025). Affective mechanisms of moral injury in trauma recovery among asylum seekers: Exploring the protective effects of mindfulness and compassion training. *Clinical Psychological Science, 14*, 60–73.

Bil & Keane, J. (2025). *The Family Circus* comic strip, 04/22/2025, by Bil & Jeff Keane.

Bitterman, M. E. (2006). Classical conditioning since Pavlov. *Review of General Psychology, 10*, 365–376.

Blanchard, R. J., Flannelly, K. J., & Blanchard, D. C. (1986). Defensive behaviors of laboratory and wild *Rattus norvegicus*. *Journal of Comparative Psychology, 100*, 101–110.

Blum, H. P. (2007). Little Hans: A centennial review and reconsideration. *Journal of the American Psychoanalytic Association, 55*, 749–765.

Blustein, D. L., Grzanka, P. R., Gordon, M., Smith, C. M., & Allan, B. A. (2025). The psychology of precarity: A critical framework. *American Psychologist, 80*, 757–770.

Bower, G. H. (1981). Mood and memory. *American Psychologist, 36*, 129–148.

Brain, W. R. (1951). *Mind, perception and science*. Blackwell Scientific Publications.

Brandon, T. H., Vidrine, J. I., & Litvin, E. B. (2007). Relapse and relapse prevention. *Annual Review of Clinical Psychology, 3*, 257–284.

Braun, S. S., Greenberg, M. T., Roeser, R. W., Taylor, L. J., Montero-Marin, J., Crane, C., Williams, J. M. G., Sonley, A., Lord, L., Ford, T., The MYRIAD Team, & Kuyken, W. (2024). Teachers' stress and training in a school-based mindfulness program: Implementation results from a cluster randomized controlled trial. *Journal of School Psychology, 104*, 101288.

Bretherton, I. (1989). Pretense: The form and function of make-believe play. *Developmental Review, 9*, 383–401.

Broadhurst, P. L. (1975). The Maudsley reactive and nonreactive strains of rats. A survey. *Behavior Genetics, 5*, 299–319.

Brogaard, B. (2015). *On romantic love: Simple truths about a complex emotion*. Oxford University Press.

Brogaard, B. (2020). *Hatred: Understanding our most dangerous emotion*. Oxford University Press.

Bronfenbrenner, U. (1979). *The ecology of human development: Experiments by nature and design*. Harvard University Press.

Brown, G. W., & Rutter, M. L. (1966). The measurement of family activities and relationships: A methodological study. *Human Relations, 19*, 241–263.

Brown, R. (1965). *Social psychology*. Free Press.

Brown, C. L., Van Doren, N., Ford, B. Q., Mauss, I. B., Sze, J. W., & Levenson, R. W. (2020). Coherence between subjective experience and physiology in emotion: Individual differences and implications for well-being. *Emotion, 20*, 818–829.

Burks, D. J., & Robbins, R. (2012). Psychologists' authenticity: Implications for work in professional and therapeutic settings. *Journal of Humanistic Psychology, 52*, 75–104.

Busch, C. J., & Evans, I. M. (1977). The effectiveness of electric shock and foul odour as unconditioned stimuli in classical aversive conditioning. *Behaviour Research and Therapy, 15*, 167–175.

Buss, A. H., & Plomin, R. (1984). *Temperament: Early developing personality traits*. Psychology Press.

Cacioppo, J. T. (2004). Feelings and emotions: Roles for electrophysiological markers. *Biological Psychology, 67*, 235–243.

Cacioppo, J. T., & Bernston, G. G. (1999). The affect system: Architecture and operating characteristics. *Current Directions in Psychological Science, 8*, 133–137.

Cacioppo, J. T., & Petty, R. E. (1981). Electromyograms as measures of extent and affectivity of information processing. *American Psychologist, 36*, 441–456.

Campbell, D. T. (1958). Common fate, similarity, and other indices of the status of aggregates of persons as social entities. *Behavioral Scientist, 3*, 14–25.

Campos, J. J., Campos, R. G., & Barrett, K. C. (1989). Emergent themes in the study of emotional development and emotional regulation. *Developmental Psychology, 25*, 394–402

Capaldi, D. M., Forgatch, M. S., & Crosby, L. (1994). Affective expression in family problem-solving discussions with adolescent boys. *Journal of Adolescent Research, 9*, 28–49.

Carr, E. G., & Durand, V. M. (1985). Reducing behavior problems through functional communication training. *Journal of Applied Behavior Analysis, 18*, 111–126.

Carver, C. S., & White, T. L. (1994). Behavioral inhibition, behavioral activation, and affective responses to impending reward and punishment: The BIS/BAS scales. *Journal of Personality and Social Psychology, 67*, 319–333.

Caspi, A., & Silva, P. A. (1995). Temperament qualities at age three predict personality traits in young adulthood: Longitudinal evidence from a birth cohort. *Child Development, 66*, 486–498.

Castonguay, L. G., Barkham, M., Jeoung Youn, S., & Page, A. C. (2021). Practice-based evidence – Findings from routine clinical settings. In M. Barkham, W. Lutz, & L. G. Castonguay (Eds.), *Handbook of psychotherapy and behavior change* (7th ed., pp. 191–222). Wiley.

Cautela, J. R., & Kastenbaum, R. (1967). A reinforcement survey schedule for use in therapy, training, and research. *Psychological Reports, 20*, 1115–1130.

Ceatha, N., Mayock, P., Campbell, J., Noone, C., & Browne, K. (2019). The power of recognition: A qualitative study of social connectedness and wellbeing through LGBT sporting, creative and social groups in Ireland. *International Journal of Environmental Research and Public Health, 16*, 3636.

Ceci, S. J. (2006). Urie Bronfenbrenner (1917–2005). *American Psychologist, 61*, 173–174.

Chan, A. S. W., Choong, A., Phang, K. C., Leung, L. M., Tang, P. M. K., & Yan, E. (2024). Societal discrimination and mental health among transgender athletes: A systematic review and meta-analysis. *BMC Psychology, 12*, 24.

Cheron, D. M., Ehrenreich, J. T., & Pincus, D. B. (2009). Assessment of parental experiential avoidance in a clinical sample of children with anxiety disorders. *Child Psychiatry and Human Development, 40*, 383–403.

Chester, D. S. (2017). The role of positive affect in aggression. *Current Directions in Psychological Science, 26*, 366–370.

Chong, L. J., Mirzadegan, I. A., & Meyer, A. (2020). The association between parenting and the error-related negativity across childhood and adolescence. *Developmental Cognitive Neuroscience, 45*, 100852.

Chorpita, B. F., Becker, K. D., & Daleiden, E. L. (2007). Understanding the common elements of evidence-based practice: Misconceptions and clinical examples. *Journal of the American Academy of Child and Adolescent Psychiatry, 46*, 647–652.

Clore, G. L., Ortony, A., & Foss, M. A. (1987). The psychological foundations of the affective lexicon. *Journal of Personality and Social Psychology, 53*, 751–766.

Corr, P. J. (2004). Reinforcement sensitivity theory and personality. *Neuroscience and Biobehavioral Reviews, 28*, 317–332.

Corr, P. J. (2011). Anxiety: Splitting the phenomenological atom. *Personality and Individual Differences, 50*, 889–897.

Coles, N. A., March, D. S., Marmolejo-Ramos, F., Larsen, J. T., Arinze, N. C., Ndukaihe, I. L. G., Willis, M. L., Foroni, F., Reggev, N., Mokady, A., Forscher, P. S., Hunter, J. F., Kaminski, G., Yüvrük, E., Kapucu, A., Nagy, T., Hajdu, N., Tejada, J., Freitag, R. M. K. ... Liuzza, M. T. (2022). A multi-lab test of the facial feedback hypothesis by the Many Smiles Collaboration. *Nature Human Behaviour, 6*, 1731–1742.

Connelly, M. L. (2001). *New directions for treating parent-adolescent conflict: Comparison of problem solving skills training and social cognitive development training.* Unpublished doctoral thesis, Department of Psychology, University of Waikato, Hamilton, New Zealand.

Cotton, J. L. (1981). A review of research on Schachter's theory of emotion and the misattribution of arousal. *European Journal of Social Psychology, 11*, 365–397.

Craske, M. G., Rauch, S. L., Ursano, R., Prenoveau, J., Pine, D. S., & Zinbarg, R. E. (2009). What is an anxiety disorder? *Depression and Anxiety, 26*, 1066–1085.

Crawford, M. T., & Salaman, L. (2012). Entitativity, identity, and the fulfilment of psychological needs. *Journal of Experimental Social Psychology, 48*, 726–730.

Cray, E. (2006). *Ramblin' man: The life and times of Woody Guthrie*. W. W. Norton.

Crivelli, C., & Fridlund, A. J. (2019). Inside-out: From basic emotions theory to the behavioral ecology view. *Journal of Nonverbal Behavior, 43*, 161–194.

Cushing, C. A., Lau, H., Hofmann, S. G., LeDoux, J. E., & Taschereau-Dumouchel, V. (2024). Metacognition as a window into subjective affective experience. *Psychiatry and Clinical Neurosciences, 78*, 430–437.

Cutting, A. L., & Dunn, J. (2002). The cost of understanding other people: Social cognition predicts young children's sensitivity to criticism. *Journal of Child Psychology and Psychiatry, 43*, 849–860.

Cyders, M. A., & Smith, G. T. (2007). Mood-based rash action and its components: Positive and negative urgency. *Personality and Individual Differences, 43*, 839–850.

Damasio, A., & Carvalho, G. B. (2013). The nature of feelings: Evolutionary and neurobiological origins. *Nature Reviews: Neuroscience, 14*, 143–152.

Daniel, K. E., Moulder, R. G., Boker, S. M., & Teachman, B. A. (2025). Trait social anxiety moderates the relationship between emotion-regulation strategy switching and state anxiety in daily life. *Clinical Psychological Science, 13*, 160–177.

Darwin, C. R. (1872). *The expression of the emotions in man and animals*. John Murray.

Darwin, C. R. (1877). A biographical sketch of an infant. *Mind. A Quarterly Review of Psychology and Philosophy, 2*, 285–294.

Davidson, R. J. (2003). Affective neuroscience and psychophysiology: Toward a synthesis. *Psychophysiology, 40*, 655–665.

Davis, M. H. (1996). *Empathy: A social psychological approach.* Westview Press.

Davitz, J. R. (1969). *The language of emotion.* McGraw-Hill.

Davitz, J. R. (1970). A dictionary and grammar of emotion. In M. B. Arnold (Ed.), *Feelings and emotions: The Loyola Symposium* (pp. 225–258). Academic Press.

de Groot, M., Schaafsma, J., Castelain, T., Malinowska, K., Mann, L., Ohtsubo, Y., Wulandari, M. T. A., Bataineh, R. F., Fry, D. P., Goudbeek, M., & Duryani, A. (2021). Group-based shame, guilt, and regret across cultures. *European Journal of Social Psychology, 51*, 1198–1212.

Deci, E. L., & Ryan, R. M. (1985). *Intrinsic motivation and self-determination in human behavior.* Plenum.

Demorest, A. P. (2020). Happiness, love, and compassion as antidotes for anxiety. *The Journal of Positive Psychology, 15*, 438–447.

Derogatis, L. R., Lipman, R. S., Rickels, K., Uhlenhuth, E. H., & Covi, L. (1974). The Hopkins Symptom Checklist (HSCL): A self-report symptom inventory. *Behavioral Sciences, 19*, 1–15.

Dignath, D., Eder, A. B., Steinhauser, M., & Kiesel, A. (2020). Conflict monitoring and the affective-signaling hypothesis: An integrative review. *Psychonomic Bulletin & Review, 27*, 193–216.

Doan, T., Ong, D. C., & Wu, Y. (2025). Emotion understanding as third-person appraisals: Integrating appraisal theories with developmental theories of emotion. *Psychological Review, 132*, 130–153.

Dodge, K. A. (1991). The structure and function of reactive and proactive aggression. In D. J. Pepler & K. H. Rubin (Eds.), *The development and treatment of childhood aggression* (pp. 201–218). Lawrence Erlbaum.

Dollard, J., Miller, N. E., Doob, L. W., Mowrer, O. H., & Sears, R. R. (1939). *Frustration and aggression.* Yale University Press.

Drake, J. E. (2023). How children can use drawing to regulate their emotions. *Theory Into Practice, 62*, 181–192.

Drake, J. E., & Winner, E. (2013). How children use drawing to regulate their emotions. *Cognition and Emotion, 27*, 512–520.

Dreisbach, G., & Fischer, R. (2015). Conflicts as aversive signals for control adaptation. *Current Directions in Psychological Science, 24*, 255–260.

Drummond, P. D. (2013). Psychophysiology of the blush. In W. R. Crozier & P. J. de Jong (Eds.), *The psychological significance of the blush* (pp. 15–38). Cambridge University Press.

Duan, X. Y., Sun, T., Lu, F., Yang, X. J., Yin, H. Y., Cao, D. P., & Zhang, S. E. (2024). Relieving depressive symptoms through Chinese relational culture among older adults with multimorbidity: Evidence from CHARLS. *Psychology Research and Behavior Management, 17*, 4331–4344.

Dunn, B. D., Galton, H. C., Morgan, R., Evans, D., Oliver, C., Meyer, M., Cusack, R., Lawrence, A. D., & Dalgleish, T. (2010). Listening to your heart: How interoception shapes emotion experience and intuitive decision making. *Psychological Science, 21*, 1835–1844.

Dweck, C. S. (2006). *Mindset: The new psychology of success.* Random House.

Edwards, D. C. (2006). Duty-to-warn-even if it may be hearsay? The implications of a psychotherapist's duty to warn a third person when information is obtained from someone other than his patient. *Indiana Health Law Review, 3*, 171–200.

Eisenberg, N. (2020). Findings, issues, and new directions for research on emotion socialization. *Developmental Psychology, 56*, 664–670.

Ekman, P. (1964). Body position, facial expression, and verbal behavior during interviews. *Abnormal and Social Psychology, 68*, 295–301.

Ekman, P. (1999). Basic emotions. In T. Dalgleish & M. J. Power (Eds.), *Handbook of cognition and emotion* (pp. 45–60). Wiley.

Ekman, P. (2003). *Emotions revealed: Recognizing faces and feelings to improve communication and emotional life.* Times Books/Henry Holt.

Elfenbein, H. A., Marsh, A. A., & Ambady, N. (2002). Emotional intelligence and the recognition of emotion from facial expressions. In L. F. Barrett & P. Salovey (Eds.), *The wisdom in feeling: Psychological processes in emotional intelligence* (pp. 37–59). The Guilford Press.

Ellis, A. (1957). Rational psychotherapy and individual psychology. *Journal of Individual Psychology, 13*, 38–44.

Ellis, A. (1962). *Reason and emotion in psychotherapy*. Stuart.

Ellis, A. (1996). The treatment of morbid jealousy: A rational emotive behavior therapy approach. *Journal of Cognitive Psychotherapy, 10*, 23–33.

Erikson, E. H. (1950). *Childhood and society*. Norton.

Evans, I. M. (1972). A conditioning model of a common neurotic pattern—fear of fear. *Psychotherapy: Theory, Research and Practice, 9*, 238–241.

Evans, I. M. (1974). A handy record-card for systematic desensitization hierarchy items. *Journal of Behavior Therapy and Experimental Psychiatry, 5*, 43–46.

Evans, I. M. (1986). Response structure and the triple response mode concept in behavioral assessment. In R. O. Nelson & S. C. Hayes (Eds.), *Conceptual foundations of behavioral assessment* (pp. 131–155). The Guilford Press.

Evans, I. M. (1993). Dynamic response relationships: The challenge for behavioral assessment. *European Journal of Psychological Assessment, 9*, 206–212.

Evans, I. M. (1996). Individualizing therapy, customizing clinical science. *Journal of Behavior Therapy and Experimental Psychiatry, 27*, 99–105.

Evans, I. M. (2005). Behavior therapy: Regulation by self, by others, and by the physical world. In C. R. O'Donnell & L. A. Yamauchi (Eds.), *Culture and context in human behavior change: Theory, research, and applications* (pp. 13–39). Peter Lang.

Evans, I. M. (2010). Positive affective priming: A behavioral technique to facilitate therapeutic engagement by families, caregivers, and teachers. *Child & Family Behavior Therapy, 32*, 257–271.

Evans, I. M. (2013). *How and why people change: Foundations of psychological therapy*. Oxford University Press.

Evans, I. M. (2015). *How and why thoughts change: Foundations of cognitive psychotherapy*. Oxford University Press.

Evans, I. M., & Galyer, K. (2009). Are you sure there isn't a monster in the closet? Regulation of children's worrying in uncertain contexts. *Child & Family Behavior Therapy, 31*, 38–53.

Evans, I. M., Galyer, K. T., & Smith, K. J. H. (2001). Children's perceptions of unfair reward and punishment. *Journal of Genetic Psychology, 162*, 212–227.

Evans, I. M., & Harvey, S. T. (2012). *Warming the emotional environment of the primary school classroom*. Dunmore.

Evans, I. M., Heriot, S. A., & Friedman, A. G. (2002). A behavioural pattern of irritability, hostility, and inhibited empathy in children. *Clinical Child Psychology and Psychiatry, 7*, 211–224.

Evans, I. M., & Kamemoto, W. S. (1973). Reliability of the short form of Betts' questionnaire on mental imagery: Replication. *Psychological Reports, 33*, 281–282.

Evans, I. M., & Moltzen, N. L. (2000). Defining effective community support for long-term psychiatric patients according to behavioural principles. *Australian and New Zealand Journal of Psychiatry, 34*, 637–644.

Evans, I. M., Okifuji, A., & Thomas, A. (1995). Home-school partnerships: Involving families in the educational process. In I. M. Evans, T. Cicchelli, M. Cohen, & N. Shapiro (Eds.), *Staying in school: Partnerships for educational change* (pp. 23–40). Paul H. Brookes.

Evans, I. M., & Pechtel, P. (2010). Phagophobia: Behavioral treatment of a complex case involving fear of fear. *Clinical Case Studies, 10*, 37–52.

Evans, I. M., & Wilson, N. (2016). Classical eyelid conditioning, psychopathy, and Hans Eysenck's grand theory. *Journal of Personality and Individual Differences, 103*, 82–90.

Evans, I. M, & Wilson, G. T. (1968). Note on the terminological confusion surrounding systematic desensitization. *Psychological Reports, 22*, 187–191.

Eysenck, H. J. (1967). *The biological basis of personality*. Charles C. Thomas.

Eysenck, H. J. (1968). A theory of the incubation of anxiety/fear responses. *Behaviour Research and Therapy, 6*, 309–322.

Eysenck, H. J., & Wilson, G. (1976). *Know your own personality*. Penguin Books.

Eysenck, M. W., & Calvo, M. G. (1992). Anxiety and performance: The processing efficiency theory. *Cognition & Emotion, 6*, 409–434.

Eysenck, S. B. G., & Eysenck, H. J. (1963). The validity of questionnaire and rating assessments of extraversion and neuroticism, and their factorial stability. *British Journal of Psychology*, *54*, 51–62.

Facci, C., Baroncelli, A., Frick, P. J., & Ciucci, E. (2024). Dimensions of parenting and children's conduct problems: The importance of considering children's callous-unemotional traits. *International Journal of Environmental Research and Public Health*, *21*, 779.

Feitosa, F., Baudewyns, P., Pilet, J-B., & Talukder, D. (2024). Who feels resentful? In L. Knops, K. Celis, V. Van Ingelgom, H. Mercenier, & F. Randour (Eds.), *Bitter-sweet democracy? Analyzing citizens' resentment towards politics in Belgium* (pp. 61–90). Open Book Publishers.

Fenichel, O. (1941). The ego and the affects. *Psychoanalytic Review*, *28*, 47–60.

Festinger, L. (1957). *A theory of cognitive dissonance*. Stanford University Press.

Festinger, L. (1962). Cognitive dissonance. *Scientific American*, *207*, 93–106.

Field, A. P. (2006). Is conditioning a useful framework for understanding the development and treatment of phobias? *Clinical Psychology Review*, *26*, 857–875.

Fitzgerald, J. M., & Richardson, H. (2002). Use of the reasons for depression questionnaire with adolescents. *Journal of Clinical Psychology*, *58*, 1045–1056.

Flusberg, S. J., Holmes, K. J., Thibodeau, P. H., Nabi, R. L., & Matlock, T. (2024). The psychology of framing: How everyday language shapes the way we think, feel, and act. *Psychological Science in the Public Interest*, *25*, 105–161.

Frankl, V. E. (1975). Paradoxical intention and dereflection. *Psychotherapy: Theory, Research & Practice*, *12*, 226–237.

Freud, S. (1901/2021). *The psychopathology of everyday life*. Fingerprint Publishing.

Frith, U., & Frith, C. D. (2025). What autism taught us about our social nature. *Current Directions in Psychological Science*, *34*, 157–162.

Fuchshuber, J., Prandstätter, T., Andres, D., Roithmeier, L., Schmautz, B., Freund, A., Schwerdtfeger, A., & Unterrainer, H-F. (2023). The German version of the Brief Affective Neuroscience Personality Scales including a LUST scale (BANPS–GL). *Frontiers in Human Neuroscience*, *17*, 1213156.

Fulghum, R. (1988). *All I really need to know I learned in kindergarten: Uncommon thoughts on common things*. Villard Books.

Furnham, A., Eysenck, S. B. G., & Saklofske, D. H. (2008). The Eysenck personality measures: Fifty years of scale development. In G. J. Boyle, G. Matthews, & D. H. Saklofske (Eds.), *The SAGE handbook of personality theory and assessment, Vol. 2. Personality measurement and testing* (pp. 199–218). Sage.

Gabriel, B. B. (2017). *An analysis of the mechanisms of change in an intervention for caregivers in New Zealand: The Fostering Security Training Programme*. School of Psychology, Massey University.

Galyer, K. T., & Evans, I. M. (2001). Pretend play and the development of emotion regulation in preschool children. *Early Child Development and Care*, *166*, 93–108.

Gao, Y., Peng, W., Xi, X., Gan, Y., & Shen, Y. (2024). Hiding uncertain me in the crowd: Avoidance-oriented affiliation defense to self-uncertainty. *Psychology Research and Behavior Management*, *17*, 3827–3840.

Gilbert, P. (1989). *Human nature and suffering*. Lawrence Erlbaum.

Gilbert, P. (Ed.). (2005). *Compassion: Conceptualisations, research and use in psychotherapy*. Routledge.

Goldfried, M. R. (2011). What constitutes "evidence" in evidence-based practice? *The Clinical Psychologist*, *63*, 1–4.

Goldfried, M. R., Arnkoff, D., & Glass, C. (2011). Integrative approaches to psychotherapy. In J. C. Norcross, G. R. VandenBos, & D. K. Freedheim (Eds.), *History of psychotherapy* (2nd ed., pp. 269–296). American Psychological Association.

Goldsmith, H. H., & Campos, J. J. (1990). The structure of temperamental fear and pleasure in infants: A psychometric perspective. *Child Development*, *61*, 1944–1964.

Golomb, C., & Galasso, L. (1995). Make believe and reality: Explorations of the imaginary realm. *Developmental Psychology*, *31*, 800–810.

Gottman, J. M. (1993). *What predicts divorce?* Lawrence Erlbaum.

Gottman, J. M. (1999). *The seven principles for making marriage work*. Weidenfeld & Nicolson.

Gottman, J. M. (2023). *What predicts divorce? The relationship between marital processes and marital outcomes*. Routledge.

Gratz, K. L., & Roemer, L. (2004). Multidimensional assessment of emotion regulation and dysregulation: Development, factor structure, and initial validation of the difficulties in emotion regulation scale. *Journal of Psychopathology and Behavioral Assessment*, *26*, 41–54.

Gray, J. A. (1964). *Pavlov's typology; Recent theoretical and experimental developments from the laboratory of B.M. Teplov*. Pergamon.

Gray, J. A. (1987). *The neuropsychology of anxiety*. Oxford University Press.

Gray, J. A., & McNaughton, N. (2000). *The neuropsychology of anxiety: An enquiry into the functions of the septo-hippocampal system* (2nd ed.). Oxford University Press.

Greenberg, L. S. (2017). *Emotion-focused therapy* (Revised ed.). American Psychological Association.

Greenberg, M. T. (2023). *Evidence for social and emotional learning in schools*. Learning Policy Institute.

Grimmer, H., Laukkonen, R., Tangen, J., & von Hippel, W. (2022). Eliciting false insights with semantic priming. *Psychonomic Bulletin & Review*, *29*, 954–970.

Gross, J. J. (1998). The emerging field of emotion regulation: An integrative review. *Review of General Psychology*, *2*, 271–299.

Gross, J. J. (2015). Emotion regulation: Current status and future prospects. *Psychological Inquiry*, *26*, 1–26.

Gross, J. J., & Ford, B. Q. (Eds.). (2024). *Handbook of emotion regulation* (3rd ed.). The Guilford Press.

Gross, J. J., & Muñoz, R. F. (1995). Emotion regulation and mental health. *Clinical Psychology: Science and Practice*, *2*, 151–164.

Grossman, P. (2023). Fundamental challenges and likely refutations of the five basic premises of the polyvagal theory. *Biological Psychology*, *180*, 108589.

Gunawardena, H., Voukelatos, A., Wilson, R., Cross, S., & Hickie, I. B. (2024). Australian school based interventions addressing child and adolescent mental disorders: A systematic review. *Journal of Mental Health Disorders*, *4*, 13–30.

Hackel, L. (2025). https://neurosciencenews.com/empathy-emotional-conditioning-29546/

Haidt, J. (2003). The moral emotions. In R. J. Davidson, K. R. Scherer, & H. H. Goldsmith (Eds.), *Handbook of affective sciences* (pp. 852–870). Oxford University Press.

Hass, N. C., Wachen, J. S., Straud, C. L., Checko, E., McGeary, D. D., McGeary, C. A., Mintz, J., Litz, B. T., Young-McCaughan, S., Yarvis, J. S., Peterson, A. L., & Resick, P. A., for the STRONG STAR Consortium. (2025). Changes in pain and related health outcomes after cognitive processing therapy in an active duty military sample. *Journal of Traumatic Stress*, *38*, 447–457.

Harlow, H. F., & Stagner, R. (1932). Psychology of feelings and emotions: I. Theory of feelings. *Psychological Review*, *39*, 570–589.

Harris, J. J., Brown, E. L., Ford, D. Y., & Richardson, J. W. (2004). African Americans and multicultural education: A proposed remedy for disproportionate special education placement and underinclusion in gifted education. *Education and Urban Society*, *36*, 304–341.

Harris, P. L., & Tang, Y. (2018). Peering into the opaque mind. *European Journal of Developmental Psychology*, *15*, 631–642.

Hatfield, E., Cacioppo, J. T., & Rapson, R. L. (1994). *Emotional contagion*. Cambridge University Press.

Hayes, S. C., Jacobson, N. S., Follette, V. M., & Dougher, M. J. (Eds.). (1994). *Acceptance and change: Content and context in psychotherapy*. Context Press.

Hayes-Skelton, S. A., & Eustis, E. H. (2020). Experiential avoidance. In J. S. Abramowitz & S. M. Blakey (Eds.). *Clinical handbook of fear and anxiety: Maintenance processes and treatment mechanisms* (pp. 116–131). American Psychological Association.

Hayran, C., & Gürhan-Canli, Z. (2022). Understanding the feeling of missing out: A temporal perspective. *Personality and Individual Differences*, *185*, 111307.

Hebb, D. O. (1955). Drives and the C.N.S. (conceptual nervous system). *Psychological Review*, *62*, 243–254.

Heritage, S. (2025, January 21). Vomiting! Fainting! Heart attacks! How dangerous can it be to watch a movie? *The Guardian*. https://www.theguardian.com/film/2025/jan/21/

Hersen, M., & Sledge, W. (Eds.) (2002). *Encyclopedia of psychotherapy*. Academic Press.

Hess, U., & Fischer, A. (2013). Emotional mimicry as social regulation. *Personality and Social Psychology Review*, *17*, 142–157.

Higgins, E. T. (1997). Beyond pleasure and pain. *American Psychologist*, *52*, 1280–1300.

Hodis, F., Johnston, M., Meyer, L. H., McClure, J., Hodis, G. M., & Starkey, L. (2015). Maximal levels of aspiration, minimal boundary goals, and their relationships with academic achievement: The case of secondary-school students. *British Educational Research Journal*, *41*, 1125–1141.

Högberg, G., & Hällström, T. (2018). Mood regulation focused CBT based on memory reconsolidation, reduced suicidal ideation and depression in youth in a randomized controlled study. *International Journal of Environmental Research and Public Health*, *15*, 921.

Hogg, M. A., Sherman, D. K., Dierselhuis, J., Maitner, A. T., & Moffitt, G. (2007). Uncertainty, entitativity, and group identification. *Journal of Experimental & Social Psychology*, *43*, 135–142.

Holzer, P. (2022). Gut signals and gut feelings: Science at the interface of data and beliefs. *Frontiers in Behavioral Neuroscience*, *16*, 929332.

Hooley, J. M. (2007). Expressed emotion and relapse in psychopathology. *Annual Review of Clinical Psychology*, *3*, 329–352.

Hooley, J. M., & Parker, H. A. (2006). Measuring expressed emotion: An evaluation of the shortcuts. *Journal of Family Psychology*, *20*, 386–396.

Howard, J. A. (2022). *Trauma aware education*. Australian Academic Press.

Hull, C. L. (1943). *Principles of behavior*. Appleton-Century-Crofts.

Hunt, E. (2024). *The Guardian*. https://www.theguardian.com/music/2024/dec/19/clairo-on-making-one-of-2024-best-albums-charm-interview?CMP=share_btn_url

Hurlburt, R. T., & Akhter, S. A. (2006). The descriptive experience sampling method. *Phenomenology and the Cognitive Sciences*, *5*, 271–301.

Hurlburt, R. T., Heavy, C. L., & Bensaheb, A. (2009). Sensory awareness. *Journal of Consciousness Studies*, *16*, 231–251.

Ip, K. I., Miller, A. L., Karasawa, M., Hirabayashi, H., Kazama, M., Wang, L., Olson, S. L., Kessler, D., & Tardif, T. (2021). Emotion expression and regulation in three cultures: Chinese, Japanese, and American preschoolers' reactions to disappointment. *Journal of Experimental Child Psychology*, *201*, 104972.

Irvine, W. B. (2015). *Aha!: The moments of insight that shape our world*. Oxford University Press.

Isaacson, R. L. (1982). *The limbic system* (2nd ed.). Springer Science.

Izard, C. E. (1977). *Human emotions*. Plenum.

Izard, C. E. (2002). Translating emotion theory and research into preventive interventions. *Psychological Bulletin*, *128*, 796–824.

Izard, C. E. (2007). Basic emotions, natural kinds, emotion schemas, and a new paradigm. *Perspectives on Psychological Science*, *2*, 260–280.

Izard, C. E., Stark, K., Trentacosta, C., & Schultz, D. (2008). Beyond emotion regulation: Emotion utilization and adaptive functioning. *Child Development Perspectives*, *2*, 156–163.

Jack, R. E., Garrod, O. B. G., & Schyns, P. G. (2014). Dynamic facial expressions of emotion transmit an evolving hierarchy of signals over time. *Current Biology*, *24*, 187–192.

Jackson, S. W. (1994). Catharsis and abreaction in the history of psychological healing. *Psychiatric Clinics of North America*, *17*, 471–491.

Jacobson, E. (1938). *Progressive relaxation*. University of Chicago Press.

James, W. (1890/1950). *Principles of psychology*. Dover Publications.

Janov, A. (1970). *The primal scream: Primal therapy: The cure for neurosis*. Delta.

Jeffries, F. W., & Davis, P. (2013). What is the role of eye movements in Eye Movement Desensitization and Reprocessing (EMDR) for post-traumatic stress disorder (PTSD)? A review. *Behavioural and Cognitive Psychotherapy*, *41*, 290–300.

Jensen, A. C., & Jorgensen-Well, M. A. (2025). Parents favor daughters: A meta-analysis of gender and other predictors of parental differential treatment. *Psychological Bulletin*, *151*, 33–47.

Ji, J. L., Heyes, S. B., MacLeod, C., & Holmes, E. A. (2016). Emotional mental imagery as simulation of reality: Fear and beyond—A tribute to Peter Lang. *Behavior Therapy*, *47*, 702–719.

Jin, R., Li, X., & Huang, H. (2025). Empathy and mental health of preschool teachers: A latent profile analysis. *Psychology Research and Behavior Management*, *18*, 255–269.

Josephides, L. (2005). Resentment as a sense of self. In K. Milton & M. Svasek (Eds.), *Mixed emotions: Anthropological studies of feeling* (pp. 71–90). Routledge.

Jost, J. T., Napier, J. L., Thorisdottir, H., Gosling, S. D., Palfai, T. P., & Ostafin, B. (2007). Are needs to manage uncertainty and threat associated with political conservatism or ideological extremity? *Personality and Social Psychology Bulletin*, *33*, 989–1007.

Kahneman, D. (2011). *Thinking, fast and slow*. Macmillan.

Kang, H., & Kim, H. (2022). Ageism and psychological well-being among older adults: A systematic review. *Journal of Gerontology & Geriatric Medicine*, *8*, 3337214221087023.

Kaplan, P. R., & Evans, I. M. (1978). A case of functional dysphagia treated on the model of fear of fear. *Journal of Behavior Therapy and Experimental Psychiatry*, *9*, 71–72.

Kaplan, S. (1995). The restorative benefits of nature: Toward an integrative framework. *Journal of Environmental Psychology*, *15*, 169–182.

Kashdan, T. B., Barrett, L. F., & McKnight, P. E. (2015). Unpacking emotion differentiation: Transforming unpleasant experience by perceiving distinctions in negativity. *Current Directions in Psychological Science*, *24*, 10–16.

Kavanagh, D. J., Freese, S., Andrade, J., & May, J. (2001). Effects of visuospatial tasks on desensitization to emotive memories. *British Journal of Clinical Psychology*, *40*, 267–280.

Kazantzis, N., Whittington, C., & Datillo, F. (2010). Meta-analysis of homework effects in cognitive and behavioral therapy: A replication and extension. *Clinical Psychology: Science and Practice*, *17*, 144–156.

Keller, H. (2013). Attachment and culture. *Journal of Cross-Cultural Psychology*, *44*, 175–194.

Kernis, M. H., & Goldman, B. M. (2006). A multicomponent conceptualization of authenticity: Theory and research. *Advances in Experimental Social Psychology*, *38*, 283–357.

Kiel, N., Samdan, G., Wienke, A. S., Reinelt, T., Pauen, S., Mathes, B., & Herzmann, C. (2024). From coregulation to self-regulation: Maternal soothing strategies and self-efficacy in relation to maternal reports of infant regulation at 3 and 7 months. *Infant Mental Health Journal*, *45*, 135–152.

Kinder, D. R., & Sanders, L. M. (1996). *Divided by color: Racial politics and democratic ideals*. University of Chicago Press.

Kingdon, D. G., & Turkington, D. (1994). *Cognitive-behavioral therapy of schizophrenia*. Psychology Press.

Kiyak, C., Simonetti, M. E., Norton, S., & Deluca, P. (2023). The efficacy of cue exposure therapy on alcohol use disorders: A quantitative meta-analysis and systematic review. *Addictive Behaviors*, *139*, 107578.

Klauer, K. C. (1997). Affective priming. *European Review of Social Psychology*, *8*, 67–103.

Klein, J. P., Rozental, A., Sürig, S., & Moritz, S. (2024). Adverse events of psychological interventions: Definitions, assessment, current state of the research and implications for research and clinical practice. *Psychotherapy & Psychosomatics*, *93*, 308–315.

Kostiuk, L. M., & Fouts, G. T. (2002). Understanding of emotions and emotion regulation in adolescent females with conduct problems: A qualitative analysis. *The Qualitative Report*, *7*, 1–15.

Krugman, P. (2024, December 10). Finding hope in an age of resentment. *The New York Times*, Section A, p. 22.

Krys, K., Kostoula, O., van Tilburg, W. A. P., Mosca, O., Lee, J. H., Maricchiolo, F., Kosiarczyk, A., Kocimska-Bortnowska, A., Torres, C., Hitokoto, H., Liew, K., Bond, M. H., Lun, V. M-C., Vignoles, V. L., Zelenski, J. M., Haas, B. W., Park, J., Vauclair, C.-M., Kwiatkowska, A., ... Uchida, Y. (2025). Happiness maximization is a WEIRD way of living. *Perspective on Psychological Science*, *20*, 874–902.

Kuusikko, S., Haapsamo, H., Jansson-Verkasalo, E., Hurtig, T., Matilla, M-L., Ebeling, H., Jussila, K., Bölte, S., & Moilanen, I. (2009). Emotion recognition in children and adolescents with Autism Spectrum Disorders. *Journal of Autism and Developmental Disorders, 39*, 938–945.

Kuyken, W., Ball, S., Crane, C., Ganguli, P., Jones, B., Montero-Marin, J., Nuthall, E., Raja, A., Taylor, L., Tudor, K., Viner, R. M., Allwood, M., Aukland, L., Dunning, D., Casey, T., Dalrymple, N., De Wilde, K., Farley, E-R., Harper, J., ... Williams, J. M. G. (2022). Effectiveness of universal school-based mindfulness training compared with normal school provision on teacher mental health and school climate: Results of the MYRIAD cluster randomised controlled trial. *British Medical Journal: Mental Health, 25*, 125–134

LaBar, K. S. (2025). Fear, learning, and the amygdala: A personal reflection in honor of Joseph LeDoux. *Cerebral Cortex, 35*, 5–10.

LaBar, K. S., & Cabeza, R. (2006). Cognitive neuroscience of emotional memory. *Nature Reviews: Neuroscience, 7*, 54–64.

Lader, M., & Mathews, A. A. (1968). A physiological model of phobic anxiety and desensitisation. *Behaviour Research & Therapy, 6*, 411–421.

Lahey, B. B. (2009). Public health significance of neuroticism. *American Psychologist, 64*, 241–256.

Lang, P. J. (1995). The emotion probe: Studies of motivation and attention. *American Psychologist, 50*, 372–385.

Lang, P. J., Bradley, M. M., & Cuthbert, B. N. (1995). *International Affective Picture System (IAPS): Affective ratings of pictures and instruction manual* (Tech. Rep. No. A-8). University of Florida.

Larroa, L. J. M. (2013). *What do I want to do and how do I get there? A possible-selves approach to motivation in education*. Massey University/Google Books.

Laski, K., Charlop, M. H., & Schreibman, L. (1988). Training parents to use the natural language paradigm to increase their autistic children's speech. *Journal of Applied Behavior Analysis, 21*, 391–400.

Laurent, J., Catanzaro, S. J., Joiner, T. E., Jr., Rudolph, K. D., Potter, K. I., Lambert, S., Osborne, L., & Gathright, T. (1999). A measure of positive and negative affect for children: Scale development and preliminary validation. *Psychological Assessment, 11*, 326–338.

Lazarus, A. A. (1989). *The practice of multimodal therapy*. Johns Hopkins University Press.

Lazarus, A. A. (2001). From insight and reflection to action and clinical breadth. In M. R. Goldfried (Ed.), *How therapists change: Personal and professional reflections* (pp. 163–183). American Psychological Association.

LeDoux, J. E. (1996). *The emotional brain: The mysterious underpinnings of emotional life*. Simon & Schuster.

LeDoux, J. E. (2000). Emotion circuits in the brain. *Annual Review of Neuroscience, 23*, 155–184.

LeDoux, J. (2012). Rethinking the emotional brain. *Neuron, 73*, 653–676.

Leff, J., & Vaughn, C. (1985). *Expressed emotion in families*. The Guilford Press.

Leistner, C., & Menke, A. (2020). Hypothalamic-pituitary-adrenal axis and stress. In R. Lanzenberger, G. S. Kranz, & I. Savic (Eds.), *Handbook of clinical neurology (Vol. 175)*, 55–64. Elsevier.

Leitman, M. W. (2016). Five new reflexes relating fear disgust breathing swallowing blinking and orienting reflex. *Biomarkers Journal, 2*, 17.

Leknes, S., & Tracey, I. (2008). A common neurobiology for pain and pleasure. *Nature Reviews: Neuroscience, 9*, 314–320.

Lengua, L. J., & Garstein, M. A. (2024). *Parenting with temperament in mind*. American Psychiatric Association.

Levinson, C. A., Christian, C., & Becker, C. B. (2025). How idiographic methodologies can move the clinical-science field forward to integrate personalized treatment into everyday clinical care and improve treatment outcomes. *Clinical Psychological Science, 13*, 69–82.

Levis, D. J. (1993). The power of extrapolating basic laboratory principles: The behavioural-cognitive approach of implosive therapy. *Behaviour Change, 10*, 154–161.

Lewinsohn, P. M. (1974). A behavioral approach to depression. In R. J. Friedman & M. M. Katz (Eds.), *The psychology of depression: Contemporary theory and research* (pp. 157–185). Wiley.

Linehan, M. M. (1993). *Cognitive-behavioral treatment of Borderline Personality Disorder*. The Guilford Press.

Lindquist, K. A. (2013). Emotions emerge from more basic psychological ingredients: A modern psychological constructionist model. *Emotion Review*, *5*, 356–368.

Linschoten, M., Weiner, L., & Avery-Clark, C. (2016). Sensate focus: A critical literature review. *Sexual and Relationship Therapy*, *31*, 230–247.

Litz, B. T. (2023a). It is time to flip the script and leverage the point of care to discover ways of improving treatment outcomes for posttraumatic stress disorder: Commentary on "A sobering look at treatment effectiveness of military-related posttraumatic stress disorder" (Levi et al., 2021). *Clinical Psychology Science*, *11*, 381–387.

Litz, B. T. (2023b). The future of moral injury and its treatment. *Journal of Military, Veteran and Family Health*, *9*(2), 1–5.

Litz, B. T., Stein, N., Delaney, E., Lebowitz, L., Nash, W. P., Silva, C., & Maguen, S. (2009). Moral injury and moral repair in war veterans: A preliminary model and intervention strategy. *Clinical Psychology Review*, *29*, 695–706.

Loev, S., Inchingolo, M., & Velasco, P. F. (2022). What is it (like) to imagine an emotion? *Humanities and Social Sciences Communications*, *9*, 440.

Lomas, T., Padgett, R. N., Pawelski, J. O., & Van der Weele, T. J. (2024). Inner peace and character strengths. In R. M. Niemiec (Ed.), *Peace psychology and character strengths: Integrating science and practice* (pp. 43–75.). Springer.

Low, R. S. T., Overall, N. C., Cross, E. J., & Henderson, A. M. E. (2019). Emotion regulation, conflict resolution, and spillover on subsequent family functioning. *Emotion*, *19*, 1162–1182.

Lumley, M. A., & Melamed, B. G. (1992). Blood phobics and nonphobics: Psychological differences and affect during exposure. *Behaviour Research & Therapy*, *30*, 425–434.

MacLean, P. D. (1955). The limbic system ("visceral brain") and emotional behavior. *Archives of Neurology & Psychiatry*, *73*, 130–134.

MacLean, P. D. (1990). *The triune brain in evolution: Role in paleocerebral functions* (9th ed.). Springer.

Mackie, K., & Evans, I. M. (2013). Parenting and fatherhood: Causal attributions and disciplinary responses for child misbehaviour. *Massey University Manawatu Doctoral Research Symposium*, *2*, 67–72.

Marks, C., Pearson, J. L., Martin, N., Werb, D., & Smith, L. R. (2022). Articulating the trauma-informed theory of individual health behavior. *Stress and Health*, *38*, 154–162.

Marks, I. M. (1987). *Fears, phobias, and rituals: Panic, anxiety, and their disorders*. Oxford University Press.

Marlatt, G. A., & Gordon, J. R. (Eds.). (1985). *Relapse prevention: Maintenance strategies in the treatment of addictive behaviors*. The Guilford Press.

Marshall, G. D., & Zimbardo, P. G. (1979). Affective consequences of inadequately explained physiological arousal. *Journal of Personality and Social Psychology*, *37*, 970–988.

Maslach, C. (1979). Negative emotional biasing of unexplained arousal. *Journal of Personality and Social Psychology*, *37*, 953–969.

Maslow, A. H. (1943). A theory of human motivation. *Psychological Review*, *50*, 370–396.

Masters, W. H., & Johnson, V. E. (1970). *Human sexual inadequacy*. Bantam Books.

Mathis, V., & Kenny, P. J. (2018). Neuroscience: Brain mechanisms of blushing. *Current Biology*, *28*, 784–802.

Mazzuchelli, T., Kane, R., & Rees, C. (2009). Behavioral activation treatments for depression in adults: A meta-analysis and review. *Clinical Psychology: Science and Practice*, *16*, 383–477.

McCleery, J., & Evans, I. M. (2001, November). *Cognitive behaviour therapy with schizophrenia: Is it more than a validated wet noodle?* Poster presented at the 35th annual conference of the Association for Advancement of Behavior Therapy, Philadelphia, PA.

McClelland, D. C., Atkinson, J. W., Clark, R. A., & Lowell, E. L. (1953). *The achievement motive*. Appleton-Century-Crofts.

McKeever, N., & Saunders, J. (2022). Irrational love: Taking Romeo and Juliet seriously. *International Journal of Philosophical Studies*, *30*, 254–275.

McNaughton, N. (2024). The legacies of the neuropsychology of anxiety for Reinforcement Sensitivity Theory. *Motivation Science*, *11*, 1–17.

McNaughton, N., & Corr, P. J. (2008). The neuropsychology of fear and anxiety: A foundation for Reinforcement Sensitivity Theory. In P. J. Corr (Ed.), *The reinforcement sensitivity theory of personality* (pp. 44–94). Cambridge University Press.

McNaughton, N, & Gray, J. A. (2024). *The neuropsychology of anxiety: An enquiry into the functions of the septo-hippocampal system* (3rd ed.). Oxford University Press.

McIver, J. A. (2011). *Will the needle make me bleed to death?* Massey University. https://mro.massey.ac.nz/server/api/core/bitstreams/eb71797a-76d1-4ebe-8dd7-5aa74eb5334a/content

Meyer, L. H. (2001). The impact of inclusion on children's lives: Multiple outcomes, and friendship in particular. *International Journal of Disability, Development and Education, 48*, 9–31.

Meyer, L. H., & Evans, I. M. (1989). *Non-aversive intervention for behavior problems: A manual for home and community.* Paul H. Brookes.

Meyer, L. H., & Evans, I. M. (1993). Science and practice in behavioral intervention: Meaningful outcomes, research validity, and usable knowledge. *Journal of The Association for Persons with Severe Handicaps, 18*, 224–234.

Meyer, L. H., McClure, J., Walkey, F., Weir, K., & McKenzie, L. (2009). Secondary student motivation and standards-based achievement outcomes. *British Journal of Educational Psychology, 79*, 273–293.

Meyer, L. H., Park H. S., Grenot-Scheyer, M., Schwartz, I. S., & Harry, B. (Eds.). (1998). *Making friends: The influences of culture and development.* Paul H. Brookes.

Michael, J. (2016). What are shared emotions (for)? *Frontiers in Psychology*, 7, 412.

Miller, N. E. (1948). Studies of fear as an acquirable drive: I. Fear as motivation and fear-reduction as reinforcement in the learning of new responses. *Journal of Experimental Psychology, 38*, 89–101.

Miller, W. R. (1983). Motivational interviewing with problem drinkers. *Behavioural Psychotherapy, 11*, 147–172.

Miller, W. R., & Rollnick, S. (1991). *Motivational interviewing: Preparing people to change addictive behavior.* The Guilford Press.

Mischel, W., Ebbesen, E. B., & Zeiss, A. R. (1972). Cognitive and attentional mechanisms in delay of gratification. *Journal of Personality and Social Psychology, 21*, 204–218.

Mitra, S., & Asthana, M. K. (2024). Investigating the effect of continuous and partial reinforcement in conceptual fear generalization. *Nature: Scientific Reports, 14*, 26305.

Modak, T., Sarkar, S., & Sagar, R. (2016). The story of Prosenjit Poddar. *Journal of Mental Health and Human Behaviour, 21*, 138–140.

Moed, A. (2024). An emotion-focused extension of coercion theory: Emerging evidence and conceptualizations for parental experienced emotion as a mechanism of reinforcement in coercive parent-child interactions. *Child Development Perspectives, 18*, 82–87.

Momeñe, J., Estévez, A., Griffiths, M. D., Macia, P., Herrero, M., Olave, L., & Iruarrizaga, I. (2023). Childhood trauma and body dissatisfaction among young adult women: The mediating role of self-criticism. *Current Psychology, 42*, 24837–24844.

Montag, C., & Davis, K. L. (2018). Affective neuroscience theory and personality: An update. *Personality Neuroscience, 1*, 1–12.

Montag, C., Solms, M., Stelzel, C., & Davis, K. L. (2022). The future of the Affective Neuroscience Personality Scales: A reflection on seven pressing matters. *Personality Neuroscience, 5*, e10, 1–6.

Mowrer, O. H. (1947). On the dual nature of learning—A reinterpretation of "conditioning" and "problem-solving." *Harvard Educational Review, 17*, 102–148

Murphy, S. T., & Zajonc, R. B. (1993). Affect, cognition, and awareness: Affective priming with optimal and suboptimal stimulus exposures. *Journal of Personality and Social Psychology, 71*, 723–739.

Nagpal, M., & Radliff, K. (2024). A systematic review of mindfulness-based school interventions on social-emotional outcomes with adolescents. *Child & Youth Care Forum, 53*, 563–610.

Neff, K. D. (2003). Development and validation of a scale to measure self-compassion. *Self and Identity*, 2, 223–250.

Nezu, A. M., & Nezu, C. M. (2018). *Emotion-centered problem-solving therapy: Treatment guidelines*. Springer.

Nezu, A. M., & Nezu, C. M. (2021). Emotion-centered problem-solving therapy. In A. Wenzel (Ed.), *Handbook of cognitive behavioral therapy: Vol.1. Overview and approaches* (pp. 465–491). American Psychological Association.

Nezu, A. M., Nezu, C. M., & Gerber, H. R. (2019). (Emotion-centered) problem-solving therapy: An update. *Australian Psychologist*, *54*, 361–371.

Nunes, C. E., Lamprianidou, E. -A., Zimmer-Gembeck, M. J., & Van Petegem, S. (2025). The relations between parents' gender equality values and (co)parenting: Examining actor-partner effects in an Australian community sample. *Journal of Family Issues*, *46*, 3–25.

NZIER (2024). *Perceptions of fairness in New Zealand. A report to the New Zealand Treasury*. New Zealand Institute of Economic Research.

Oakey-Frost, D. N., Moscardini, E. H., Russell, K., Rasmussen, S., Cramer, R., & Tucker, R. P. (2022). Defeat, entrapment, and hopelessness: Clarifying interrelationships between suicidogenic constructs. *International Journal of Environmental Research and Public Health*, *19*, 10518.

Öhman, A., Flykt, A., & Esteves, F. (2001). Emotion drives attention: Detecting the snake in the grass. *Journal of Experimental Psychology-General*, *130*, 466–478.

Ortony, A., Clore, G. L., & Collins, A. (2022). *The cognitive structure of emotions* (2nd ed.). Cambridge University Press.

Osgood, C. E., Suci, G. J., & Tannenbaum, P. H. (1957). *The measurement of meaning*. University of Illinois Press.

Otterpohl, N., Wild, E., Havinghurst, S. S., Stiensmeier-Pelster, J., & Kehoe, C. E. (2022). The interplay of parental response to anger, adolescent anger regulation, and externalizing and internalizing problems: A longitudinal study. *Research on Child and Adolescent Psychopathology*, *50*, 225–239.

Padilla, C. M., Hines, C. T., & Ryan, R. M. (2020). Infant temperament, parenting and behavior problems: Variation by parental education and income. *Journal of Applied Developmental Psychology*, *70*, 10179.

Palermo, M. T. (2003). Preventing filicide in families with autistic children. *International Journal of Offender Therapy and Comparative Criminology*, *47*, 47–57.

Panksepp, J. (1992). A critical role for "affective neuroscience" in resolving what is basic about basic emotions. *Psychological Review*, *99*, 554–560.

Panksepp, J. (1998). *Affective neuroscience: The foundations of human and animal emotions*. Oxford University Press.

Panksepp, J. (2015). Toward the constitution of emotional feelings: Synergistic lessons from Izard's differential emotions theory and affective neuroscience. *Emotion Review*, *7*, 110–115.

Papez, J. W. (1937). A proposed mechanism of emotion. *Archives of Neurology and Psychiatry*, *38*, 725–743.

Paton, D., & Johnston, D. (Eds.). (2017). *Disaster resilience: An integrated approach*. Charles C. Thomas.

Patterson, G. R. (1982). *Coercive family process*. Castalia.

Patterson, G. R., & Reid, J. B. (1970). Reciprocity and coercion: Two facets of social systems. In C. Neuringer & J. Michael (Eds.), *Behavior modification in clinical psychology*. Appleton-Century-Crofts.

Pearlstein, J. G., Johnson, S. L., Timpano, K. R., Stamatis, C. A., Robison, M., & Carver, C. S. (2024). Emotion-related impulsivity across transdiagnostic dimensions of psychopathology. *Journal of Personality*, *92*, 342–360.

Pemau, A., Marin-Martin, C., de la Torre-Luque, A., Ayad-Ahmed, W., Lopez-Villatoro, J. M., Fernandez-Rodriques, V., Mola, P., Carrasco, J. L., & Diaz-Marsa, M. (2024). Relationship between the feeling of emptiness and suicide reattempt: Conclusions from cross-sectional and longitudinal analyses. *Clinical Psychology & Psychotherapy*, *32*, e70000.

Persons, J. (2008). *The case formulation approach to cognitive-behavior therapy*. The Guilford Press.

Philips, K. H., Brintz, C. E., Moss, K., & Gaylord, S. A. (2019). Didgeridoo sound meditation for stress reduction and mood enhancement in undergraduates: A randomized controlled trial. *Global Advances in Health and Medicine*, *8*, 1–10.

Phillips, J. (1987). *A man's country? The image of the pakeha male—A history*. Penguin Books.

Piotrowski, K., Mikolajczak, M., & Roskam, I. (2023). I should not have had a child: Development and validation of the Parenthood Regret Scale. *Journal of Family Psychology*, *37*, 1282–1293.

Pizzagalli, D. A. (2014). Depression, stress, and anhedonia: Toward a synthesis and integrated model. *Annual Review of Clinical Psychology*, *10*, 393–423.

Planalp, E. M., & Goldsmith, H. H. (2020). Observed profiles of infant temperament: Stability, heritability, and associations with parenting. *Child Development*, *91*, 563–580.

Plutchik, R. (1962). *The emotions: Fact, theories, and a new model*. Crown Publishing Group/Random House.

Plutchik, R. (1980). A general psychoevolutionary theory of emotion. In R. Plutchik (Ed.), *Emotion: Theory, research, and experience, Volume 1: Theories of emotion* (pp. 3–33). Academic Press.

Plutchik, R. (2003). *Emotions and life: Perspectives from psychology, biology, and evolution*. American Psychological Association.

Pons, F., Harris, P. L., & de Rosnay, M. (2004). Emotion comprehension between 3 and 11 years: Developmental periods and hierarchical organization. *European Journal of Developmental Psychology*, *1*, 127–152.

Porges, S. W. (2022). Polyvagal theory: A science of safety. *Frontiers in Integrative Neuroscience*, *16*, 871227.

Porges, S. W. (2023). *Polyvagal theory: Summary, premises & current*. Unpublished paper. https://www.polyvagalinstitute.org/_files/ugd/8e115b_f8f82f01065b41dc85e7698fd4f99818.pdf?index=true

Proudfit, G. H. (2015). The reward positivity: From basic research on reward to a biomarker for depression. *Psychophysiology*, *52*, 449–459.

Qi, C., Wang, Y., Lai, J., & Jiao, Y. (2023). Hidden hurt: A qualitative study of microaggressions experienced by disabled children in education in China. *Child Abuse & Neglect*, *141*, 106200.

Quansah, J. E., & Gagnon, J. (2025). Toward an integrative approach to the study of positive-affect-related aggression. *Perspectives on Psychological Science*, *20*, 357–370.

Quay, H. C. (1988). Attention deficit disorder and the behavioral inhibition system: The relevance of the neuropsychological theory of Jeffrey A. Gray. In L. M. Bloomingdale & J. Sergeant (Eds), *Attention deficit disorder: Criteria, cognition, intervention* (pp. 117–125). Pergamon Press.

Quinn, N., & Mageo, J. M. (Eds.). (2013). *Attachment reconsidered: Cultural perspectives on a Western theory*. Palgrave Macmillan/Springer Nature.

Rachlin, H. (2000). *The science of self-control*. Harvard University Press.

Reilly, H. (2023). The story of Freud's patient Anna von Lieben—as told by Anna von Lieben. *Journal of the Royal College of Physicians, Edinburgh*, *53*, 57–64.

Rinck, M., & Becker, E. S. (2007). Approach and avoidance in fear of spiders. *Journal of Behavior Therapy and Experimental Psychiatry*, *38*, 105–120.

Robinson, M. J. F., Zumbusch, A. F., & Anselme, P. (2022). The incentive sensitization theory of addiction. *Oxford Research Encyclopedia: Psychology*, published on line 1/28/2022. Oxford University Press.

Robinson, T. E., & Berridge, K. C. (1993). The neural basis of drug craving: An incentive-sensitization theory of addiction. *Brain Research Review*, *18*, 247–291.

Robinson, T. E., & Berridge, K. C. (2008). The incentive sensitization theory of addiction: Some current issues. *Philosophical Transactions of the Royal Society*, *363*, 3137–3146.

Rose, N., & Abi-Rached, J. (2014). Governing through the brain: Neuropolitics, neuroscience and subjectivity. *Cambridge Anthropology*, *32*, 3–23.

Roskam, I., Brianda, M. E., & Mikolajczak, M. (2018). A step forward in the conceptualization and measurement of parental burnout: The Parental Burnout Assessment (PBA). *Frontiers in Psychology*, *9*, Article 758.

Round, A., Baker, W. J., & Rayner, C. (2017). Using visual arts to encourage children with Autism Spectrum Disorder to communicate their feelings and emotions. *Open Journal of Social Sciences, 5*, 90–108.

Rozin, P., & Schiller, D. (1980). The nature and acquisition of a preference for chili pepper by humans. *Motivation and Emotion, 4*, 77–83.

Rump, K. M., Giovannelli, J. L., Minshew, N. J., & Strauss, M. S. (2009). The development of emotion recognition in individuals with autism. *Child Development, 80*, 1434–1447.

Russell, A., & Russell, G. (1989). Warmth in mother-child and father-child relationships in middle childhood. *British Journal of Developmental Psychology*, 7, 219–235.

Russell, J. A., & Barrett, L. F. (1999). Core affect, prototypical emotional episodes, and other things called *emotion*: Dissecting the elephant. *Journal of Personality and Social Psychology, 76*, 805–819.

Ryan, R. M., & Deci, E. L. (2000). Self-determination theory and the facilitation of intrinsic motivation, social development, and well-being. *American Psychologist, 55*, 68–78.

Saarni, C. (1984). An observational study of children's attempts to monitor their expressive behavior. *Child Development, 55*, 1504–1513.

Saarni, C., & Harris, P. L. (Eds.). (1989). *Children's understanding of emotion*. Cambridge University Press.

Salisbury, C. L., Evans, I. M., & Palombaro, M. M. (1997). Collaborative problem-solving to promote the inclusion of young children with significant disabilities in primary grades. *Exceptional Children, 63*, 195–209.

Salmon, K., Evans, I. M., Moskowitz, S., Grouden, M., Parkes, F., & Miller, E. (2013). The components of young children's emotion knowledge: Which are enhanced by adult emotion talk? *Social Development, 22*, 94–110.

Salmela, M., & Nagatsu, M. (2017). How does it really *feel* to act together? Shared emotions and the phenomenology of we-agency. *Phenomenology and the Cognitive Sciences, 16*, 449–470.

Salovey, P., & Mayer, J. D. (1990). Emotional intelligence. *Imagination, Cognition and Personality*, 9, 185–212.

Sametband, I., Chiara, G., Gaete-Silva, J., & Strong, T. (2024). Negotiating cultural relevance from within therapy conversations. *Human Systems: Therapy, Culture and Attachments, 4*, 3–20.

Samoilov, A., & Goldfried, M. R. (2000). Role of emotion in cognitive-behavior therapy. *Clinical Psychology: Science and Practice*, 7, 373–385.

Sanders, M. R., Divan, G., Singhal, M., Turner, K. M. T., Velleman, R., Michelson, D., & Parel, V. (2022). Scaling up parenting interventions is critical for attaining the Sustainable Development Goals. *Child Psychiatry & Human Development, 53*, 941–952.

Schachter, S., & Singer, J. (1962). Cognitive, social, and physiological determinants of emotional state. *Psychological Review, 69*, 379–399.

Seidman, A. J., George, C. J., & Kovacs, M. (2025). Aging and the self-regulation of sadness: A longitudinal study of individuals with and without histories of depression. *Clinical Psychology Science*, 21677026251338752.

Seligman, M. (2011). *Flourish: A new understanding of happiness and well-being and how to achieve them*. Nicholas Brealey Publishing.

Seligman, M. E., & Maier, S. F. (1967). Failure to escape traumatic shock. *Journal of Experimental Psychology*, 74, 1–9

Shapiro, M. B. (1969). A clinically orientated strategy in individual-centred research. *British Journal of Social and Clinical Psychology*, 8, 290–291.

Sheehan, P. W. (1967). A shortened form of Betts' Questionnaire upon mental imagery. *Journal of Clinical Psychology, 23*, 386–389.

Silverman, W. K., Rey, Y., Marin, C. E., Boutris, P., Jaccard, J. & Pettit, J. W. (2024). Boundaries on parent involvement in their child's anxiety cognitive-behavioral-treatment outcome: Parent reinforcement and relationship behaviors moderate outcome. *Clinical Psychological Science, 12*, 936–944.

Simmonds, A. D., & Bobo, L. D. (2019). Understanding "no special favors": A quantitative and qualitative mapping of the meaning of responses to the Racial Resentment Scale. *Du Bois Review, 15*, 323–352.

Simons, J. S., & Gaher, R. M. (2005). The Distress Tolerance Scale: Development and validation of a self-report measure. *Motivation and Emotion, 29*, 83–102.

Sloboda, J. A. (2010). Music in everyday life: The role of emotions. In P. N. Juslin & S. A. Sloboda (Eds.), *Handbook of music and emotion: Theory, research, applications* (pp. 493–514). Oxford University Press.

Smetana, J. G. (1995). Parenting styles and conceptions of parental authority during adolescence. *Child Development, 66*, 299–316.

Smith, E. E., Reznik, S. J., Stewart, J. L., & Allen, J. B. (2016). Assessing and conceptualizing frontal EEG asymmetry: An updated primer on recording, processing, analyzing, and interpreting frontal Alpha asymmetry. *International Journal of Psychophysiology, 111*, 98–114.

Smith, K. E., Woodard, K., & Pollak, S. D. (2025). Arousal may not be anything to get excited about. *Emotion Review, 17*, 3–15.

Smith, W. A., Allen, W. R., & Danley, L. L. (2007). "Assume the position . . . you fit the description": Psychosocial experiences and racial battle fatigue among African American male college students. *American Behavioral Scientist, 51*, 551–578.

Smits-van der Nat, M., van der Wilt, F., Meeter, M., & van der Veen, C. (2024). The value of pretend play for social competence in early childhood: A meta-analysis. *Education Psychology Review, 36*, Article 46.

Solly, M. (2021, March 12). How the 1996 Dunblane massacre pushed the U.K. to enact stricter gun laws. *Smithsonian Magazine*. https://www.smithsonianmag.com/history/how-1996-dunblane-massacre-pushed-uk-enact-stricter-gun-laws-180977221/

Solomon, S. (2020). Mourning in Trump's America: An existential account of political grief. In D. L. Harris (Ed.), *Non-death loss and grief: Context and clinical implications* (pp. 61–71). Taylor & Francis.

Solomon, S., Pyszczynski, T., & Greenberg, J. (2015). *The worm at the core: On the role of death in life*. Random House.

Speed, B. C., Goldstein, B. L., & Goldfried, M. R. (2018). Assertiveness training: A forgotten evidence-based treatment. *Clinical Psychology Science and Practice, 25*, 1–20.

Staats, A. W. (1972). Language behavior therapy: A derivative of social behaviorism. *Behavior Therapy, 3*, 165–192.

Staats, A. W. (1983). *Psychology's crisis of disunity: Philosophy and method for a unified science*. Praeger.

Staats, A. W. (1990). Paradigmatic behavior therapy: A unified framework for theory, research, and practice. In G. H. Eifer & I. M. Evans (Eds.), *Unifying behavior therapy: Contributions of paradigmatic behaviorism* (pp. 14–56). Springer.

Staats, A. W. (1996). *Behavior and personality: Psychological behaviorism*. Springer.

Staats, A. W. (2012). *The marvelous learning animal: What makes human nature unique*. Prometheus Books.

Staats, A. W., & Eifert, G. H. (1990). A psychological behaviorism theory of emotions: A basis for unification. *Clinical Psychology Review, 10*, 1–40.

Staats, C. K., & Staats, A. W. (1957). Meaning established by classical conditioning. *Journal of Experimental Psychology, 54*, 74–80.

Stampfl, T. G., &Levis, D. J. (1967). Essentials of implosive therapy: A learning-theory-based psychodynamic behavioral therapy. *Journal of Abnormal Psychology, 72*, 496–503.

Staub, E. (2003). *The psychology of good and evil: Why children, adults, and groups help and harm others*. Cambridge University Press.

Steffen, P. R., Hedges, D., & Matheson, R. (2022). The brain is adaptive not triune: How the brain responds to threat, challenge, and change. *Frontiers in Psychiatry, 13*, 802606.

Stephenson-Jones, M., Bravo-Rivera, C., Ahrens, et al. (2020). Opposing contributions of GABAergic and glutamatergic ventral pallidal neurons to motivational behaviors. *Neuron, 105*, 921–933.

Steptoe, A. (2019). Happiness and health. *Annual Review of Public Health, 40*, 339–359.

Stern, J. A., Kelsey, C. M., Krol, K. M., & Grossmann, T. (2023). Maternal recognition of positive emotion predicts sensitive parenting in infancy. *Emotion, 25*, 1506–1512.

Sternberg, R. J. (1986). A triangular theory of love. *Psychological Review, 93*, 119–135.

Sternberg, R. J. (2021). Toward a triangular theory of love for one's musical instrument. *Psychology of Music*, *49*, 1747–1757.

Sue, D. W. (Ed.). (2010). *Microaggressions and marginality: Manifestation, dynamics, and impact*. Wiley.

Szasz, T. (1975). *The age of madness*. Routledge and Kegan Paul.

Szasz, T. (1988). *Pain and pleasure: A study of bodily feelings* (2nd ed.). Syracuse University Press.

Tangney, J. P., & Dearing, R. L. (2002). *Shame and guilt*. The Guilford Press.

Tarren-Sweeney, M. (2007). The Assessment Checklist for Children – ACC: A behavioral rating scale for children in foster, residential and kinship care. *Children and Youth Services Review*, *29*, 672–691.

Tellegen, C. L., & Sanders, M. R. (2013). Stepping Stones Triple-P—positive parenting program for children with disability: A systematic review and meta-analysis. *Research in Developmental Disabilities*, *34*, 1556–1571.

Tessier, J., Joussemet, M., Kurdi, V., & Mageau, G. A. (2021). Adolescents "walking the talk": How value importance and enactment relate to well-being and risk-taking. *Motivation & Emotion*, *45*, 249–264.

Thomas, A., & Chess, S. (1977). *Temperament and development*. Brunner/Mazel.

Thomas, R., Deighton, R., Mizuno, M., Yamaguchi, S., & Fujii, C. (2020). Shame and self-conscious emotions in Japan and Australia: Evidence for a third shame logic. *Culture & Psychology*, *26*, 622–638.

Thompson, R. A. (1994). Emotion regulation: A theme in search of a definition. In N. A. Fox (Ed.), *The development of emotion regulation: Biological and behavioral considerations*, (pp. 25–52). *Monographsof the Society for Research in Child Development*, 59 (2–3, serial No. 240).

Thompson, R. F., & Spencer, W. A. (1966). Habituation: A model phenomenon for the study of neuronal substrates of behavior. *Psychological Review*, *73*, 16–43.

Tran, M. A. Q., VoThan, T., Soliman, M., Ha, A. T., & Pham, M. V. (2024). Could mindfulness diminish mental health disorders? The serial mediating role of self-compassion and psychological well-being. *Current Psychology*, *43*, 13909–13922.

Trimble, D. G., & Chandran, A. (2021). Associations between sad feelings and suicide behaviors in the 2019 Youth Risk Behavior Survey: A call for action. *Frontiers in Pediatrics*, *9*, 694819.

Tronick, E. Z. (1989). Emotions and emotional communication in infants. *American Psychologist*, *44*, 112–119.

Twardawski, M., Angerl, E-M., & Lobbestael, J. (2024). The effect of aggressive fantasizing on aggressive inclinations: Moderating effects of dispositional anger expression. *Aggressive Behavior*, *50*, e22143.

Ulloa, M. L., Evans, I. M., & Jones, L. (2016). The benefit of emotional awareness training on teachers' ability to manage preschool children's affect: An experimental study. *Escritos de Psicología*, *9*, 1–14.

Unger, W., Evans, I. M., Rourke, P., & Levis, D. J. (2003). The S-S construct of expectancy versus the S-R construct of fear: Which motivates the acquisition of avoidance behavior? *The Journal of General Psychology*, *130*, 131–147.

Van den Hout, M. A., van der Molen, G. M., Griez, E., & Lousberg, H. (1987). Specificity of interoceptive fear to panic disorders. *Journal of Psychopathology and Behavioral Assessment*, *9*, 99–106.

van der Kolk, B. (2014). *The body keeps the score: Brain, mind, and body in the healing of trauma*. Penguin.

van Heijst, K., Ploeger, A., & Kret, M. E. (2023). Basic emotions or constructed emotions: Insights from taking an evolutionary perspective. *Perspectives on Psychological Science*, *20*, 377–391.

van Heijst, K., Ploeger, A., & Kret, M. E. (2025). Beyond right and wrong: Fostering connection in emotion theory debates. *Perspectives on Psychological Science*, *20*, 1029–1032.

Van Hoeck, N., Watson, P. D., & Barbey, A. K. (2015). Cognitive neuroscience of human counterfactual reasoning. *Frontiers in Human Neuroscience*, *9*, 00420.

Van Holen, F., Vane Hove, L., Clé, A., Verheyden, C., & Vanderfaeillie, J. (2022). The feelings and coping strategies of children placed in Flemish family foster care. *Adoption & Fostering*, *46*, 24–40.

van Kleef, G. A., & Côté, S. (2022). The social effects of emotion. *Annual Review of Psychology, 73*, 629–658.

Van Loo, K. J., & Rydell, R. J. (2013). On the experience of feeling powerful: Perceived power moderates the effect of stereotype threat on women's math performance. *Personality and Social Psychology Bulletin, 39*, 387–400.

Vanman, E. J., Kappas, A., & Ito, T. A. (2021). Social neuroscience is more than the study of the human brain: The legacy of John Cacioppo. *Social Neuroscience, 16*, 1–5.

Vernon, J. (1965). *Inside the black room: Studies of sensory deprivation*. Penguin Books.

Vinnell, L. J., Milfont, T. L., & McClure, J. (2023). Natural hazard versus natural disaster: Does framing the event affect preparedness intentions, attitudes, and behaviour? *Social Psychological Bulletin, 18*, 1–26.

Voeltz, L. M., & Evans, I. M. (1982). The assessment of behavioral interrelationships in child behavior therapy. *Behavioral Assessment, 4*, 131–165.

Vogelmann-Sine, S. (2025). *Personal communication*. https://www.psychologytoday.com/us/therapists/silke-vogelmann-sine-ph-d-inc-honolulu-hi/213919

Volo, S. (2021). The experience of emotion: Directions for tourism design. *Annals of Tourism Research, 86*, 103097.

Wahler, R. G. (1980). The insular mother: Her problems in parent-child treatment. *Journal of Applied Behavior Analysis, 13*, 207–219.

Warmingham, J. M., Duprey, E. B., Handley, E. D., Rogosch, F. A., & Cicchetti, D. (2023). Patterns of childhood maltreatment predict emotion processing and regulation in emerging adulthood. *Development and Psychopathology, 35*, 766–781.

Wareham, P., & Salmon, K. (2006). Mother-child reminiscing about everyday experiences: Implications for psychological interventions in the preschool years. *Clinical Psychology Review, 26*, 535–554.

Watkins, P. L., & Clum, G. A. (Eds.) (2008). *Handbook of self-help therapies*. Taylor & Francis/Routledge.

Watson, D., Clark, L. A., & Tellegen, A. (1988). Development and validation of brief measures of positive and negative affect: the PANAS scales. *Journal of Personality and Social Psychology, 54*, 1063.

Watson, D. L., & Tharp, R. G. (1977). *Self-directed behavior: Self-modification for personal adjustment*. Brooks/Cole.

Watson, J. B., & Rayner, R. (1920). Conditioned emotional reactions. *Journal of Experimental Psychology, 3*, 1–14.

Wedding, D., & Corsini, R. (Eds.). (2018). *Current psychotherapies* (11th ed.). Cengage.

Westlund, K. (2024). *My problems with the Constructed Theory of emotions*. https://illis.se/en/constructed-theory-of-emotions/

Weisner, T. S., & Gallimore, R. (1977). My brother's keeper: Child and sibling caretaking. *Current Anthropology, 18*, 169–190.

Weiss, A., & Deary, I. J. (2020). A new look at neuroticism: Should we worry so much about worrying? *Current Directions in Psychological Science, 29*, 92–101.

Weiss, A. A., & Evans, I. M. (1978). Process studies in language conditioning: I Counterconditioning of anxiety by "calm" words. *Journal of Behavior Therapy and Experimental Psychiatry, 9*, 115–119.

Werner, K., & Gross, J. J. (2010). Emotion regulation and psychopathology. A conceptual framework. In A. M. Kring & D. M. Sloan (Eds.), *Emotion regulation and psychopathology: A transdiagnostic approach to etiology and treatment* (pp. 13–37). The Guilford Press.

Whiteside, S. P., & Lynam, D. R. (2001). The five-factor model and impulsivity: Using a structural model of personality to understand impulsivity. *Personality and Individual Differences, 30*, 669–689.

Wilson, N., & Evans, I. M. (2002). Relationship between reward-dominant response style and ratings of boys' conduct problems. *New Zealand Journal of Psychology, 31*, 59–64.

Wilson, T. D, & Gilbert, D. T. (2005). Affective forecasting: Knowing what to want. *Current Directions in Psychological Science, 14*, 131–134.

Winett, R. A., & Winkler, R. C. (1972). Current behavior modification in the classroom: Be still, be quiet, be docile. *Journal of Applied Behavior Analysis*, *5*, 499–504.

Wolpe, J. (1958). *Psychotherapy by reciprocal inhibition*. Stanford University Press.

Wolpe, J. (1969). *The practice of behavior therapy*. Pergamon Press.

Wolpe, J., & Rachman, S. (1960). Psychoanalytic "evidence": A critique based on Freud's case of Little Hans. *Journal of Nervous and Mental Disease*, *131*, 135–148.

Wong, A. H. K., & Lovibond, P. F. (2018). Excessive generalisation of conditioned fear in trait anxious individuals under ambiguity. *Behaviour Research and Therapy*, *107*, 53–63.

Wright, J. S., & Panksepp, J. (2012). An evolutionary framework to understand foraging, wanting, and desire: The neuropsychology of the SEEKING system. *Neuropsychoanalysis*, *14*, 5–39.

Yaakov, O. B., Schlomo, S. B., & Keini, N. L. (2023). Parental stress among parents of young children: The contribution of parental self-awareness, attachment orientation, quality of couple relationship and child's temperament. *Current Psychology*, *42*, 13669–13679.

Yeung, R. C., Sokolowski, H. M., Fan, C. L., Fernandes, M. A., & Evine, B. (2025). The curse of imagery: Trait object and spatial imagery differentially relate to symptoms of Posttraumatic Stress Disorder. *Clinical Psychological Science*, *13*, 903–916.

Zanette, L. Y., Frizelle, N. R., Clinchy, M., Peel, M. J. S., Keller, C. B., Huebner, S. E., & Packer, C. (2023). Fear of the human "super predator" pervades the South African savanna. *Current Biology*, *33*, 4689–4696.

Zastrow, B. L., Martel, M. M., & Widiger, T. A. (2018). Preschool Oppositional Defiant Disorder: A disorder of negative affect, surgency, and disagreeableness. *Journal of Clinical Child & Adolescent Psychology*, *47*, 967–977.

Zhang, Y., & Hackel, L (2025). Reward association with mental states shapes empathy and prosocial behavior. *Psychological Science*, *36*, 691–712.

INDEX

For the benefit of digital users, indexed terms that span two pages (e.g., 52–53) may, on occasion, appear on only one of those pages.